Translating Petrarch's Poetry
L'Aura del Petrarca from the
Quattrocento to the 21st Century

LEGENDA

LEGENDA is the Modern Humanities Research Association's book imprint for new research in the Humanities. Founded in 1995 by Malcolm Bowie and others within the University of Oxford, Legenda has always been a collaborative publishing enterprise, directly governed by scholars. The Modern Humanities Research Association (MHRA) joined this collaboration in 1998, became half-owner in 2004, in partnership with Maney Publishing and then Routledge, and has since 2016 been sole owner. Titles range from medieval texts to contemporary cinema and form a widely comparative view of the modern humanities, including works on Arabic, Catalan, English, French, German, Greek, Italian, Portuguese, Russian, Spanish, and Yiddish literature. Editorial boards and committees of more than 60 leading academic specialists work in collaboration with bodies such as the Society for French Studies, the British Comparative Literature Association and the Association of Hispanists of Great Britain & Ireland.

The MHRA encourages and promotes advanced study and research in the field of the modern humanities, especially modern European languages and literature, including English, and also cinema. It aims to break down the barriers between scholars working in different disciplines and to maintain the unity of humanistic scholarship. The Association fulfils this purpose through the publication of journals, bibliographies, monographs, critical editions, and the MHRA Style Guide, and by making grants in support of research. Membership is open to all who work in the Humanities, whether independent or in a University post, and the participation of younger colleagues entering the field is especially welcomed.

ALSO PUBLISHED BY THE ASSOCIATION

Critical Texts
Tudor and Stuart Translations • *New Translations* • *European Translations*
MHRA Library of Medieval Welsh Literature

MHRA Bibliographies
Publications of the Modern Humanities Research Association

The Annual Bibliography of English Language & Literature
Austrian Studies
Modern Language Review
Portuguese Studies
The Slavonic and East European Review
Working Papers in the Humanities
The Yearbook of English Studies

www.mhra.org.uk
www.legendabooks.com

TRANSCRIPT

Transcript publishes books about all kinds of imagining across languages, media and cultures: translations and versions, inter-cultural and multi-lingual writing, illustrations and musical settings, adaptation for theatre, film, TV and new media, creative and critical responses. We are open to studies of any combination of languages and media, in any historical moments, and are keen to reach beyond Legenda's traditional focus on modern European languages to embrace anglophone and world cultures and the classics. We are interested in innovative critical approaches: we welcome not only the most rigorous scholarship and sharpest theory, but also modes of writing that stretch or cross the boundaries of those discourses.

Editorial Committee
Chair: Matthew Reynolds (Oxford)
Robin Kirkpatrick (Cambridge)
Laura Marcus (Oxford)
Patrick McGuinness (Oxford)
Ben Morgan (Oxford)
Mohamed-Salah Omri (Oxford)
Tanya Pollard (CUNY)
Yopie Prins (Michigan)

Advisory Board
Jason Gaiger (Oxford)
Alessandro Grilli (Pisa)
Marina Grishakova (Tartu)
Martyn Harry (Oxford)
Linda Hutcheon (Toronto)
Calin-Andrei Mihailescu (London, Ontario)
Wen-Chin Ouyang (SOAS)
Clive Scott (UEA)
Ali Smith
Marina Warner (Birkbeck)
Shane Weller (Kent)
Stefan Willer (Berlin)

Managing Editor
Dr Graham Nelson
41 Wellington Square, Oxford OX1 2JF, UK

www.legendabooks.com/series/transcript

TRANSCRIPT

1. *Adapting the Canon: Translation, Visualisation, Interpretation*, edited by Ann Lewis and Silke Arnold-de Simine
2. *Adapted Voices: Transpositions of Céline's Voyage au bout de la nuit and Queneau's Zazie dans le métro*, by Armelle Blin-Rolland
3. *Zola and the Art of Television: Adaptation, Recreation, Translation*, by Kate Griffiths
4. *Comparative Encounters between Artaud, Michaux and the Zhuangzi: Rationality, Cosmology and Ethics*, by Xiaofan Amy Li
5. *Minding Borders: Resilient Divisions in Literature, the Body and the Academy*, edited by Nicola Gardini, Adriana Jacobs, Ben Morgan, Mohamed-Salah Omri and Matthew Reynolds
6. *Memory Across Borders: Nabokov, Perec, Chamoiseau*, by Sara-Louise Cooper
7. *Erotic Literature in Adaptation and Translation*, edited by Johannes D. Kaminski
8. *Translating Petrarch's Poetry: L'Aura del Petrarca from the Quattrocento to the 21st Century*, edited by Carole Birkan-Berz, Guillaume Coatalen and Thomas Vuong
9. *Making Masud Khan: Psychoanalysis, Empire and Modernist Culture*, by Benjamin Poore
10. *Prismatic Translation*, edited by Matthew Reynolds
11. *The Patient, the Impostor and the Seducer: Medieval European Literature in Hebrew*, by Tovi Bibring
12. *Reading Dante and Proust by Analogy*, by Julia Caterina Hartley
13. *The First English Translations of Molière: Drama in Flux 1663-1732*, by Suzanne Jones
14. *After Clarice: Reading Lispector's Legacy in the Twenty-First Century*, edited by Adriana X. Jacobs and Claire Williams
15. *Uruguayan Theatre in Translation: Theory and Practice*, by Sophie Stevens
16. *Hamlet Translations: Prisms of Cultural Encounters across the Globe*, edited by Márta Minier and Lily Kahn
17. *The Foreign Connection: Writings on Poetry, Art and Translation*, by Jamie McKendrick
18. *Poetics, Performance and Politics in French and Italian Renaissance Comedy*, by Lucy Rayfield

Translating Petrarch's Poetry

L'Aura del Petrarca from the Quattrocento to the 21st Century

Edited by Carole Birkan-Berz,
Guillaume Coatalen and Thomas Vuong

Transcript 8
Modern Humanities Research Association
2020

*Published by Legenda
an imprint of the Modern Humanities Research Association
Salisbury House, Station Road, Cambridge* CB1 2LA

ISBN 978-1-78188-663-2 (HB)
ISBN 978-1-78188-664-9 (PB)

First published 2020

All rights reserved. No part of this publication may be reproduced or disseminated or transmitted in any form or by any means, electronic, mechanical, photocopying, recording or otherwise, or stored in any retrieval system, or otherwise used in any manner whatsoever without written permission of the copyright owner, except in accordance with the provisions of the Copyright, Designs and Patents Act 1988, or under the terms of a licence permitting restricted copying issued in the UK by the Copyright Licensing Agency Ltd, Saffron House, 6–10 Kirby Street, London EC1N 8TS, *England, or in the USA by the Copyright Clearance Center, 222 Rosewood Drive, Danvers MA 01923. Application for the written permission of the copyright owner to reproduce any part of this publication must be made by email to legenda@mhra.org.uk.*

Disclaimer: Statements of fact and opinion contained in this book are those of the author and not of the editors or the Modern Humanities Research Association. The publisher makes no representation, express or implied, in respect of the accuracy of the material in this book and cannot accept any legal responsibility or liability for any errors or omissions that may be made.

Trademark notice: Product or corporate names may be trademarks or registered trademarks, and are used only for identification and explanation without intent to infringe.

© *Modern Humanities Research Association 2020*

Copy-Editor: Dr Nigel Hope

CONTENTS

Acknowledgements   ix

List of Contributors   xi

Introduction   1
CAROLE BIRKAN-BERZ, GUILLAUME COATALEN, AND THOMAS VUONG

PART I: EARLY MODERN VERSIONS AND APPROPRIATIONS OF PETRARCH

1   Petrarch in Parts: Scattered Rhymes in Sixteenth-Century English Books   13
CHRIS STAMATAKIS

2   The New Asclepius: Fragmentation and Reassemblage in Du Bellay's *L'Olive*   31
MYRON MCSHANE

3   Petrarch and the French Reception of the *Triumphi*: An Age of Transition   48
ALESSANDRO TURBIL

4   The Translation of Lexical-Semantic Elements in Enrique Garcés's *Los sonetos y canciones del Petrarcha*: The Case of *Sestina RVF* 30   63
FRANCISCO JOSÉ RODRÍGUEZ MESA

5   Translating the *Canzoniere* into Images: The Petrarca Queriniano Incunable   82
GIULIA ZAVA

6   Petrarch and the Pastoral Design of Luca Marenzio's *Madrigali a quattro voci [...] Libro primo* (1585)   103
MASSIMO OSSI

PART II: CLAIMING PETRARCH FOR MODERN TIMES

7   Georges and Madeleine de Scudéry: Two Polite Commentators of Petrarch   127
DOMINIQUE CHAIGNE

8   The Untranslatable Laura: Nineteenth-Century French Perspectives   139
JENNIFER RUSHWORTH

9   Orpheus versus Hermes: On a Few Twentieth-Century French Translators of the *Canzoniere*   152
RICCARDO RAIMONDO

10 Echoes of the Petrarchan *Innamoramento* in Tim Atkins's *Petrarch Collected* and Emmanuel Hocquard's *Un Test de solitude*: Two Poets between Subversion and Dialogue   171
    THOMAS VUONG

11 'Petrarch's Love Clangs her Triumphal Car': Following Petrarch in Geoffrey Hill's Mid- to Later Work   191
    CAROLE BIRKAN-BERZ

PART III: PRACTICE-BASED CRITICISM AND ORIGINAL TEXTS

12 How Petrarch Can Speak to Contemporary Poetry: Yves Bonnefoy as Petrarch Translator and Critic   209
    THOMAS VUONG

13 Elements of the History of the Sonnet from its Italian Sources: Formal Aspects   215
    JACQUES ROUBAUD

14 Seven Types of Translation: An Overview and Arrangement of Avant-Garde Translation Practice with Reference to Tim Atkins's *Petrarch Collected Atkins*   222
    TIM ATKINS

15 'Era il giorno ch'al sol si scoloraro': A Derivative Dérive into/out of Petrarch's Sonnet 3   245
    ROBERT SHEPPARD

Appendix: EUROPETRARCA: The Relevance of a Database of Translations of the *Canzoniere*   263
GUILLAUME COATALEN

Index   271

ACKNOWLEDGEMENTS

This book began as a Young and Early Career Researchers' network project devoted to the sonnet in translation, as part of the Tract and Prismes research groups of the Université Sorbonne Nouvelle and with the associated doctoral schools devoted to language and literature. This network gathered a number of scholars from various universities in Paris and around Europe. A full list of the members of this network can be accessed on the project's webpage: <sonnetintranslation.wordpress.com>. We are grateful for Tract, Prismes, and the Université Sorbonne Nouvelle's Research Board for funding the research associated with this book.

More particularly, we would like to thank the following members of this network for providing much-needed support and assistance, as well as extremely valuable intellectual feedback on various aspects of this book. Four of the following scholars were also consultants for this book. Corinne Noirot lent us her expertise in early modern French poetry. Riccardo Raimondo allowed us to benefit from his knowledge of Italian language and literature and of the French translations of Petrarch in the early modern and contemporary eras. Jennifer Rushworth provided much of the initial inspiration and enthusiasm as well as invaluable scholarly input on the French reception of Petrarch. Finally, we would like to thank Fanny Quément for her outstanding work in this project, which included editing and translating two of the chapters into English, as well creating the project's website.

We would also like to thank Jean-Yves Masson for being a guiding light in this project, as well as Philippe Guérin and Jean Vignes for their kind and learned support. We are also grateful to the music community — especially Kate Van Orden and David Rothenberg — for helping us find authors and peer reviewers for our chapter on Petrarch's musical settings. Further acknowledgements are given in the individual chapters. We also warmly thank all the anonymous reviewers who kindly assisted in the peer review process for this volume. Finally, we would like to thank everyone at Legenda and MHRA, Nigel Hope for his meticulous copy-editing and — most importantly — Matthew Reynolds and Graham Nelson for giving our book a home.

Our gratitude extends to the late Yves Bonnefoy and to Jacques Roubaud for letting us reproduce their work. We also thank the Queriniana Library, Brescia and the British Library for allowing us to reproduce images from their collections. We are thankful to Antony S. Kline and Adam Kline for permission to reproduce poems from *The Complete Canzoniere*. We are grateful to the following parties for allowing us to reproduce all or part of the following works: Cover image by Nadia Berz, reproduced by permission of Nadia Berz. Poems and excerpts from Petrarch, *The Complete Canzoniere, a Translation into English*, by A.S. Kline, reproduced by permission of Adam Kline (www.poetryintranslation.com). Egerton MS 2711, f. 70r (Thomas Wyatt), reproduced by permission of the British Library. Images from the Petrarca Queriniano incunable reproduced by permission of Biblioteca Queriniana, Brescia, Italy. Petrarch, *Chansonnier, Rerum vulgarium fragmenta*, ed. by Giuseppe Savoca, trans. by Gérard Genot, reproduced by permission of Les Belles Lettres éditions. 'Pétrarque, *Le Chansonnier*: extraits trad. par Jean-Yves Masson', *Europe*, 82 (2004), 902–03. Reproduced by permission of *Europe, revue littéraire mensuelle*. Poems and excerpts from Poems and excerpts from Emmanuel Hocquard, *Un Test de solitude* and *A Test of Solitude*, trans. by Rosmarie Waldrop reproduced by permission of P.O.L. éditions and Rosmarie Waldrop respectively. Jacques Roubaud, 'Elements of the History of the Sonnet from its Italian Sources', reproduced by permission of Jacques Roubaud, Martine Aboucaya and Yvon Lambert. Poems from Robert Sheppard, *Petrarch 3*, reproduced by permission of Crater Press. Excerpts from *Petrarch Collected Atkins*, by Tim Atkins, reproduced by permission of Crater Press. Images 'frog pond plop' by Gary Barwin and Derek Beaulieu, reproduced by permission of Gary Barwin and Derek Beaulieu. Further debts are acknowledged in individual chapters.

Lastly, heartfelt thanks to our respective spouses — Boris, Judit, and Aurélie — without whose patience and encouragement this volume would never have been completed.

LIST OF CONTRIBUTORS

Tim Atkins has been a member of the summer faculty at The Jack Kerouac School of Disembodied Poetics at Naropa University, and a member of Carla Harryman's Poets' Theatre in San Francisco. He is the author of many books, including *Atkins Collected Petrarch* (a Times Literary Supplement and Salon.com book of the year), *Deep Osaka* (a photobook), *Koto Y Yo* (all from Crater Press), *On Fathers < On Daughtyrs* (Boiler House Press), *25 Sonnets* (The Figures), *Petrarch* (Book Thug), and *Horace* (O Books). *A Girl is a Machine Made of Birds*, a collaborative collection of concrete & visual poems and assemblages made with his daughter, Yuki, has just been published by Canary Woof. He teaches at the University of Roehampton.

Carole Birkan-Berz is Senior Lecturer in Literary Translation and Translation studies at Université Sorbonne nouvelle. As part of her research at the Sorbonne nouvelle, she put together an international research network on the sonnet in translation, one of whose outcomes is the present volume. She is currently co-editing the next collection of essays to come out of this project, entitled *New Perspectives on Translating and Adapting the Sonnet*. Carole is the author of several articles on the sonnet as practised by Geoffrey Hill and other contemporary British poets and has written much on poetry in translation. She is now working on a monograph on the contribution of translation studies to literary criticism.

Guillaume Coatalen is Senior Lecturer in early modern English literature at the University of Cergy-Pontoise (France) with a strong interest in unedited material in manuscripts. His latest publication is *Two Elizabethan Treatises on Rhetoric: Richard Rainold's Foundacion of Rhetoricke (1563) and William Medley's Brief Notes in Manuscript (1575)* (Brill, 2018). He is currently working on Queen Elizabeth I's French correspondence and on a book on the image of poets in early modern English plays.

Dominique Chaigne holds an *agrégation* and a PhD in French literature. He is the author of several articles on the seventeenth-century French sonnet.

Myron McShane is Postdoctoral Fellow at the Centre for Renaissance and Reformation Studies at the University of Toronto, currently researching French Renaissance poetry and its relationship to New World travel literature. Recently, he pursued the same subject as a Long-Term Postdoctoral Fellow at the John Carter Brown Library at Brown University. His unabridged bilingual edition of Giannozzo Manetti's *Apologeticus*, the first full-length treatise on translation theory, has been published as *A Translator's Defense* for the I Tatti Renaissance Library at Harvard University Press. Among recent conferences, he has presented on Renaissance translation theory at the Casa Petrarca in Arezzo.

Massimo Ossi is Professor of Musicology at Indiana University. He is the author of *Divining the Oracle: Claudio Monteverdi's Seconda Prattica* (University of Chicago Press, 2003). Current research includes a book-length project, *Music in the Time of War: Monteverdi's madrigali guerrieri et amorosi*; narrative and intertextuality in the Italian madrigal; programme music before 1750; and musicians' social networks in Venice, 1600–1650. He edits the series 'Music and the Early Modern Imagination' (Indiana University Press).

Riccardo Raimondo holds a PhD in French and Italian Literatures from USPC Paris (2018). He was Visiting Researcher at Ottawa (2016) and Oxford (2017), as well as Post-doc Associate at UZH Zurich (2018–19). He is now Marie Skłodowska-Curie Global Fellow at Montréal and Oslo with a project entitled *Translational Traditions and Imaginaries: A Comparative History of Petrarch's Canzoniere in France and England* (2020–2023). He is interested in several areas of Intellectual history and book history, as well as the reception of Italian literature from a European transnational and translational perspective.

Francisco José Rodríguez Mesa is Senior Lecturer in Italian Studies at the University of Córdoba (Spain). His research focuses on different aspects of Italian Medieval and Renaissance literature, mainly Petrarchan poetry and its diffusion during the fourteenth and fifteenth centuries (particularly in the Kingdom of Naples and in the Iberian peninsula) and medieval short narrative forms. He has also studied the role of women in some fourteenth-century Italian works, such as Boccaccio's *Decameron* and *De mulieribus claris* and Petrarch's *De insigni obedientia et fide uxoria*.

Jacques Roubaud is a renowned French poet, essayist, novelist, and mathematician. A member of Oulipo since 1966, he is a specialist in the mathematical structure of the sonnet and other fixed forms. His encyclopaedia of the sonnet *Quasi-cristaux* was published in 2013 by Yvon Lambert et Martine Aboucaya Editions and is also available online at http://blogs.oulipo.net/qc/description/chapitre-3-rerum-vulgarum-fragmenta/. Roubaud has received the Grand prix national de la poésie and the French Academy Grand prix de littérature Paul-Morand.

Jennifer Rushworth is Lecturer in French and Comparative Literature at University College London, having previously been a Junior Research Fellow at St John's College, Oxford. She has published two books, *Discourses of Mourning in Dante, Petrarch, and Proust* (Oxford University Press, 2016) and *Petrarch and the Literary Culture of Nineteenth-Century France* (Boydell, 2017). For essays on Proust she won the Society for French Studies's Malcolm Bowie Prize 2015 and the *Paragraph* Essay Prize 2016.

Robert Sheppard's poetry books include *History or Sleep*, his selected poems, and his co-created 'anthology' of fictional European poets *Twitters for a Lark: Poetry of the European Union of Imaginary Authors*, both published by Shearsman. Shearsman also publishes *The Robert Sheppard Companion*, edited by James Byrne and Christopher Madden. Since *Petrarch 3*, Sheppard has continued his transpositions of sonnets, now called 'The English Strain', of which *Hap* from Knives Forks and Spoons has been published. Sheppard is Emeritus Professor at Edge Hill University, UK, and his critical work *The Meaning of Form* is published by Palgrave.

Chris Stamatakis is Associate Professor in Renaissance English Literature at University College London, and author of *Sir Thomas Wyatt and the Rhetoric of Rewriting: Turning the Word* (Oxford University Press, 2012). Besides a co-edited volume on *Shakespeare, Italy, and Transnational Exchange* (Routledge, 2017), recent publications have addressed Gabriel Harvey's Italian reading, English sonnet culture, and early Tudor literary criticism. Forthcoming works include chapters on sixteenth-century sonnets for *The Oxford History of Poetry in English* and on Sidney and visual culture for *The Oxford Handbook of Philip Sidney*, and an edition of Thomas Nashe's *Christs Teares over Jerusalem* (Oxford University Press).

Alessandro Turbil recently completed a doctorate at the University of Turin and the Sorbonne Nouvelle on the first French translations of the *Triumphi*. His two main areas of research are the history of the dissemination of Petrarch's work in fifteenth- and sixteenth-century France and their influence on cultural and intellectual debate in the French Renaissance; his second line of research is focused on the acquisition of the rhetoric and linguistic peculiarities of Petrarch's literary language by French Petrarchist poets. He currently lectures at the University of Tours.

Thomas Vuong has a PhD in comparative literature (University of Paris 13). He studies twentieth and twenty-first-century poetry, with a specific focus on the sonnet, in Italy (Pier Paolo Pasolini, Giorgio Caproni), the UK (Tony Harrison), the United States (Natasha Trethewey, Garth Brooks) and France (Jacques Roubaud and Oulipo). He also has an interest in translation studies, where he considers the importance of the imaginary in the translating process.

Giulia Zava is a PhD candidate in Italian studies at Università Ca' Foscari Venezia and Université de Genève. Her doctoral research aims to provide a new critical edition of the *Motti e facezie del Piovano Arlotto*, an anonymous collection of witticisms from the end of the fifteenth century. For her master's thesis, she studied the Petrarca queriniano incunable. Her main research interest is Renaissance Italian literature, with a particular focus on the vernacular production of the second half of the fifteenth century.

INTRODUCTION

*Carole Birkan-Berz, Guillaume Coatalen,
and Thomas Vuong*

Translators are the invisible actors of literary history
— Jean-Yves Masson

'd'un corps naistre un corps de mesme face'
[from one body to birth a body with the same face]
— Jacques Peletier du Mans[1]

I am one who delights in imitation but not in sameness
— Petrarch, *Familiarum Rerum Libri*, XXII, 2

S'Amore o Morte non dà qualche stroppio
a la tela novella ch'ora ordisco,
et s'io mi svolvo dal tenace visco,
mentre che l'un coll'altro vero accoppio,

i' farò forse un mio lavor sí doppio
tra lo stil de' moderni e 'l sermon prisco,
che, paventosamente a dirlo ardisco,
infin a Roma n'udirai lo scoppio. (*RVF* 40)

[If Love or Death do not bring some flaw
to this new cloth that I now weave,
and if I can keep free of clinging lime,
while I twine the one truth with the other,

perhaps I will create a double work
in modern style but with ancient content,
so that, I'm fearful of saying it too boldly,
you'll hear the noise even as far as Rome.][2]

In Petrarch's time, translation was not primarily aimed at people unversed in the source language. Readers were generally proficient in many languages and dialects and did not need to have texts translated for them. Petrarch, for one, knew Latin, French, and Provençal in addition to Tuscan, the basis of literary Italian. Hence, any author who embarked on a translation enterprise did so knowing the value of their contribution would be assessed. In this perspective, translation — especially between Romance languages — was often carried out as imitation from a master. Petrarch imitated many Latin sources, both Classical and Christian. In sonnet 40 of the *Rerum Vulgarium Fragmenta* (*RVF*), he entreats his anonymous correspondent to send him back the source book — possibly Augustine's *Confessions* — arguing that he will create a work '*si doppio*' ('so double'), weaving together 'modern style' and 'ancient content', that it will be heard as far as Rome. In his *Letters on Familiar Matters* (*Rerum Familiarum Libri*), Petrarch details his theory of imitation, explaining that he must not repeat Virgil's poems or other sources word-for-word although he is extremely well versed in them (XXII, 2), and arguing that his source should be a 'guide', not one that binds the poet to him (ibid.). Much like his translator Jacques Peletier du Mans, quoted in our epigraph, he compares imitation to the likeness 'between a son and a father' (XXIII, 19).[3] In Petrarch's sonnet quoted above, the 'original' is still present in the 'imitation' — being recognized by readers, it gives authority to the work — but it is the labour of binding it together with novelty that ensures the imitator's renown to the wider world. Much in the same way, it was through translations and imitations of Petrarch that the sonnet soared across Europe, remodelling its poetic landscape — so much so that even the most avant-garde poetry still finds itself in debt to the author of the *Canzoniere*.

When translation was not done as imitation, it often took place in the spirit of gloss or interpretation.[4] This was quickly carried out with Petrarch's sonnets, whose first commentaries appeared in his lifetime, with Boccaccio's biographical writings on his friend or in Trecento translations of the *Canzoniere* into Latin such as Coluccio Salutati's. In the Quattrocento, as Petrarch's fame as a vernacular poet began to grow, Bembo was the one who shaped the *RVF* into a 'Canzoniere' — or a volume known as *petrarchino* — according to the wishes of the author, unlike what previous editors had done.[5] He also canonized Petrarch as the shaper of a uniform Italian language over Italy's many dialects. Bembo's edition of the *RVF* gave rise to many glosses and commentaries, the first by Alessandro Vellutello in 1525, and to glossaries of Petrarch's language and poetics. To this day, most Italian editions of the *Canzoniere* include copious commentaries and glosses. Thus, from the appearance of the first printed books, translating Petrarch implied 'carrying over' not just a poetical message, but also a rich, complex poetics, woven together with the personae of Laura and Petrarch, and conveyed by multiple exegetes and interpreters. As Teolinda Barolini and Wayne Storey put it in their study *Petrarch and the Textual Origins of Interpretation*: 'Petrarch, more than most authors, more for instance than Dante or Boccaccio, created an opus that in fact *requires* would-be interpreters'.[6] This is true of interlinguistic Petrarch as well, as is shown by McLaughlin, Panizza, and Hainsworth's recent study documenting seven centuries of 'Interpretation, Imitation, and Translation' in Britain alone. Just as in the case of the Bible, to translate Petrarch — especially the *Canzoniere* — is to engage with a tremendous exegetical tradition. In this respect, although our study begins in the Quattrocento, it seems undeniable that, from Chaucer to the avant-garde, translation and Petrarch are almost as intricately linked as translation and the Bible.[7]

The aim of this volume is to trace the multiple ways in which Petrarch has been translated, imitated, interpreted, and adapted from the Quattrocento to the present day. The essays collected in the following pages look at translation not only as the attempt at word-for-word or sense-for-sense correspondence but as a wide spectrum that includes commentary, gloss, editing, quotation, versioning, adaptation, and metamorphosis. Beyond the concept of Petrarchism as it is traditionally understood, we aim to demonstrate the continuing influence and *aura* of Petrarch's poetry in Europe through these processes of translation, adaptation, and re-creation. In this volume — arranged mostly chronologically and with a final section featuring original critical and poetic texts — we hope to demonstrate the poetic vitality of the Petrarchan legacy up to the present day, and to shed further light on the people the scholar and translator Jean-Yves Masson has called 'the invisible actors of literary history'.[8]

Until the present publication and especially since Petrarch's 700th anniversary in 2004, most studies of Petrarch's reception have assessed the assimilation of Petrarch and Petrarchism in various national settings, especially in Britain and France.[9] Much as the *Canzoniere* as a masterpiece of vernacular literature was a response to the language question in Italy, Petrarch in translation was instrumental in shaping French and English national poetics. Following on from this, studies have focused on myth-making and national-ideological or religious-national sentiment.[10] In a more expansive movement, some studies have shown the existence of a European Petrarch in the Renaissance and sometimes beyond.[11] In keeping with these works, we bring together and interweave chapters from Italian, English, French, and Spanish literature specialists, as a means to suggest parallels between those traditions. Within the literature cited, certain periods have been studied more than others: there are authoritative studies on Petrarch as an early modern model or as a Romantic or post-Romantic source in England or France.[12] We wish to show that Petrarch's aura extends well into the present day, and demonstrate this by representing a number of works about and by contemporary poets. Finally, much work has been done on intertextuality, on the *Canzoniere* as a source book for Western poetics, on the spread of the sonnet form, the emergence of the lyric self, and the specific use of the sequence, as well as on Petrarchism and anti-Petrarchism.[13] We wish to explore less trodden paths by devoting closer attention to the intricate processes of translation at work and also shed further light on poetic forms that appear in conjunction with the sonnet, such as the *canzone*, the madrigal and the sestina, or to works that have enjoyed less contemporary renown such as the *Triumphi* (It. *Trionfi*) or Petrarch's Latin works.[14] Since translation is conceived as a cross-disciplinary field, the authors of these essays use a variety of scholarly approaches, such as comparative literature, corpus linguistics, manuscript studies, visual studies, musicology, and especially translation studies to bring new perspectives to some classic works.

For the early modern era, this volume demonstrates the many mechanisms by which translations or versions of Petrarch's poetry were produced and wishes to foster reflection on translation as/and poetic composition and artistic interpretation. Our first two contributions examine the earliest well-known imitators and adaptors of Petrarch in England and France, as well as the initial theorizing about Petrarchan imitation that took place concomitantly. Chris Stamatakis's contribution, focusing on Wyatt, Puttenham, and other lesser-known writers, is entitled 'Petrarch in Parts: Scattered Rhymes in Sixteenth-Century English Books'. The chapter deals with the peculiar tendency for writers, in both manuscript and print culture, to render Petrarch's lyrics in fragmented, excerpted snippets — as atomized versions of already short forms. Rather than seeking to replicate the original in its entirety, these English translators favour the single-line fragment, the distich, and the quatrain. Because of the occasionally haphazard nature of commonplacing, many of these partial translations of the *Canzoniere* have received little attention to date. In parallel, Myron McShane's chapter, 'The New Aesclepius: Fragmentation and Reassemblage in Du Bellay's *L'Olive*', which follows it, focuses on Du Bellay, France's first composer of a *Canzoniere* in the style of Petrarch, as well as the first writer to theorize about imitation from the Italians. McShane — also a specialist in early modern translation, this time in French — uses the metaphor of the Greek hero and god of medicine to reassess Du Bellay's poetics of literary imitation and show how fragments from various Petrarchan, anthological, and Ariostan intertexts are reintegrated in *L'Olive*, especially in the first lines of poems.

The second strand of early modern translation practices uncovered in this book is the hermeneutic, exegetical one. The next two contributions use a philological approach and explore the contribution of translation to language itself. In 'Petrarch and the French Reception of the *Triumphi*: An Age of Transition', Alessandro Turbil investigates how these translations composed in the late fifteenth and early sixteenth centuries contributed to the more general phenomenon of renewal that revived the style, literary language and form of French poetry of this period. Using a lexicological approach, the author traces a few particular French syntagms specifically derived from these translations of the *Triumphi*. Following the previous contributions about France and England, Francisco José Rodríguez Mesa's chapter looks at Spanish Petrarchism, specifically through the lens of the first complete translation of the *RVF* into Spanish composed by the Portuguese translator Enrique Garcés in 1591 as he was employed in the mining industry in Peru. This study is of particular interest as it brings Petrarch into an Iberian and Latin American context and examines how to translate languages that are philologically close to one another in the context of such intricate rhetorical devices as the *senhal*. The author also shows an attempt towards semantic faithfulness, in contrast to the practices of imitation evoked above.

The practice of translation as interpretation is most significantly at work in the kind of intersemiotic translation that occurs in musical settings or in visual illuminations of poetic works. Our last two contributions on the late medieval and early modern era touch upon this most crucial aspect. Giulia Zava's chapter 'Translating the *Canzoniere* into Images: The Petrarca queriniano incunable' looks at the only fully illuminated incunable in the entire Petrarchan visual tradition — a unique volume in that its illustration is not only decorative but interpretative. In this particular historical period, at the dawning of Petrarch's European fame explosion, this interpretation might not display Bembo's thorough reading, but the anonymous illuminator was however able to provide a deep original exegesis. In her close reading, the author considers the volume within the context of the encounter of poetry and imagery.[15]

Modern literary critics sometimes forget that Petrarch's verse was often heard in a musical setting. This is true even when the text itself is not retained, as in Liszt's case, when the Romantic composer recreates the reader's interpretation of the sonnet musically.[16] In the last chapter of the first section, 'Petrarch and the Pastoral Design of Luca Marenzio's *Madrigali a quattro voci [...] Libro primo* (1585)', Massimo Ossi examines the interplay between literary and musical trends in Renaissance secular polyphony. The author offers a new explanation for the preponderance of texts by Petrarch and Sannazaro within the stylistic discourse of the pastoral genre. Ossi provides an insightful analysis of the coexistence of different stylistic registers in Marenzio's only madrigal book for four voices in relation to the broader question of interpreting madrigal books as 'books' interweaving literary and musical narratives.

Our section on the modern and contemporary era — with its companion section consisting in 'Practice-Based Criticism' — looks at what happens when Petrarch becomes a classic to be discussed, appropriated, reconstructed, subverted, and transmuted. This section starts with a study on seventeenth-century French literature. Dominique Chaigne's 'Georges and Madeleine Scudéry: Two Polite Commentators of Petrarch' discusses the Scudéry siblings' rewriting of Petrarch's poetry and myth, first as sonnets, then as narrative. The 'Description of the Famous Fontaine de Vaucluse' by Georges de Scudéry epitomizes in twelve sonnets the main stages of Petrarch and Laura's story in Provence while his sister Madeleine de Scudéry tells of an amorous initiation of her character Mathilde d'Aguilar with the two fictionalized characters of 'Laure' and 'Pétrarque' in the Avignon gardens. Their conversations draw on some sonnets of the *Canzoniere* which Mathilde comments upon among others. In both cases, interpretation is yoked with fiction and a debate is staged on the reception of Petrarch's sonnets in the context of polite conversation and banter. Moving on to late eighteenth-century and nineteenth-century France, Jennifer Rushworth expounds on a particular aspect of the French appropriation of Petrarch — 'The Untranslatable Laura: Nineteenth-Century French Perspectives'. Examining translations by Voltaire and the Abbé de Sade, she argues that Petrarch was understood by French nineteenth-century readers as a 'poet of Provence'. Subsequent political events, such as the Unification of Avignon with the rest of France at the French Revolution, encouraged Avignonese readers and writers to claim both Petrarch and Avignon as newly French. Finally, Rushworth focuses on one particular Petrarchan 'untranslatable', the polysemous name of the beloved Laura, and traces the different creative ways in which French nineteenth-century translators responded to this linguistic challenge.

Delving into twentieth- and twenty-first-century poetics, Riccardo Raimondo, in 'Orpheus versus Hermes: On a few Twentieth-Century French Translators of the *Canzoniere*', introduces the new concept of the translator's 'imaginary'. For this specialist of translation studies, the opposite mythical figures of Hermes and Orpheus epitomize the ways in which translation is practised. One represents hermeneutic translations that transpose meaning, while the other figure 'gropes his way around poetic forms in the dark'. Raimondo also contemplates a third way, that of Apollo, a mysteriously recreating and revealing translator. The three metaphors are illustrated by a study of four French translations of the first sonnet of Petrarch's *Canzoniere* — those of Louis Aragon, Gérard Genot, Yves Bonnefoy, and Jean-Yves Masson. Next in the volume is Thomas Vuong's contribution, a comparative study of two contemporary poets, Emmanuel Hocquard and Tim Atkins, one French, the other British. Both poets have composed a collection of so-called 'sonnets' that subvert most of Petrarch's work and legacy, while maintaining a poetical dialogue with the notion of lyric. Thomas Vuong's chapter compares these wholly different projects, which both tap into the Petrarchan tradition, especially that of the *innamoramento*, in order to shed a new light on the poetics of daily life. He concludes that echoes of Petrarch, however distorted, still inform contemporary poetry. Closing the scholarly section on twentieth- and twenty-first-century poetics is Carole Birkan-Berz's case study of the Petrarchan intertext in Geoffrey Hill's mid- to later work. She argues that Geoffrey Hill struggles with the inheritance of Petrarchism in the Western lyric by engaging with some lesser-known aspects of Petrarch. Following the traces of Hill's wide-ranging Petrarchan intertext, she shows the Poet Laureate to be a significant, if paradoxical presence, better gauged by examining Hill's mode of translation and adaptation, and his attraction to untranslatability. Looking at two core Petrarchan images in Hill — those of the triumph and the Virgin Mary — leads her to examine the exchanges between Hill and other poet-translators, be they Italian, English, or French.

Our third section is intended to be paired with the second section of the volume. We are grateful to Jacques Roubaud for granting us permission to reproduce his seminal work. Thomas Vuong's pithy presentation of Bonnefoy's critical texts on translating Petrarch for modern times shows the many poetic or philosophical ways in which he wished to show the Trecento master as being closer to the modern reader than might be imagined. This summary also brings to light many of the aspects highlighted by the critics in the book, and thus doubly testifies to Petrarch's enduring aura. In contrast, Jacques Roubaud seems to encode the writing of a sonnet in mathematical language and demonstrates how 'every sonnet is a sonnet by Petrarch'. In 'Elements of the History of the Sonnet from its Italian Sources', a short excerpt taken from chapter 3 of *Quasi-cristaux*, Roubaud studies what he deems to be the third phase of the invention of the sonnet: its use by Petrarch. Having analysed the various aspects of the form in the *RVF*, he offers his conclusions in his trademark style — a blend of erudition, polemic, and cheeky wit. He derives from his study of these sonnets both a meditation on the form's variability — especially as seen through translations — and an assessment of Petrarch's influence on the genre's rise throughout Europe.

Following Roubaud's contribution are two pieces emanating from two poets greatly influenced by Oulipo and by constraint literature generally. In a self-reflexive essay, the poet Tim Atkins gives readers an overview of the experimental translation methods he used in translating Petrarch. These methods, which partly stem from Oskar Pastior's Petrarch-inspired experiments in German and include 'Allusive Referential Translation', 'Derangement of the Senses Translation', and 'Hoax, Parody and Persona Translation', show how fruitful or explosive the encounter between Petrarch and the avant-garde can be. Despite his playfulness and subversive bent, Atkins engages with Petrarch and the particular language of Petrarchism in its historicity. In the same vein, the contemporary poet and critic Robert Sheppard, in '"Era il giorno ch'al sol si scoloraro": A Derivative Dérive into/out of Petrarch's Sonnet 3', relates his own attempt to translate Petrarch's *RVF* 3 using various online versions and cribs. Sheppard produces fourteen versions of the same Petrarch poem which include 'Pet' (in dog voice, V. 3), 'Petrak: the first English sonnet, Good Friday 1401' in mock middle English (V. 4), 'Wow' (a riff on Rimbaud's 'Voyelles' (V. 11), and 'National Poetry Day' (V. 15).[17] Sheppard's chapter accounts for the composition of the pieces, their relation to the works of the poet Peter Hughes (the author of *After Petrarch*), to Atkins, and to avant-garde poets Harry Mathews and Nicholas Moore. According to Sheppard, the more the texts seem intertextually dependent upon others, the more 'original' the results — which harks back to the process of late medieval and early modern imitation evoked at the beginning of this introduction. Finally, in the last 'appendix' section of this book, new digital tools are also envisioned with Guillaume Coatalen's proposed creation of a EUROPETRARCA database gathering translations of the *RVF* into Latin and into Europe's many vernacular languages, which would be extremely helpful for research but also of use in teaching.[18] A comprehensive digital database of Petrarch's sonnets in translation would surely help scholars grasp the complexity of one of the most successful literary modes in European culture. Indeed, we also intend our volume to pave the way for further research on translating and adapting the sonnet.[19]

We hope that readers will benefit from some of the parallels drawn between the different eras surveyed in this volume. One point of intersection is the tension between gathering and scattering previously noted by literary scholars such as Heather Dubrow.[20] In particular, the collaging practices of the avant-garde mirror commonplacing in the Renaissance. We hope that this look at Petrarch's poetry and its translation helps readers change their vision of the sonnet, as a form which could historically be fragmented, and not just monumental. Another practice present in all eras is the exegetical dimension of translation, which one can also find in the contemporary recreations of contemporary poets, such as Jean-Yves Masson and Geoffrey Hill. Finally, beyond the question of Petrarchism and anti-Petrarchism, parodying and exercises in style can be found throughout the volume, as highlighted in Jennifer Rushworth's chapter on Voltaire and Sade and in Robert Sheppard's practice-based excursion. Above all, we hope to demonstrate the relevance of translation studies in the field of literary scholarship. In terms of theory, the concepts of the 'untranslatable' or that of the translator's 'imaginary' are particularly relevant in building bridges between the practices of translation, adaptation, and literary creation. In practice, we hope that the volume, with its close analyses and practice-based chapters, offers a glimpse into how poetry is made.

Notes to the Introduction

1. Jacques Peletier du Mans, 'Douze sonnetz de Pétrarque', in *Œuvres poétiques* (Paris: Michel de Vascosan, 1547), pp. 47–59 (p. 47).
2. Francesco Petrarca, *Canzoniere*, ed. by Marco Santagata (Milan: Mondadori, 1996), p. 220. Petrarch, *The Complete Canzoniere*, trans. by A. S. Kline (Birmingham: Poetry in Translation, 2001). Unless otherwise stated, A. S. Kline's translation is the one used in this volume. This is available at <https://www.poetryintranslation.com/PITBR/Italian/Petrarchhome.php>.

3. For in-depth exploration of Petrarch's and others' views on imitation, see Martin L. McLaughlin, *Literary Imitation in the Italian Renaissance: The Theory and Practice of Literary Imitation in Italy from Dante to Bembo* (Oxford: Clarendon Press, 1995).
4. For an in-depth look at these two aspects of translation, see Frederick M. Rener, *Interpretatio: Language and Translation from Cicero to Tytler* (Amsterdam: Rodopi, 1989).
5. Ernest H. Wilkins, *The Making of the Canzoniere and other Petrarchan Studies* (Rome: Edizioni di Storia e Letteratura, 1951).
6. Teodolinda Barolini and H. Wayne Storey, *Petrarch and the Textual Origins of Interpretation*, Columbia Studies in the Classical Tradition, 31 (Boston: Brill, 2007), p. 17.
7. Martin McLaughlin, Letizia Panizza, and Peter Hainsworth (eds), *Petrarch in Britain: Interpreters, Imitators, and Translators* (Oxford: Oxford University Press, 2007).
8. Jean-Yves Masson and others, *Histoire des traductions en langue française* (Lagrasse : Verdier, 2012) p. 10.
9. For England, see McLaughlin and others, *Petrarch in Britain* and Jackson Campbell Boswell and Gordon Braden, *Petrarch's English Laurels, 1475–1700* (Farnham: Ashgate, 2012). For France, see Eve Duperray, *La Postérité répond à Pétrarque: sept siècles de fortune pétrarquienne en France* (Paris: Beauchesne, 2006) and idem, *L'or des mots: une lecture de Pétrarque et du mythe littéraire de Vaucluse des origines à l'orée du XXe siècle* (Paris: Publications De La Sorbonne, 1997).
10. See for example William J. Kennedy, *The Site of Petrarchism: Early Modern National Sentiment in Italy, France, and England* (Baltimore: Johns Hopkins University Press, 2003), as well as Deirdre Serjeantson, 'Milton and the Tradition of Protestant Petrarchism', *Review of English Studies*, 65 (2014), 831–37, and Mike Hodder and Anne O'Connor, 'Petrarch Goes West: Translation and the Literary Canon', *Italian Studies*, 72 (2017), 345–60.
11. Loredana Chines, *Il petrarchismo: un modello di poesia per l'Europa* (Roma: Bulzoni, 2006); Carlo Ossola, *Pétrarque et L'Europe* (Grenoble: Millon, 2006); Gordon Braden, *Petrarchan Love and the Continental Renaissance* (New Haven: Yale University Press, 1999); Dino S. Cervigni, *Petrarch and the European Lyric Tradition* (Chapel Hill: Annali D'Italianistica, 2004), as well as the proceedings from European Petrarchism: Reading and Writing Petrarch in the Renaissance gathered by Stefano Jossa in *Italique*, 15 (2012), <https://journals.openedition.org/italique/342> [accessed 1 August 2018].
12. Edoardo Zuccato, *Petrarch in Romantic England* (Basingstoke: Palgrave Macmillan, 2008); Jennifer Rushworth, *Petrarch and the Literary Culture of Nineteenth Century France: Translation, Appropriation, Transformation* (Woodbridge: Boydell, 2017).
13. Thomas P. Roche, *Petrarch and the English Sonnet Sequence* (New York: AMS Press, 1989); Heather Dubrow, *Echoes of Desire English Petrarchism and its Counterdiscourses* (Ithaca, NY and London: Cornell University Press, 1995); Roland Greene, *Post-Petrarchism: Origins and Innovations of the Western Lyric Sequence* (Princeton, NJ: Princeton University Press, 1991); Leonard Forster, *The Icy Fire: Five Studies in European Petrarchism* (Cambridge: Cambridge University Press, 1969).
14. Eve Duperray notes that Petrarch's Latin works have enjoyed a revival in Italy and France in the 1990s (*L'Or des mots*, p. 16). This revival of interest can be witnessed in the Anglophone world with the publication of the recent volumes Victoria Kirkham and Armando Maggi (eds), *Petrarch: A Critical Guide to the Complete Works* (Chicago: University of Chicago Press, 2009) and Albert Russell Ascoli and Unn Falkeid, *The Cambridge Companion to Petrarch* (Cambridge: Cambridge University Press, 2015).
15. For overviews of Petrarch in the visual arts, including the ample iconography created after the *Triumphi*, see 'Petrarch Illustrated', in J. B. Trapp, *Studies of Petrarch and his Influence* (London: Pindar Press, 2003), pp. 1–278, as well as Jean Seznec, 'Petrarch and Renaissance Art', in *Francesco Petrarca, Citizen of the World*, ed. by Aldo S. Bernardo (Padua: Editrice Antenore, 1980), pp. 133–50.
16. For a wide-ranging survey of Petrarch in music, see Andrea Chegai and Cecilia Luzzi, *Petrarca in musica: Atti del Convegno internazionale di studi: VII centenario della nascita di Francesco Petrarca* (Lucca: Libreria musicale italiana, 2005).
17. Robert Sheppard, *Petrarch 3: A Derivative Dérive* (Izmir and Minneapolis: Crater Press, 2017). This is published in an unpaginated double-sided format (folded like a map).

18. In this way, we see this volume and the proposed database as emerging in kinship with the varied approaches (textual, historical, comparative, etc.) proposed in Christopher Kleinhenz and Andrea Dini, *Approaches to Teaching Petrarch's Canzoniere and the Petrarchan Tradition* (New York: The Modern Language Association of America, 2014).
19. A new critical and anthologizing tradition seems to be slowly emerging, helping us envision the sonnet form beyond national framings and calling for new translational approaches. See Friedhelm Kemp, *Das europäische Sonett* (Göttingen: Wallstein, 2002); John Fuller, *The Sonnet* (London: Methuen, 1972); François Jost, *Le sonnet de Pétrarque à Baudelaire* (Berne: Peter Lang, 1989); Dominique Moncond'huy, *Le Sonnet* (Paris: Gallimard, 2005); Don Paterson, *101 Sonnets from Shakespeare to Heaney* (London: Faber and Faber, 1999; 2nd edn 2012); Eavan Boland and Edward Hirsch, *The Making of a Sonnet* (New York: W. W. Norton, 2008).
20. Heather Dubrow, '"You may be wondering why I called you all here today": Patterns of Gathering in the Early Modern Print Lyric', in *The Work of Form: Poetics and Materiality in Early Modern Culture*, ed. by Elizabeth Scott-Baumann and Ben Burton (Oxford: Oxford University Press, 2014), pp. 23–38.

PART I

Early Modern Versions and Appropriations of Petrarch

CHAPTER 1

Petrarch in Parts: Scattered Rhymes in Sixteenth-Century English Books

Chris Stamatakis

The practice of translating Petrarch's lyric verse into English stretches back to at least the 1530s and 1540s, in the pioneering poetic experiments of Sir Thomas Wyatt and Henry Howard, Earl of Surrey, inaugurating an English tradition of Petrarchan verse that was duly theorized by literary critics from the period itself. Petrarch's presence in early modern England has been thoroughly documented over recent years, and the contours of his reception precisely traced through both critical studies and bibliographic finding-aids.[1] Yet one under-studied aspect of the sixteenth-century Englishing of Petrarch lies in the curious tendency for writers, in both manuscript and print, to render Petrarch's lyrics in piecemeal, fragmented form — not as whole, integral poems that aim to approximate the original, but as deliberately incomplete, excerpted snippets intent on capturing and nativizing no more than a part of their Petrarchan source. Entrenched associations between Petrarch and the short lyric form (especially the sonnet) are pushed even further, as sixteenth-century English translators reveal a fondness for atomizing already succinct forms into even smaller units: disembodied quatrains, distichs, even single-line fragments. This practice of wilful excerpting gestures to aesthetic tensions between whimsical *selectio* and faithful *imitatio* — between scattering of parts and gathering into new wholes — and reconfigures Petrarch's literary and cultural status in England. In this intertextual ecosystem, Petrarch's authority is both reaffirmed and brought under duress through these acts of fragmentary translation.

This decontextualizing translation of Petrarch's lyrics has received little attention to date, leaving a critical lacuna in the history of his English reception and, more broadly, the translational habits of his English readers. In this atomistic poetics of deracinating and recontextualizing, early modern writers and readers co-opt Petrarch for what might be called a culture of epigrammatic concision at the end of the sixteenth century and the turn of the seventeenth, the epigram (by some accounts) having 'displaced the sonnet in popularity' at this juncture.[2] Studying these fragmented Petrarchan excerpts reveals much about writers' habits of translating and (an often coterminous activity) readers' habits of commonplacing: both agents respond to the literary, moral, or cultural authority of an anterior master-text. Furthermore, these translation fragments are instrumental in the sixteenth-century formation of English vernacular poetics: enriched with these Petrarchan excerpts, English literary culture is both conscious of and occasionally resistant to its Petrarchan heritage. The sixteenth-century cult of Petrarchism in England, manifested in both single-author compositions and multiple-contributor anthologies, is consonant with a vogue for miniaturization and lyric economy, attested by the primacy of the epigram and couplet as compressed, nimble articulations enabling translational invention. Focusing on English translation fragments of Petrarch's Italian lyric verse, principally the sonnets in his *Canzoniere*, this chapter addresses some uses to which such fragmentary renditions were put: establishing a literary genealogy between European vernacular cultures; recognizing a tension between cultural rupture and cultural continuity; acknowledging literary belatedness, perhaps even an anxiety of influence; defining a native literary culture founded (avowedly or grudgingly) on the ruins of an inherited intertext; formulating a self-conscious critical commentary on the compositional process itself; and, finally, voicing a kind of resistance to Petrarchan borrowing in the very act of Petrarchan borrowing and reuse, revealing Petrarch's vexed affinity with the short lyric form in English over the sixteenth century.

Fragmentary poetics

The 'tradition of Petrarch translation in English', as Peter Hainsworth quips, 'is not a glorious one overall'. The poems selected for translation in the sixteenth century suggest an interest in a small number of favoured sonnets, 'mostly ones celebrating Laura's beauty and ones built up around paradoxes', and an even smaller number of *canzoni*. In short, his oeuvre is reducible to 'commonplace choices' beyond which early modern English translators seemed reluctant to venture. At times this timidity resulted in an intertextual echo chamber, whereby poems translated or imitated by Wyatt and Surrey would be retranslated or re-imitated by their Elizabethan acolytes.[3] There is, ostensibly, no logic to Wyatt's or Surrey's patterns of selection: their earliest editor, G. F. Nott, observes with bafflement that 'the sonnets [Wyatt] has selected from Petrarch are for the most part the worst that Petrarch wrote'.[4] The literary merits of these sonnets notwithstanding, one notable feature of their curious choices is that Wyatt and Surrey consistently deracinate local parts from Petrarch's lyric whole: poems are plucked from Petrarch's (admittedly loose) sequence in a seemingly sporadic, irregular fashion without regard for the compilational architecture of the source or its structural, biographical, or narrative contexts.

This aleatory principle of selection may derive its inspiration from Petrarch's own 'poetics of fragmentation'.[5] Readers have long registered Petrarch's obsession with the dialectic principles of 'particularization (*parte*) and scattering (*sparte*)' as binary poles around which his *Canzoniere* is constructed, in terms drawn from *RVF* 308.[6] On his collection in its manuscript incarnation Petrarch bestowed the Latin title *Rerum vulgarium fragmenta* (*RVF*) [fragments written in the vernacular], in what

Robert Durling posits as the first use of 'fragment' to describe a kind of art, as if inaugurating a new genre.[7] This title offers an equivalent of sorts to the Italian label, *Rime sparse* [scattered rhymes], by which the collection also circulated, alluding to the opening sonnet's opening line, 'Voi ch'ascoltate in rime sparse il suono' [You who hear in scattered rhymes the sound] (*RVF* 1.1). As a self-professed gathering of scattered fragments, Petrarch's malleable oeuvre distinguishes itself from Dante's more rigid, prescribed sequence in the *Vita nuova* whose lyric units are connected by prose ligatures; by contrast, Petrarch's *Rime sparse* resembles a more appealingly permissive work espousing a looser organizational syntax. Comparably, the Neapolitan Jacopo Sannazaro presented his *Sonetti e canzoni* as a series of 'frammenti' [fragments] rescued from obscurity, 'hinting at a process of deconstruction of former unities'.[8] Petrarch's continual revisionary interventions, re-editing his own oeuvre over decades, transformed what Armando Petrucci has called a 'libro d'autore' into a 'libro-archivio', one 'consecrated to the always impending work of copying and recopying'.[9] Petrarch's *Canzoniere*, by this reckoning, is no more an embodiment of literary capital and cultural *auctoritas* than a repository of detachable parts available for imitative redeployment and translational reuse. The publishing history of Petrarch's lyrics exploited and even fostered this impression of fluid reusability. Many of the sixteenth-century print editions of his vernacular verse — for instance Giolito's 1553 edition featuring a commentary by Giulio Camillo and textual machinery by Lodovico Dolce glossing Petrarch's distinctive 'concetti' [conceits] — were issued with in-text commentaries identifying his intertextual borrowings, lexical apparatuses indexing rhymes (in the form of a 'rimario'), and paratextual supplements that 'targeted the reader as potential writer'.[10]

Answering these implicit or explicit invitations, the fragmentary poetics cultivated by English translators — combining anatomized selection and reassembly — can be located, generally, in broader early modern habits of reading and commonplacing and, specifically, in a European context of Petrarchan excerpting. Cultural historians and historians of reading have remarked on an early modern 'delight in particularization' symptomatic of a 'culture of dissection', noting also the inherently 'tight conjunction of reading and selecting' implicit in the 'intertwined meanings of the Latin *legere* (gather, select, read)'.[11] A burgeoning of compendia in the print marketplace attests these readerly biases sanctioned by humanist precepts: Ann Moss places Dominicus Nanus Mirabellius's *Polyanthea opus suavissimis floribus exornatum* (Savona, 1503), an encyclopaedic reference work featuring excerpts from modern vernacular authors including Petrarch and Dante, in the context of 'the humanists' investigation of the resources of language'.[12] Petrarch's *Rime sparse* encouraged aspiring writers to commonplace quotations in an Erasmian mould (Erasmus' ever-expanding *Adagia* representing a canonical repository of *loci communes*). As JoAnn Della Neva remarks, the *Rime sparse* became the 'source for several rhetorical handbooks', especially from the mid-sixteenth century onwards, as in Ludovico Beccadelli's dictionary of Petrarchan idioms (*Epiteti del Petrarca*, 1555–1560) or the anonymous *Annotationi brevissime sovra le Rime di m. F. P.* (1566), an encyclopaedic record of 'ornamenti artificiosi del Petrarca', the constituent ingredients of

Petrarchismo.[13] In part, the utility of such compendia of Petrarch and other Italian poets lay in their privileging of aesthetic criteria: in his *Bellezze del Furioso* (Venice, 1574), Orazio Toscanella favours over the allegorical and moral import of Lodovico Ariosto's *Orlando furioso* (1532) the poem's 'artificii' and 'bellezze', what Robert Cummings calls its 'evidences of artistry and its ornaments'. In their aesthetic compulsions, these publications often imply and propagate a practice of 'reading for beauties' that tends to be neglected in scholarly accounts of sixteenth-century reading as something primarily pragmatic or 'goal-oriented'.[14]

Serving as functional aids for aspirant writers learning to 'write copiously', such handbooks proffered exemplary rhetorical ornaments as 'point[s] of departure' for lyric composition. Writers who redeployed culled excerpts necessarily denied 'the integrity of previous authoritative texts', viewing them 'chiefly as repositories of fragments which could be reordered'. This reconfiguration of fragments is congruous with an Erasmian poetics of iconoclastic imitation, a practice likewise recommended in Joachim du Bellay's *La Deffence et illustration de la langue francoyse*, advocating that the literary past 'be broken up for aspiring writers to use these fragments in their own discourse'.[15] In this vein, the selective emulation of Petrarch provoked Cornelio Castaldi's dismay, at the turn of the sixteenth century, at those '*imitatori del Petrarca*' who valued the quotable part over the inimitable whole:

> *Udite servi di vane parole,*
> *Che più stimate i remi che la Barca*[16]

[Listen, slaves of empty words, you who consider the oars more valuable than the boat]

Yet Petrarch seems to have espoused just such a practice of fragmentary *imitatio*. In his *Familiarum rerum libri*, he recommends that the imitative reader not only gather selected gleanings but also transform them, and his injunctions even sanction something approaching outright *dissimulatio*: the writer who borrows in this way produces something idiosyncratic out of many sources ['ex multis unum suum ac proprium conflabit'] and conceals the imitation ['imitationem [...] celabit'].[17] Petrarch's early sixteenth-century commentators detected these allusive manoeuvres in his own poetry: in his commentary on the *Rime e trionfi* (1541), Bernardino Daniello placed Petrarch in an intertextual matrix formed of authors 'both classical and contemporary', tracing literary debts and 'reconstructing fragments from the classical past' to collate with Petrarch's tessellated compositions.[18] Accordingly, Petrarch's habits of borrowing from anterior literary models had already attained some level of literary-critical recognition and cultural notoriety by the time the first translations of his works were being composed in early Tudor England.

Quoting Petrarch

Through the editorial and exegetical efforts of Petrarch's early sixteenth-century Italian commentators, such as Pietro Bembo in his 1525 *Prose della volgar lingua*, Petrarch was promoted as the chief vernacular model above the other two 'corone' (Dante and Boccaccio), and his oeuvre elevated to the status of a glorified florilegium — a canon of authoritative pre-texts and minable *exempla* ready for imitation and appropriation. Conscripted within a broader constellation of intertextual borrowing, Petrarch's vernacular works — prophylactics against belatedness and cultural entropy — bestowed on his imitators some degree of literary authority or authentication. Fit for exemplary imitation as not just a neo-Latin moralist but also a paragon of vernacular literature, Petrarch prompted among his early English translators a type of *imitatio* that manifested itself less through wholesale translation of entire works than through isolated, synecdochic bursts of interlingual engagement in which the part substituted for an implied whole. Petrarch's Tudor translators treated his vernacular lyric corpus as a thesaurus of metaphors and oxymoronic formulations to be lifted, piecemeal, into a new literary culture, in which they would reverberate with new inflections. For instance, through this feedback loop, the opening line of Petrarch's *RVF* 248 ('Chi vuol veder quantunque pò Natura' [Whoever wishes to see what things Nature can achieve]) is excerpted as the lyric *point de départ* for Thomas Watson's *Hekatompathia*, passion xxi ('Who list to vewe dame *Natures* cunning skil'), Sir Philip Sidney's *Astrophel and Stella*, sonnet 71 ('Who will in fairest booke of Nature knowe'), and the manuscript 'exhortation to the reader' in Henry Constable's *Diana* ('Eyes curiouse to behold what nature can create').[19] In each case, Petrarch's latently bookish metaphor acquires, like a self-replicating meme, new and explicit resonances that challenge readers to view and judge the merits of the literary compositions before them.

Commenting on Petrarch's early English reception, George Puttenham traces a genealogy of indebtedness to Wyatt's and Surrey's first forays in translating Italian poetry. Epitomizing exemplary *imitatio*, Wyatt and Surrey, 'hauing trauailed into Italie, and there tasted the sweete and stately measures and stile of the Italia[n] Poesie', resemble 'nouices newly crept out of the schooles of *Dante Arioste* and *Petrarch*' whose exemplarity offered the instruments for renovating English poetics and enriching the expressive capabilities of the vernacular.[20] Wyatt's and Surrey's Elizabethan successors perpetuate this mode of allusive mining. Deploying the same vocabulary of a literary novitiate, George Gascoigne, in his presentation manuscript of *The Grief of Joye* (1576/77), a metaphrase of Petrarch's *De remediis utriusque fortunae*, styled himself '*Petrarks* jorneyman' (or apprentice), and elsewhere fashioned his authorial identity as an avowed imitative gatherer — a belated, post-Petrarchan aftercomer reanimating passages borrowed from a master-text.[21] Gascoigne's *A Hundreth Sundrie Flowres* is, self-professedly on its title-page, a collection of sundered, sundry, 'gathered' items — texts assembled 'partely (by translation) in the fyne outlandish Gardins of Euripides, Ouid, Petrarke, Ariosto, and others' and 'partly by inuention'.[22] Such 'gathering' by excerpted translation produces both the first stanza of Gascoigne's 'A cloud of care hath coured all my coste', indebted to

RVF 189, and two other poems, namely 'Dame Cinthia hir selfe' and 'O Curteous Care', which imitate in their complex stanza form the first eleven lines of *RVF* 23, Petrarch's *canzone delle metamorfosi*, a catalogue of the speaker's Ovidian transformations.[23] Little wonder, then, given these magpieish sensibilities, that the almost certainly fictitious 'M. A. Perugino' should, in a commendatory epistle prefacing the expanded volume of *Posies*, commend Gascoigne as 'vn' Immitatore di Petrarcha'.[24]

Comparably, Gabriel Harvey lauds Petrarch's quotable exemplarity in *Pierces Supererogation* by enumerating his traits. Petrarch is 'the lyfe of Poetry; the grace of Arte; a precious tablet of rare conceits, & a curious frame of exquisite workemanship; nothing but neate Witt, and refined Eloquence'.[25] Theorized in this way as a paradigm of striking 'conceits', Petrarch becomes a model of technical craft and artful refinement in a compressed, diminutive medium, and a 'tablet' — a surface for writing on, something intended to bear an inscription — such that, by implication, his writings become available for rewriting as much as for rereading. Attesting these possibilities of fragmentary quotation, Harvey cites the first two lines of Petrarch's *RVF* 263 as evidence of the 'loftinesse of [Petrarch's] conceite' in his 'Letter IV' to Edmund Spenser, in which, moreover, four hexameters (beginning 'Noble *Alexander*, when he came to the tombe of Achilles') by Gabriel's brother John translate the opening three lines of Petrarch's *RVF* 187 ('*Giunto Alessandro ala famosa tomba*'), accompanied by the comment that the poem is 'quoted' in the 'Glose of your *October*' in Spenser's *Shepheardes Calender*.[26] In each case, the Italian subtext, deracinated from its original moorings, serves in the new context as a kind of *incipit* or introit — an instantly (or at least implicitly) recognizable and authoritative tag proffering a new point of origin for English writers. Petrarch's cultural authority, immediate recognizability, and associations with literary craft as asserted by Harvey become formally, materially inscribed in the late sixteenth century in works of literary criticism and Italian–English language-learning manuals. In his dialogue books, John Florio reproduces fragments from Petrarch's oeuvre, translating them in a parallel column to demonstrate the proverbial, idiomatic capabilities of English. Florio plunders lines for translation from the *Canzoniere* (*RVF* 232.12–14, 272.1–2) in his *Firste fruits*, and supplies a line-for-line *terza rima* translation of a fragment from Petrarch's *Trionfo della pudicizia* ('With her the virtues all') in *Florios Second Frvtes*, demonstrating his own prosodic skill, the copiousness of English as a literary vernacular, and Petrarch's translingual reach as a quotable proverbialist.[27]

Remembering, Forgetting

Evidence for this practice of excerpting and scattering Petrarch's already self-consciously 'scattered rhymes' survives in several European canons. For instance, the first of the sonnets in the *Canzoniere* translated into French, *RVF* 134 ('Pace non trovo'), gave rise only to a partial, fragmentary translation, and in a form other than the sonnet.[28] In Tudor engagements with Petrarch's *Rime sparse*, Englished fragments — whether accompanied by the corresponding lines of the Italian original, or rendered into English devoid of identificatory context or marginal citation — support Mary Thomas Crane's compelling thesis that 'gathering' and 'framing' constituted the dominant discursive modes, readerly practice, and compilational habits in this period. Remembering and re-membering borrowed fragments in new arrangements involves forgetting the original contexts from which verse units have been lifted: these procedures imply a move towards a 'true intertextuality of fragments'.[29] This type of fragmentary translation, elsewhere called a 'rhétorique des citations' ('quotation rhetoric') by Marc Fumaroli, is extensively illustrated by Du Bartas's *Les Semaines*, an encyclopedic amalgam of fragments accumulated over the last quarter of the sixteenth century.[30] In one of the few critical engagements with this citational rhetoric, Robert Cummings ventures the compelling case that, since *Les Semaines* were inherently fragmented, their chief purpose for readers was not moral, as a repository of improving *sententiae* or doctrine, but aesthetic, affording translators 'detachable "beauties"' that could be transplanted to new contexts.[31] The practice recalls Puttenham's celebration of gleaning pithy 'gnomes' (*sententiae*), whereby writers cite or 'alleage textes or authorities of wittie sentence'.[32] The emphasis falls as much on the manner and aesthetic achievement as on the moral, doctrinal import of the sentence itself.

Fragmented translation of this kind negates (or at least dispenses with) original contexts and exploits the openness to recontextualization on which humanistically sanctioned practices of commonplacing rely — lifting reusable quotations from their encasing structural syntax and reconfiguring them in new thematic, conceptual collocations. The translator of fragments comes to resemble Genette's *bricoleur*, creating new structures from the residues of previous structures, and interposing new contexts for these relocated units. In Tudor literary practice, these newly recontextualized fragments invite readers to ponder the implications of the redeployment. Sixteenth-century English poetry is peppered with Petrarchan borrowings silently implanted within larger lyric forms, and these redeployed snippets, in their new contexts, often reveal a metaliterary concern with the poetic speaker's disorientation or with the operations of memory in activating dormant residues of the past — a concern with, in other words, a kind of alienation or displacement consequent on the reuse or replication of an anterior fragment in a new textual environment. Perhaps most famously, Petrarch's 'Non so mio, no' [I am not my own], from his notoriously metamorphic *RVF* 23, is transplanted by Sidney as a canonically recognizable Petrarchan tag in *Astrophel and Stella*, as 'I am not I, pitie the tale of me' (sonnet 45), an articulation at one remove from itself.[33] Drawing on the recognizability and mobility of Petrarch's verse, Tudor translators and imitators betray a particular fondness for culling the opening lines of his lyrics, as trademark, signature introits. Wyatt's personal manuscript contains the following abortive fragment in his own hand (see Fig. 1.1):

> ffrom thowght to thowght / from hill to hill Love dothe me lede
> clene co[n]trary from restfull lyff / thes co[m]mon path[es] I trede[34]

Wyatt closely repackages the opening three lines of Petrarch's 72-line canzone, *RVF* 129, a poem aptly shot through with buried allusions to Orphic wandering and dislocation. The couplet, in Wyatt's untethered version now shorn of the encasing context enjoyed by Petrarch's original, intimates not only the speaker's

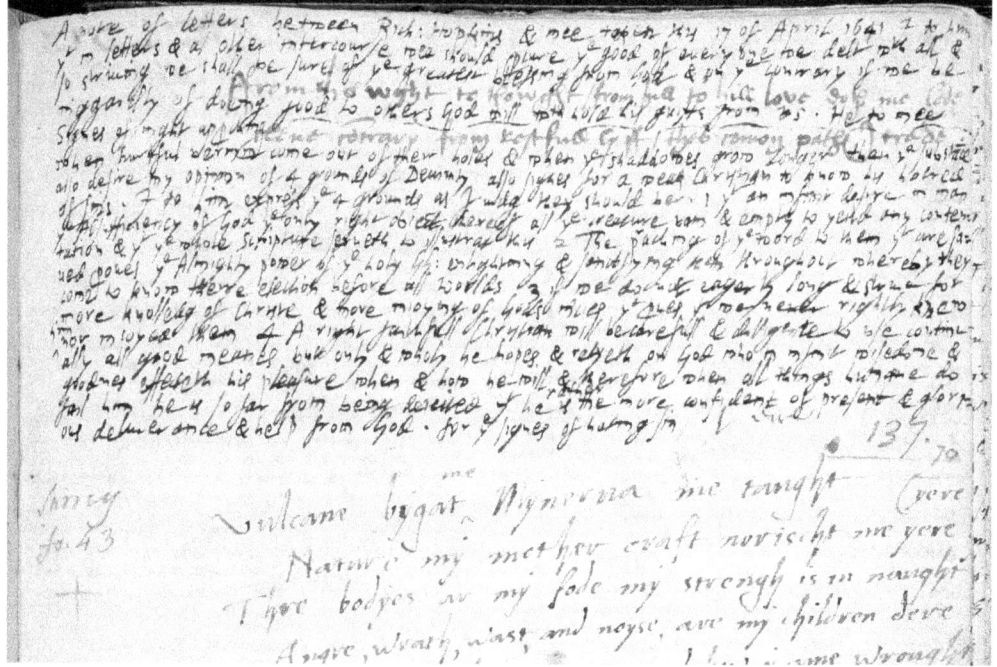

Fig. 1.1. The verse fragment, 'ffrom thowght to thowght', in Wyatt's own handwriting, breaks off after the second line. A gap is left in the manuscript before Wyatt's son enters the next poem, 'Vulcane bygat me', in his italic hand further down the page. The verse fragment has been written over in darker ink by the manuscript's later owners.
© The British Library Board (Egerton MS 2711, f. 70r, detail)

sense of restlessness but also the fragment's displacement and nomadic wandering in a centreless literary universe.

These dispersive manoeuvres, occasionally acquiring a kind of metatextual self-consciousness about the very act of literary reuse, are amply illustrated in Thomas Watson's collection of eighteen-line 'sonnets'. In his *Hekatompathia* (1582), arguably the first sustained Petrarchan sequence in English, Watson's favoured *mise en page* — a relatively static pattern of prose headnotes and, at times, marginal citations — advertises the fragmentary borrowings from (*inter alia*) Petrarch. Entry XXXIX, for instance, reproduces the sestet of Petrarch's *RVF* 20 in italics as an avowed source from which 'The second part of this Passion is borrowed'. Watson's poem, in gothic black-letter, is typographically and strophically distinct, although it clearly sits in a dynamic relationship with its source, against which it is implicitly to be collated by the reader:

> *Piu volte gia per dir le labbra apersi:*
> *Poi rimase la voce in mezz'l petto:*
> *Ma qual suon poria mai salir tant'alto?*
> *Piu volte incominciai di scriuer versi.*
> *Ma la penna, e la mano, e lo'ntelletto*
> *Rimaser vinto nel primier assalto.*

> I haue attempted oft to make complainte,
> And with some dolefull wordes to tell my griefe,
> But through my fearefull heart my voyce doth fainte,
> And makes me mute where I shoulde craue releife:
>   An other while I thinke to write my paine,
>   But streight my hand laies downe the pen againe.[35]

This curtailed, fragmentary exchange becomes inevitably autoreferential: it seems to reflect on the stilted processes of elegiac composition, the limits of rhetorical invention, and the shackles on articulation that are both consequent on and, paradoxically, alleviated by fragmentary plundering. By decontextualizing fragments from Petrarch, Watson, like other Tudor translators, displaces the text from itself, leaving readers in doubt as to the identity of the lyric voice (Petrarch? Watson? A fictional persona? The Orphic fragment itself?) and the role of the strophic casing in which those voices are newly animated.

Particularly dense illustrations of these principles of fragmentation, displacement, and self-referentiality are offered by poems that resemble a *cento* — synoptic mosaics of stolen parts. Disconnected moments are, through programmatic eclectic imitation, synthesized into a new form. The practice, indebted to Senecan and Erasmian models of apian foraging and transformative recombination, is witnessed on the continent in the sixteenth-century Italian vogue for *centoni*, an 'interleaving of texts from different sources', as manifested in Giulio Bidelli's 1588 *Centoni di verse del Petrarca*. The typically 'fragmented, discrete nature of Petrarchan discourse' finds obvious English equivalents in, for instance, Watson's eclectic, 'lapidary' composites of borrowed Italian fragments.[36] Sonnet XXI in his *Hekatompathia* combines fragments from Petrarch's aforementioned 'Chi vuol veder quantunque' (*RVF* 248) and Serafino Aquilano's sonnet 'Chi vuol veder gran cose altiere e nuove'.[37] Pre-Elizabethan *centi* are readily in evidence in Surrey's slender oeuvre, which texturally enacts his motto, 'sat superest' (enough survives) — implicitly an apologia for and assertion of the potency of the ruined fragment that yet endures. For instance, Surrey's 'Svche waiward waies hath loue' translates lines from Ariosto's *Orlando furioso* (II.i), Petrarch's *Trionfo d'amore* (III.151–87, IV.139–53), and his *Canzoniere* (*RVF* 206.10–11).[38] Perhaps the most sustained example is Surrey's *terza rima* poem 'The sonne hath twise brought furth', constructed from a series of allusions and nods to *Troilus and Criseyde* and Petrarch's *Rime*. Possibly refracting a sonnet (*RVF* 224) already translated by Wyatt as 'Yf amours faith',[39] Surrey's poem echoes a solitary line from Petrarch's poem, 's'arder da lunge et agghiacciar da presso' (*RVF* 224.12), in 'At hand to melt, farre of[f] in flame to burne' (l. 18). Other close correspondences announce themselves throughout the poem: ll. 21–23 of Surrey's cento ('All thing aliue [...] the dayes vnrest') render *RVF* 22.1–6, and ll. 47–49 ('And yf I flee I carie with me still | The venomde shaft, whiche dothe his force restore | By hast of flight') recall *RVF* 209.9–11. Beyond these seemingly incidental moments of close borrowing littered throughout Surrey's poem, some of the translated excerpts appear more intensely autoreferential. Employing a vocabulary indebted simultaneously to the realms of architecture and commonplacing, Surrey's speaker expresses a desire to

> [...] withdraw from euery haunted place,
> Lest by my chere my chance appere to playn:
> And in my mynde I measure pace by pace,
> To seke the place where I my self had lost (ll. 32–35)

rendering the opening quatrain of Petrarch's sonnet that begins

> Solo et pensoso i più deserti campi
> vo mesurando a passi tardi et lenti,
> et gli occhi porto per fuggire intenti
> ove vestigio uman la rena stampi. (*RVF* 35.1–4)

[Alone and careworn, I go through the most desolate fields measuring out hesitant, slow paces, and keep my eyes primed to flee any place where human footprints mark the sand]

and the opening two lines from another sonnet,

> Quando mi vène inanzi il tempo e 'l loco
> ov' i' perdei me stesso (*RVF* 175.1–2)

[When I remember that time and place where I lost my self]

Here, Surrey's assembly of fragments — this nexus of thematic preoccupations relating to the speaker's disorientation and displacement, an attempt at memorial tracing, efforts to retreat from a resurgent past that indelibly bears the vestiges of previous occupants — silently but self-reflexively acknowledges its own genealogy of indebtedness. Surrey's borrowings repeatedly reflect on the practice of borrowing itself: these fragmentary translations, often pointedly revolving around the resources of poetic memory, bring to the fore the implications of fragmentary translation for the compositional process itself.

Surrey's practice brings under duress assumptions that the sixteenth century witnesses a movement away from overt, reverential quotation towards silent, combative assimilation. Montaigne, at the end of the century, is often invoked by historians of intertextuality in this connection, in propounding a mode of conscious forgetting that Marilyn Randall deems 'symptomatic of a transition in Renaissance aesthetics from a poetics of memory and memorization, to one of forgetting'.[40] Whether the result of unconscious literary reminiscences or designed amnesia, Surrey's unobtrusive assimilations in the aforementioned *cento* evidence a type of *dissimulatio* that sits uneasily with enduring critical assumptions that early sixteenth-century translators subserviently seek to appropriate or replicate established *auctoritates*. Indeed, much of the literary, rhetorical theory of the early 1500s recommends this very type of silent assimilation: Erasmus' *Ciceronianus* (1528), for instance, actively privileges the deft, inconspicuous, eclectic amalgamation of fragments that masks the appearance of a derivative mosaic.[41]

Fragmentary Couplets

Italian literature in general and Petrarch in particular are typically central to late sixteenth-century reflections on the disreputable poetics of theft. The debates tend to reveal a radical unease about the status of the literary fragment as a diminutive, possibly trite, form, and about the merits of its intertextual reuse. Ben Jonson levelled the disparaging accusation that Samuel Daniel merely seasoned his pastoral drama with a 'few *Italian Herbs*',[42] and Sidney's Sonnet 15 in *Astrophel and Stella* impugns the method of Ciceronian imitation espoused by other English poets who mine Petrarch's oeuvre only to import quotable turns of phrase, indigested and untransformed, into their 'rimes'. This 'Dictionaries methode' indiscriminately plucks out 'euery flowre not sweet perhaps' from among 'poore *Petrarchs* long deceased woes'. Sidney implicitly distances himself from this dilettantist pretence of poetic skill: subservience to an impoverished, depleted source of inspiration finally reveals incomplete or unskilful assimilation — 'at length stolne goods do come to light'.[43] Comparably, Michael Drayton professes inventive autonomy, boasting,

> Yet these mine owne, I wrong not other men,
> Nor trafique further then thys happy Clyme,
> Nor filch from *Portes* nor from *Petrarchs* pen,
> [...]
> I am no Pickpurse of anothers wit.[44]

The last line of this sonnet mischievously borrows from Sidney's *Astrophel and Stella* 74 ('I am no pick-purse of anothers wit').[45] The ideal of *imitatio* has been debased, and literary authorities reduced to caricatures of excerptable, trite conceits. In a more sustained critique, some Elizabethan commentators conceive of derivative literary genealogies as entropic. In William Scott's *Modell of Poesye* (1599), a post-Sidneian literary-critical manuscript treatise, the discussion of Petrarch's contribution to the subgenre of elegiac lyric leads to a wider commentary on the vogue for Petrarchan borrowings among English translators. Focusing on 'the complaynts vttered in the rymes and sonnets of Petrarch, some saye the father or refyner of our vulgar kyndes', Scott recounts how there are 'some English admyrers of their sundry starres, with greate felicitie of witt that followe him; but', he laments, 'it were to be wisht some conceipts had neuer bene borne'.[46] Scott implies that faithful, sensitive *imitatio* has yielded to a poetics of trite reproduction of the most obvious or exaggerated Petrarchan *topoi*, the kind of neo-Petrarchan excess lampooned on the continent nearly half a century earlier by Joachim du Bellay, in a pithy (and possibly insincere) avowal of a poetics of sincerity: 'J'ay oublié l'art de petrarquizer.'[47]

These literary-critical reflections point to a radical ambivalence in the cultural status of the fragment, a term used increasingly in bookish, lectorial capacities to refer to *textual* excerpts. On the one hand, the literary fragment is readily dismissed as something trivial, insincere, and the most easily imitable or transferable unit in poetic production, as when John Harvey speaks disparagingly of some 'stale poeticall fragment, or other antique record'.[48] On the other hand, the fragment enjoys a vogue, a by-product of the humanistic approbation of commonplacing — hence Erasmus's fond recollection of 'certayne fragmentis of myne olde study'.[49] As an epigrammatic, compact form demanding the writer's skill in economical expression on a diminutive scale, the fragment fulfils Henry Peacham's stylistic imperative, in his rhetorical handbook *The Garden of Eloquence*, that a proverbial 'gnome' should display 'apt breuitie'.[50] Elizabethan critical theory seems divided on where 'Forceablenes and efficacye' (the 'last vertue and grace in style', in William Scott's terms) reside. Arguing at first, with Quintilian, that *enargeia* arises from *amplificatio*, Scott then ventures the countervailing claim that similar rhetorical vigour derives from short, compressed expression — from 'entringe into particulers, breakinge the whole into his partes, anatomizing euery lymme' in order to 'compact our conceiptes in shorte and pithie termes', thereby fulfilling a numismatic axiom that, in a linguistic economy, 'the excellencye of speach consisteth in signifyinge much by fewe wordes'.[51] This same ambivalence colours Roger Ascham's posthumously published *Scholemaster* (1570) in its account of the 'vse or misuse' of the 'Epitome' for the 'encreace of eloquence'. At first, the 'epitome' — a term emerging in the sixteenth century to denote a formal genre ('epitome, n.', *OED Online*, first citation from 1529) or literary activity ('epitome, v.', first citation from 1596) — is symptomatic of 'a silie poore kinde of studie' that privileges a trivial, superficial mode of reading.[52] Yet later Ascham acknowledges its ability to rein in the excesses of the 'inuentiuest heades', curbing their lexical enthusiasm: in a play on the word's etymology (partly cognate with *anatomy*), Ascham contends that 'a wise learned man, by this way of *Epitome*, in cutting away wordes and sentences' produces a text half the size 'but twise as good as it was, both for pleasure and also commoditie' — a kind of Occam's razor pruning sources down to their elementary essences, thereby heightening readerly delight and utility.[53]

In Tudor literary practice, anatomical commonplacing of Petrarch's verse shows a particular affinity with the couplet, a form implicitly recognized as central to native English poetics, as when Puttenham traces the use of the '*distick* or couple' to Chaucer and Gower.[54] As Cathy Shrank notes, there is a certain show of 'wit in reducing into two lines of verse the self-pitying laments of Petrarchan lovers, already clichéd by the 1560s'.[55] In these fragmented bursts, translating Petrarch is as much about displaying skill in adapting foreignness to an English form as about finding lexical equivalents for Petrarch's words. For instance, Thomas Kyd's *The Householders Philosophie* (1588), a translation of Torquato Tasso's *Padre di famiglia*, renders embedded excerpts from Petrarch's *Rime* in fourteener couplets.[56] Beyond offering opportunities to display the translator's prosodic virtuosity, translation of Petrarchan fragments into English couplets often invites critical self-reflexiveness, registering a penchant for selecting fragments from Petrarch that are imbued with some literary-critical import or which, self-consciously or not, seem to reflect on the processes of commonplacing and literary composition itself. For instance, the personal commonplace book compiled by William Withye (*c.* 1570–1590) is peppered with bursts from Petrarch and Tasso, in a collational poetics that quotes the original source immediately before the accompanying English translation. In one instance, Withye copies the last tercet of *RVF* 56 and adjoins an accompanying Latin tag to his English translation:

>Petrar: pri: part.
>*Canzon 43.*

Et hor di qual ch'io ho letto mi souene
Che'nanzi al di' de l'vltima partita
Huom beato chiamar non si conuene.

It often me recalles to minde, that oft I red.   { nemo se beatus
N'one happye be, saue they w[hi]ch happely ar ded   { ante obitum⁵⁷

On a page densely laced with scattered rhymes (from Petrarch's *Trionfo d'amore* and Torquato Tasso's *Aminta*) in which each fragment is accompanied by an English translation in couplets, this two-line excerpt (dating to *c.* 1578–81) becomes necessarily self-referential: it dwells on an act of recollection, textualizing memory as the speaker recalls what has been 'oft [...] red'; and it comments indirectly on the intertwined processes of reading, commonplacing, and composition. In a *mise en page* that gestures to a *mise en abyme*, Withye then annotates his new couplet composition in the margin with a proverbial Latin tag (paraphrasing the second line) that implicitly bestows on his English fragment some kind of literary and cultural authority.

Anti-quoting Petrarch

That the couplet should be chosen as the form for housing Petrarchan excerpts is not unfitting. It is, from the earliest sixteenth-century translations of his sonnets, inherently imbued with a sense of the distinctively English character of English Petrarchism: one of Wyatt's foundational innovations in Englishing Petrarch's sonnets was in the deployment of a final couplet (at strophic odds with the two-tercet format of the typical Petrarchan sestet). Translators of Petrarchan fragments, typically opting to encase their source-text in this patriotically English habiliment, seem to have exploited the couplet's associations with epigrammatic integrity and apophthegmatic authority. Yet the couplet form is used on occasions for anti-epigrammatic ends in translating Petrarchan fragments, and points to a fundamental typology of contradiction in the English reception of Petrarch's verse. Speaking of aphorisms as attenuated, without beginning or end, Derrida argues that they exist always in a state of unstable reworking.[58] Exploiting that ontological uncertainty, sixteenth-century English fragments of Petrarch occasionally interrogate the authority of the Petrarchan master-text from which they derive. In Robert Tofte's *Blazon of Jealousie*, a translation of Benedetto Varchi's sixteenth-century Italian treatise on love and jealousy, Tofte juxtaposes two couplet fragments from Petrarch when discussing verbs of provocation. After a digression on Dante, first *RVF* 207.70 and then *RVF* 23.7 are quoted in quick succession:

And *Petrarcq* (after the same manner) writeth thus:

>Hor de miei danni à me medessimo incresse, &c.
>Now to my selfe, I grieue for this my losse,
>Though by her lookes she shewed she sorry was.

Yet neuerthelesse, the same Poet in the first Stanza of his Canzon, of his transformations, taketh it in this our sense, when he saith:

> Poi se giuro si come à me n'increbbe, &c.
> *Then sware she that to me she did no wrong,*
> *Although she vext me for to stay, and looke so long.*

And this is worth the noting (as I said a little before) that one Tuscan word alone, should signifie two things; and those so much different one from another.[59]

The illusion of epigrammatic veracity is exposed, as a second couplet translation disrupts the authority of the first. That it should be Petrarch's metamorphic canzone (the aforementioned *RVF* 23) that is plundered to counterpoint the first quotation seems fitting: one bit of disembodied text interrogates the authority of another, transforming meaning as Petrarch's source-text is broken apart and re-embodied in a new form at odds with its predecessor. *RVF* 23 famously dwells on the resources of verbal memory, the transformation of voice, and a baffling succession of reinscribed selves, betraying an Ovidian fondness for transmogrification into variant forms.

Deployed in this dynamic, self-contradictory way, translated fragments from Petrarch suggest a kind of anti-commonplacing or anti-quoting — quoting an authority disruptively, and at a cynical distance. As with Montaigne's self-mythologizing practice of eclectic burrowing and borrowing of axioms, 'ever heer and there picking and culling, from this and that booke, the sentences that please me, not to keepe them (for I have no store-house to reserve them in) but to transport them into this: where [...] they are no more mine, then in their first place', this anti-commonplacing of Petrarch does not claim ownership over the borrowings so much as imply a critical distance — a disavowal rather than a covert assimilation, and ironizing rather than appropriating.[60] That all Petrarchism is already post-Petrarchism and keeps 'regenerating itself, even as each of the reproductions deconstructs the original', has become a critical truism.[61] Petrarch's characteristic rhetoric of impasse and irresolution is inflected anew in these bitty translations which attest what Christine Hutchins has called 'anti-Petrarchan Petrarchism', a feature arguably distinguishing the English reception of Petrarchan poetics from its Italian or French afterlife.[62] This disruptive quotation of Petrarch's oeuvre questions the veracity and utility of excerptable fragments as excerptable fragments.

The 1598 English translation by 'I.K.' (probably John Keper) of Annibale Romei's *Discorsi cavallereschi* (first published Venice 1585), a treatise on (intellective) beauty that is larded with quotations from Dante, Ariosto, and Petrarch, adopts a bivalent approach to Petrarch's literary and cultural authority, subjecting it to both celebration and interrogation. Admittedly, part of the dialectic tension derives from the Italian original itself, whose speakers are engaged in a dialogue about reading the literary past. These rhetoricized readers of Petrarch are alert to the aporia that lies within dislocated moments lifted from his oeuvre, even as Petrarch's authority and facility for concise, apophthegmatic expression are openly praised. Speakers routinely acknowledge how '*Petrarch* wittily expresseth' a conceit, as in I. K.'s couplet rendering of *RVF* 134.1–2,

> *I find no peace, and yet to warre, dare not be bold:*
> *I feare, and hope, I burne, and yet like ice am cold.*[63]

just as, two years previously, Thomas Lodge illustrated how 'diuine *Petrarch* most wittily singeth' with a deft couplet rendering of *RVF* 7.1–2:

> *La gola il somno, & l'otiose piume,*
> *Hanno dol mundo ogni virtus bandita.*
> Incontinence, dull sleepe, and idle bed,
> All vertue from the world haue banished.[64]

Yet beyond these approving citations of Petrarchan excerpts — excerpts worthy of commonplacing for their utility as *sententiae* or their aesthetic merits of pithy concision — Elizabethan translators readily engage in a more disruptive, belligerent form of quotation. In Romei's extended disquisition on reciprocal love, Petrarch's status as an incontrovertible authority is called into doubt:

> we may coniecture how vainely it was spoken by our Poet;
> Although thou hast thy heart placed full high aboue,
> Waile not, though die thou doost, and languish in her loue.
> For it had beene a truer sentence to haue said:
> Who placed hath his heart mounting too neare the skie,
> May well lament, if he languish through want, and die.[65]

Rent and rendered into fragments, Petrarch's lyric oeuvre is transformed into a contestable source — one that might be improved upon in epigrammatic concision by a countervailing fragment.

Ostensibly canonical and quotable, Petrarch's lyric corpus seems particularly susceptible to these combative revisions, as if inviting a kind of *aemulatio* by which translators contest its constituent parts and scatter them anew in novel formulations. On the continent, Maurice Scève's *Délie* (1544), for all its overt debts to Petrarch, agonistically turned Petrarchan fragments against themselves: in 'borrowing Petrarch's words', Scève 'almost defiantly reverses the meaning of Petrarch's discourse', assigning his words 'a new significance'.[66] In English literary culture, in his commentary on Surrey's translation of *RVF* 145, George Puttenham ventures an epigrammatic, couplet epitome to replace both Petrarch's original sonnet and Surrey's English intermediary ('translated with very good grace'). After reproducing Surrey's sonnet in full, Puttenham opines,

> All which might haue bene said in these two verses.
> *Set me wheresoeuer ye will,*
> *I am and wilbe yours still.*[67]

Whether the result of competitive one-upmanship, a penchant for epigrammatic economy, a demonstration of the possibilities of verse form in the service of vernacular eloquence, or a bold claim to the 'grace' that he attributes to Surrey's rendition of the whole sonnet — achieving the expressive agility, uncoerced elegance, and technical difficulty mastered with apparent ease that are variously connoted by the Italian ideal of *grazia* — Puttenham's couplet exposes tensions between originary literary authority and the vagaries of reception; between a poetic conceit and its formal articulation; and between unitary whole and epigrammatic part. Reducing a sonnet to a couplet fragment, Puttenham's synecdoche is both homage to and critique of Petrarch's literary status as a quotable authority. The couplet form promises epigrammatic authenticity but brings that very ideal into jeopardy.

The Petrarchan fragment, shorn of its original context, is turned against itself. By the end of the sixteenth century, the project of epigrammatizing Petrarch's conceits reaches something of a crisis point. Translating a fragment from Petrarch quoted in Montaigne, Florio succinctly warns against over-curious, *'newfangled inventions'*. When Englishing Montaigne's *Essaies*, Florio supplements Montaigne's quotation of *RVF* 105.48 (left untranslated by Montaigne) with a self-consuming English couplet. We might recall the 'co[m]mon path[es]' trodden earlier by Wyatt:

> Keepe your selves in the common path, it is not good to be so subtil, and so curious. Remember what the Italian proverbe saith,
>
> | *Chi troppo s'assottiglia, si scavezza.* | *Petr.* p. I. canz. |
> | Who makes himselfe too fine, | 13.48. |
> | Doth breake himselfe in fine.[68] | |

Playing on the senses of super-subtlety ('too fine') and finality ('in fine') yoked by the homophonic no-rhyme, Florio's couplet undermines its own epigrammatic status by epigrammatically admonishing the very epigrammatic subtlety it embodies. Florio sets the fragment's aphoristic quotability at odds with its pragmatic implementation. If English sonnet sequences exposed how the sonnet might exhaust its Petrarchan wellsprings (revealing '*Petrarchs* long deceased woes'), the cynical, anti-commonplacing practice of translating Petrarchan fragments was, it seems, no less instrumental in unfolding the expressive limitations of the epigram that notionally succeeded the sonnet as the favoured lyric form in English literary history.

Notes to Chapter 1

1. See, respectively, *Petrarch in Britain: Interpreters, Imitators, and Translators over 700 years*, Proceedings of the British Academy, 146, ed. by Martin McLaughlin, Letizia Panizza, and Peter Hainsworth (Oxford: Oxford University Press, 2007) and *Petrarch's English Laurels, 1475–1700*, ed. by Jackson C. Boswell and Gordon M. Braden (Farnham: Ashgate, 2012).
2. John Mulryan, 'Jonson's Classicism', in *The Cambridge Companion to Ben Jonson*, ed. by Richard Harp and Stanley Stewart (Cambridge: Cambridge University Press, 2000), pp. 163–74 (p. 169).
3. Peter Hainsworth, 'Translating Petrarch', in *Petrarch in Britain*, ed. by McLaughlin, Panizza, and Hainsworth, pp. 341–58 (p. 341).
4. *The Works of Henry Howard, Earl of Surrey, and of Sir Thomas Wyatt the Elder*, ed. by G. F. Nott, 2 vols (London: T. Bensley, 1815–16), II, 118.
5. Giuseppe Mazzotta, 'The "Canzoniere" and the Language of the Self', *Studies in Philology*, 75.3 (1978), 271–96 (p. 274).
6. Nancy J. Vickers, 'The Body Re-membered: Petrarchan Lyric and the Strategies of Description', in *Mimesis: From Mirror to Method, Augustine to Descartes*, ed. by John Lyons and Stephen Nichols (Hanover, NH: New England University Press, 1982), pp. 100–09 (p. 102).
7. *Petrarch's Lyric Poems: The Rime Sparse and Other Lyrics*, ed. by Robert M. Durling (Cambridge, MA: Harvard University Press, 1976), p. 26.

8. Letizia Panizza, 'Literature in the Vernacular', in *The Cambridge History of Italian Literature*, ed. by Peter Brand and Lino Pertile (Cambridge: Cambridge University Press, 1999), pp. 152–77 (p. 162).
9. Olivia Holmes, *Assembling the Lyric Self: Authorship from Troubadour Song to Italian Poetry Book* (Minneapolis: University of Minnesota Press, 2000), p. 171, quoting Armando Petrucci, 'Minuta, autografo, libro d'autore', *Il Libro e il testo: Atti del convegno internazionale (Urbino, 20–23 settembre 1982)*, ed. by Cesare Questa and Renato Raffaelli (Urbino: Università degli studi di Urbino), pp. 399–414 (p. 412).
10. JoAnn Della Neva, 'An Exploding Canon: Petrarch and the Petrarchists in Renaissance France', *Annali d'Italianistica*, 22 (2004), 189–206 (p. 190). See *Il Petrarca novissimamente revisto [...] Con alcuni dottiss. avertimenti di m. Giulio Camillo et indici del Dolce*, ed. by Lodovico Dolce (Venice: G. Giolito, 1553).
11. Respectively, Jonathan Sawday, *The Body Emblazoned: Dissection and the Human Body in Renaissance Culture* (London: Routledge, 1995), pp. 2–3; and Randall Ingram, 'Lego Ego: Reading Seventeenth-Century Books of Epigrams', in *Books and Readers in Early Modern England: Material Studies*, ed. by Jennifer Andersen and Elizabeth Sauer (Philadelphia: University of Pennsylvania Press, 2002), pp. 160–76 (p. 162).
12. Ann Moss, *Printed Commonplace-Books and the Structuring of Renaissance Thought* (Oxford: Clarendon Press, 1996), p. 94.
13. JoAnn Della Neva, 'Scattered Rhymes: Petrarchan Fragments in Scève's *Délie 60*', *French Studies*, 41.2 (1987), 129–40 (pp. 135–36).
14. Robert Cummings, 'Reading Du Bartas', in *Tudor Translation*, ed. by Fred Schurink (New York: Palgrave Macmillan, 2011), pp. 175–96 (p. 185).
15. Della Neva, 'Scattered Rhymes', p. 136.
16. Cornelio Castaldi, *Poesie volgari e latine di Cornelio Castaldi* (Paris: Prault, Briasson, e Tilliard Librari, 1757), p. 65.
17. *Le Familiari*, ed. by Vittorio Rossi and Umberto Bosco, 4 vols (Florence: Sansoni, 1933–42), I.8.23, 23.19.10.
18. William J. Kennedy, 'Petrarchan Poetics', in *The Cambridge History of Literary Criticism*, III: *The Renaissance*, ed. by Glyn P. Norton (Cambridge: Cambridge University Press, 1999), pp. 119–26 (p. 122).
19. Thomas Watson, *The Hekatompathia or Passionate Centurie of Loue* (London: John Wolfe, 1582), C3^r; Philip Sidney, *The Countesse of Pembrokes Arcadia* (Edinburgh: Robert Waldegrave, 1599), Yy4^v–Yy5^r; Henry Constable, *Diana*, in London, Victoria and Albert Museum, Dyce MS 44, 16^r.
20. George Puttenham, *The Arte of English Poesie* (London: Richard Field, 1589), H4^v.
21. George Gascoigne, *The Grief of Joye*, London, British Library, Royal MS 18 A.LXI.
22. George Gascoigne, *A hundreth sundrie flowres* (London: Richard Smith, 1573), A1^r.
23. Respectively, ibid., D1^{rv}, E2^v–E3^v, Hh1^r–Hh2^r.
24. George Gascoigne, *The Posies of George Gascoigne Esquire* (London: Richard Smith, 1575), ¶¶¶3^v.
25. Gabriel Harvey, *Pierces supererogation* (London: John Wolfe, 1593), F4^v–G1^r.
26. Gabriel Harvey, *Three proper, and wittie, familiar Letters* (London: Henry Bynneman, 1580), E1^v–E3^v.
27. John Florio, *Florio his firste fruites* (London: Thomas Woodcock, 1578), L2^v, L3^v; Florio, *Florios second frutes* (London: Thomas Woodcock, 1591), Cc2^v–Cc4^r.
28. Marcel Françon, 'Une Imitation du Sonnet de Pétrarque: Pace non Trovo', *Italica*, 20.3 (1943), 127–31.
29. Mary Thomas Crane, *Framing Authority: Sayings, Self, and Society in Sixteenth-Century England* (Princeton: Princeton University Press, 1993), p. 17.
30. Marc Fumaroli, *L'Age de l'éloquence: Rhétorique et 'res literaria' de la Renaissance au seuil de l'époque classique* (Geneva: Droz, 1980).
31. Cummings, p. 176.
32. Puttenham, Dd1^r.
33. Sidney, Xx6^{rv}.
34. Thomas Wyatt, London, British Library, MS Egerton 2711, 70^r.

35. Watson, E4^r.
36. Stephen Clucas, 'Thomas Watson's *Hekatompathia* and European Petrarchism', in *Petrarch in Britain*, ed. by McLaughlin, Panizza, and Hainsworth, pp. 217–27 (pp. 224–25).
37. Watson, C3r.
38. Henry Howard, *Songes and Sonettes written by the [...] late Earle of Surrey, and other* (London: Richard Tottel, 1557), A3^r–A4^r.
39. Wyatt, MS Egerton 2711, 12^v.
40. Marilyn Randall, *Pragmatic Plagiarism: Authorship, Profit, and Power* (Toronto: University of Toronto Press, 2001), p. 41.
41. Desiderius Erasmus, *Il Ciceroniano*, ed. by Angiolo Gambaro (Brescia: La Scuola, 1965), p. 290.
42. Ben Jonson, *Hymenæi* (London: Valentine Sims, 1606), A3^v.
43. Sidney, Xx1^v.
44. Michael Drayton, *Ideas Mirrovr* (London: Nicholas Ling, 1594), ★2^r.
45. Sidney, Yy5^v.
46. William Scott, *The Modell of Poesye*, London, British Library, MS Add. 81083, 15^v.
47. Joachim du Bellay, *Recueil de poësie* (Paris: G. Cauellat, 1553), no. XVIII.
48. John Harvey, *A Discoursiue Probleme concerning prophesies* (London: Richard Watkins, 1588), B1^v.
49. Desiderius Erasmus, *Enchiridion militis christiani* (London: Wynkyn de Worde, 1533), C7^r.
50. Henry Peacham, *The Garden of Eloquence* (London: Richard Field, 1593), Cc3^r.
51. Scott, 38^v, 39^v.
52. See *OED Online*, Oxford University Press [accessed December 2016].
53. Roger Ascham, *The Scholemaster* (London: John Day, 1570), N2^v–N3^v.
54. Puttenham, M1^v.
55. Cathy Shrank, '"Matters of love as of discourse": The English Sonnet, 1560–1580', *Studies in Philology*, 105.1 (2008), 30–49 (p. 39).
56. Thomas Kyd, *The Householders Philosophie* (London: John Charlewood, 1588), A3^r, D3^r.
57. William Withye, *Commonplace book*, London, British Library, Sloane MS 300, 23^v.
58. Jacques Derrida, '52 aphorismes pour un avant-propos', *Mesure pour mesure: architecture et philosophie*, special issue of *Cahiers du CCI* (1987), 7–13.
59. Robert Tofte, *The Blazon of Jealousie* (London: John Busby, 1615), H2^v.
60. John Florio, *Essays written in French by Michael Lord of Montaigne* (London: Edward Blount, 1613), G1^v.
61. Barbara L Estrin, *Laura: Uncovering Gender and Genre in Wyatt, Donne, and Marvell* (London: Duke University Press, 1994), p. 29.
62. Christine E Hutchins, 'English Anti-Petrarchism: Imbalance and Excess in "the Englishe straine" of the Sonnet', *Studies in Philology*, 109.5 (2012), 552–80 (p. 558).
63. Annibale Romei, *The Courtiers Academie [...] translated into English by I.K.* (London: Valentine Sims, 1598), F2^r.
64. Thomas Lodge, *Wits Miserie* (London: Cuthbert Burby, 1596), O4^v.
65. Romei, F3^r.
66. Della Neva, 'Scattered Rhymes', p. 134.
67. Puttenham, Bb3^v.
68. Florio, *Essays*, Ee1^v.

CHAPTER 2

The New Asclepius: Fragmentation and Reassemblage in Du Bellay's *L'Olive*

Myron McShane

Introduction

Anyone interested in the history of European Petrarchism, or more particularly in the near half-millenium French history of translating and adapting Petrarch's *Canzoniere*, ranging from Clément Marot to Yves Bonnefoy, cannot overlook Du Bellay's *L'Olive*. To begin with, this 1549 work is the first sonnet sequence written in French. Next, the collection of fifty sonnets, expanded one year later to 115, accompanies — or, more precisely, is accompanied by — the same author's celebrated manifesto, *La Deffense et illustration de la langue françoyse*, in which he constructs an elaborate argument for the superiority of imitation over translation. In addition, there is a significant socio-political dimension to the collection insofar as its addressee is Marguerite de France, King Henry II's sister and a notable patron of letters. Yet, despite these features, for many years *L'Olive* chiefly was considered the unloved precursor to *Les Regrets*, Du Bellay's much more favoured sonnet sequence. Not that, in the interim, this lack of admiration prevented considerable scholarship from being written on the subject.[1] However, the sonnet collection was persistently evaluated as tiresome or as essentially a translation of minor Italian 'sonneteers'.[2] Moreover, the Petrarchan sensibility of *L'Olive* was called into question by scholars who saw its primary source in Ariosto and more than thirty poets in contemporary Italian Petrarchist anthologies.[3] From the start, Du Bellay seemingly confused readers by confessing in the preface to the 1549 version of *L'Olive* that he imitated Petrarch, Ariosto, and other modern Italians, before then claiming in a later second preface to the expanded *L'Olive augmentée* that his models were Virgil, Horace, Ovid, and Petrarch.[4] More recently, the critical pendulum has swung back to claiming that *L'Olive* indeed represents a *Pétrarque français*. This perspective has found broad agreement among subsequent commentators.[5]

Given that *L'Olive* has provoked such disparate views, it is worth re-examining the question of how the various intertextual strands found in the collection function. Can a re-examination of the numerous paratexts to the sonnet sequence clarify Du Bellay's aims? Does he have distinct methods in imitating Petrarch? If so, how does this relate to the role of the Petrarchists or Ariosto? In this reanalysis of *L'Olive* and the poetics of literary imitation, I propose to first reassess certain paratextual features of the two editions of the sonnet sequence before considering how fragments from various Petrarchan, anthological, and Ariostan intertexts eventually are reintegrated in *L'Olive*. In reflecting on this poetic process of fragmentation and reassemblage, I have found it useful to emphasize Du Bellay's own fondness in both his theoretical and poetic works for the myth of Asclepius and Hippolytus, in which the god of medicine, on finding the limbs of the celibate youth scattered along the shoreline, miraculously restores him to wholeness. Du Bellay was not the only Renaissance figure to be captivated by this example of division and unity, fragment and totality, the Many and the One. There is frequent recourse to the legend among several generations of Italian humanists familiar to Du Bellay.[6] As there also is in both classic works on Renaissance literary imitation and subsequent scholarship on Du Bellay's *L'Olive*.[7] By contrast, in thus framing the imitative techniques of *L'Olive*, I would like to employ the myth to underline the innovative nature of Du Bellay's sonnet sequence. The old Asclepius, struck dead by lightning for his hubristic act, shows the perils of attempting a miraculous restoration. Du Bellay, in his own reconstitution of poetic fragments, will restore the restorer in the guise of a *nuovo Esculapio*.

The Intention of the Author: Paratexts in *L'Olive*

Unlike most present-day adaptations of Petrarch's *Rerum Vulgarium Fragmenta* (*RVF*), such as the recent volume by Tim Atkins, the text of *L'Olive* did not simply speak for itself.[8] In opposition to present-day notions on how textual interpretation has freed itself from authorial intentionality, Du Bellay quite explicitly entitles the first chapter of the second book of *La Deffense* thus: 'L'intention de l'Aucteur'. Intricate paratexts were to be found in each of the two quite distinct versions of the sonnet sequence. Indeed, throughout this chapter it will be imperative to distinguish between the original *L'Olive* of 1549 comprising fifty sonnets and *L'Olive augmentée* of 1550, which included sixty-five additional ones. It should also be remembered that both collections of sonnets were published in a volume with satires and odes. Even by the era's standards, *L'Olive*'s paratext was markedly elaborate. For *La Deffense*, the treatise championing imitation over translation, was allegedly conceived as a foreword to the 1549 *L'Olive*. According to Du Bellay himself, his large-scale 93-page manifesto was meant to be a liminary text to his smaller 78- page volume of poetry. One year later, in the preface to *L'Olive augmentée*, he explains his reasoning:

> Je craignoy' [...] que telle nouveauté de poësie pour le commencement seroit trouvée fort etrange et rude. Au moyen de quoy, voulant prevenir cete mauvaise opinion, [...] je mis en lumiere ma *Deffence et illustration de la langue françoise*; ne pensant toutefois au commencement faire plus grand oeuvre qu'*une epistre et petit advertissement au lecteur*.[9]

> [I was afraid [...] that such a novel kind of poetry would initially seem very strange and harsh. Because I wanted to avoid this negative view, [...] I brought out my *Defence and Illustration of the French Language*; at the outset, however, I did not consider composing anything larger than an epistle and a short introduction to the reader.]

The claim here is that in order to prevent a poor reception of the novelty ('nouveauté') of *L'Olive*, Du Bellay only intended to write a short foreword ('petit advertissement') to explain his unfamiliar poetry. The preconceived brevity of the foreword seemingly metastasized into a full-length tract arguing for the advantages of imitation over translation for future French poets. The implications of this passage are significant. Rather than consider, as we might expect, that *La Deffense* is a stand-alone work which acts as a catalyst for Du Bellay's poetry, theory in fact follows practice. The primacy of *L'Olive* elevates the volume of poetry to a much higher status if it is seen as the begetter of such an influential treatise. Should we believe this claim? Although the sincerity of Du Bellayan prefatory material has often been doubted, and his assertion that poetry preceded theory is retroactively dated after the first edition of *L'Olive*, there is — speculation aside — no counter evidence against his declaration. Indeed, as François Rigolot was first to emphasize, *La Deffense* functions as a long preface to the first edition of *L'Olive*.[10] That being the case, it should be expected that Du Bellay's manifesto, in keeping with its prefatory nature, will explain how literary imitation in *L'Olive* works. However, the treatise frustrates these expectations. Despite the granular detail that is sometimes found in the work, *La Deffense* is generally more concerned with a conception of literary imitation in its broadest sense as opposed to a thoroughgoing description of intertextual processes. To be sure, explicit reference is made in the text to Petrarch five times. In the first instance, Du Bellay critiques the poet's previous translators:

> Et ce, que je dy des Langues Latine et Greque, se doit reciproquement dire de tous les vulgaires, dont j'allegueray seulement un Petrarque, du quel j'ose bien dire, que si Homere, et Virgile renaissans avoint entrepris de le traduyre, ilz ne le pouroint rendre avecques la mesme grace et nayfveté, qu'il est en son vulgaire Toscan. Toutesfois, quelques uns de notre Tens ont entrepris de le faire parler Françoys.[11]
>
> [And what I say of the Latin and Greek languages can be equally said of all the vulgar tongues, of which I will only cite Petrarch, of whom I daresay that if a reborn Homer and Virgil undertook to translate him, they could not render him with the same grace and freshness that he has in his native Tuscan. Yet some in our time have tried to make him speak French.[12]]

As he does habitually in *La Deffense*, Du Bellay does not specify which poets he means by the vague description 'quelques uns'. He could have intended any one of the previous French translators of Petrarchan sonnets such as Marot, Saint-Gelais, Peletier du Mans and, most extensively, Vasquin Philieul. Later, in discussing various genres, Du Bellay again has recourse to the indefinite in saying: 'Pour le Sonnet donques, tu as Petrarque, et quelques modernes Italiens.'[13] Beyond the anonymous nature of this reference to contemporary 'petrarchisti', this passage also reveals how Du Bellay implicitly suppresses 175 years of the Petrarchist tradition in

Italy. The French poet ruptures the continuity of Petrarchism by banishing, among others, the Quattrocento Petrarchists to oblivion. For Du Bellay, nothing comes between the master of the sonnet and his Italian contemporaries.

Despite its renown as a work of literary theory, however, *La Deffense* in certain respects can be considered a failure in achieving Du Bellay's stated aim of explaining the novelty of his approach in *L'Olive*. For over 400 years, critics continually held him responsible for word-for-word translations. In the very same year that *L'Olive* was published, Thomas Sébillet, his theoretical adversary, accused him of translating word-for-word rather than imitating his models.[14] Again and again, the same charge is repeated by modern scholars.[15] However, within the text itself, the manifesto attempts to forestall these critics. Apart from explicit references to Petrarch, *La Deffense*'s greatest contribution to understanding Du Bellay's views on literary imitation is in its conception of genres. In the chapter entitled *Quelz genres de Poëmes doit elire le Poëte Françoys*, he concludes a list of various forms of poetry and their respective authors, including the citation above on the connection between Petrarch and the sonnet, with the expression 'tu sçais où en doibs trouver les Archetypes'.[16] As Emmanuel Buron has convincingly shown, the essential point in Du Bellay's argument is both to present an archetypal model, as Italian humanists did with Petrarch, and to expand the concept of imitation to include multiple authors.[17] This process leads to an example such as *L'Olive*, where Petrarch represents the overall archetype, while composite imitation of 'quelques modernes Italiens' is also permissible.

One way in which Du Bellay conceives of composite imitation can be found in his revision of a passage from an earlier work championing the vernacular by Sperone Speroni entitled *Dialogo delle lingue*. Now, since the research of Pierre Villey, it is well known that the text of *La Deffense* assiduously imitated the Italian humanist's earlier work.[18] Nearly one-sixth of the treatise is drawn from Speroni's dialogue. Yet, Du Bellay's process of revising the Italian theorist's work provides a valuable perspective on how he alters the foreign text. In a celebrated passage, the figure of the Courtier reports a critique of those who think they can merely gather various words from Latin authors for their own Neo-Latin compositions: 'Il che facendo, se voi sperate (quasi *nuovo Esculapio*) che il porre insieme cotai fragmenti possa farla risuscitare, voi v'ingannate [...].'[19] It is clear that Du Bellay has this passage in mind, when he writes 'Et si vous esperez (*comme fist Esculape* des Membres d'Hippolyte) que par ces fragments recuilliz elles puyssent estre resuscitées, vous vous abusez'[20] Here, Speroni's phrase, 'new Asclepius', has been glossed in the French text with the addition of 'the limbs of Hippolytus' in order to explain the reference. While the meaning of the passage itself is not entirely altered, the suppression of *nuovo* superficially seems to weaken the force of the original phrase. Du Bellay's substitution is significant insofar as his revision shows he was not simply passively retranscribing Speroni's text, but took note of the phrase through an act of glossing. Unlike Speroni's negative example of failed Neo-Latin poets, whose works of resuscitation are a 'chose impossible', inherent in Du Bellay's rewritten version is the existence of a vernacular counter-example.[21] The title of the eleventh chapter from which this citation derives, 'Qu'il est impossible d'egaler les Anciens en leurs Langues', implies that it is in fact entirely possible to rival past writers in French. While other commentators have remarked on the relevance of this passage to its applicability to Du Bellay's manner of imitation in *L'Olive*, I want to emphasize not just how Du Bellay is performing an Asclepian task of reassemblage, but rather to accent the radical novelty of his enterprise as the *new* version of the divine restorer. The theory becomes practice in *L'Olive augmentée*. In this second version of *L'Olive*, published without *La Deffense*, Asclepius is directly addressed in what has justly been described as a riddlingly allusive text:

> Toy, qui fis voir la lumiere incongnue
> Au chaste filz du jaloux inhumain,
> Quand tu pillas d'une trop docte main
> La proye en vain de Pluton retenue.[22] (*OA* 90.1–4)

[You showed the unknown light of the jealous inhuman one to the virginal son, when you too cleverly snatched the prey held back in vain from Pluto.]

For the hubristic deed of thwarting Pluto ('jaloux inhumain') and restoring ('d'une trop docte main') Hippolytus ('chaste filz'), Asclepius is struck ('te foudroyant') in the second quatrain by the vengeful bolts ('traictz vengeurs') of Jupiter ('l'horrible Dieu'). But the new Asclepius, the poet-lover of *L'Olive*, manages — unlike the god of medicine — to foil Pluto:

> Las moy chetif! qui l'oblivieux bord,
> Malgré L'Enfer, Acheron et son port,
> Ay depouillé de sa plus riche proye! (*OA* 90.9–11)

[Alas I, the wretched, have robbed the oblivious shore of its richest prey, in spite of Hell, Acheron and its port!]

In this first tercet, the new Asclepian narrator, now in the guise of Orpheus, has dispossessed ('depouillé') Pluto ('L'Enfer') on the shore of Lethe ('oblivieux bord') of Olive herself, allusively embedded in the adjective 'oblivieux' (ObLIViEux).[23] In the concluding tercet, Orpheus, as the new Asclepius, immortalizes his *innamorata*:

> Celle que j'ay faict compagnie des Dieux,
> Me bat, me poingt, me brusle, me foudroye
> Par les doulx traictz qui sortent de ses yeulx. (*OA* 90.11–14)

[*That* one, whom I made companion of the Gods, beats, grabs, burns, and strikes me with the sweet bolts that radiate from her eyes.]

The narrator of *L'Olive* raises his lady ('celle') to divine status ('faict compagnie des Dieux') only to be punished by the sweet bolts ('doulx traictz') of Olive's eyes rather than the previously mentioned vengeful ones of Jupiter. Thus Du Bellay has transformed the presence of Asclepius from *La Deffense*, the prosaic prefatory text of the 1549 *L'Olive*, to the poetic sonnet in *L'Olive augmentée*.

La Deffense may be the largest element of the preface to *L'Olive*, but there are other aspects of Du Bellay's paratextual machinery that are worth attending to. There is no need to revisit the overall structure of the paratexts, since Cécile Alduy has already provided an overview of the symmetry between *La Deffense*'s own paratexts and those of *L'Olive*.[24] However, certain essential details of the prefatory material to the 1549 sonnet sequence have yet to be explored. The title of the initial edition, *L'Olive et quelques autres oevvres poêticques*, immediately reveals that the sonnets are but one single part of Du Bellay's overall poetic vision at that time. In addition to *Cinquante sonnetz à la louange de L'Olive* there is also a satire and odes: *L'Anterotique de la vieille, & de la jeune Amye* and *Vers lyriques*. In this respect, Du Bellay's Petrarchan project is only part of an ambition to execute a trio of works. The emphasis on the triadic nature of the 1549 *L'Olive* is worth underlining. There is a justifiable tendency to place an emphasis on the pairing of the sonnets and odes, due to Du Bellay's own remarks in the preface to *L'Olive augmentée*: 'à la persuasion de Jaques Peletier, je choisi le Sonnet, et l'Ode' [at the urging of Jacques Peletier, I chose the Sonnet and the Ode].[25] Yet, a closer examination of the relationship between these three works will provide a further insight into Du Bellay's conception of the overall structure of the original version of *L'Olive*. *L'Anterotique* certainly functions in an aesthetic sense to vary the tone of the volume, as the invective against an old woman has rightly been thought of as a *Contre-Olive*.[26] Indeed, this work foreshadows Du Bellay's later satire on the banalities of the Petrarchan tradition in his poem 'Contre les Pétrarquistes'. But *L'Anterotique* is also a vital component in the strikingly symmetrical structure of the three works. Let us re-emphasize that the overall title of the work, *L'Olive et quelques autres oevvres poêticques*, establishes the primacy of the sonnet sequence in relation to the other two works, as does its initial placement in the subseqent list of contents. Yet, the respective length of each work suggests that the *Vers lyriques* (36 pages/866 lines) is more substantial than either the *Cinquante sonnetz à la louange de l'Olive* (23 pages/700 lines) or *L'Anterotique* (8 pages/214 lines). In a skilful arrangement that has, to my knowledge, gone unremarked by previous commentators, the numerical total of *L'Anterotique*, counted as one poem, and the *Vers lyriques*, comprising thirteen separate poems, equals in number the fourteen lines which make up each of the fifty sonnets. In this way, Du Bellay's clever parallelism between the sonnet form and the number of other poems in the volume formally creates a symmetry between the three works which re-emphasizes the importance of the sonnets in relation to *L'Anterotique* and the *Vers lyriques*. Such numerological correspondences were not unfamiliar to Du Bellay. Several scholars have noted that the collection of fifty sonnets ($7 \times 7 + 1$) has Minervan and Pythagorean overtones.[27] In addition, it should be noted that the total number of sonnets in *L'Olive augmentée* also has a resonance with the number seven (115 or $1 + 1 + 5 = 7$).

Du Bellay is not the sole author to appear in *L'Olive*. In fact, two Neo-Latin poets, Jean Dorat and Salmon Macrin, respectively, wrote liminary poems to the two editions of the sonnet sequence. Dorat's dedicatory poem, 'Ioannes Auratus In Olivam', marks the only time the name Petrarch appears in verse in the 1549 edition of *L'Olive*. The mentor to the Pléiade makes the claim that Petrarch surpassed *'scripta vetusta'* ('the writings of the ancients') and that Du Bellay's Olive 'comitatur' ('accompanies') Petrarch's Laura. Already, the future royal poet is busy establishing a relationship of equality between Petrarch and his student Du

Bellay. Dorat concludes his elegiacs by further reinforcing connections between the pagan gods and Franco-Italian poets: 'Phoebus amat Laurum, glaucam sua Pallas Olivam' ('Phoebus loves Laura, just as Pallas Athena loves the green-grey Olive').[28] Similarly, Du Bellay will emphasize from the opening sonnet of *L'Olive*, 'Egal un jour au Laurier immortel' (*O* 1.14), to the conclusion of *L'Olive augmentée*, 'Jusq'à l'egal des Lauriers tousjours verds' (*OA* 115.14), that he will equal Petrarch. Notably, the French poet does not claim that he will surpass the Tuscan. Even in *La Deffense*, which is frequently described as polemical, the emphasis is on equalling Greek and Latin, 's'egaler aux superbes langues Greque, et Latine', rather than surpassing the classical languages.[29] In the broader context of Renaissance imitation theory, Du Bellay was probably aware of Bartolomeo Ricci's *De Imitatione*, published eight years earlier, where the Italian humanist outlined his tripartite model of literary imitation as either following (*sequi*), imitation (*imitari*) or emulation (*aemulari*).[30] Although Du Bellay will imply in Sonnet 3 that he can surpass the *RVF* by favourably comparing the tributaries of his Loire ('Loire fameux, qui ta petite source | Enfles de maintz gros fleuves et ruysseaux') to Petrarch's Italian river ('le Pau envieux'), his explicit position throughout *L'Olive* echoes Dorat's emphasis on equality rather than dominance.

Imitating Petrarch: Canzone 70

A key to understanding how Du Bellay employs Petrarch intertextually is recognizing that the *RVF* functions, like *L'Olive*, as a polyglot text.[31] By this claim, I do not wish merely to emphasize that the name of Petrarch's sonnet sequence is in Latin. Rather, it is the fleeting presence of Provençal which provides a clue, heretofore unremarked, to the principal way in which Du Bellay incorporates fragments from Petrarch's own words in his sonnet sequence. To understand Du Bellay's main imitative process, it is worth starting with some overlooked words of the poet himself. This brief description of imitative procedures in the preface to *L'Olive augmentée* may have been previously neglected due to the context, where he is speaking of his alleged imitation of French poets. Du Bellay's comments, however, equally apply to his direct citations from Petrarch:

> Combien voit on entre les Latins immitateurs des Grecz, et entre les modernes Italiens immitateurs des Latins, de commmencemens et de fins de vers, de couleurs et figures poëtiques quasi semblables?' (*OA* 51)
>
> [Among Latin imitators of the Greeks and modern Italian imitators of the Romans, how similar are the beginning and ending of verses and the rhetorical colours and figures?]

Among the three ways of imitation Du Bellay enumerates, the initial portion of his first example specifies the beginnings of lines of verse. This observation about how Roman poets copy the *incipits* of Greek poets and how, in turn, contemporary Italians copy their countrymen, underlines the long-established practice of imitating first lines of poems in the three literary cultures Du Bellay prized in *La Deffense*. Given the initial emphasis about this technique, it is not surprising to find that a majority of Du Bellay's intertextual borrowings from Petrarch are *incipits* from the *RVF*. While this method escaped the notice of *L'Olive*'s earlier editors, whose focus was on the enumeration of figures, a later critic included the presence of *incipits* from the *RVF* in a fourfold categorization of imitative strategies in Du Bellay's sonnet sequence.[32] The text's recentest editor has greatly extended this analysis by determining that more than half of the references to the *RVF*, thirty-five of sixty-five, are of this type.[33] Remarkably, the imitation of Petrarchan first lines is found in 30 per cent of *L'Olive augmentée*. Sonnet 3 of *L'Olive* offers an example of this ubiquitous process: 'Loyre fameux, qui ta petite source | Enfles' transposes Petrarch's 'Rapido fiume, che d'alpestra vena' to Du Bellay's home province. The intertextual link is made more fitting by considering that *RVF* 208 proceeds to make a pun on the Rhone ('rodendo intorno') before urging the river to flow onward ('vattene innanzi') to Avignon, thereby emphasizing the shared literary geography of the two poets.

This predilection of Du Bellay's for citing the first line of Petrarchan sonnets has been attributed to several factors, such as the wish to re-create a Petrarchan ambience, the desire to prompt the reader's memory of the *RVF*, or as a reflection of Renaissance editorial practices, with their detailed appendices of first lines in editions of the Italian sonnets.[34] While these considerations are all valid in accounting for this practice, there is also a noted precedent for this textual operation in the *RVF* itself, if the above-mentioned reference to Occitan is further explored.

If we turn to canzone 70 in the *RVF*, Petrarch's own fondness for this technique will become apparent:

> Lasso me, ch' i' non so in qual parte pieghi
> la speme ch' è tradita omai più volte!
> Che se non è chi con pietà m'ascolte,
> perché sparger al ciel si spessi preghi?
> Ma s'egli aven ch'ancor non mi si nieghi
> finir anzi 'l mio fine
> queste voci meschine,
> non gravi al mio signor perch'io il ripreghi
> di dir libero un dì tra l'erba e i fiori:
> *Drez et rayson es qu'ieu ciant e·m demori.* (RVF 70.1–10)[35]

> [Oh what to do with all that hope of mine
> by now betrayed so many, many times!
> Since no one offers me an ear of pity,
> why cast so many prayers into the air?
> But should it be that I not be denied
> an end to my poor words,
> before my end has come,
> I beg my lord it please him let me say
> again one day, free in the grass and flowers:
> 'It's right and just that I sing and be joyful.'[36]]

The last line of this first stanza happens to be the first verse of a canzone attributed to either William of St Gregory or Arnaut Daniel. What makes this citation of an *incipit* even more apt is that the Italian poet cites the line in Provençal, thereby providing an example of Du Bellay's oft-used technique in a language geographically associated with France. The next Petrarchan stanza concludes with the initial line from a Cavalcanti canzone: *Donna mi priegha, per ch'io voglio dire* (70.20). The first line of one of Dante's stony rhymes ends the third stanza *così nel mio parlar voglio esser aspro* (70.30), while Cino da Pistoia's *La dolce vista e 'l bel guardo soave*, concluding the fourth stanza, is the initial line of his canzone on the death of his lady (70.40). Finally, Petrarch ends with an autocitation: *nel dolce tempo de la prima etade*, quoting the beginning line from his very own canzone 23. Notably, this early poem by Petrarch occupies a privileged place as the first canzone in the *RVF*.

Clearly, canzone 70 is a poetic manifesto in which Petrarch pays homage to his Italian and Provençal forebears. It is highly unlikely that Du Bellay would not have noticed the Italian poet's use of five *incipits* in this text. On the contrary, he could rely on cultivated readers of the *RVF* to make the association between Petrarch's imitative techniques and his own. Indeed, in certain cases Du Bellay does not just quote the opening line of a sonnet from the *RVF*, but concludes his own sonnet with an *incipit*. Witness sonnet 4 of *L'Olive*, where the last line, 'Par leur doulceur angelique et seraine', refers to the opening line of Petrarch's sonnet 276: 'Poi che la vista angelica serena'. It should also be noted that this Du Bellayan penchant for the first lines of Petrarchan sonnets becomes more pronounced when one compares the original version of *L'Olive* to its subsequent 1550 edition. Petrarchan *incipits* are imitated more than twice as often in *L'Olive augmentée* (twenty-four out of thirty-five).[37] When critics characterize the 1550 edition as having a more noticeable Petrarchan nature, the use of *incipits* contributes actively to Du Bellay's creation of a dense verbal association with the vernacular poetry of his Italian predecessor.[38] Yet, despite this frequent recourse to first lines from the *RVF*, Du Bellay's reluctance to imitate entire Petrarchan sonnets in *L'Olive*, excepting an example discussed below, indicates his fragmentary perspective on the relationship between the part to the whole in imitating his Italian predecessor.

Selective Stratification: Petrarchism and the Giolito Anthologies

At the very beginning of the twentieth century, Henri Chamard, the first modern editor of Du Bellay's complete works, did not mention how much the poet relied on two contemporary collections of Petrarchist poetry known as the Giolito anthologies. This oversight is not as surprising as it may seem. Du Bellay's most hostile contemporary critics, such as Aneau and Sébillet, as well as admirers like the humanist Etienne Pasquier, were well aware of their existence, but curiously did not directly mention them either. Indeed, Du Bellay himself left the matter vague, as we have seen, by speaking of the influence of 'quelques modernes italiens'. The discovery that he closely imitated over thirty poets from two volumes of Giolito's *Rime diverse*, published respectively in 1545 and 1547, had to wait for Joseph Vianey's publication on the Italian sources of *L'Olive*. In subsequent decades, this painstaking investigative work was further refined in order to indicate whom, among the various authors in the anthologies, Du Bellay had followed.[39] Faced with such seemingly overwhelming evidence, researchers concluded that the Giolito anthologies, rather than Petrarch, were the principal source for *L'Olive*.[40] And later commentators agreed.[41] Later still, for reasons outlined above, a reaction against such a reductive reading of the sonnet sequence took hold. Indeed, an injunction was given to forget the sources in order to better grasp the singular nature of *L'Olive*.[42] To put it in Renaissance rhetorical terms, Du Bellay may have followed the 'verba' of the Petrarchists, but overall he imitated the 'res' of Petrarch.

Significant scholarship has been devoted to discussing the Giolito anthologies themselves.[43] Furthermore, Du Bellay's imitations of over thirty poets from the Giolito anthologies, though seemingly word for word, have been shown to be actually far more artful than originally thought. Although demonstrations of Du Bellay's skill in imitative transposition could be extended to all the examples he borrows and adapts from the anthologies, there is no reason to repeat here what previous analyses have already indicated.[44] Nor is there a need to re-examine how Du Bellay borrows exclusively from volume 1 of the *Rime diverse* in the first version of *L'Olive*, while employing both volumes in the expanded version of the sonnet sequence.[45]

What is worth insisting upon is the enduring existence of the verbal traces of the Giolito poets in *L'Olive augmentée*. On the one hand, it is certainly true that the explicit textual presence of Petrarch increases in *L'Olive augmentée* while that of the *Rime diverse* recedes.[46] Yet, despite the double movement towards Petrarch both conceptually and stylistically in the 1550 edition of *L'Olive*, the ongoing presence of Petrarchism is worth noting. Even one of the concluding sonnets of *L'Olive augmentée*, which begins with the celebrated line 'Si nostre vie est moins qu'une journée' (*OA* 113), closely follows Bernardino Daniello's 'Se 'l viver nostro è breve oscuro giorno'. As previous analyses have shown, Du Bellay's Neoplatonic conclusion to his sonnet sequence is more sophisticated than the work of his Italian predecessor.[47] Yet vestiges of the Giolito poets remain. Some have emphasized the relationship between Petrarch and Petrarchism as that of archetype and ongoing tradition.[48] Others have noted the juxtaposition between the fragmentary nature of Petrarch's eponymous single-author *RVF* and the multi-author fragmentation intrinsic to anthologies.[49] I would like to note further how *L'Olive* selectively represents the Petrarchist tradition. In favouring the Giolito poets, Du Bellay disrupts the continuity of the Petrarchan lineage as much as he faithfully reproduces Petrarch's imitators. He excises Quattrocento Petrarchists, such as Tebaldeo and Aquilano, in the same way that he leaves Dante unmentioned in his literary treatise. If these aesthetic choices can ultimately be traced back to the influence of Pietro Bembo, whom Du Bellay explicitly invokes in *La Deffense*, ('Je me contenteray de nommer ce Docte Cardinal Pierre Bembe'), their significance goes beyond the matter of theoretical genealogy.[50] Rather, the French poet discriminates among the sedimentary layers of Petrarchan tradition to produce a selective stratification. The benefit of imitating the Giolito poets is that Du Bellay is able to avoid relying too closely on Petrarch while, at the same time, invoking an anthological model that resists attaching a specific identity to any of the poets representing the Petrarchist tradition.

Tri-Generic Imitation: Ariosto, Virgil, and Petrarch

If the Giolito poets dedicated themselves to perpetuating the Petrarchan sonnet form, Ariosto's generic multiplicity represented a more complex imitative model for Du Bellay. Early commentators were quick to notice how both Ariosto's sonnets and epic *Orlando Furioso* influenced Du Bellay.[51] In fact, the Italian poet is cited twenty-one times in *L'Olive*. Overall, the epic is favoured slightly over the sonnets (twelve to nine). In the chapter on epic poetry in *La Deffense*, Du Bellay ranks Ariosto so highly that he hastens to add a disclaimer to temper his enthusiasm:

> si tu as quelquefois pitié de ton pauvre Langaige, si tu daignes l'enrichir de tes Thesors, ce sera toy veritablement qui luy feras hausser la Teste, et d'un brave sourcil s'egaler aux superbes Langues Greque, et Latine, comme a faict de nostre Tens en son vulgaire un Arioste Italien, que j'oseroy' (n'estoit la saincteté des vieulx Poëmes) comparer à un Homere et Virgile.[52]

> [If you at times pity our impoverished language, if you deign to enrich it with your treasures, it will truly be you who will make it lift its head and with a gallant brow match those proud Greek and Latin languages, as in our time an Italian Ariosto has done in his vulgar tongue, whom I would dare (were it not for the sanctity of the old poems), compare to a Homer and Virgil.[53]]

Only the prestigious antiquity of the classical epics prevents Du Bellay from declaring the Italian epic poet the equal to his Greek and Latin forebears. As for the sonnets, several critics have already indicated how Du Bellay both closely follows and subtly adapts Ariosto's shorter poems in *L'Olive*.[54] My goal here is to demonstrate not only how Du Bellay verbally imitates Ariosto's poetry, but also how his adaptations establish the presence of multiple genres relating to Petrarch and Virgil.

In Ariosto's tenth sonnet, he employs the figure of *praeteritio* to speak of his powerlessness before his *innamorata*:

> Com'esser può che dignamente io lodi
> vostre bellezze angeliche e divine,
> se mi par ch'a dir sol del biondo crine
> volga la lingua inettamente e snodi? (*Rime* 10.1–4)[55]

> [How can it be that I should fittingly praise your angelic and divine beauties if, in only speaking of your blond mane, my tongue moves awkwardly and I become undone?]

Although Du Bellay's version seems to be a close translation, there are both subtle and conspicuous alterations:

> Auray'-je bien de louer le pouvoir
> Ceste beauté, qui décore le monde,
> Quand pour orner sa chevelure blonde
> Je sens ma langue ineptement mouvoir? (*O* 8.1–4)

> [Would I have the power to praise this beauty who adorns the world, when I feel my tongue move awkwardly in beautifying her blonde hair?]

In the first quatrain, the French adaptation goes beyond the narrow confines of the speaker and his lady by claiming that her hair is not merely angelic in itself, but that her locks enhance the world itself ('qui decore le monde'). Du Bellay proceeds to follow Ariosto's original sonnet quite closely. However, a comparison of the final tercet in both versions reveals a significant substitution:

> Deh! morso avess'io, come Ascreo, l'alloro.
> Di queste, se non d'altro, direi tanto,
> che morrei cigno, ove tacendo io moro. (*Rime* 10.11–14)

[O that I had bitten the laurel, like the Ascrean! On these matters, if not others, I could say so much that I would die a swan whereby, remaining silent, I die.]

> Puis que pour vous (cheveulx) j'ay tel martyre,
> Que n'ay-je beu à la fontaine saincte?
> Je mourroy' cygne, où je meurs sans mot dire. (*O* 8.11–14)

[Since for you, hair, I have such suffering, why didn't I drink at the sacred fountain? I would have died a swan, whereas I die without saying a word.]

In the Italian version, Ariosto's striking phrase about biting the laurel ('morso avess'io') refers to the tradition where Greek poets received poetic inspiration by ingesting laurel leaves. In comparing himself to the Ascraean ('come Ascraeo'), the Italian poet employs a Virgilian epithet to refer to Hesiod (*Georgics* 2.176), whose traditional birthplace was in the town of Ascra in Boeotia. The text also alludes, of course, to the Petrarchan laurel ('l'alloro') whose poetic significance derives from the opening of Hesiod's *Theogony*, where the Greek didactic poet mentions that the Muses 'gave him a sceptre of laurel' ('καί μοι σκῆπτρον ἔδον δάφνης' [30]). In his own version, Du Bellay has chosen to replace the overt Petrarchan symbol in Ariosto's sonnet with another reference to the *Georgics*. In mentioning the sacred fountain ('la fontaine saincte'), Du Bellay is referencing *Castaliam* or the Castalian spring on Mount Parnassus (*Georgics*, 3.293). This substitution both erases an overt reference to Petrarch's laurel/Laura while at the same time subtly reproducing Ariosto's intertextual use of the *Georgics*. In such a way, Ariosto and Du Bellay each incorporate an element from the Virgilian didactic genre of the *Georgics* in their sonnets.

In the 1550 version of *L'Olive*, Ariosto's presence, like that of the Giolito Anthology, recedes in favour of the *RVF*. In fact, the Italian poet's role diminishes in a more marked fashion (sixteen references in fifty sonnets in *L'Olive*, compared to only five in the sixty-five sonnets in *L'Olive augmentée*). Despite this significant reduction, Du Bellay borrows from Ariosto in nearly 20 per cent of the sonnets (twenty-one of 115 sonnets). If there is a quantitative decrease in Ariostan imitation in *L'Olive augmentée*, the qualitative consequences of these borrowings nevertheless remain significant. In sonnet 93, Du Bellay, as has long been known, imitates an entire sonnet by Petrarch for the first and only time. Here are the opening quatrains:

> Cantai, or piango, et non men di dolcezza
> del pianger prendo che del canto presi,
> ch'a la cagion, non a l'effetto, intesi
> son i miei sensi vaghi pur d'altezza.

> Indi et mansuetudine et durezza
> et atti feri, et umili et cortesi
> porto egualmente, né me gravan pesi,
> né l'arme mie punta di sdegni spezza. (*RVF* 229.1–8)

[I sang, and now I weep, and I take no less
delight in weeping than I took in singing,
for the cause and not the effect, is in
my senses, longing for my noble one.

So I bear mildness and severity,
cruel or humble or courteous actions,
equally, no weight burdens me,
no weapon tipped with disdain touches me.[56]]

> Ores je chante, et ores je lamente,
> Si l'un me plaist, l'autre me plaist aussi,
> Qui ne m'areste à l'effect du souci,
> Mais à l'object de ce qui me tormente.
>
> Soit bien ou mal, desespoir ou attente,
> Soit que je brusle ou que je soy' transi,
> Ce m'est plaisir de demeurer ainsi:
> Egalement de tout je me contente. (*OA* 93.1–8)[57]

[Now I sing and now I lament; if I like one, I like the other too. I don't linger over the result of my trouble, but the author of my torment. Whether good or bad, despairing or expectant, whether I burn or am numb, it's a pleasure to remain like this: I am equally happy with either.]

The French version, while close to the original, slightly modifies the Italian by avoiding the military metaphor of armour ('spezza', *RVF* 229.8) present in Petrarch. But, as in sonnet 8 above, Du Bellay provides a notable interpolation in the sestet:

> Tengan dunque ver' me l'usato stile
> Amor, madonna, il mondo et mia fortuna,
> ch'i' non penso esser mai se non felice.
>
> viva o mora o languisca, un più gentile
> stato del mio non è sotto la luna
> si dolce è del mio amaro la radice. (*RVF* 229.9–14)

[Let Love, my lady, world and fortune
treat me as they have always done,
and I will never think myself unhappy.

Alive, or dead, or languishing, there's no
state better than mine beneath the moon,
so sweet is the root of my bitterness.[58]]

> Madame donc, Amour, ma destinée,
> Ne changent point de rigueur obstinée,
> Ou hault ou bas la Fortune me pousse.
>
> Soit que je vive ou bien soit que je meure,
> Le plus heureux des hommes je demeure,
> Tant mon amer a la racine doulce. (*OA* 93.9–14)

[So let my lady, Love, my fate, never change their unyielding severity, whether Fortune thrusts me high or low. Whether I live or whether I die, I live as the happiest of men, as long as my bitterness has so sweet a root.]

In the first tercet, Du Bellay exchanges Petrarch's broad emphasis on both the world and fortune ('il mondo et mi fortuna' [world and fortune]) for a narrower focus on destiny ('Ou hault ou bas la Fortune me pousse' [whether Fortune thrusts me high or low]). This selective emphasis on Fortuna is not merely a case whereby *L'Olive augmentée* rephrases lines from the 1549 edition such as 'Ou hault ou bas me pousse la fortune' (*O* 33.2 [*OA* 35.2]). Such phrasal reworkings happen to be a signature technique in the expanded sonnet sequence, as can be seen by the last line of sonnet 93, where 'Tant mon amer a la racine doulce' had been, in an earlier formulation, 'De mon amer la tant doulce racine' (*OA* 77). Instead, Du Bellay's transposition of word order using 'pousser' and 'Fortune' finds an analogue in Ariosto's own transpositional self-referentiality. Notably, Du Bellay inserted an Ariostan line employed in both Capitolo 13 and in his *Rime*: 'alto o basso Fortuna che mi ruote'. Or, alternatively, the French poet cited a third transposition by Ariosto from *Orlando Furioso*: 'o me Fortuna in alto o in basso ruote' (44.56.4).

Du Bellay's imitation of Ariosto's multiple genres matches a similar process he pursues in his citational strategy of Virgilian genres. In Sonnet 45 of *L'Olive*, the poet under the 'arbre pasle' recalls *Eclogue* 5, where the shepherd Menalcas compares the yielding of the pale olive tree ('pallenti olivae') to Amyntas' inclinations for Mopsus.[59] As the text of *L'Olive* imitates three Ariostan genres (epic, sonnet, capitolo), so too does it reference three major Virgilian genres, (bucolic, didactic, epic). In turn, Du Bellay would have found a model for this tri-generic strategy in Petrarch's own use of Virgil in the *RVF*. For the Italian poet explicitly cites, among many examples, the Roman epic in sestina 22.26 ('l'amorosa selva' [the amorous wood]; *Aeneid* 6.442), the didactic poem in sonnet 24.8 ('l'inventrice de le prime olive' [the inventress of the olive tree]; 'oleacque Minerva inventrix' [and Minerva, inventress of the olive tree], *Georgics* 1.18) and bucolics in sonnet 185 ('un liquido sottile | foco' [a subtle liquid fire]; 'et liquidi simul ignis' [and like liquid fire], *Eclogues* 6.33). In the preface to *L'Olive augmentée*, Du Bellay pays homage to the Mantuan by placing his name at the head of a revised list of sources: 'Encor' diray-je bien que ceulx qui ont leu les oeuvres de Virgile, d'Ovide, d'Horace, de Pétrarque, et beaucoup d'aultres' [I would say again that those who have read the works of Virgil, Ovid, Horace, Petrarch, and many others].[60] The expansive nature of the Petrarchan sonnet form, in allowing for a tri-generic Virgil, finds an analogous process in Du Bellay's *L'Olive*, through reference to the multiple genres in Ariosto, Virgil, and Petrarch.

Conclusion

The impact of *L'Olive* on Du Bellay's fellow poets can readily be seen in the many volumes of sonnets produced over the next fifty years in France by, among many others, Ronsard, Pontus de Tyard, Baïf, Magny, and Desportes. In the final nine years of a truncated life, Du Bellay would reverse three positions he upheld when composing *L'Olive*. For personal and socio-literary reasons, he wound up ridiculing Petrarchists, translating rather than imitating poets, and authoring Neo-Latin verse. Yet, at the time Du Bellay wrote *L'Olive* and *L'Olive augmentée*, his views on imitation allowed for a wide-ranging series of methods to adapt Petrarch in French. A brief perusal of the recentest edition of *L'Olive* will reveal that Du Bellay went beyond the primary models discussed in this chapter.[61] Nevertheless, the way in which he gathers fragments from Petrarch, the Petrarchist tradition, and Ariosto demonstrates an original way in which to balance the requirements of archetype and composite. Fittingly, the Renaissance attachment to the metaphor of Asclepius began with philology, as Poliziano drew upon the figure of the divine healer in an attempt to restore the mutilated manuscripts of Cicero's *De natura deorum*.[62] Similarly, modern-day critics have adopted divergent views when confronted with the disconnected procedures at work in *L'Olive*. In the form of a learned dialogue, Speroni had the god of medicine represent the futility of classicism confronted by nascent vernaculars. A new Asclepius was deemed an unachievable figure until the appearance of the first sonnet sequence in French.[63]

Notes to Chapter 2

1. Michel Magnien, 'Bibliographie des Agrégations de Lettres 2008, Du Bellay: *Deffence et illustration de la langue française* et *L'Olive* (1549–1550)', *Seizième siècle*, 4 (2008), 325–40 (pp. 334–40).
2. See Henri Chamard, *Joachim Du Bellay, 1522–1560* (Lille: Travaux et mémoires de l'Université de Lille, 1900; reprint, Geneva: Slatkine, 1969), p. 199; and Thomas Greene, *The Light in Troy: Imitation and Discovery in Renaissance Poetry* (New Haven: Yale University Press, 1982), p. 220.
3. See Joseph Vianey, *Le Pétrarquisme en France au XVIe siècle* (Montpellier: Coulet, 1909; reprint, Geneva: Slatkine, 1969), pp. 85–97; and Ernesta Caldarini, 'Nuove fonti italiane dell'*Olive*', *Bibliothèque d'Humanisme et Renaissance*, 12 (1965), 395–434 (p. 433).
4. See Joachim Du Bellay, *L'Olive*, ed. by Ernesta Caldarini (Geneva: Droz, 1974). For the 1549 preface, see the Appendice, p. 168. For the second preface, see p. 50. All references to *L'Olive* are from this edition. References in the text to the 1549 edition of *L'Olive* are indicated by the abbreviation O, while those from the 1550 edition, *L'Olive augmentée*, are cited as OA.
5. For the phrase *Pétrarque français*, see Joachim Du Bellay, *Oeuvres poétiques*, ed. by Daniel Aris and Françoise Joukovsky, 2 vols (Paris: Classiques Garnier, 1993), I, p. xviii. Subsequent commentators include Olivier Millet, 'Du Bellay et Pétrarque, autour de *l'Olive*', in *Les poètes français de la Renaissance et Pétrarque*, ed. by Jean Balsamo (Geneva: Droz, 2004), pp. 253–66; Cécile Alduy, 'L'Arbre et la branche: croissance du recueil et défense de la langue française (1549–1550)', in *Du Bellay, une révolution poétique? La Deffence, et Illustration de la langue françoyse & L'Olive*, ed. by Bruno Roger-Vasselin (Paris: CNED/PUF, 2007), pp. 35–57; and Emmanuel Buron and Nadia Cernogora, *Du Bellay: La Deffence et illustration de la langue françoyse, L'Olive* (Neuilly: Editions Atlande, 2007).
6. See Angelo Poliziano, *Miscellaneorum centuria secunda*, ed. by Vittore Branca and Manlio Pastore Stocchi (Florence: Olschki, 1978), p. 3; and Sperone Speroni, *I dialogi di Messer Speron Speroni* (Venice: Aldus, 1542), p. 130.
7. See Greene, *Troy*, pp. 147–71, and subsequently Perrine Galand-Hallyn, *Le 'Génie' latin de Joachim Du Bellay* (La Rochelle: Rumeur des Ages, 1995), pp. 32–34; Buron and Cernogora, *Du Bellay*, p. 158; and Cynthia Nazarian, 'Du Bellay's Petrarchan Politics: Violence and Imitation in the *Olive* and the *Deffence*', *Modern Language Quarterly*, 74 (2013), 1–28 (pp. 15–20).
8. Tim Atkins, *Petrarch* (Toronto: BookThug, 2013).
9. Du Bellay, *L'Olive*, p. 46; my emphasis. All translations are mine unless otherwise indicated.
10. François Rigolot, 'Esprit critique et identité poétique: Du Bellay préfacier', in *Du Bellay. Actes du*

colloque international d'Angers du 26 au 29 mai 1989, 2 vols (Angers: Presses de l'université d'Angers, 1989), I, 285–300 (p. 289).
11. Joachim Du Bellay, *La Deffence, et illustration de la langue françoyse & L'Olive*, ed. by Jean-Charles Monferran and Ernesta Caldarini (Geneva: Droz, 2007), p. 88.
12. Richard Helgerson, trans., *Joachim Du Bellay* (Philadelphia: University of Pennsylvania Press, 2006), p. 336.
13. Du Bellay, *La Deffence*, p. 136.
14. Ibid., p. 282.
15. Chamard, *Du Bellay*, p. 175; Vianey, *Pétrarquisme*, p. 96; and Greene, *Troy*, p. 220.
16. Du Bellay, *La Deffence*, p. 138.
17. Buron and Cernogora, *Du Bellay*, pp. 166–69.
18. Pierre Villey, *Les sources italiennes de la Deffense et illustration de la langue françoise de Joachim Du Bellay* (Paris: Champion, 1908; reprint, Geneva: Slatkine, 1969), pp. 101–10.
19. Speroni, *Dialogi*, p. 130^r. My emphasis.
20. Du Bellay, *La Deffence*, pp. 112–13. My emphasis.
21. Ibid., p. 113.
22. On the sonnet's allusiveness, see Buron and Cernagora, *Du Bellay*, p. 306.
23. François Rigolot, *Poétique et onomastique. L'exemple de la Renaissance* (Geneva: Droz, 1977), p. 145.
24. Alduy, 'L'Arbre', pp. 39–42.
25. On the pairing of sonnets and odes, see Millet, 'Autour', p. 261. For the passage citing Peletier du Mans, see Du Bellay, *L'Olive*, p. 44.
26. Du Bellay, *Oeuvres*, ed. by Aris, I, p. xxxi.
27. Dorothy Gabe Coleman, 'Minerve et *l'Olive*', in *Du Bellay. Actes du colloque international d'Angers du 26 au 29 mai*, 2 vols (Angers: Presses de l'université d'Angers, 1989), 161–70 (p. 163); and Michel Magnien, 'La première *Olive* (1549)', in *L'Olive de J. Du Bellay. Actes des Séminaires d'analyse textuelle Pasquali (Lucelle 1er-4 déc. 2005)*, ed. by Ruggero Campagnoli, Eric Lysøe, and Anna Soncini Fratta (Bologna: Casa Editrice CLUEB, 2007), pp. 7–45 (p. 16).
28. Dorat's eight-line liminary poem can be found in Du Bellay, *L'Olive*, p. 170.
29. Du Bellay, *La Deffence*, p. 139.
30. See Bartolomeo Ricci, *De Imitatione libri tres* (Venice: Manutius, 1545 [1541]), p. 43^v. On Du Bellay's familiarity with Ricci, see Marc Bizer, *La poésie au miroir. Imitation et conscience de soi dans la poésie latin de la Pléiade* (Paris: Champion, 1995), p. 45. On Ricci's tripartite model, see George W. Pigman, 'Versions of Imitation in the Renaissance', *Renaissance Quarterly*, 33 (1980), 1–32 (p. 3).
31. William Kennedy, *The Site of Petrarchism* (Baltimore: Johns Hopkins University Press, 2003), p. 105.
32. On rhetorical figures in *L'Olive*, see Chamard, *Du Bellay*, pp. 175–76; and Du Bellay, *L'Olive*, ed. by Caldarini, pp. 20–31. On a suggested taxonomy of *incipits*, see JoAnn DellaNeva, 'Variations in a Minor Key: Du Bellay's Imitations of the Giolito Anthology Poets', *French Forum*, 14 (1989), 133–46 (pp. 141–44).
33. Millet, 'Autour', p. 266.
34. DellaNeva, 'Variations', p. 143; Millet, 'Autour', pp. 264–65.
35. All quotations from the *RVF* are from Francesco Petrarca, *Rime*, ed. by Marco Santagata (Milan: Mondadori, 1999). As in this edition, the concluding lines of each cited stanza of canzone 70 have been italicized.
36. Mark Musa, trans., *The Canzoniere* (Bloomington: Indiana University Press, 1996), p. 109.
37. Millet 'Autour', pp. 264–66.
38. On the Petrarchan nature of the 1550 edition, see Alduy, 'L'Arbre', p. 53; and Buron and Cernogora, *Du Bellay*, p. 188.
39. Vianey, *Pétrarquisme*; Caldarini, 'Fonti'.
40. Vianey, *Pétrarquisme*, p. 93; Caldarini, 'Fonti', p. 433.
41. Greene, *Troy*, p. 220.
42. Du Bellay, *Oeuvres poétiques*, ed. by Aris and Joukovsky, p. xxvi.
43. See Louise George Clubb and William G. Clubb, 'Building a Lyric Canon: Gabriel Giolito and the Rival Anthologists (1545–1590)', *Italica* 68 (1991), 332–44; and Monica Bianco and Elena

Strada, eds, *I più vaghi e i più soavi fiori: studi sulle antologie di lirica del Cinquecento* (Alessandria: Edizioni dell'Orso, 2001).
44. DellaNeva, 'Variations', pp. 134–41.
45. Buron and Cernogora, *Du Bellay*, p. 188.
46. Buron and Cernogora, *Du Bellay*; Alduy, 'L'Arbre'.
47. JoAnn DellaNeva, 'An Exploding Canon: Petrarch and the Petrarchists in Renaissance France', *Annali d'Italianistica*, 22 (2004), 189–206.
48. Buron and Cernogora, *Du Bellay*.
49. Cécile Alduy, *Politiques des 'Amours'. Poétique et genèse d'un genre français nouveau (1540–1560)* (Geneva: Droz, 2007), pp. 80–86.
50. Du Bellay, *La Deffence*, p. 176.
51. On Du Bellay's imitation of Ariosto' sonnets, see Chamard, *Du Bellay*, p. 176; on his use of Ariosto's epic, see Vianey, *Pétrarquisme*, pp. 90–93.
52. Du Bellay, *La Deffence*, p. 139.
53. Helgerson, trans., *Du Bellay*, p. 378.
54. JoAnn DellaNeva, 'Teaching Du Bellay a Lesson: Ronsard's Rewriting of Ariosto's Sonnets', *French Forum* 24 (1999), 285–301; and Klaus W. Hempfer, 'Traditions discursives et réception partielle: *Le Roland Furieux* de l'Arioste dans *L'Olive* de Du Bellay', in *L'Arioste et le Tasse en France au XVIe siècle* (Paris: Editions rue d'Ulm, 2003), pp. 53–74.
55. Citations from Ariosto are from Ludovico Ariosto, *Opere: Carmina, Rime, Satire, Erbolato, Lettere*, III, ed. by Mario Santoro (Turin: Unione Tipografico-Editrice Torinese, 1989).
56. A. S. Kline, *The Complete Canzoniere*, <www.poetryintranslation.com>, p. 335.
57. Henri Chamard first called attention to this direct imitation in his *Du Bellay*.
58. Kline, *The Complete Canzoniere*, p. 335.
59. See Joachim Du Bellay, *Oeuvres completes*, II: *L'Olive*, ed. by Olivier Millet (Paris: Champion, 2003), p. 306. For a broader treatment of Du Bellay's use of Virgil, see Olivier Millet's 'Présence de Virgile dans *l'Olive* de Du Bellay', in *Les Fruits de la saison: mélanges de littérature des XVIe et XVIIe siècles offerts au Professeur André Gendre*, ed. by Philippe Terrier and others (Geneva: Droz, 2000), pp. 105–18.
60. Du Bellay, *L'Olive*, p. 50.
61. See the valuable list of textual sources in Millet's edition of *L'Olive* in Du Bellay, *Oeuvres complètes*.
62. Poliziano, *Miscellaneorum*, p. 3.
63. The research and writing of this chapter were made possible through a postdoctoral fellowship funded by the Social Sciences and Humanities Research Council of Canada. I am grateful to the editors of this volume, as well as to the anonymous reviewer and Timothy Reiss for comments on earlier drafts.

CHAPTER 3

❖

Petrarch and the French Reception of the *Triumphi*: An Age of Transition

Alessandro Turbil

During the sixteenth century Petrarch obtained great fame in France, becoming one of the main protagonists of the French cultural *milieu*. In particular, his literary works in the vernacular became for the French poets an example to follow in the renovation of their literary language. As has been demonstrated over the years by Paola Cifarelli, Gabriella Parussa and Elina Suomela-Härmä, the fortune of Petrarch's *Triumphi* in France is linked to two main factors: firstly, a renewed interest in the Italian poet's works; secondly, the perceived need for a renewal of style and literary form in French poetry.[1] After a century, the fifteenth, that had celebrated Petrarch through his various works in Latin as *philosophus moralis*, *orator* and *poeta*, the sixteenth century saw his consecration as a lyric poet thanks to the circulation in France of his best-known vernacular work, the *Canzoniere*. However, at the beginning, it was the *Triumphi* rather than the *Canzoniere* that made the very specific language of the Italian poet known in France.[2] French translators, while transposing the tercets of the *Triumphi* between the last quarter of the fifteenth century and the first half of the sixteenth century, not only attempted to imitate metres and forms of Petrarch's versification, they also solved problems concerning language and vocabulary issues, coining words, expressions, and poetic images that will be typical of the new lyric poetry.[3] In fact, from the reign of Louis XII to that of Henry II, this poem in *terza rima* was subjected to a number of different and systematic translations (both in prose and in verse), while the *Canzoniere* spread only later in France and was mainly read in Italian.

Even before the wide diffusion of the *Triumphi* and the *Canzoniere* beyond the Alps, Petrarch's literary works in the vernacular were already known by the French literati, but his first imitators still did not undertake a systematic use of his poetic formulas.[4] Petrarch's name was considered as a symbol of moral authority trustworthy in matters of love.[5] His name was listed with Alain Chartier and the authors of the *Roman de la Rose* among the founders of a modern *ars amandi*.[6] Nevertheless, the *Triumphi* were interpreted primarily as an interesting compendium of historical and erudite knowledge, similar in a certain way to the *De viris illustribus*. Little attention was paid at first to formal and metrical aspects of Petrarch's poetry. We have to wait until Clément Marot's school in order to witness the introduction in France of a form of Petrarchism also characterized by the imitation of a conventional literary language.[7]

As Dario Cecchetti has demonstrated, the popularity of the *Triumphi* among sixteenth-century French readers stemmed from the poem's allegorical content and form.[8] Petrarch at this time was still regarded, as he had been in the previous century, more as a moral philosopher and a Latin scholar than as a lyric poet, and the *Triumphi* were more compatible with such a view than the *Canzoniere*.[9] This is even more the case, when we consider how much the Italian verses of this poem are paraphrased and amplified in the French translations. This is valid both for the translations in prose and for the translations in verse, even if the amplification appears distinctly more perceptible in the prose adaptations, maybe to satisfy the preferences of French readers of the late fifteenth century still influenced by the prevailing view of Petrarch as moral philosopher and author of Latin treatises.[10] Indeed, many of the translators of the *Triumphi* examined here seem still to regard Petrarch as a moral philosopher rather than a lyric poet. Evidently, the vision described in the poem, its allegorical and moral content and the endless succession of great men and women of the past inserted in the various triumphs, encouraged a sense of continuity.[11]

Following Cecchetti, I would argue that the *Triumphi* represented, in the eyes of French literati, a moment of transition between the erudition of Petrarch's Latin writings and the lyricism of the *Canzoniere*.[12] Translations of the *Triumphi* represent a particularly interesting case not only for the genesis of a literary myth but also in relation to the linguistic code used by different translators to 'Frenchify' the Italian text. Leaving aside for the moment the complex situation related to the first reception of the *Triumphi* by French readers and the circulation of some reductions in Latin couplets at the end of the fifteenth century, then translated into French, the *Triumphi* were quite popular in sixteenth-century France. This is attested by translations of the poem (the subject of this chapter) and by the presence of the triumphal scenes in visual arts.[13] When some illuminated manuscripts containing the *Triumphi* arrived in France from Italy in the last decades of the fifteenth century, the text immediately aroused great interest. This was mostly because, in the late fifteenth century, French readers were still deeply fascinated by encyclopaedic knowledge, classical culture and medieval allegorical tradition. Nevertheless, it is known that even before 1495 some Italian manuscripts containing Petrarch's vernacular works circulated in France, as attested by the presence of the text in French aristocratic library records.[14]

According to Gabriella Parussa, it is possible that some translations of these texts already existed before the 'golden age' of the *Triumphi*. Thanks to the information discovered in an inventory drawn up in 1496, Parussa reported news of the existence in the library of Charles d'Angoulême of a manuscript of the *Triomphe de Renommée* which had been already noticed by Gianni Mombello but on which we have no further precise information, even about the language used in the text.[15] Moreover, she also reported the French translation of an unidentified manuscript prepared in 1456 and containing one or more unspecified texts of Petrarch. The translation was commissioned by Charles d'Orléans and mentioned in a book of accounts of the Duke.[16] In any case, the limited availability of manuscripts containing the *Triumphi* and/or the *Canzoniere* in aristocratic libraries was soon remedied by a more substantial spread of printed editions, as a result of the great influence acquired by the Tuscan poet.

Between the end of the reign of Louis XII and the beginning of the reign of Henri II, Petrarch's poem becomes the object of two adaptations in prose and three adaptations in verse. This result was achieved through the efforts of five different translators, who competed at different times in the systematic attempt to make the text and the lexicon of the Italian poem 'French'.[17] Regarding the French translations examined in this essay, our attention will be focused on the following texts: the prose translation, called 'short version', attributed to Georges de la Forge and dated to the late fifteenth century; the verse translation of Simon Bourgouin, from the early sixteenth century; the anonymous translation in prose, called 'long version', published in 1514 in Paris by Barthélemy Vérard; and the two verse translations from the mid-sixteenth century, one by Jehan Maynier baron of Oppède (printed in Paris in 1538) and the other by Vasquin Philieul (printed in Avignon in 1555).[18]

The aim of this chapter is to investigate how these translations contributed to the more general phenomenon of renewal that revived the style, literary language and form of French poetry of this period. My hypothesis is that the process of filtering and adaptation that concerned the *Triumphi* involved from the start not only the thematic dimension of the Petrarchan model but also its unique poetic language. Despite the vast erudition shown by Petrarch in the *Triumphi* through endless lists of characters and anecdotes, the poem uses a language that is still strongly related to the rarefied linguistic code that had been developed by the Italian poet for the preparation of the *Canzoniere*. This chapter seeks to ascertain the role played by the first translators of the *Triumphi*, both in the cultural transmission of the old French poetic tradition and in its renovation under the growing influence of Petrarch's literary works in the vernacular. Such an analysis will enable the discovery and identification of a trace of Petrarchist language before the birth of the school of Marot, or the movement of the Pléiade.

Before proceeding any further, I will first specify the method underpinning my analysis. My aim is to present a series of pieces of evidence which demonstrate how the translators of the *Triumphi* worked in a dimension of continuity (or discontinuity) with poetic experiences of the past. The purpose is to situate a certain phrase or a certain 'poetic expression' in the context of a poetic vocabulary already employed by French literati in order to explain lexicographically certain choices made by Petrarch's translators. The peculiarity of certain linguistic structures has to balance the recovery of an earlier literary tradition with the innovation of style, form and vocabulary of French poetry. Once again, this particular process of 'renewal' suggests the transitional character of these first experiments in translating Petrarch's *Triumphi*. With this perspective in mind, a certain number of key-terms were chosen from within the five translations with the purpose of discovering with which adjective or noun they were usually associated in the earlier French literary tradition.

The Sweet Memory

The first example I would like to propose regards the beginning of the first chapter of the *Triumphus Cupidinis*, which introduces us to Petrarch's most typical lyrical lexicon.

> Nel tempo che rinnova i mei sospiri
> Per la dolce memoria di quel giorno
> Che fu principio a sì longhi martiri
> (PETRARCH, *Trionfi*, *Triumphus Cupidinis* I, vv. 1–3)[19]

> [It was the time, when I doe sadly pay
> My sighs, in tribute to that sweet-sowre-day,
> Which first gave being to my tedious woes:[20]]

The first case considered, according to the aforementioned methodology, is the phrase 'dolce memoria' related to the target texts of Jehan Maynier and Simon Bourgouin.

> En ce temps que mes souspirs estoint renouvelléz par le doulz souvenir d'ycelluy jour qui fut mon commencement en amour au long martire et tourment de ma vie.
> (GEORGES DE LA FORGE, *Triumphus Cupidinis* I, f. 1r)

> Au temps que Mes souspirs en moy se renouvellent | Par les doulx souvenirs qui les jours me revellent | Lesquelz aux longz martirs furent commancement
> (SIMON BOURGOUIN, *Triumphus Cupidinis* I, f. 2v)

> Au temps que se renouvellent mes souspirs, par la doulce memoire de cellui jour qui fut commencement et si long martir [...]
> (Translation B, VÉRARD, *Triumphus Cupidinis* I, f. 2r)

> En ce beau temps qui mon mal renouvelle | Par souvenir estant en ma cervelle | Du jour qui fut maulvais commancement | A m'engendrer une peyne cruelle, | Longue douleur, penitence immortelle
> (JEHAN MAYNIER, manuscript version, *Triumphus Cupidinis* I, f. 15r)

> Au temps qu'on voit le grief dueil rappeller, | Et mes souspirs tousjours renouveller | Par la memoyre et doulceur seurement | De celluy jour, qui fut commencement | Du long martir, et que Sol s'efforçoit
> (JEHAN MAYNIER, printed version, *Triumphus Cupidinis* I, f. 1r)

> Au temps, le quel mes souspirs renouvelle | Par souvenir de ta doulce journee, | Qui fut la source a ma playe mortelle
> (VASQUIN PHILIEUL, *Triumphus Cupidinis* I, f. 342)

More specifically, it is interesting to note a contrast between the manuscript versions of Maynier's translation and the printed one. The translation closer to the original 'dolce memoria' can be found only in the version that was recast in view of the printed edition of 1538.[21] In the manuscript version there appears instead a verse ('par souvenirs estant en ma cervelle') which is much closer to the sentence discovered in all other translations, except of course for the *mise en prose* published by Vérard in 1514. It seems not very surprising that the author of translation B adopts this expression because at least one of the French translations of Ilicino's commentary on the *Triumphi* shows also this particular syntagm, the 'doulce memoire'.[22] The author of translation B knew the commentary and perhaps its French translation, dated around 1504. He had therefore no reason to adopt another formula that was not a literal translation of 'la dolce memoria', which in any case enjoyed a certain success at that time.[23] In the process of reformulation of the Provençal author's text aforementioned, the syntagm 'per la dolce memoria' thus assumes a special intertextual value since an expression very similar to that contained in the printed version of Maynier's translation appears previously only in the Vérard edition of the second prose translation (1514). According to Paola Cifarelli, it is highly probable that the reviser Jean Chaperon had this text in front of him, while preparing the manuscript version of Maynier's text for the printed edition.[24]

Equally impressive is the fact that we find a very similar translation of this concept in another translation of the *Triumphi*, which is the oldest *mise en prose* dating from the late fifteenth century. It is possible to read in this version, in the second chapter of the *Triumphus Mortis*, the following phrase: 'j'ay eu le doulz neu de ta memoire en mon cueur. car ton beau [nom] m'a pleu' [I have the sweet knot of your memory in my heart, for your beautiful name pleased me].[25] The syntagms 'doulz neu' and 'memoire en mon cueur' seem to refer to the same register and to the same semantic field as the expression 'doulce memoire'.

Why did Simon Bourgouin (who made his translation around the early years of the sixteenth century) prefer to use the phrase 'doulx souvenirs' in his translation? The reason is immediately evident on comparison of Bourgouin's work with two other adaptations in verse of the *Triumphi* (i.e. the manuscript version of Maynier's translation and Philieul's translation printed in 1555): the coexistence of two parallel forms is attested in equal measure in our corpus.

Through a search in the electronic database of Garnier's *Corpus de la Littérature médiévale*, it seems clear that the phrase 'doulx souvenirs' represents an alternative to the syntagm 'doulce memoire' (closer to the original 'dolce memoria').[26] Given a certain number of comparisons with medieval texts, it seems that the use of the expression 'doulx souvenirs' by Bourgouin and other translators might arise from a desire to respect a traditional use. Occurrences of this phrase recur in the *Miracles de Nostre Dame*, more specifically in the *Miracle de l'enfant donné au diable*,[27] in the works of Eustache Deschamps[28] and in those of Christine de Pizan,[29] in the *Ballades* of Charles d'Orléans,[30] and in Arnoul Gréban's *Mystère de la Passion*.[31]

This case can demonstrate the coexistence of two specific trends in the translation work of our translators. Sometimes we find the introduction of a certain number of phrases derived directly from Petrarch's linguistic code and sometimes we can witness the recovery of a previous literary tradition that responds to the reuse of a poetic code that already exists, 'comme si l'écriture était modélisée par des expressions héritées. La littérature médiévale est en effet fondée, pour une large part, sur la réécriture de thèmes et de motifs attendus' [as if the writing were modelled on inherited expressions. Medieval literature is indeed founded in a large part on the rewriting of themes and motifs].[32] This phenomenon can also be explained by the following remark by Michael Riffaterre: 'd'une part [on a] la compréhension du mot selon les règles du langage et les contraintes du contexte, et d'autre part [on a] la connaissance du mot comme membre d'un ensemble où il a déjà joué ailleurs un rôle défini' [on the one hand, we have the comprehension of the word according to the rules of language and the constraints of the context, and on the other hand, the knowledge of the word as belonging to a set in which it has already played a well-defined part elsewhere].[33] It is consequently essential to consider first intertextuality when seeking to understand the lexical universe of these translations.

The Love Knot

> quando una giovenetta ebbi dallato,
> pura assai più che candida colomba.
> Ella mi prese; ed io, che avrei giurato
> difendermi d'un uom coverto d'arme,
> con parole et con cenni fui legato
> (PETRARCH, *Trionfi*, *Triumphus Cupidinis* III, vv. 89–93)

> [When by my side I spi'd a lovely maide,
> (No Turtle ever purer whitenesse had)
> And straight was caught (who lately swore I would
> Defend me from a man at Armes) nor could
> Resist the blowes of words with motion grac't;
> The image yet is in my phansie plac't.][34]

In the third chapter of the *Triumphus Cupidinis*, the verses quoted above testify once again to a strong concentration of lyrical vocabulary. In this case, one particular combination of words deserves to be analysed in detail. For the Italian past participle 'legato', the different translations propose the syntagms 'lié', 'prins et lié', 'lié et pris' and 'prins'. In three cases the target texts have been subjected to a phenomenon of coordination of two French verbs, *prendre* and *lier*, while in the source text the verb is only one, *legare*.

> Quant je vy une jouvencelle clere resplendissant et plus blanche que ne fut onques coulombe. Celle la me print. Je desiroye bien estre contre elle defendu d'ung homme armé de tout harnoys. Mais de parolles et d'ung bauldrier [f.6r°] je fuz tresestroit lié.
> (GEORGES DE LA FORGE, *Triumphus Cupidinis* I, f. 5v–6r)

> Quant une gente fille au corps plaisant et beau | S'en vint a mon costé avecq voulenté franche, | Pure assez beaucoup plus que une columbe blanche, | Laquelle me prist. Lors je, qui eusse affermé| Et juré resister contre homme tout armé, | Fus tost pris et lié par parolle et les signes| Et les beaultéz de celle dame insignes.
> (SIMON BOURGOUIN, *Triumphus Cupidinis* II, vv. 162–68)

> [...] quant je vi de costé moi, une belle jeune fille clere resplendissant, pure et plus blanche que une colombe, laquelle me print. Et moi, qui eusse bien juré me deffendre d'ung homme armé de tout harnois de parolles et signes, je fus lié et prins.
>
> (Translation B, Vérard, *Triumphus Cupidinis* IV, f. 24r)

> Et tout à coup je veis à mon costé | Une nymphe qui m'eust tantost osté | Tout le povoir qu'avoye de me deffendre | À tout aultre qui m'eust voulu offendre. | Mais sa beauté, sa grace et sçavoir | Affoiblirent mon cueur et mon povoir, | Dont je fuz prins de l'amoureuse corde
>
> (Jehan Maynier, manuscript version, *Triumphus Cupidinis* II, vv. 153–59)

> Quand je vis prés de moy, plus blanche que columbe | Une jeune fillette, au regard tresplaisante | Plus qu'au ciel le soleil n'a clarté reluysante, | Le mantien gracieux, en cueur treschaste et pure | Laquelle tost me print, pourtant j'atteste et jure | Que j'avois le povoir vifvement me deffendre | Contre tout homme armé, se on m'eust voulu surprendre | Mais pour dire le vray je fuz lié et pris | Par sa doulce parolle et sur moy eust le pris
>
> (Jehan Maynier, printed version, *Triumphus Cupidinis* IV, vv. 8–16)

> Quand a costé j'eus une jouvencelle | Plus pure asses que blanche Colombette. | Ceste me prit, qui tant estois rebelle, | Qu'aurois juré d'homme armé me defendre, | Par beaulx semblans et beaulx dicts fus a elle.
>
> (Vasquin Philieul, *Triumphus Cupidinis* II, f. 356)

The text of Simon Bourgouin seems once again influential.[35] It proves often to be the best model for measuring how different translations of this Italian poem serve to transmit stereotyped forms of lyrical lexicon from one poetic language to another. The occurrence of the phrase 'pris et lié' found in Bourgouin (and also traced in two other cases, but with an inversion of the terms) is encountered quite commonly in other texts of the fourteenth and fifteenth centuries. Instances of this same pairing can be found, for example, in the works of Eustache Deschamps[36] and in the *Farce de trois amoureux de la Croix*.[37] In the context of a poetic tradition in search of stylistic renewal, this particular case shows well how the Petrarchan linguistic code is filtered in a dimension of continuity with the French literary tradition. Bourgouin shows more than other translators, in fact, a certain sensitivity to the poetic phrases of the preceding French literary tradition.

The Beautiful Eyes and the Beautiful Golden Hair

> Perseo era l'uno; e volsi saper come
> Andromeda gli piacque in Ethïopia,
> vergine bruna i begli occhi e le chiome
>   (F. Petrarca, *Trionfi*, *Triumphus Cupidinis* II, vv. 142–44)

> [*Perseus* was one, and well you know the way
> How he was catched by *Andromida*:
> She was a lovely brownet, black her haire
> And eyes.[38]]

The last case taken into account here regards the translation into French of the verse 'vergine bruna i begli occhi e le chiome' proposed by the selected translators.

> Le roy Perseus estoit l'ung de ceulx qui veult sauvoir et pense comment luy pleut en Ethyope celle jeune noire Andrometa aveques ses beaux yeulx.
>
> (GEORGES DE LA FORGE, *Triumphus Cupidinis* I, f. 14r)

> L'un estoit Perseüs, par quoy vouluz sçavoir | Comme bien il ayma et tant luy pleut à veoir | Au pays de Ethïope Andromeda, la belle | Et clere et brune vierge en amours non rebelle, | Avecq ses beaulx cheveulx dorez et ses doulx yeulx.
>
> (SIMON BOURGOUIN, *Triumphus Cupidinis* IV, vv. 253–55)

> Le roy Perseus estoit l'ung d'iceulx qui veult sçavoir et penser comment lui pleut en Ethiope celle jeune noire Andromeda avec les beaulx yeulx.
>
> (Translation B, VÉRARD, *Triumphus Cupidinis* II, f. 4v).

> La j'aperceu le puissant roy Percés | D'Andromeda en Ethïope prins | Par grand amour, qui l'eut si fort surprins, | Qu'estant noyre, elle luy pleut assez
>
> (JEHAN MAYNIER, manuscript version, *Triumphus Cupidinis* IV, vv. 269–72)

> La j'aperceus Perceüs de valeur, | D'Andromeda en Enthiope prins, | Par grand amour qui bien tost l'a surprins, | Ce nonobstant qu'elle eust noire couleur
>
> (JEHAN MAYNIER, printed version, *Triumphus Cupidinis* II, vv. 259–62)

> La Perseus estoit pris et servile | D'Adromeda, qui, la Couchiquy danse, | Pucelle brune aux beaux yeux et gentile
>
> (VASQUIN PHILIEUL, *Triumphus Cupidinis* II, f. 352)

In the oldest prose translation, attributed to Georges de la Forge, and in the second oldest one, published by Vérard in 1514, as well as in that of Philieul published in 1555, this passage is still present. Conversely, the syntagm relating to the beautiful eyes does not even appear in the two versions of Maynier's translation. However, perhaps assuming a more general knowledge of the vernacular works of the Tuscan poet than is provable at present,[39] it is possible to detect how Bourgouin expands Petrarch's tercet to five alexandrines interpolating in his text two new attributes, 'beaulx' and 'dorez', to describe Andromeda's hair ('le chiome').

It must be emphasized here that, in Bourgouin's translation, there is a misreading which is particularly interesting for us and it occurs as a result of misunderstanding the source text. In his translation, the *rhétoriqueur* shows that he did not understand the implicit and erudite reference to Ovid.[40] Andromeda is wrongly considered blonde and dark-skinned at once. Nevertheless, the particular reformulation of the source text undertaken by Bourgouin may also have been induced by knowledge of the vernacular works of Petrarch and by the fact that the link between the golden hair of Laura ('Erano i capei d'oro a l'aura sparsi') and her character of beloved lady *par excellence* in the *Canzoniere* is common. However, this link may seem very unusual in the *Triumphi* in which the colour of Laura's hair is never specified. In fact, in the poem, the word 'chiome' is only employed in two verses: 'vergine bruna i begli occhi e le chiome' (*Triumphus Cupidinis* II, v. 144) which refers to Andromeda and 'le chiome accolte in oro o sparse al vento' (*Triumphus Cupidinis* III, v. 136) which refers to Laura. The latter is indeed the only case where the words 'chiome' and 'oro' are found together.[41] This verse is translated by Bourgouin as follows: 'Encore, qui plus est, ses beaulx cheveulx tressez, | plus que or luysans, [...]' (*Triumphus Cupidinis* II, vv. 237–38).[42] It seems obvious that the translator, here, did not understand completely the meaning of the source text by wrongly extending the adjective of the hairnet, which is defined as gilded, to the hair of Laure.[43] Paradoxically, it would be the second time in the same triumph that he makes a mistake of interpretation of this kind.

Returning to the case of Andromeda, the effort of the translator, which aims to reproduce the poetic universe of Petrarch also from an existing lexicon, has demonstrated an important flaw in the translation. This fault has allowed us to realize the 'stereotypical nature' of several figures and expressions, which already exist in this first translation in verse dated to the beginning of the sixteenth century, and which therefore belong to a period which still precedes Marot's first attempts to translate into French a few of Petrarch's sonnets.

For the attribute 'dorez', a search in the *Corpus de la Littérature Médiévale* to find which word was the most frequently associated with this adjective in medieval texts reveals that for forty-five occurrences recovered, none is related to the noun 'cheveulx' (we found instead the syntagms 'blondz cheveulx' or 'beaulx cheveux'). Turning to Myriam Rolland-Perrin's work dedicated to the study of the presence of women's hair in the literature of the Middle Ages, similar occurrences have been found in *Florence de Rome*, in the *Blason des cheveulx* of Jean de Vauzelles, in the French translation of the *Théséide* datable to the fifteenth century,[44] in the *Roman de la Rose* and also in the *Fotéor*.[45] In conclusion, the insertion of this phrase could reflect an original interpolation truly *à la manière de Pétrarque*, even if the final result must actually be considered erroneous.

It has been possible to identify at least ten occurrences of the phrase 'beaulx yeulx' in the *Corpus de la Littérature Médiévale*. It is well known that this phrase will also be very popular in the sixteenth century. The syntagm 'beaulx yeulx' is also widely used in the works of the major Petrarchist poets of the century such as Scève, Ronsard, Du Bellay and Labé.[46] We therefore find a correspondence in relation to the phrase 'beaulx cheveulx dorez'.[47] Finally, one last case seems to be particularly interesting. In the text of the thirteenth sonnet of Du Bellay's *Sonnetz de l'honneste amour*, the phrase 'beaulx cheveulx dorez' is not too far in the text from the syntagm 'beaux yeux', recalling Bourgouin's translation. This example proves the necessity of analysing the lexicon of the first French translations of this poem not only in relation to the previous literary tradition but also in relation to the lexicon of the poets of the high period of French Petrarchism.

Conclusions

All these cases demonstrate the existence of a specific process of codification of the language of poetry among the first imitators of Petrarch. This process can be traced even in the first translations of the vernacular works of Petrarch. It is clear that the *Triumphi* played in France a different role in comparison with the other works of Petrarch. Firstly, because the French translations of the poem were accompanied by a very specific process of transition, which also concerned the perception of the image of the Italian poet (a transitional phase that lasted nearly three decades).[48] Secondly, because the interest in the *Triumphi* determined the earliest systematic translations in French of the extremely refined linguistic code of Petrarch, long before the dissemination and imitation in France of the *Canzoniere*. If the French myth of Petrarch found its roots in the interest in his Latin works, the translations of the *Triumphi* clearly had the role of promoting a further phase leading to the circulation and imitation of both his vernacular works beyond the Alps.

The two prose adaptations clearly show how the first interest in France for this poem was mainly related to its topic (allegories, moral instructions and the incomparable erudition of the author) rather than to the formal aspect of the text. The prose translations, avoiding the particular obstacle of a translation in verse, confirmed once again how the first interest for the *Triumphi* was based on its content. However, it has been observed how certain linguistic patterns, already included in prose, have been reused in the printed edition of Jehan Maynier's verse translation, showing the existence of strong intertextual relations. With the *rhétoriqueur* Simon Bourgouin the erudite and moral aims became less important, although still present. Starting from the first verse translation, the moral aims were followed by artistic purposes, such as the imitation of the rhymes and of the rhythmic structure of Petrarch's poetry. The work of this translator tells us a lot about the rise of an aesthetic issue, as evidenced also by the last two verse translations.

This long history of translations which involved the *Triumphi* can be considered, in this sense, as a moment of transition between the erudition of Petrarch's Latin writings and the lyricism of the *Canzoniere*. Although the attention to the work of the Italian humanist was initially (with prose translations) directed exclusively to philosophical and erudite topics, it moved gradually (with verse translations) onto the assimilation and imitation of style, themes and tropes of the Italian poet.[49] For this reason, all these translations can be considered as the pillars of a bridge that links the past with the future. Careful studies of this kind, regarding a corpus of texts which are mostly still unpublished and sometimes difficult to consult, will make it possible in the future not only to study these adaptations from the point of view of literature and translation studies, but also to discover how these first repositories of poetic invention could have inspired the sixteenth-century lyric poets who approached the linguistic code of Petrarch more and more systematically.[50] The best way to demonstrate it is by finding semantic relations between words. In a word: with lexicology. This corpus of prose and verse translations can, then, help us understand how the language of the Italian poet was gradually assimilated and *Frenchified* at the turn of the Middle Ages and Renaissance.

Notes to Chapter 3

1. The *Triumphi* have a different meaning from the other works of Petrarch in French literature because they represent very well the moment of transition between the spread of Latin writings and the fortune of the *Canzoniere*. Cf. Elina Suomela-Härmä, 'Note sulla prima traduzione francese dei 'Trionfi' di Petrarca', *Studi Francesi*, 129 (1999), 545–53; Gabriella Parussa, 'I Trionfi di Petrarca tra l'Italia e la Francia: le metamorfosi di un testo', in *Atti VII congresso degli Italianisti Scandinavi*, ed. by Enrico Garavelli and Elina Suomela-Härmä (Helsinki: Société Néophilologique, 2005), pp. 71–87; Paola Cifarelli, 'Jean Maynier d'Oppède et Pétrarque', in *Les poètes français de la Renaissance et Pétrarque*, ed. by J. Balsamo (Geneva: Droz, 2004), pp. 85–104; Paola Cecchetti, Dario. 'Petrarca in Francia prima del Petrarchismo: un mito polemico', *Franco-Italica*, no. 11 (1997), 7–31. In the writing of this chapter I have benefited from the help and support of Carole Birkan-Berz and Jennifer Rushworth to whom I wish to express my gratitude.
2. The French literati saw in the *Triumphi* the last representative of a specific literary tradition that could ideally go back to the *Roman de la Rose*. It is also known that the first readers who become interested in the text of the *Triumphi* in the late fifteenth century could still consider Petrarch in his status of *philosophus moralis*. This is proved by the fact that, in the first French translations of the *Triumphi*, moral and allegorical aspects are always magnified over the aesthetic value of the text. Cf. Dario Cecchetti, 'Petrarca in Francia prima del Petrarchismo: un mito polemico', *Franco-Italica*, 11 (1997), 7–31 (p. 8).
3. Dario Cecchetti, *Il Petrarchismo in Francia* (Torino: Giappichelli, 1970), p. 15.
4. In other words, syntagms or phrasemes (clichés) used repetitively. The first imitators of Petrarch in France were content to replicate purely from a thematic point of view what the language of Petrarch had expressed about the theme of love. Cf. Jean Balsamo, 'Nous l'avons tous admiré, et imité: non sans cause. Pétrarque en France à la Renaissance: un livre, un modèle, un mythe', in *Les poètes français de la Renaissance et Pétrarque*, ed. by Jean Balsamo (Geneva: Droz, 2004), pp. 13–32; Dario Cecchetti, *Il Petrarchismo in Francia* (Torino: Giappichelli, 1970); Mia Cocco, *La tradizione cortese ed il petrarchismo nella poesia di Clément Marot* (Florence: Olschki, 1978).
5. Jean Balsamo, 'Le "premier cercle" du pétrarquisme français', in *La Postérité répond à Pétrarque*, ed. by Eve Duperray (Paris: Beauchesne, 2006), pp. 127–45 (p. 128).
6. The presence of Petrarch among the poets of love dates back to the *Concorde des deux langages* of Jean Lemaire de Belges: 'Mettoit en avant plusieurs acteurs renommez et auctorizes, si comme Dante, Petrarque et Boccace, tous trois Florentins, Philelphe, Seraphin, et assez d'autres Ytaliens' (Jean Lemaire de Belges, *La Concorde des deux langages*, ed. by J. Frappier (Geneva: Droz, 1947), p. 2). This quotation may well represent the very starting point of the construction of the French myth of Petrarch.
7. Cf. Jean Balsamo, 'Nous l'avons tous admiré, et imité: non sans cause. Pétrarque en France à la Renaissance: un livre, un modèle, un mythe', *Les poètes français de la Renaissance et Pétrarque*, ed. by Jean Balsamo (Geneva: Droz, 2004), pp. 13–32; Mia Cocco, *La tradizione cortese ed il petrarchismo nella poesia di Clément Marot* (Florence: Olschki, 1978).
8. Cf. Cecchetti, *Il Petrarchismo in Francia*.
9. Cf. Cecchetti, 'Petrarca in Francia prima del Petrarchismo'; Luigi Foscolo Benedetto, 'Il "Roman de la Rose" e la letteratura italiana', *Beihefte zur Zeitschrift für Romanische Philologie*, 12 (1910), 164–71.
10. The aim of the two translations in prose was clearly to make this text easily accessible to the interested French public, who at the end of the fifteenth century were accustomed to reading prose rather than verse, as attested by some texts of the time quoted by Georges Doutrepont in his 1939 work (Georges Doutrepont, *Les mises en prose des épopées et des romans chevaleresques du XIVe au XVIe siècle* (Brussels: Palais des Académies, 1939)). It can be assumed that a process of simplification was undertaken at first with a nearly *mot à mot* translation of the Italian text. This seems evident from reading the first prose translation, which is dated from the last decades of the fifteenth century and attributed to Georges de la Forge. At a later date, the second prose translation satisfies once more the need to reveal the implications of the Italian text, this time in a much more radical way including a large part of Bernardo Ilicino's commentary on

the *Triumphi* and making use also of other more or less identified sources. Cf. Paola Cifarelli, 'Su alcuni personaggi del mito in una traduzione francese tardomedievale dei "Triumphi" di Petrarca', *Elaborazioni poetiche e percorsi di genere. Miti, personaggi e storie letterarie. Studi in onore di Dario Cecchetti*, ed. by Michele Mastroianni (Alessandria: Edizioni dell'Orso, 2010), pp. 251–77.

11. It is very likely that the same consideration can also explain the assertion of Jean Robertet, who wrote in 1476: 'J'ay regardé és Triumphes Pétrarque | Qui d'hystoires reciter fut monarque, | Où j'ay trouvé maint homme de renom' (Jean Robertet, *Oeuvres*, ed. by C.-M. Zsuppan (Geneva: Droz, 1970), p. 174).
12. It is important to recall that the transmission of the *Rerum Vulgarium Fragmenta* was achieved through the contribution of translations. Even if highly valuable translations in French were made by Clément Marot, Jacques Peletier du Mans, and Vasquin Philieul, the audience of these translations was still sensitive to the Petrarch myth. Around the middle of the sixteenth century, it was common for the reading of the vernacular works of Petrarch to take place principally in Italian, now considered a classical language 'alla stregua del latino e del greco' (Cecchetti, 'Petrarca in Francia prima del Petrarchismo', p. 31).
13. Cf. Jean Balsamo, 'Nous l'avons tous admiré, et imité', p. 21.
14. The first approach to Petrarch's poetry in France was oriented by the limited availability of Italian manuscripts and then of Italian incunabula containing the vulgar works of the Tuscan poet. As Jean Balsamo observed, a preliminary simplification was necessary to make possible the reception and understanding of these works, especially in relation to the *Triumphi*. The prose translations of the poem represent this need to 'filter' the Italian text in order to render it more accessible to French readers. The exact date of the entry of the first codices in French territory is not known. It was noted that before the arrival of Charles VIII in Italy many aristocratic libraries had been enriched with books containing sometimes only the text of the *Triumphi*, sometimes only the text of the *Canzoniere*, and sometimes both in the same volume. Cf. Suomela-Härmä, 'Note sulla prima traduzione francese dei "Trionfi" di Petrarca',; Gabriella Parussa, 'I Trionfi di Petrarca tra l'Italia e la Francia: le metamorfosi di un testo', *Atti VII congresso degli Italianisti Scandinavi*, ed. by Enrico Garavelli and Elina Suomela-Härmä (Helsinki: Société Néophilologique, 2005), pp. 71–87; Gianni Mombello, *I Manoscritti delle opere di Dante, Petrarca e Boccaccio nelle principali librerie francesi del secolo XV* (Florence: Olschki, 1971); Elizabeth Pellegrin, *La bibliothèque des Visconti et des Sforza, ducs de Milan au XVe siècle* (Paris: Publications de l'IRHT, 1955); Elizabeth Pellegrin, *Manuscrits de Pétrarque dans les bibliothèques de France* (Padua: Antenore, 1966).
15. Cf. Parussa, 'I Trionfi di Petrarca tra l'Italia e la Francia', p. 82; Gianni Mombello, *I Manoscritti delle opere di Dante, Petrarca e Boccaccio nelle principali librerie francesi del secolo XV* (Florence: Olschki, 1971), p. 144.
16. Léon De Laborde, *Les ducs de Bourgogne. Etudes sur les lettres, les arts et l'industrie pendant le XVe siècle*, III (Paris:Plon frères, 1852).
17. 'Aussy Petrarque aura nouveau renom | Quand il sera Françoys' (Vasquin Philieul, *Laure d'Avignon* (Paris: J. Gazeau, 1548), f. A²v).
18. For more detailed information, see Alessandro Turbil, 'Le fil rouge de la doulce mémoire: pour une analyse du langage amoureux des plus anciennes traductions françaises du Triumphus Cupidinis', *Petrarchesca*, no. 3 (2015), 89–108.
19. The reference source text is always Francesco Petrarca, *Trionfi, Rime Estravaganti, Codice degli Abbozzi*, ed. by Vinicio Pacca et Laura Paolino (Milan: Mondadori, 1996).
20. Anna Hume; Francesco Petrarca, Dans *The Triumphs Of Love: Chastity: Death*, 1–2 (Edinburgh: 1644).
21. The choice of dividing the syntagm 'dolce memoria' in two can be explained by metrical reasons. The sense of the syntagm 'dolce memoria' is preserved by the anticipation of the noun 'memoyre', placed in main position in Italian, and located also in first position in the French décasyllabe, followed in this case, because of the presence of an 'e' mute, by the syntagm beginning with vocal 'et dulceur'. All of these arrangements are made with the purpose of maintaining the metrical placements of the verses 4+6.
22. I quote here in its entirety the extract of the French commentary translation where it is possible

to find the same syntagm: 'Texte. Que eu temps que en lui se renouveloient les amoureux souspirs par la *doulce memoire* du premier iour que il se estoit en amoure qui fut le commencement de l'enflambement de amours le soleil estoit monté l'une et l'autre corne de thor' (BnF Fr. 594, f. 8v).

23. Some years later, the expression is quoted in the title of a famous song by Pierre Regnault (*c.* 1490–after 1561), which was among the best known at that time: 'Car la vertu croistra sa renommée, | Luy despartant pour si loyal devoir | *Doulce mémoire* en plaisir consommée' (Pierre Sandrin. 'Doulce Mémoire.' *Second livre contenant XXVII chansons nouvelles a quatre parties [...]* (Paris: P. Attaingnant et H. Jullet, 1538); this syntagm also appears in a letter written by Marguerite de Navarre on 7 February 1543 in answer to her brother the king of France Francis I: 'Nom de grand père après honneur et gloire | Dont l'humble seur par la *doulce mémoire*' (François Génin, *Nouvelles Lettres de la Reine de Navarre: Adressées au Roi François Ier, Son Frère* (Paris: Renouard, 1842), p. 282 [ms. fr. 2286, f. 116]). The expression is quoted also in a verse written by Bonaveture Des Périer ('Le Nombril' — Blasons du corps féminin): 'Duquel tresheureux touchement | La doulce Memoire recente' (Albert-Marie Schmidt, *Poètes du XVIe siècle* (Paris: Gallimard, 1969), p. 336).

24. The revision of the manuscript text of Maynier's translation was carried out by the cleric Jean Chaperon for the printed version. Cf. Paola Cifarelli, 'Jean Maynier d'Oppède et Pétrarque', in *Les poètes français de la Renaissance et Pétrarque*, ed. by Jean Balsamo (Geneva: Droz, 2004), p. 89; Claire Le Brun-Gouanvic, *Jean Chaperon, Le Chemin de long estude de Dame Cristine de Pizan (1549)* (Paris: Champion, 2008).

25. BnF Arsenal 3086, f. 25v° (my translation). It follows the italian text of the *Triumphus Mortis* II, vv. 127–30:

> S'al mondo tu piacesti agli occhi miei,
> questo mi taccio; pur quel dolce nodo
> mi piacque assai che intorno al cor avei
> e piacemi il bel nome, se vero odo
>
> [If to
> My partiall eye, the world esteemed you:
> I held me quiet, being throughly blest
> In that true-love knot lockt within my brest:]

Anna Hume, Francesco Petrarca, *The Triumphs Of Love: Chastity*.

26. Claude Blum, *Corpus de la Littérature Médiévale des origines au 15ᵉ siècle* (Paris: Champion Électronique, 2001). The expression 'doulce mémoire' appears in the *Corpus* in only one case: 'Le Badin commence | Doulce memoire en plaisir consommée'. It is the incipit of the *Farce nouvelle a troys personnages, c'est assavoir le badin, la femme et la chambriere*, composed around fifteenth–early sixteenth century; 1st edition between 1530 and 1550.

27. 'Que le cueur me doie partir: | Se ne fust le *doulx souvenir* | De la royne glorieuse | Morte fusse de mort hontheuse; | Mais sa grace si me soustient' (Anonymous, *Miracles de Nostre Dame par personnages*, ed. by Gaston Paris and Ulysse Robert, I (Paris: Librairie Firmin Didot & C., 1876), p. 20).

28. Philippe Alexandre De Queux de Saint-Hilaire, *Œuvres complètes d'Eustache Deschamps*, ed. by the Marquis de Queux de Saint-Hilaire and Gaston Raynaud (Paris: Librairie Firmin Didot & C., 1878–1903). Note the following excerpts: 'C'est uns plaisirs conceuz par vision, | Continuez par un *doulx souvenir* | De la biauté d'aucune retenir' (III, 272); 'Las, je ne puis reposer ne dormir, | Joye, deduit, ne nul repos avoir, | Pour le penser et le *doulx souvenir* | Qu'Amour me fait en mon cueur concevoir' (III, 281); '*Doulx Souvenir*, veoir ce que j'endure | Et concevoir mon tresdouloureux plour' (III, 347); 'Pour ma douleur assouagier | Qui me fait chascun jour languir | Veul faire d'un *doulx souvenir*' (IV, 187); 'De Desir suy garnis sanz effreer, | *Doulx Souvenir* me vient reconforter' (X, p. xvii); '*Doulx Souvenir* tient son cuer moistement' (X, p. lxxxii).

29. 'De te cuidier fouyr, car sy m'entrappe | *Doulx Souvenir* que mucié ne savoye' (Maurice Roy, *Œuvres poétiques de Christine de Pisan*, I (Paris : Librairie Firmin Didot & C., SATF, 1886), p. 262); 'Pour ce je tiens que vous en tout temps dure | *Doulx souvenir*, qui departir ne laisse | Loyal

amour de vous, et que maistresce' (Maurice Roy, *Œuvres poétiques de Christine de Pisan*, I (Paris: Librairie Firmin Didot & C., SATF, 1886), p. 267).

30. 'Pour ce, reclus me tendray en penser | Treshumblement, de toute ma puissance. | *Doulx Souvenir*, chierement je vous pry, | Escrivez tost ceste balade cy' (Pierre Champion, *Charles d'Orléans, Poésies*, I (Paris : Librairie ancienne Honoré Champion, CFMA, 1923), pp. 63–64); 'Et pour plus abregier ta voye, | Prens ta guide *Doulx Souvenir*' (Pierre Champion, *Charles d'Orléans, Poésies*, I (Paris: Librairie ancienne Honoré Champion, CFMA, 1923), p. 231).

31. 'Helas, mon tres *doulx souvenir*, | jadis te souloye tenir | en desir | en plaisir | au temps de ta tendre jeunesse' (Arnoul Greban, *Le Mystère de la Passion*, ed. by Omer Jodogne, I (Brussels: Palais des Académies, 1965), p. 361).

32. Myriam Rolland-Perrin, *Blonde comme l'or. La chevelure féminine au Moyen Âge* (Aix-en_Provence: Publications de l'université de Provence, 2010), p. 8.

33. Michel Riffaterre, 'L'intertexte inconnu', *Littérature*, no. 41 (1981), 4–7 (p. 6).

34. Hume; Petrarca, *The Triumphs Of Love: Chastity*.

35. In his translation, Bourgouin employs this formula in five places (using only one time the expression 'lié et pris'): 'Petrarque dit qu'il fut lié et pris | D'Amour avecq une fille très belle'; 'Qui luy narra qu'il seroit sans desdit | Pris et lié d'Amour par faict et dict'; 'Et de simple femme est pris et lié en Pouille'; 'fus tost pris et lié par parolle et les signes | Et les beaultéz de celle dame insignes'; 'de son mal, mesmes celluy voyant | Dont suys pris et lié, par qui fus forvoyant'.

36. Philippe Alexandre De Queux de Saint-Hilaire, *Œuvres complètes d'Eustache Deschamps*, ed. by Marquis de Queux de Saint-Hilaire and Gaston Raynaud (Paris: Librairie Firmin Didot & C., 1878–1903). Note the following excerpts: 'Tant que l'un d'eulx, par un mauvais motif, | Prins et lié sera en sa contrée' (v, 330); 'Par son parler, par sa blandice, le treuve si mol et si nice, | Qu'elle le rouille comme un œuf, | Prins et lié comme le beuf' (IX, 189).

37. 'Las ! je suis prins et si hardement lié | De vostre amour. Si n'en suis delié | Bref, par vostre doulceur' (André Tissier, *Recueil de farces (1450–1550)*, XI (Paris: Droz, 1997), p. 140).

38. Hume ; Petrarca, Dans *The Triumphs Of Love: Chastity*.

39. The Zani edition used by Bourgouin did not cointain the *Canzoniere*. If Bourgouin knew it was probably thanks to the manunscript tradition.

40. Cf. Petrarca, *Trionfi, Rime Estravaganti, Codice degli Abbozzi*, ed. by Pacca et Paolino, p. 122.

41. These verses were translated by Bourgouin in this way: 'Encore, qui plus est, ses beaulx cheveulx tressez, | plus que or luysans, au vent espenduz et dressez' (Bourgouin, *Triumphus Cupidinis* II, vv. 237–38). It is clear that here the translator has not understood the text, misinterpreting the colour of the gold wire crown with the hair colour of the woman. Inside the same triumph it is the second time that a similar mistake appears. My search in the Italian source text has also included the word 'capei'.

42. Cf. Gabriella Parussa, and Elina Suomela-Härmä, *Les Triomphes: traduction française de Simon Bourgouin* (Geneva: Droz, 2012).

43. Just one final point about this issue. In a few verses of the *Blason des cheveulx*, written by Jean de Vauzelles and dated to 1536, we encounter the same phrase (vv. 85–88): 'beaulx cheveulx, plus reluysans q'or fin, | Desquelz ne puis, ne pourroys faire fin, | Je vous supplye en vos tresses dorées, | Par mille noeudz haultement decorées' (Dominique-Martin Méon, *Blasons, poésies anciennes des XV et XVImes siècles, extraites de différens auteurs imprimés et manuscrits* (Paris: Guillemot, 1809), p. 4).

44. Cf. Musée Condé, manuscrit 601.

45. Cf. Rolland-Perrin, *Blonde comme l'or*. Here are some excerpts: 'L'empereriz de Romme o les cheveus dorez: | Il n'ot plus belle femme en soissante citez' (*Florence de Rome*, v. 5026–27); 'Cheveulx dorez, rayans sur le soleil | Si très-luysantz, qu'ilz font esblouyr l'œil | Qui les regarde, et les voit coulorez | Non pas d'or fin, mais encor mieulx dorez | [...] Donc beaulx cheveulx, plus reluysans qu'or fin, | Desquelz ne puis, ne pourroys faire fin, | Je vous supplye en vos tresses dorées, | Par mille noeudz haultement decorées, | Tenir lié ce mien cueur despourveu | Avec les yeulx de ceulx qui vous ont vue' (*Blason des cheveulx*, vv. 13–16 et vv. 85–90); 'les cheveulx dorez relevez | sans tresse autour | de sa teste' (*La Théséide*, f. 80v); 'Les biaus crins de la teste blonde' (*Le Roman de la Rose*, v. 13289); 'Et voit les biaus crins blondoianz/

Comme ondes ensamble ondoianz' (*Le Roman de la Rose,* v. 21139–40); 'Les biaus crinz de la teste blonde, | Ou s'il couvient que l'en la tonde | Par aucune grant maladie, | Dont biauté est tost enlaidie' (*Le Roman de la Rose,* vv. 13287–90); 'Durement li plot a veoir, | Qu'il avoit les crins biaus et blons, | A merveille les avoit Ions' (*Le Fotéor,* vv. 106–08).

46. Cf. Cecchetti, *Il Petrarchismo in Francia.* Here are some excerpts: 'Ses *beaulx yeulx* clers par leur privé usage' (Maurice Scève, *Delie,* CCCCIX); 'Seulz voz *beaulx yeulx* (où le certain archer, | Pour me tuer, d'aguet e vint cacher | Devant le soir finissent ma journée' (Pierrre de Ronsard, *Les Amours,* CXXI); 'Les *beaux yeux* de sa Dame' (Joachim Du Bellay, *Divers jeux rustiques,* XV); 'Quand vos *beaux yeulx* Amour en terre incline' (Joachim Du Bellay, *L'Olive,* XCIV). Cf. Keith Cameron, *Concordance des œuvres de Joachim Du Bellay* (Geneva: Droz, 1988). Here are some excerpts: 'Pour avoir paix avecques voz *beaulx yeulx*' (Joachim Du Bellay, *L'Olive,* LXX, 4); 'Ô *beaux yeux* de crystal ! ô grand' bouche honoree' (Joachim Du Bellay, *Les Regrets,* XCI); 'Le sainct rayon qui part des *beaux yeux* de ta dame' (Joachim Du Bellay, *Les Regrets,* VIII).

47. Cf. Keith Cameron, *Concordance des œuvres de Joachim Du Bellay* (Paris : Droz, 1988). It follows some excerpts: 'Ô belle main ! ô beaux cheveux dorez' (Joachim Du Bellay, *L'Olive,* XXIII); 'Ce ne sont pas ces beaux cheveux dorez | Ny ce beau front, qui l'honneur mesme honnore, | Ce ne sont pas les deux archets encore, | De ces beaux yeux de cent yeux adorez' (Joachim Du Bellay, *XII Sonnetz de l'Honneste Amour,* II).

48. Cecchetti, 'Petrarca in Francia prima del Petrarchismo', p. 31; Suomela-Härmä, 'Note sulla prima traduzione francese dei 'Trionfi' di Petrarca', p. 546.

49. Cf. Lionello Sozzi, 'Presenza del Petrarca nella letteratura francese', *Petrarca e la cultura europea,* ed. by Luisa Rotondi Secchi Tarugi (Milan: Nuovi Orizzonti, 1997).

50. Some pieces of evidence were published in 2015. For details, cf. Turbil, 'Le fil rouge de la doulce mémoire''.

CHAPTER 4

The Translation of Lexical-Semantic Elements in Enrique Garcés's *Los sonetos y canciones del Petrarcha*: The Case of *Sestina RVF* 30

Francisco José Rodríguez Mesa

Spanish is a language in which a wide range of Italian-style — or even Petrarchan — verse was produced during the so-called *Siglo de Oro*. In contrast to other European countries however, Italian-style poetry in Spain was not promoted by the diffusion of translated texts, but by the direct contact of Spanish poets with original Italian works, mainly as a consequence of the historical and political links between Italian and Iberian peninsulas from the fifteenth century onwards, which started with the coronation of Alfonso the Magnanimous as King of Naples (1443) and became even more intense with the annexation of the Kingdom of Naples to the Crown of Aragon (1503).[1]

Verse in the Italian style became completely established in Spain in the first half of the sixteenth century, as attested by the famous letter that Boscán addressed to the duchess of Soma (1540–41)[2] or the existence of an anti-Petrarchan reaction led by Cristóbal de Castillejo (d. 1550). In addition, among the authors belonging to the first generation of Italianist Spanish poets are Hurtado de Mendoza, Gutierre de Cetina, or Hernando de Acuña, who were born before 1520, whereas the second generation comprises poets such as Gregorio Silvestre, Jorge de Montemayor, or Ramírez Pagán, who died before 1570, when Fernando de Herrera was in the most important period of his production.[3] Considering how deeply rooted Italian models were among Spanish poets from the first decades of sixteenth century, it is astonishing that the first almost-complete translation of Petrarch's *Rerum vulgarium fragmenta* (*RVF*), Enrique Garcés's *Los sonetos y canciones del Petrarcha*,[4] was not published until 1591.

In a volume containing various studies about Petrarch's fortune in Europe and America, Furio Brugnolo stated that the work that first set out the problem of translation of vernacular works into other languages as well as its limits and possibilities was Petrarch's Canzoniere.[5] At this moment, a new and particular problem arose in Spain, since the poetic task no longer was how to imitate Petrarch, but how to *translate* his poems. The author had to find a strategy so as to respect both meaning and form and keep a certain degree of faithfulness to the Source Text (ST), regardless of the target culture or audience.[6]

Garcés carries out his translation within a context in which Petrarch was not considered an author who could be influential for Spanish poetry, but an *authority* as far as lyrical poetry is concerned who was already venerated by most poets even if his works — in spite of numerous imitations — were not available in Spanish at the time. It is also remarkable that *Los sonetos y canciones*, even though published in Madrid, started to be translated in Peru. Indeed, in the last decades of the sixteenth century and early seventeenth centuries, there was a vivid interest for Humanism and Italianist poetry in the Americas, as the foundation of the Academia Antártica and the publication of Diego Dávalos's *Miscelánea austral* (1602) or Diego Mexía de Fernangil's *Parnaso antártico* (1608) prove.[7]

This makes Garcés's translation an extremely interesting text, especially considering the context in which it was produced. In order to understand in a more detailed and specific way the author's *modus traducendi*, an especially complex poem has been chosen as the subject of this analysis: the *sestina RVF* 30. In this composition the general difficulties of poetic translation are combined with the constraints of the stanza and its iterative rhyme scheme, which provides an amount of six words which are relevant in terms of both meaning and form. In addition, taking into account the closeness of both source and target languages, the study of Garcés's strategies in order to minimize the intrinsic problems of this text could be relevant for the reflection on poetic translation and translation studies in general.

Enrique Garcés: The Portuguese Engineer Who First Translated Petrarch's Canzoniere into Spanish

Not much is known about Garcés's childhood and youth, and neither his biographers nor the scholars who have studied his life agree on the veracity of the details concerning the first two decades of his existence.[8] Enrique Garcés was born around 1525 in Porto to an important family belonging to the Portuguese nobility. After the date of his birth, it can only be deduced from some official documents that he had left Portugal by 1545, and that in 1547 he was already settled in Peru along with his brother.

In addition to his literary activity, Garcés became famous in his lifetime because of his discoveries in the field of mining; as a matter of fact, he is still remembered nowadays as a "precursor en las Ciencias y las Letras peruanas del siglo XVI".[9] As far as mining is concerned, Garcés discovered the existence of cinnabar deposits in Huamanga from which mercury could be extracted. Later, during a visit to New Spain, he found out that mercury was used to extract silver and he started working on this field, taking advantage of the cinnabar mines he had discovered in Huamanga and inventing a furnace to extract mercury from cinnabar. These activities implied the optimization of Peruvian silver mines, from which the author himself obtained great benefits.[10] Actually, almost all official documents issued in the New World that provide some information about Garcés's life have to do with his mining activity.

Some scholars have pointed out that Garcés may have studied mining in Spain before his departure to America,[11] but there is no documentary evidence for it; in fact, he could have acquired knowledge in this discipline later, once he had arrived in Peru, since the first evidence about his mining occupation appears in 1558. Until that moment, the official documents used to sketch out the translator's life only mention his activity as a trader or as a bookseller in Guayaquil and Lima.

As for his literary career, it must be said that there is no evidence about the moment in which Garcés started composing verse or translating foreign works into Spanish. Nevertheless, it is widely accepted that his poetic activity began in America and that, when he came back to Spain in 1589, all his translations were ready — or almost ready — for publication.

Before analysing the content of Garcés's works, it is necessary to emphasize the intimate link existing between both his literary career and his mining activity, at least during the last decade of his life. As a matter of fact, being around seventy years old and having worked the whole of his life in a field that had notably enriched the Spanish Empire, Garcés decided to ask for an economic reward in order to retire and to be able to live comfortably until his death. At first, he wrote to the Spanish authorities from Peru, but very soon he realized that his requests would be more easily fulfilled if he came back to the Iberian Peninsula and managed to present them directly to Philip II's Court.[12]

Faced with this situation and being completely aware of the difficulties of convincing the monarch to grant the requested salary, Garcés might have conceived the publication of his three translations into Spanish, all of them in 1591, in Madrid and dedicated to King Philip II, as a way of underlining his services to the Crown and his skills both in Sciences and in Arts.

Garcés's Three Translations

In spite of his important activity as a translator, Garcés's career as a poet or as a writer — if it really existed — is almost completely unknown and has been only preserved in some poems used to introduce his translations.[13]

As mentioned, the three Garcés translations that we know of were published in Madrid in 1591 and dedicated to King Philip II. Nevertheless, these works can be divided into two different groups according to the nature and the subject of their STs.

The first category comprises only one of these three texts: the translation of Francesco Patrizi's *De Regno et Regis Institutione*, a fifteenth-century political essay with didactic purposes that could be included within the genre of the so-called *speculum principis* (Mirror for Princes). In fact, it was originally composed by his author — one of the most relevant Humanists of fifteenth-century Naples and

Bishop of Gaeta — for Alfonso of Aragon, Duke of Calabria and heir to the Neapolitan throne. It was published by the printer Luis Sánchez and its complete title is *Francisco Patricio De Reyno y de la institucion del que Ha de Reynar, y de como deue auerse con los subditos, y ellos con el. Donde se traen notables exemplos, e historias, y dichos agudos, y peregrinos. Materia gustosissima para todo genero de gentes. Traduzido por Henrique Garces de Latin en Castellano. Dirigido a Philippo Segundo deste nombre y primer Monarca de las Españas y de las Indias. En Madrid, por Luis Sanchez MDXCI*.[14]

The second group of works is formed by two verse translations: Camões's *Os Lusiadas* and Petrarch's *RVF*. These two works also share the printer who published them: Guillermo Drouy, who may have been chosen by the translator because of the kind of works that his printing house brought into the open.

Camões's epic poem, translated as *Los Lusiadas de Lvys de Camoes, Traduzidos de Portugues en Castellano por Henrique Garces dirigidos a Philippo Monarcha primero de las Españas, y de las Indias. En Madrid. Impresso con licencia en casa de Guillermo Drouy impressor de libros. Año 1591*[15] is the only one of Garcés's works in which his mother tongue is involved — in this case as the source language. Maybe for this reason, it has been considered by modern scholars as the best, most faithful, and most fluent among his three translations.[16] As a matter of fact, the translator manages to maintain the *ottava rima* pattern in Spanish with a notable adherence and respect to the content of the ST.

Nevertheless, *Los Lusiadas* is also the only work translated by Garcés of which there had been a Spanish version before 1591. In effect, the Portuguese *editio princeps* was put to press in 1572, and eight years later two different Spanish versions of the text appeared.[17]

Los sonetos y canciones del poeta Francisco Petrarcha, que traduzia Henrique Garces de la lengua Thoscana en Castellana is the title with which *RVF* was brought out by Guillermo Drouy in Madrid in 1591. As in the case of Camões's masterpiece, it is a metrical translation that, in general terms, respects the structure of the stanzas used in the ST. It was also the most complete version of Petrarch's Canzoniere of its age in Spain, since it lacks only five poems: the *canzone* 'Verdi panni sanguigni oscuri, o persi' (*RVF* 29), which Garcés decided not to translate because of its difficulty, and the four sonnets composing the so-called Babylonian cycle (*RVF* 114; 136–38), which the translator may not have known since they had been prohibited.[18]

As can be easily deduced from these brief descriptions, *De Regno* is a Latin and Humanist work written in prose and with an educational aim, four features that are not shared by the two other masterpieces Garcés decided to translate into Spanish. This fact may not be incidental, since through the translation of this wide variety of themes, the author might have meant to underline his mastery in different fields. It cannot be forgotten that this seems to be the way of thinking that led Garcés to try to obtain his reward showing both his mastery of mining and of the arts.

3. *Los sonetos y canciones del poeta Francisco Petrarcha* and Garcés's awareness as a translator

The Petrarch translation, as it was common in Garcés's time, is introduced by a certain number of poetic paratexts, most of them sonnets,[19] the first of which is extremely useful in order to understand some meaningful features of the Target Text (TT):[20]

> Siendo este mi trabajo detenido
> Algunos años más que Horacio manda
> Entró mi pensamiento en demanda
> Que le traía de antes affligido:
> Y viendo claramente quan metido
> El mundo quasi todo por ser anda
> Parnasino, también se me desmanda
> Haziendo del valiente y atrevido.
> Porfiando ser tiempo ya que el arca
> Olvide, y sin recelo a ti le embíe
> O ínclito invencible gran monarcha.
> (Que en Poesía lo es también Petrarcha)
> Y que en ser Portugués no desconfíe
> Pues me assegura el hierro de tu marca.

[Since my work was stopped for some years more than those advised by Horace, my thoughts started thinking on issues I had been thinking before, and because I see that almost the entire world does its best to become Parnassian, I run the risk of being considered as brave and daring. I hope the time to forget has arrived and, without mistrust, it sends you this, oh, illustrious and invincible King (in the same way that Petrarch was in poetry)! And do not be suspicious if I am Portuguese, since I was branded by your iron.]

The first clue that could be guessed through this sonnet has to do with the period during which Garcés worked on his translation. It has already been said that the Portuguese translator came back to Europe in 1589 and that his translation of Petrarch's Canzoniere was published two years later, but it is unlikely that the whole work was translated during those two years.

In effect, in the first two lines of this sonnet, the author reports that he decided to publish his work after having kept it aside for a period which was longer than that recommended by Horace: the lines make an indirect quotation of *Ars poetica* 385–90, where the Roman poet asserts that this period should be of nine years. Taking this point as a basis, scholars such as Garribba[21] contend that Garcés's translation was entirely made in Peru and that this work may have taken place during the decade of 1570. This hypothesis is also supported by the fact that Cervantes talks about Garcés's translation in the sixth book of his *Galatea*, which was published in 1585 with a *privilegio* of 1584:

> De un Enrique Garcés, que al piruano
> reino enriquece, pues con dulce rima,
> con sutil, ingeniosa y fácil mano,
> a la más ardua empresa en él dio cima,

> pues en dulce español al gran toscano
> nuevo languaje ha dado y una nueva estima,
> ¿quién será tal que la mayor le quite,
> aunque el mesmo Petrarca resuscite?²²

[Enrique Garcés makes richer the Peruvian kingdom, since he carried out the hardest work in tender rhymes, with fine, witty and elegant hand, because he gave to the great Tuscan a new language, the tender Spanish, and a new fame. Who could deny him this merit even if Petrarch himself were to be resurrected?]

Paradoxically, the fact that Garcés's translation was carried out in Peru was no more than a circumstantial event that had no influence on the final configuration of his TT. This fact might be explained, in our view, for two main reasons. On the one hand, intellectuals in the Spanish New World during the period in which Garcés lived had to face a high degree of isolation; as a matter of fact, the first academy that worked in Peru, the so-called 'Academia Antártica' operated only between 1596 and 1608, when Garcés had already come back to Spain.²³ This solitude made it impossible for the intellectual to have any cultural exchanges that could lead to a modification of the way of thinking he brought with him on his arrival from Europe. On the other hand, it is likely that Garcés intended his translation to be published in Spain and it is extremely plausible that King Philip was thought of as the addressee at a very early moment of composition, so that — regardless of the cultural situation in Peru — he might be interested in the creation of a TT the closest to the Spanish style as possible. In other words, apart from the ink and the paper Garcés used for the first drafts, the Peruvian elements in this translation could be said to be non-existent.

Coming back to the first sonnet, the encomiastic and practical dimension of *Los sonetos y canciones* is also underlined in it. In fact, lines 11–12 constitute an exaltation of the addressee, emphasizing the King's power, greatness and invincibility and establishing a parallel with Petrarch. This strategy is quite original and relevant because, on the one hand, it links the person to whom the work is dedicated and the content of the work, and, on the other hand, because by taking this association as a basis, the content of the Canzoniere is ennobled and dignified so that its rejection or criticism could imply an attack on the addressee himself. Furthermore, it should be taken into account that Petrarch was one of the most influential authors in Spanish poetry at the end of the sixteenth century, so, in a certain way, the connection that these lines imply may be read as an additional praise to the King as well.

From the point of view of translation, *Los sonetos y canciones* implies a process of transposition between two foreign languages for the translator: Italian as SL and Spanish as TL. It could be thought that a similar phenomenon took place when Garcés decided to translate Patrizi's political essay into Spanish, but it must be borne in mind that *De Regno* was originally written in Latin and that, both in the sixteenth-century Spanish territories — when it was translated by Garcés — and in fifteenth-century Italy — when it was originally composed by Patrizi — Latin was not strictly considered a foreign language for a cultivated person. It is also true that the mastery that the Portuguese translator must have had of Spanish was not inferior at all to the one he might have had of the language of Rome, since (as previously said) Garcés left Portugal when he was around twenty and lived the rest of his life in territories where Spanish was the official language.[24] In fact, this idea appears in the two last lines of this first sonnet, when the translator assures the addressee that his work has no linguistic shortcomings deriving from his mother tongue.

Apart from the poem opening the paratextual presentation of the work, the composition closing this section is also important for understanding Garcés's mentality as a translator. It is a long composition (72 lines) written in *ottava rima* and preceded with the title 'El traductor a su trabajo' ('The Translator to his Work'). As Garribba says, this is the only composition in which the translator talks with a certain openness of his work, explaining some of its characteristics and making references to his own poetic style.[25] In effect, throughout this poem, Garcés confesses to be old, not to be a professional poet, but a mere bearer of texts which are at the same time both useful and beautiful[26] (ll. 6–8; 15). He also insists that his mother tongue is not involved in the translation process (ll. 25–32)[27] and justifies the lack of translation of *RVF* 29 (the 'Verdi panni' *canzone*), encouraging — or challenging — other poets to translate it (ll. 59–64). Lines 65–68 may be the most relevant ones in terms of Garcés's criteria for translating:

> Al que supliere en esto mi rudeza
> Supplico que conserve la harmonía
> Del texto, no olvidando la agudeza
> Del artificio, y de la poesía.

[I beg the person who could correct my coarseness to keep the harmony of the text without leaving aside the wittiness of the artifice and the poetry.]

Taking this passage as a basis, it could be perfectly said that the 'wittiness of the artifice and the poetry' are the most important aspects of the ST according to Garcés;[28] in other words, according to these lines, the translator has done his best to compose a TT in which both meaning ('harmonía | del texto') and structural and aesthetic form ('la agudeza | del artificio, y de la poesía') are kept.

From 'Giovene donna sotto un verde lauro' to 'Una dama debaxo de un verde lauro': Garcés's translation of *RVF* 30

The validity of the guidelines mentioned by Garcés in his paratextual poem will be checked with one of the most difficult compositions of the whole Canzoniere: *RVF* 30,[29] which Garcés translated in this way:

> Una dama debaxo de un verde lauro
> vide más blanca y fría que la nieve,
> nunca del Sol herida en hartos años:
> su hablar, y sus cabellos, y su vista
> me agradaron ansí, que ante mis ojos
> la traigo, o sea en llano, o en alta cima.
>
> Mis pensamientos creo havrán su cima
> quando sin verdes hojas se halle lauro,

y quando se enxugaren estos ojos
verán elarse el fuego, arder la nieve:
que todo me es contrario, do la vista
o manos pongo, y sélo ha muchos años.

Mas porque buelva el tiempo con los años
y en un punto el bivir llega a su cima,
con el cabello negro, o blanco en vista,
la sombra seguiré del dulce lauro
por el ardiente Sol, y por la nieve,
hasta cerrar del todo aquestos ojos.

No se han visto jamás tan lindos ojos
en los presentes ni en pasados años
que me derriten como el Sol la nieve,
y dello es el arroyo que esta cima
divide de lo llano, y riega el lauro,
que es un diamante, aunque es blando a la vista.

Yo temo de mudar antes mi vista
que con piedad me muestre sus dos ojos
el ídolo que adoro en bivo lauro:
que si al contar no yerro, oy ha siete años
que sospirando voy de cima en cima,
la noche y día, al Sol, y al viento, y nieve.

Mas dentro fuego, y fuera blanca nieve
con estos pensamientos y otra vista,
llorando siempre iré por qualquier cima:
quiçá que haré bolver píos los ojos
de alguno, que vendrá de aquí a mil años,
si tanto bivir puede un verde lauro.

Al auro, y aun al Sol que da en la nieve,
vence el cabello en vista, que mis ojos
y mis años conduzen a su cima.

[I saw a lady under a green laurel, she was whiter and colder than the snow that has not been touched by the sun for years. Her speech, her hair and her face pleased me to such an extent that I always walk with them, both in flatland and in high peaks. || I think that my thoughts will reach their peaks when the laurel losses its green leaves and when my eyes are dry they will see an icy fire and burning snow, since everywhere I look becomes contrary to me, and I knew that a long time ago. || But since time goes by with the years, and in a certain moment life reaches its peak, regardless of my black or white hair, I will follow, either in the burning sun or in the snow, the shadow of that sweet laurel until the day in which my eyes will be forever closed. || Such beautiful eyes have never been seen, either in the present or in past years; they melt me like the sun melts the snow, what gives birth to the brook that divides this peak from the flatland and that waters the laurel which, even if it seems to be soft, is a diamond. || I am afraid that I will get old before the idol I admire in an alive laurel lets me see her merciful eyes, since — if I am not wrong — I have been sighing from peak to peak, night and day, in the sun, under the wind and in the snow for seven years today. || But with fire inside me and white snow outside, with these thoughts and a different aspect, I will always go crying through every peak. Maybe I will make someone's eyes merciful in one thousand years if a green laurel can live that long. || The air and the sun beating on the snow are defeated by that hair, whose peak my eyes and my years lead to.]³⁰

The analysis of the TT will be divided into two different parts, the first one dealing with the metric and structural form of the stanza and the second one studying the elements concerning the meaning of the poem. It is true, however, that given the metric and rhetorical particularities of the *sestina* this distinction between form and content cannot be drawn always in a clear way, especially as far as the rhyme words are concerned, but the words themselves and their translation will be analysed in the first section, whereas the modification of the content that these translations imply will be studied in the second part.

The patterns of Garcés's sextina and Petrarch's sestina

In terms of metrical patterns, Garcés, in the translation of Petrarchan sonnets, very often uses the strategy of changing the order of the ST to avoid the difficulties of the original in terms of structure (mainly as far as rhyme is concerned). As a matter of fact, while in Petrarch easy or derivative rhymes (especially by collocating verbal forms at the end of the line) are extremely unusual, these constitute a very frequent strategy in Garcés's TT. This has also been a further reason to analyse the way in which the Portuguese author faced the translation of a *sestina*, since the structure of the stanza itself does not allow for the implementation of this mechanism.³¹

The mere reading of Garcés's TT demonstrates that the translation respects the metric features of the ST. As a matter of fact, most of the lines are hendecasyllabic, and the exceptions are not very relevant, as can be seen on line 1 ('Una dama debaxo de un verde lauro'), a dodecasyllable whose reduction to eleven syllables is impossible, or on line 6 ('la traigo, o sea en llano, o en alta cima'), whose adherence to the hendecasyllabic pattern forces the poet to admit a series of infrequent synalephes.

As previously said, the *sestina* implies an important limitation in which the boundaries between form and content are not clear at all: the fact that rhyme structure is a word-basis one and not a syllabic or phonic one. In effect, this phenomenon involves an extreme rigidity of every single line from the ST to the TT, since the way in which the final words of a single stanza are translated modifies and conditions the structure and the rhythm of the whole composition.³²

RVF 30 consists of a *sestina* with *congedo*³³ according to the scheme (A= 'L'auro' ['lauro']) B= 'neve' (D= 'chiome') E= 'occhi' (C= 'anni') F= 'riva'. Garcés's TT maintains the same structure as the ST as far as the rhyme pattern is concerned and also in terms of the configuration of the *tornada*; that is to say, the translator manages to respect the rules of the *retrogadatio cruciata* also in his poem.³⁴ Nevertheless, there are some essential modifications concerning some of the words in rhyme position; Garcés translates these words in this way:

Petrarch	Garcés
Lauro [=*laurel*]	Lauro [=*laurel*]
Neve [=*snow*]	Nieve [=*snow*]
Anni [=*years*]	Años [=*years*]
Chiome [=*hair*]	Vista [=*sight, aspect*]
Occhi [=*eyes*]	Ojos [=*eyes*]
Riva [=*shore*][35]	Cima [=*peak*]

It can be easily seen that some of the translations do not mean any semantic modification, but a mere transposition from Italian to Spanish, which is facilitated by the lexical similarities between both languages. This is the case of 'neve > nieve', 'anni > años' or 'occhi > ojos'. The maintaining of the term 'lauro' also in the TL follows different criteria than the three previous cases. In effect, whereas words like 'nieve', 'años' or 'ojos' were completely frequent in the common speech of sixteenth-century Spain (as they are nowadays), 'lauro' was a term used only in poetic contexts (substituting for the more common 'laurel'). However, the most important differences between the ST and the TT are to be found in the other two terms: 'chiome > vista' and 'riva > cima'.

In both cases the process followed by Garcés to select the key term to use as a rhyme word in the TT could not be defined as a translation process, but as one of substitution, since there is no semantic correspondence between the terms in the ST and in the translation. Anyway, the reasons for Garcés's lexical selections may be originated by the contexts in which 'chiome' and 'riva' appear in the first stanza of the ST:

> Giovene donna sotto un verde lauro
> vidi più biancha et più fredda che neve
> non percossa dal sol molti et molt'anni;
> e'l suo parlare e'l bel viso, et le *chiome*
> mi piacquen sì ch'i' l'ò dinanzi agli occhi,
> ed avrò sempre, ov'io sia, in poggio o'n *riva*.

> ['I saw a girl under green laurel | colder and whiter than the snow | untouched by the sun for many years: | and her speech, her lovely face, her hair | so please me that she's before my eyes | and will be always, wherever, on sea or shore.'][36]

Line 4, where 'chiome' appears for the very first time in the poem, shows a term whose semantic value in Petrarch seems to be closer than 'chiome' to the Target 'vista': 'viso'; in effect, in the *Enciclopedia dantesca* the term 'viso' is defined as 'sight'.[37] In addition, on line 6, 'riva' appears forming a phrase ('in poggio o'n riva') with its opposite in this context, and it is the antonym itself that is the element that shares more similarities with the Target Term ('cima') in the whole line. Hence, the translation/adaptation strategy followed by Garcés with these terms seems to be clear: he decided to invert the order of these two lines in the ST in order to collocate in the rhyme position two words that, being more semantically malleable than the ones chosen by Petrarch, may have facilitated the translation of the rest of the lines in the *sestina* where they appear. Actually, as it will be seen later, most of the semantic differences between the ST and the TT and almost all the important reformulations of content involve lines whose rhyme words in the ST are either 'chiome' or 'riva'.

Content variations

The way in which the content of the poem is structured in the ST and in the TT could be defined, in general terms, as the result of a strategy of line-by-line translation, which — as previously said — is the most frequent process of meaning transposition in this kind of stanza. In fact, in most of the lines Garcés's modifications are minimal — even if sometimes this should not be understood as a proof of the translator's mastery, but as a consequence of the closeness of Italian and Spanish in the configuration of the poetic speech.

Despite these linguistic parallelisms, if there is a passage in which Garcés's attention and care are stressed in a particular way, it is throughout the first stanza. In fact, compared to the Petrarchan original, there is an almost complete adherence both to meaning and to structural form. The only relevant exceptions are the previously mentioned changes in the order of the words on lines 4 and 6, which do not have any consequences in the interpretation of the fragment. In my opinion, it might be possible that this faithfulness to the ST arises from the fact that the choices shown in this first stanza determine the structure — and, in a certain way, also the meaning — of the whole composition.

As a matter of fact, this conscientious task seems to evaporate in the very first line of the second stanza, which starts with a modification — the first one of the TT — as far as the ST is concerned, since Garcés ignores the adverb 'allor' ('then, in that moment') and decides to introduce a subjective verb 'creo' ('I think') where Petrarch's line expresses a certainty 'saranno'[38] ('they will be'). A similar effect can be found on line 9, where the TT eliminates — for obvious metrical reasons — the allusion to the peace of the poet's heart, which will not arrive because of the lady's steadfastness.[39] Nevertheless, the greatest modification of this stanza arrives with the last two lines, where Petrarch's original ('non ò tanti capelli in queste chiome | quanti vorrei quel giorno attender anni': 'and there's not as many strands in my hair | as the years I'd wait to see that') is completely modified. In fact, whereas the ST makes reference to the poet's patience — and even hope — while he is waiting for a change in the lady's mind, the TT presents two lines that have nothing to do with any future hope, but that underline the poet's pessimism. This change in perspective (hope vs negative certainty) can also be traced through the verb tenses and aspects in these lines: present and conditional in the ST and present with a past value in the TT.

In essence, the third stanza does not show any substantial divergence between the ST and the TT, and in general terms its fidelity to the original is comparable to the one of the first sixain. In this sense, it must be said that the way in which Garcés manages to reproduce the metaphor of the passage of time and of age on line 15 is praiseworthy considering that Petrarch builds this line on the basis of the semantic value of the term 'chiome' ('hair') ('o colle brune o colle bianche chiome': 'either with dark or with white hair'), which the Portuguese translator changes into 'vista' ('sight'). The solution for reformulating line 18 ('fin che l'ultimo dì chiuda quest'occhi': 'until the last day closes my eyes') in order to maintain both the hendecasyllable and the meaning of the ST is also commendable. What is more, there is one line in this stanza where the TT even improves on its source: the Petrarchan line 14 ('sì ch'a la morte in un punto s'arriva': 'so that death comes to us') is even nowadays an example of a remarkable irregularity for a *sestina*,[40] since — as previously said (see note 29) — the word in rhyme position in this kind of stanza should be disyllabic and not be a verb; it is impossible to say if it was done consciously or not, but Garcés's line keeps the disyllabic noun set from the beginning of the composition.

A hyperbaton on line 16 ('*la sombra seguiré* del dulce lauro' where the ST shows '*seguirò l'ombra* di quel dolce lauro')[41] which is not due to metric reasons, could be marked as a minor divergence from the Petrarchan original in these six lines. Of a deeper relevance seems to be one feature of line 13: while in *RVF* we read 'Ma perché *vola* il tempo et fuggon gli anni' ('But since time flies and they vanish, those years'), what is the very first appearance in the whole of the Canzoniere of the classic topos of *tempus fugit*, the TT shows 'Mas porque *buelva* el tiempo con los años', substituting the original verb 'vola' ('flies') with 'buelva' ('comes back'), so that the identification of the motif is almost completely lost or — in the best of the cases — deeply hidden. Nevertheless, the solution to this lack of semantic correspondence between the ST and the TT is shown in one of the paratexts published together with Garcés's translation. In effect, on folio 3 of Guillermo Drouy's edition, there is an 'Erratas' section, where misprints are shown and the author specifies that this 'buelva' should be read as 'buela', literal translation of the source term.

The first three lines of the fourth stanza do not show any relevant peculiarities of translation, even if this fidelity to the ST radically changes between lines 22 and 24. Taking as a basis the melting snow on line 21, the ST makes reference to the poet's tears using one of the words in rhyme position that Garcés changed: 'riva'; this strategy seems to be the origin of three lines whose meaning notably differs from the ST. As a matter of fact, Garcés's line 22 ('y dello es el arroyo en esta cima') does not allude to the lover's crying in such a transparent way as Petrarch ('onde procede lagrimosa riva': 'from which proceeds a tear-drenched shore') and, as a consequence, the brook watering the laurel does not come from the tears yielded by love, but could be interpreted as a natural one. This modification implies some important losses, such as the impossibility of identifying Petrarch and Laura's story with Apollo and Daphne and also the unfeasibility of understanding that the brook of tears (the laurel representing Laura) grows because it is nourished by the tears themselves.

Also the reference to love on Petrarch's line 23 is lost in this translation, presumably because of metric reasons whereas the choice of translating 'chiome' as 'vista' since the first stanza provokes a semantic alteration on line 24: where Petrarch describes both Laura's beauty and chastity taking as a basis for her skin and her hair ('ch'à i rami di diamante, et d'òr le chiome': 'that has branches of steel,[42] and golden hair'), Garcés is forced to reformulate the last part of the line to introduce his rhyme word, and the solution ignores the reference to Laura's blond hair to stress the grace that the poet proves in looking at her ('que es un diamante, aunque es blando a la vista').

The fifth stanza in both the ST and the TT returns to the idea of the passage of time and the lack of hope for the lover presented in the second sixain. As far as the content is concerned, the translation is once more quite faithful to the Petrarchan original, and the alterations or omissions can be frequently justified for metrical reasons: 'volto et chiome' ('face and hair') > 'vista' (line 25) or 'che con *vera* pietà mi mostri *gli* occhi' ('I see real pity in her eyes') > 'que con piedad me muestre sus *dos* ojos' (line 26). In the same way, the double opposed pairs on line 30 in the ST ('la notte e'l giorno, al caldo ed a la neve': 'night and day, in heat and snow') modify their structure because of the need for additional syllables to complete the hendecasyllabic pattern in Spanish ('la noche y día, al Sol, *y al viento*, y nieve'). Only in one line of the TT does Garcés show a higher degree of freedom in his translation: this is the case of line 27, where the original 'l'idolo mio, scolpito in vivo lauro' ('my idol, sculptured from living laurel'), which could be perfectly translated literally into Spanish keeping the original hendecasyllabic structure ('mi ídolo esculpido en/con[43] vivo lauro') becomes 'el ídolo *que adoro* en bivo lauro'.[44]

These same criteria are valid for the analysis of the last of the sixains, where only two features are remarkable: on the one hand and once more, the ability of Garcés to keep the metaphor of the coming of old age on line 32 maintaining the use of 'vista' as the word in rhyme position, and on the other hand the semantic transformation of line 36 due to the change of the adjective modifying 'lauro': 'ben cólto' in the ST, 'verde' in the TT. This phenomenon is, in my opinion, much more relevant than the previous one, since the Petrarchan line seems to refer to the amount of time that Laura could be remembered through the verses the poet wrote in her honour; hence, the adjectival phrase 'ben cólto' ('cultured') is to be understood as a metaphor — even a metaliterary one — of the activity of Petrarch as a love poet. With the solution proposed by Garcés, however, this dimension is completely lost, since the adjective 'verde' seems to focus on the natural appearance and the vitality of the laurel as a plant.

The translation of the *tornada* shows deeper differences between both texts, and some of them betray the fidelity to the ST that Garcés has maintained from the very beginning of his *sestina*. Almost the totality of these changes belongs to the first line of the stanza: line 37, and the modifications, could be considered as the consequence of a linguistic characteristic of the ST.

Petrarch writes in line 37 'L'auro e i topacii al sol sopra la neve' ('The laurel,[45] topaz in sun on snow'). For the second time in this *sestina*, the Italian poet does not follow the prescriptions of composition for this kind of stanza. If — as previously said — on line 14 the word in rhyme position was 's'arriva' instead of the disyllabic noun 'riva', in the opening of this *tornada* a noun phrase formed by an article plus a noun ('L'auro') is found instead of the single noun 'lauro', which was repeated throughout the poem. It is obvious that Petrarch can use this mechanism because both elements, even if semantically different and without relation, are homophonic in Italian, but this feature is not shared by the Spanish language, so that Garcés cannot imitate the strategy of the ST in his translation as he usually does. In contrast, the Portuguese translator opts to respect the meaning of the Italian phrase, even if it implies a further problem in Spanish: the addition of a syllable and the use of a noun which were not frequent either in the Spanish language or in poetic speech ('Al *auro*'). Anyway, this is only the first of the difficulties which should be faced on this line, because the transposition of all the elements of the ST into a hendecasyllable in Spanish seems to be impossible.[46] In fact, Garcés decides to omit the reference to the topaz, even if it implies, on a visual level, the loss of the reference to the lady's eyes and, on a metaphorical one, the omission of the symbol of chastity.[47]

In spite of the difficulties for translating the *tornada*, Garcés's version must be once more praised because of a good solution found for the translation of line 38, where the TT omits only one adjective of the ST in order to reach to insert the rhyme word 'chiome' ('vincon le *bionde* chiome presso agli occhi': '[it] is exceeded by bond hair near the eyes' > 'vence el cabello en *vista*, que mis ojos'). Furthermore, it must be said that this omission does not cause any internal incoherence, since the previous allusions to the lady's blond hair were also eliminated from Garcés's TT ('et d'òr le chiome' > 'aunque es blando a la vista' line 24). In conclusion, even in this aspect — and again it is impossible to determine if in a conscious way or not — the solution of the translator is coherent and well-motivated.

Conclusions

Throughout this study the inherent difficulties of the *sestina* as a stanza have been repeatedly pointed out. In spite of these obstacles, concerning both the structural and semantic levels, one could conclude that Garcés's translation of *RVF* 30 is quite satisfactory. In addition, the high degree of fidelity that the TT shows if compared to the Petrarchan original and, at the same time, the attentiveness with which the translator complies with the exigencies of Spanish sixteenth-century metrics could make us think that Garcés is a translator whose mastery is substantially shown in difficult texts. In fact, the literary levels reached by his *sestina* are much higher and more delicate than the results obtained in the translation of freer kinds of stanzas, such as the sonnet or the *canzone*, where lines are manipulated to such an extent that, sometimes, it is no longer possible to find a single Petrarchan vestige and rarely does it happen because of an aesthetic observance.

Unfortunately for Garcés, this high mastery in poetry — and also in translation — is only shown on the very few occasions in which he has to face such a difficult element as a *sestina*, and it is in these occasions that the combination of 'harmony in the text and acuity and craft in poetry', as he says in his paratextual and translatological poem, are really implemented. For the rest of *Los sonetos y canciones* and in spite of his great potential, he has always been considered a poet with 'capacità poetiche non eccelse'.[48]

Nevertheless and despite the scarcity of flattering words dedicated to Garcés until today, it must be taken into account that his task cannot be considered as merely translational or equivalent to the one carried out by other European poets translating Petrarch for the very first time into their mother tongues in the sixteenth century. Firstly, because Spanish was not Garcés's mother tongue, but above all because Petrarch was so famous — and even read — among Spanish sixteenth-century poets that providing a translation of *RVF* could not simply be oriented to make available the text to the Spanish audience, but to prove the mastery of the translator, and to achieve this goal the translator had to show a wide range of strategies apart from the mere reproduction of the ST or the literal translation.

As far as these strategies are concerned, Garcés might have found very useful his own experience in mining, since a good translation in the sixteenth century should follow a parallel path: it consisted in the extraction of some raw materials from the ST in order to manipulate them with accuracy and care so that they become a good which fulfils the needs of the target audience in terms of utility and beauty and whose possession makes them richer.

Notes to Chapter 4

1. On the historical and political contexts of the Hispanic kingdoms during the last part of the Middle Ages and in their relationships with the Italian states, see among other works José Carlos Rovira, *Humanistas y poetas en la corte napolitana de Alfonso el Magnánimo* (Alicante: Instituto de Cultura Juan Gil-Albert, 1990), Francisco José Rodríguez Mesa, *'Qui risorga ogni laude del Petrarca' Petrarquismo y lírica culta en Nápoles hasta el ocaso de la monarquía aragonesa* (Córdoba: Universidad de Córdoba, 2012) or the recent María D'Agostino, *La nobil città de la sirena. Cultura napoletana e poesia spagnola del Cinquecento* (Rome: Salerno, 2017).
2. Boscán most likely wrote this letter in 1540 or 1541 and made it as a preface to the second book of his complete works. Throughout the epistle he defends himself from the criticism his poetry has received because of the important differences between the Italian style of poetry and the traditional Castilian one, especially regarding sonority:

   [P]oniendo las manos en esto, me topé con hombres que me cansaron. Y en cosa que toda ella consiste en ingenio y en juicio, no teniendo estas dos cosas más vida de cuanto tienen gusto, pues cansándome había de desgustarme, después de desgustado, no tenía donde pasar más adelante. Los unos se quejaban que en las trovas de esta arte los consonantes no andaban tan descubiertos ni sonaban tanto como en las castellanas; otros decían que este verso no sabían si era verso, o si era prosa, otros argüían diciendo que esto principalmente había de ser para mujeres y que ellas no curaban de cosas de sustancia sino del son de las palabras y de la dulzura del consonante [...] ¿quién ha de responder a hombres que no se mueven sino al son de los consonantes? ¿Y quién se ha de poner en pláticas con gente que no sabe qué cosa es verso, sino aquél que calzado y vestido con el consonante os entra de un golpe por el un oído y os sale por el otro? [...] Si a éstos mis obras les parecieren duras y tuvieren soledad de la multitud de los consonantes, ahí tienen un cancionero, que acordó de llamarse general para que todos ellos vivan y descansen con él generalmente.

   [Setting my hands to this, I ran into men who tired me. And in a practice that depends entirely on wit and on judgement, neither of which have life apart from pleasure, once I became tired, I necessarily became displeased, and once displeased, I had no way of proceeding. Some complained that in the songs of this art the consonance did not proceed as openly, nor did it sound out in the manner of the Castilian songs; others said that they did not know if this verse was verse or prose, others argued that this must be principally for women, who cared nothing for matters of substance but only for the sound of the words and the sweetness of the rhyme... [...] who needs to respond to men who are not moved but by the soundings of consonance? And who needs to engage in conversation with people who do not know what verse is unless it be that which, shod and saddled with its consonantal rhyme, enters you with one blow to the ear, and departs with another? [...] If my works seem rough to these men, and they feel bereft of a multitude of rhymes, they have a *cancionero* that kindly called itself 'general' so that all men of that sort might live and take repose with it generally.]

>   For further information on the letter and its political reading, see Leah Middlebrook, *Imperial Lyric: New Poetry and New Subjects in Early Modern Spain* (University Park: Pennsylvania State University Press, 2009), especially pp. 41–47.

3. The first generation of Spanish Italianist poets is formed by noblemen who were poets and soldiers at the same time and very frequently took part in the Italian wars or in Italian politics. For instance, Hernando de Acuña fought in the Piedmont War, Hurtado de Mendoza was a diplomat in Rome, and Gutierre de Cetina worked at the court of the Prince of Ascoli. The division between the first and the second school is merely based on chronological aspects. As for the way in which these authors reproduce Petrarchan models, the deeper changes arrive in Spain at the end of the century, when Fernando de Herrera (and also Fray Luis de León) rebuild in their poems a poetic tension that leads to the failure of the 'poetic I' as a consequence of the impossibility to achieve their goals (in aesthetic terms in the case of Herrera and in religious terms for Fray Luis). For further information, see Álvaro Alonso, *La poesía italianista* (Madrid: Laberinto, 2002).

4. Garcés's translation only lacks the *canzone* 'Verdi panni, sanguigni oscuri, o persi' (*RVF* 29) and the so-called Babylonian sonnets (*RVF* 114 and 136–38).

5. Furio Brugnolo and Aviva Garribba, 'Enrique Garcés traductor del *Canzoniere* (1591): aspectos lingüísticos, estilísticos y métricos', in *Petrarca y el petrarquismo en Europa y América*, ed. by Mariapia Lamberti (Mexico City: Universidad Nacional Autónoma de México, 2006), pp. 289–306 (pp. 289–91).

6. Alfonso D'Agostino ('Traduzione e rifacimento nelle letterature romanze medievali', in *Testo medievale e traduzione*, ed. by Cammarota, Maria Grazia and Maria Vittoria Molinari (Bergamo: Bergamo University Press, 2001) pp. 151–72) defined translation during the Middle Ages as a process which could be summarized using the formula '$T_1\ (L_1,\ R_1) \rightarrow T_2\ (L_1/L_2,\ R_2)$', where T stands for the text, L for the language and R for the whole of rhetorical strategies which are typical and inherent of every literary culture. The main contribution of this new approach for translation consists in a clear reduction of the elements containing 'R', which are those which could justify or even require a higher degree of separation between ST and TT. Therefore, this implies a higher degree of manipulation.

7. For an overview of the so-called Peruvian Petrarchism, see Alicia Colombí's works, especially *Petrarquismo peruano: Diego Dávalos y Figueroa y la Miscelánea Austral* (London: Támesis, 1985) and *Del exe antiguo a nuestro nuevo polo, una década de literatura virreinal (Charcas 1602–1612)* (Berkeley, CA: Centro Cornejo Polar y Latinoamericana Editores, 2003).

8. Garcés's life and production have been widely studied in the last decade by Aviva Garribba ('La prima traduzione completa del Canzoniere di Petrarca in spagnolo: *Los sonetos y canciones del Petrarcha, que traduzía Henrique Garcés de lengua thoscana en castellana* (Madrid, 1591)', *Artifara — Addenda*, 3 (2003), 1–74; 'La prima traduzione completa del Canzoniere di Petrarca in spagnolo: *Los sonetos y canciones del Petrarcha, que traduzía Henrique Garcés de lengua thoscana en castellana* (Madrid, 1591). Edizione', *Artifara — Editiones*, 3 (2003), 1–182; 'Il petrarchismo in America Latina nel Cinquecento: il caso di Enrique Garcés', *Confronto letterario*, 40 (2003), 247–61; 'Aspectos léxicos de la traducción del *Canzoniere* por Enrique Garcés', *Cuadernos de filología italiana*, extra 12 (2005), 115–32). Apart from Garribba, Estuardo Núñez devoted some studies to the poetic translations of this author ('El primer traductor de Petrarca y Camoens en América', *Cuadernos americanos*, 18.1 (1959), 234–42; *Las letras de Italia en Perú* (Lima: Universidad Nacional Mayor de San Marcos, 1968); 'Henrique Garcés múltiple hombre del Renacimiento', in *La tradición clásica en el Perú virreinal*, ed. by Teodoro Hampe Martínez (Lima: Universidad Nacional Mayor de San Marcos, 1999) pp. 129–44). Guillermo Lohmann Villena's article about Garcés's

biography ('Enrique Garcés descubridor del mercurio en el Perú, poeta y arbitrista', *Anuario de estudios americanos*, V (1948), 439–82) is still the main source used by scholars.

9. Guillermo Lohmann Villena, 'Enrique Garcés descubridor del mercurio en el Perú, poeta y arbitrista', *Anuario de estudios americanos*, 5 (1948), 439–82 (p. 439).
10. Garcés obtained the concession of silver extractions for twelve years, and after that, in 1572, he was appointed tax collector in Huamanga.
11. Garribba, 'La prima traduzione completa del Canzoniere di Petrarca in spagnolo', p. 1.
12. These documents are kept in the Archivo General de Indias and the Archivo Nacional de Perú and constitute the basis for Lohmann Villena's study ('Enrique Garcés descubridor del mercurio en el Perú, poeta y arbitrista', *Anuario de estudios americanos*, V (1948), 439–82).
13. In the translation of Camões's *Os Lusiadas*, Garcés includes some paratextual sonnets that he composed himself: two dedicated to King Philip II, a certain number of them in a poetic exchange with Diego de Aguilar, and a last one in which he explains the reasons why he decided to translate the Portuguese epic poem. At the beginning of *De Reyno y de la institucion del que ha de Reynar*, the translator introduces just one sonnet to dedicate the work to the King, whereas the paratextual presentation of Petrarch's *RVF* contains an initial group of three sonnets dedicated to the King, a total of eight sonnets included in a poetic exchange with others authors and a metapoetic composition in *ottava rima* closing the section.
14. *Francisco Patricio on the Kingdom and on the Institution of Who Shall Reign, and on How He Should Behave with his People and They with him, Telling some Famous Examples and Stories, and Witty and Comical Anecdotes, Being a Pleasant Reading for every Kind of People, Translated by Henrique Garcés from Latin into Spanish, Addressed to Philip II, First King of Spain and the Indias, in Madrid, by Luis Sánchez MDXCI*. According to Aviva Garribba ('La prima traduzione completa del Canzoniere di Petrarca in spagnolo: *Los sonetos y canciones del Petrarcha, que traduzía Henrique Garcés de lengua thoscana en castellana* (Madrid, 1591)', p. 62), this is Garcés's translation of which a highest number of copies is kept.
15. There are fifteen copies of this translation in different libraries of Europe and America. These fifteen copies are the result of the thirteen that Yolanda Clemente San Román (*Tipobibliografía madrileña. La imprenta en Madrid en el siglo XVI (1566–1600)*, 3 vols (Kassel: Reichenberger, 1998), II, 541–42) studied plus two more that Garribba ('La prima traduzione completa del Canzoniere di Petrarca in spagnolo: *Los sonetos y canciones del Petrarcha, que traduzía Henrique Garcés de lengua thoscana en castellana* (Madrid, 1591)', p. 61) found in the Biblioteca Nacional de Lisboa and the Biblioteca Nacional de Rio de Janeiro.
16. Modern scholars, such as José Toribio Medina (*Escritores americanos celebrados por Cervantes en el canto de Calíope* (Santiago de Chile: Ateneo, 1926)), Luis Alberto Sánchez (*Los poetas de la colonia y de la revolución* (Lima: PTCM, 1947)), or Núñez ('Henrique Garcés múltiple hombre del Renacimiento'), have considered this translation as Garcés's masterpiece, even if some of the sixteenth-century poets criticized the poetic quality of the text (Alicia Colombí-Monguió, 'Las visiones de Petrarca en la América virreinal', *Revista Iberoamericana*, 48 (1982), 536–86).
17. By Benito Caldera (Alcalá de Henares) and Luis Gómez de Tapia (Salamanca).
18. In Spain, these sonnets were first prohibited in the 1583 *Indice*, whereas they do not appear in the previous version of 1551–59. Nevertheless, the Roman *Indice* censored them in 1559.
19. There are twenty-five poems, numbered by Garribba ('La prima traduzione completa del Canzoniere di Petrarca in spagnolo: *Los sonetos y canciones del Petrarcha, que traduzía Henrique Garcés de lengua thoscana en castellana* (Madrid, 1591). Edizione', pp. 5–13).
20. All the quotations from Garcés included in this study come from Garribba's edition ('La prima traduzione completa del Canzoniere di Petrarca in spagnolo: *Los sonetos y canciones del Petrarcha, que traduzía Henrique Garcés de lengua thoscana en castellana* (Madrid, 1591). Edizione').
21. Garribba, 'La prima traduzione completa del Canzoniere di Petrarca in spagnolo: *Los sonetos y canciones del Petrarcha, que traduzía Henrique Garcés de lengua thoscana en castellana* (Madrid, 1591)', p. 4.
22. Miguel de Cervantes, *La Galatea* (Madrid: Aguilar, 2003). Luis Monguió (*Sobre un escritor elogiado por Cervantes. Los versos del perulero Enrique Garcés y sus amigos (1591)* (Berkeley: University of California Press, 1960)) provides further information about this mention of Garcés.

23. José de la Riva Agüero in his classic *El Perú histórico y artístico* (Santander: J. Martínez, 1921) identifies 1570 as the turning point of Peruvian politics and culture with the arrival in Lima of Francisco de Toledo, representative of King Philip II (p. 84). Even if it is true that de Toledo started a series of reforms including the secularization of the University of Lima, the actual change of the colonial society took more than two decades, as the creation of the Academia Antártica proves. For further information on the Academia and on its main author, Dávalos y Figueroa, see Carmen de Mora Valcárcel, 'Un raro del siglo XVII: la Miscelánea Austral de Pedro Dávalos y Figueroa', in *Andalucía y América en el siglo XVII* ed. by Torres Ramírez, Bibiano (Huelva: Diputación, 1985), pp. 231–50.
24. It must be also taken into account that, in sixteenth- and seventeenth-century Portugal, Spanish was widely spoken, mainly among the highest social classes.
25. Garribba, 'La prima traduzione completa del Canzoniere di Petrarca in spagnolo: *Los sonetos y canciones del Petrarcha, que traduzía Henrique Garcés de lengua thoscana en castellana* (Madrid, 1591)', p. 6.
26. The Horatian influence is also present in different parts of this composition.
27. Apart from the first sonnet, this idea also appears in IX, 6–7 and XIV, 9–10).
28. Garribba, 'La prima traduzione completa del Canzoniere di Petrarca in spagnolo: *Los sonetos y canciones del Petrarcha, que traduzía Henrique Garcés de lengua thoscana en castellana* (Madrid, 1591)', p. 7.
29. The ST of *RVF* 30 according to Marco Santagata's edition (Francesco Petrarca, *Canzoniere*, Milan: Mondadori, 2010) is provided here in order to facilitate the reading of the analysis. All the quotations from *RVF* in Italian in this study come from Santagata's edition. The separation between the different stanzas is shown with a double vertical line (||): Giovene donna sotto un verde lauro | vidi più biancha et più fredda che neve | non percossa dal sol molti et molt'anni; | e'l suo parlare e'l bel viso, et le chiome | mi piacquen sì ch'i'l'ò dinanzi agli occhi, | ed avrò sempre, ov'io sia, in poggio o'n riva. || Allor saranno i miei pensieri a riva | che foglia verde non si trovi in lauro; | quando avrò queto il core, asciutti gli occhi, | vedrem ghiacciare il foco, arder la neve: | non ò tanti capelli in queste chiome | quanti vorrei quel giorno attender anni. || Ma perché vola il tempo et fuggon gli anni, | sì ch'a la morte in un punto s'arriva, | o colle brune o colle bianche chiome, | seguirò l'ombra di quel dolce lauro / per lo più ardente sole et per la neve, | fin che l'ultimo dì chiuda quest'occhi. || Non fur già mai veduti sì begli occhi, | o ne la nostra etade o ne' prim'anni, | che mi struggon così come'l sol neve, | onde procede lagrimosa riva, | ch'Amor conduce a pie' del duro lauro | ch'à i rami di diamante, et d'òr le chiome. || I' temo di cangiar pria volto et chiome, | che con vera pietà mi mostri gli occhi | l'idolo mio, sculpito in vivo lauro: | che s'al contar non erro, oggi à sett'anni | che sospirando vo di riva in riva | la notte e'l giorno, al caldo ed a la neve. || Dentro pur foco, et for candida neve, | sol con questi pensier', con altre chiome, | sempre piangendo andrò per ogni riva, | per far forse pietà venir negli occhi | di tal che nascerà dopo mill'anni, | se tanto viver pò ben cólto lauro. || L'auro e i topacii al sol sopra la neve | vincon le bionde chiome presso agli occhi | che menan gli anni miei sì tosto a riva.
30. Taking into account the syntactic differences between English and Spanish it is not possible to carry out a line-by-line translation of the *sestina*. This translation has been done by trying to preserve the most meaningful elements of every stanza in order to achieve a better comprehension of the particularities discussed later. The separation between the different stanzas is shown with a double vertical line (||).
31. It must be kept in mind that the rhetoric codification of the *sestina* requires that all the rhyme-words are disyllable and, in addition, prohibits the use of verb forms in this position.
32. It should be borne in mind that this process (almost a word-by-word translation) presents serious problems when the word in the ST is used with any polysemic value.
33. The *congedo* or *tornada* is the last stanza of the *sestina*, generally three lines long, in which the six words in rhyme position throughout the poems appear.
34. The *retrogradatio crociata* or 'backward crossing' is the scheme which determines the rotation of rhyme words in the different stanzas of a *sestina*.
35. Actually 'riva' is one of the hardest words of the poem to translate due to its polysemy in the

different contexts it appears. For instance, 'plain' in opposition to 'mount' in line 6 or 'stream' and 'brook' in line 22. This semantic variety complicates the task and explains the fact that Garcés cannot find a univocal term in order to carry out a literal translation and to keep the meaning of the ST.

36. All the English versions of *RVF* shown in this chapter come from the translation by A. S. Kline in Francesco Petrarch, *The Complete Canzoniere* (New York: PiT, 2002).
37. http://www.treccani.it/enciclopedia/viso_(Enciclopedia_Dantesca) [accessed 4 April 2016].
38. It must be also remembered that in Petrarch this line could have a funereal reading, as happens on line 39 and in other passages of the *RVF* showing similar terms (82, 3 or 164, 12).
39. The phonic and syllabic differences between the Italian 'cor(e)' ('heart') and the Spanish 'corazón' together with the high recurrence of the Italian term in lyric Renaissance poetry is one of the hardest problems of poetic translation from Italian to Spanish.
40. Pietro G. Beltrami, *La metrica italiana* (Bologna: Il Mulino, 2002), p. 266.
41. It must be said that without this hyperbaton, Garcés's hendecasyllable would be stressed on the third syllable, which is not normal.
42. In spite of Kline's translation, the ST shows diamond and not steel branches.
43. To keep the hendecasyllable, the original 'in vivo lauro' could be translated as 'en vivo lauro' if a diaeresis was done between 'mi^{v}ídolo' (taking as a basis that the initial vowel of the noun is stressed) or as 'con vivo lauro' if a synalephe was made between these two words.
44. One should also note the redundant meaning in the TT phrase 'ídolo que adoro'.
45. The ST shows 'l'auro' ('the air'), and not 'Lauro' ('The laurel'). Kline's decision keeps the right structure for the *tornada*, maintaining the words in rhyme position throughout the *sestina*.
46. As a matter of fact, not only Garcés, but all the Spanish translations of the Canzoniere used to carry out this study omit or transform any of the terms present in the Petrarchan original.
47. According to Robert M. Durling ('Giovene Donna Sotto Un Verde Lauro', *Modern Language Notes*, 86, (1971), 1–20), the gold refers to Laura's hair and the topazes (in plural) to the lady's eyes. In addition, in *RVF* 190, 10 the topaz appears as a reference to chastity.
48. Garribba, 'La prima traduzione completa del Canzoniere di Petrarca in spagnolo: *Los sonetos y canciones del Petrarcha, que traduzía Henrique Garcés de lengua thoscana en castellana* (Madrid, 1591)', p. 1.

CHAPTER 5

Translating the *Canzoniere* into Images: The Petrarca Queriniano Incunable

Giulia Zava

Adapting Petrarch can mean many things; it does not only imply the conversion of the poet's vernacular into another language, but can sometimes involve the translation of words into images.[1] Unlike the iconography of the *Triumphi*, the *Rerum Vulgarium Fragmenta* (*RVF*) do not seem to offer great adaptability for representation. As Joseph Burney Trapp writes of the former:

> the reason for this is not far to seek. They are narrative rather than lyric, and so lent themselves more easily both to literal translation into pictures and to variation *ad lib.*; they were graphic in their presentation of procession, people and situation; they used familiar *exempla*, to which others could be added; and their adaptability for artists who wished to elaborate on their imagery and *dramatis personae* or to use them for decoration stood them in good stead.[2]

However, there are some exceptions. The *Canzoniere* was also represented in images, and the most interesting example of this practice is the first edition of Petrarch's vernacular works (printed in Venice in 1470), now preserved in the Biblioteca Queriniana of Brescia.[3]

The incunable is a real *unicum*, since it is the only *Canzoniere* to be fully illuminated in the entire Petrarchan visual tradition and because its illustration is interpretative, not only decorative. As a matter of fact, this particular copy was annotated and illustrated by an anonymous man of letters at the end of the fifteenth century. This unknown intellectual provides us with an extraordinary visual translation of Petrarch's poems. He interpreted the author's poetry and transposed it in simple drawings, which indeed are not the result of a skilled hand, but are the work of an inexperienced painter, yet an astute commentator. Over the years, scholars have focused mainly on uncovering the annotator's identity: from 1904 to the late 1980s, different theories followed one another, until Ennio Sandal, Giuseppe Frasso and Giordana Mariani Canova published a masterful work in 1990, supporting the identification of Antonio Grifo, the author of a collection of poetry preserved in the Biblioteca Marciana (shelf mark It. Z 64 [4824]).[4]

Grifo was a Venetian *literatus* at the court of Ludovico Sforza, where he proved to be a refined poet (and perhaps a capable man-at-arms too, if we identify him as the contestant who took part in a competition in Padua in 1466). He gained the respect of Gasparo Visconti and illustrated Dante's *Commedia* for Moro's family and courtiers, as Vincenzo Calmeta witnesses.[5] In their essays, which respectively analyse the philological and the artistic aspect of the volume, Frasso and Mariani Canova outline the features of this vague figure, who probably devoted his decoration on Petrarch's volume to Beatrice d'Este, Ludovico's wife. Grifo is also presumed to be the decorator of both a *Petrarchino* preserved at the Bodleian Library and of a *Commedia* housed in the Casa di Dante in Rome.[6] Yet, as Pietro Gibellini has shown, this hypothesis, rooted in handwriting analysis and stylistic similarities in such a conventional age as the Courtly one, cannot be considered certain.[7] Thus, Gibellini proposed to resolve every doubt by referring to the anonymous as 'Maestro Queriniano' or 'Dilettante Queriniano': indeed, the work in the queriniano incunable is worthy of being appreciated regardless of the author's identity. This chapter will refer to the anonymous author as 'Dilettante Queriniano', reflecting the declaration he makes at the beginning of the volume, where he admits that he is no professional painter. His dilettantism in painting is clear, but it is also clear that he was a real master in both poetry and interpretation.

Indeed, contrary to first impressions, the analysis of the relationship between the text and pictures reveals the paintings as vehicles of an innovative translation of Petrarch's text into images.[8] Initially, the artwork might appear to show the more amorous events of Petrarch's life in a rather enjoyable reading, devised for the predominantly feminine audience of the Sforza environment. Valchiusa is depicted here as a peaceful natural scene, with well-maintained fields, pruned trees, and green hills crossed by paths leading to houses and castles, but this does not mean that the Dilettante offers us a simplistic reading.

This chapter provides an overview of the illumination of the queriniano volume. I will begin by introducing the book's decoration; I will then focus on the fundamental and typical symbolism through which the anonymous represents Petrarch and Laura. After that, I will point out some recurring features of his work's interpretation, in order to pinpoint the key of his exegesis.

This illustration's interpretative intention can be first of all appreciated in the representation of Petrarch and Laura. The poet, in his human guise, can be seen staring back at Cupid, aiming a confrontational gaze at him (as in the picture near *Quel'antiquo mio dolce empio signore*, at the *recto* of the folio 128r), or lying under a tree deep in thought in *L'aere gravato et l'importuna nebbia* (*RVF* 66, f. 27r). In the latter, the Dilettante understands the meditative essence of the sestina, while in the former, he appreciates the improper feeling Petrarch blames his enemy for. So does Laura: she can appear reassuring and merciful, as in the image which narrates her apparition in Petrarch's dream in *Già fiammeggiava l'amorosa stella* (*RVF* 33, f. 14v), or naked and shameless, as we can see in the picture to the left of *Chiare, fresche et dolci acque* (*RVF* 126, f. 51v).[9] The two protagonists of the *fragmenta* meet each other as they would in a novel, and they enact the events described by the poet, as it can be seen in the courting scene between Francesco and Laura in *Nova angeletta sovra l'ale accorta* (*RVF* 106, f. 43v). Although his work is always enjoyable and delicate, it is nevertheless essential to acknowledge that the images of the Petrarca queriniano are never unsophisticated.

84 GIULIA ZAVA

FIG. 5.1. *Brescia, Biblioteca Queriniana, Inc. G.V. 15, f. 51v, Rvf CXXVI*

Translating the *Canzoniere* into Images 85

che ben muor chi morendo esce di doglia
Canzon mia fermo in campo
staro ch'egli è disnor morir fuggendo
et me stesso reprendo
di tai lamenti si dolce è mia sorte
pianto sospiri & morte
seruo damor che queste rime leggi
ben non al mondo chel mio mal pareggi

Rapido fiume che dalpestra uena
rodendo intorno ondel tuo nome prendi
nocte & di meco disioso scendi
ou amor me te sol natura mena
uattene innanzi el tuo corso non frena
ne stancheza ne sonno & pria che rendi
suo dritto al mar fixo usi mostri attendi
lerba piu uerde & laria piu serena
Iui e quel nostro uiuo & dolce sole
cha dorna e nfiora latua riua manca
forse o che spero el mio tardar le dole
basciai el piede o laman bella & bianca
dille el basciar sia nuece di parole
lo spirto e promto ma la carne e stanca

Dolci colli ouio lasciai me stesso
partendo onde partir giamai non posso
mi uano innanzi & emmi ognor adosso
quel caro peso chamor ma comesso
meco di me mi merauiglio spesso
chi pur uo sempre & non son ancor mosso

FIG. 5.2. *Brescia, Biblioteca Queriniana, Inc. G.V. 15, f. 81r, Rvf CCVIII-CCIX*

One way to appreciate the critical attitude of the Dilettante lies in his symbolism. Petrarch and Laura certainly appear in their human aspects on occasion, but in most cases they abandon them in favour of metaphorical ones. Allegory, as one would expect, is one of the main features of the incunable, conferring a meaningful and coherent visualization on the Dilettante's reading. First of all, the figure of Petrarch is represented through a precise symbolism: from the *verso* of the first leaf appears a pictogram with which the volume's edges will be studded. This particular symbol consists of a red book, often pierced with an arrow and tormented by a lustful snake. The individual attributes that compose it demonstrate that the Dilettante was used to reading the poet's lyric through an intertextual perspective: the arrow — an obvious signal of Love's action — is already mentioned in the second and third sonnets of *Canzoniere*; the serpent is notoriously a biblical and classical emblem and is also cited by Petrarch in his *Trionfo d'Amore* as well.[10]

The red volume becomes an incisive symbol for the poet's feelings, and is pictured time and again: it is carried by the snake in pursuit of Laura (so in *Sì travïato è 'l folle mi' desio*, *RVF* 6, f. 2r), it can show Petrarch's wounded heart or also weep (in *Amor co la man dextra il lato manco*, *RVF* 228 and in *Cantai, or piango, et non men di dolcezza*, *RVF* 229). Again, it can be tortured by snakes in *Non à tanti animali il mar fra l'onde* (*RVF* 237, f. 88v), or travel to Laura in a sonnet distinguished by a strong desire for her ('Basciale 'l piede, o la man bella et bianca; | dille, e 'l basciar sie 'nvece di parole', says Petrarch in *Rapido fiume che d'alpestra vena*). Conversely, it can evolve from symbolical book stages to human ones, when the poet moves from Laura in the following poem, *I dolci colli ov'io lasciai me stesso* (*RVF* 209). The pictogram changes because Petrarch's feelings change: in the first sonnet, the poet moves to the places where Laura lives (and the Dilettante draws the book with its instigator attributes). In the second, Petrarch abandons his inappropriate thoughts — inspired by the prospect of seeing her — and, with them, his negative companions.

Laura's allegorical system is deployed in a similar way. First and foremost, the woman is methodically represented by laurel: this emblem of poetry, of glory and unsatisfied love echoes back to her throughout the whole volume. Each initial which heads the poems of the incunable is twisted around a laurel branch — luxuriant in the *Rime in vita*, dried out in the *in morte* section (and in the first poem of the second part both types of branches appear).[11] Moreover, the laurel almost always appears in the images that the Dilettante places alongside the texts. The anonymous illustrator proves to be an able translator of the poet's work into images. In *Apollo, s'anchor vive il bel desio* (*RVF* 34, f. 15r), the laurel oak is the scene's focal point: mythology and allegory intertwine in a sonnet that associates Petrarch with Apollo. Besides, as in Petrarch's verses, the laurel is emphasized and acquires new characteristics, combining both botanical and human features. For example, the portrait of the woman in *Del cibo onde 'l signor mio sempre abonda* (*RVF* 342, f. 122v) is green and gold-coloured: even in her human aspect, Laura must be laurel-like, and vice versa.

Still, even leaving aside the fundamental image of the bay tree, the metaphorical aspects of Petrarch's poetry are continuously conveyed through allegorical

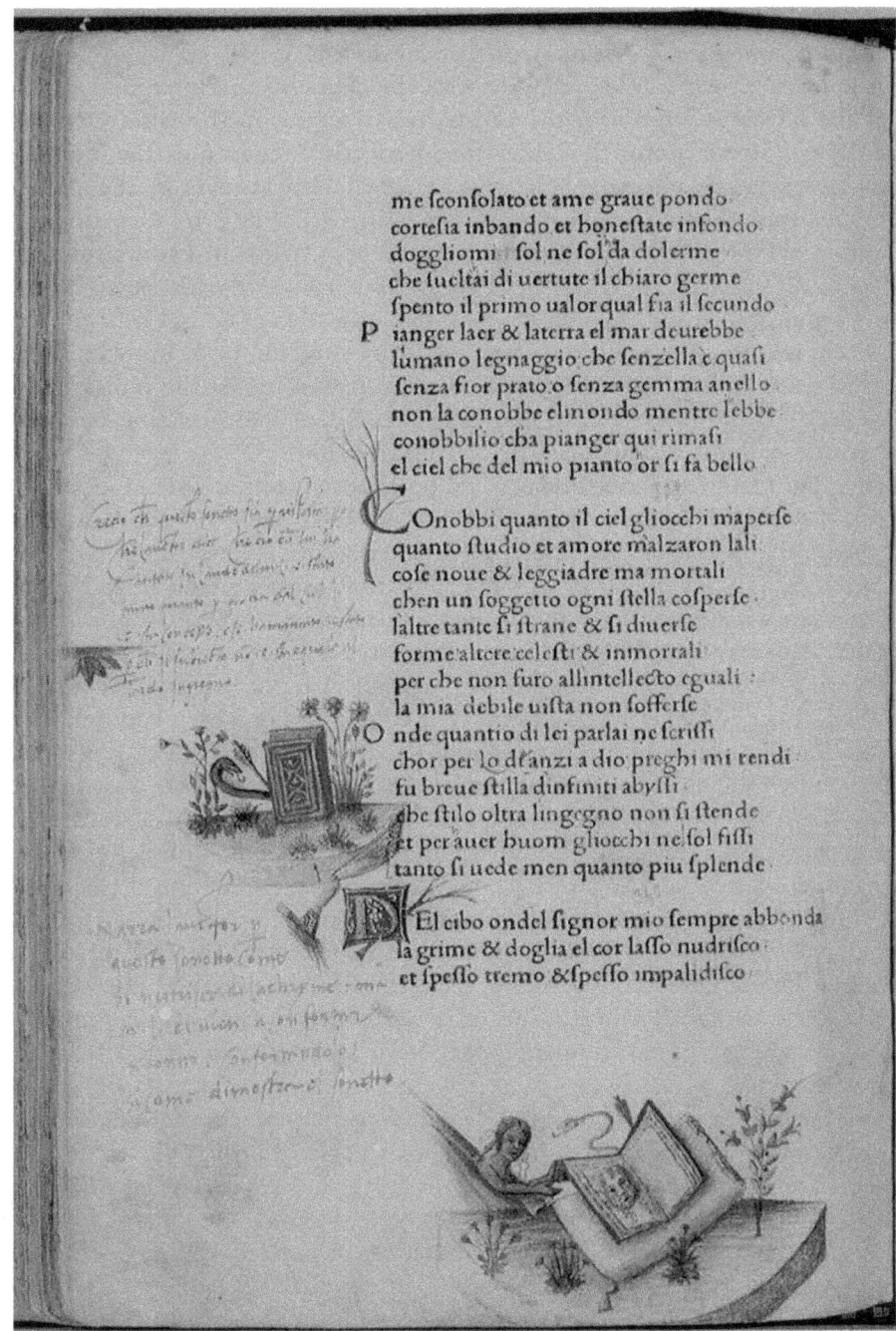

FIG. 5.3. *Brescia, Biblioteca Queriniana, Inc. G.V. 15, f. 122v, Rvf CCCXXXIX-CCCXLII*

representations. Laura is everywhere in the Vauclusian environment, she embodies Vauclusian nature itself, with its streams, its hills and trees.[12] If we evaluate once again the picture near sonnet 34, we notice the elements that surround the laurel, such as the brook and the hill; they all represent Laura, in the same way they do in the *RVF*. Furthermore, the Dilettante perfectly understands the significance Petrarch gave to the phoenix. The mythological bird appears in the *Canzoniere* in rare but meaningful circumstances, changing according to the context, but constantly heralding its profound meaning: the poet's faith in Laura's resurrection and, with it, in poetry's enduring fame.[13] According to this perspective, the phoenix's appearance on the side of *Arbor victoriosa triumphale* (*RVF* 263, f. 96r) is particularly telling. The sonnet makes no mention of the bird, but the illustrator decides to paint it there nonetheless. We find ourselves beside the transition to the *in morte* section, and he wishes to deliver his confident interpretation of the poet's work, which will not exhaust itself with Laura's death.

Indeed, faith and hope are fundamental perspectives in the Dilettante's exegesis. He trusts Petrarch's poetry and believes that God supports the poet's work: this appears to be one of the most stable interpretative keys of the anonymous artist. Interestingly, evidence of this interpretation can be found in the confident representation which the illustrator decides to place next to *Anzi tre dì creata era alma in parte* (*RVF* 214, f. 82v). This intricate and pensive sestina is actually translated into a clarifying painting — the only one in the whole volume which does not extend freely, but is limited by clear boundaries. The dark wood of which Petrarch speaks is made of sporadic trees, and the book representing the author is taller, in perspective, than they are. Every discouraged aspect of the poet's lyric is lost, and this, in my opinion, thanks to the appearance of a goat's face in the sky. This creature, in the tradition of animal symbolism, could signify many different things (both positive and negative) and could also just be a reference to the astronomical period of the year.[14] However, it is fundamental to remember that the goat was a traditional symbol for the eye of God. Since the Dilettante believes that the salvation prayer of the poet will be heard ('ma Tu, Signor, ch'ài di pietate il pregio, | porgimi la man dextra in questo bosco: | vinca 'l Tuo sol le mie tenebre nove', says Petrarch — vv. 28–30),[15] every dark signal must disappear from his icon and, of course, from his interpretation.

If we leaf through the incunable, we can find many examples of this positive reading, which are for many reasons matched to this historical period and to this precise environment. Let us take a look at the image near *In quel bel viso ch'i' sospiro et bramo* (*RVF* 257, f. 94v). In this sonnet, the gaze of the poet, who is watching Laura, is interrupted and obstructed by the 'honorata man che second'amo' (v. 4), placed in the middle by Love; however, Petrarch can visualize what his eyes cannot see. The painting the Dilettante created here is particularly interesting. The pictogram which represents the poet is held by a hand that grows from the hat typically worn by cardinals. The poet's symbol stares at a laurel branch: there is no physical obstacle between Petrarch and Laura — quite the contrary, the hand helps the book carry on with his contemplation of the laurel tree. Moreover, in the sky Christ's head appears with twelve other faces: the Dilettante's interpretation, once again, is rooted in the

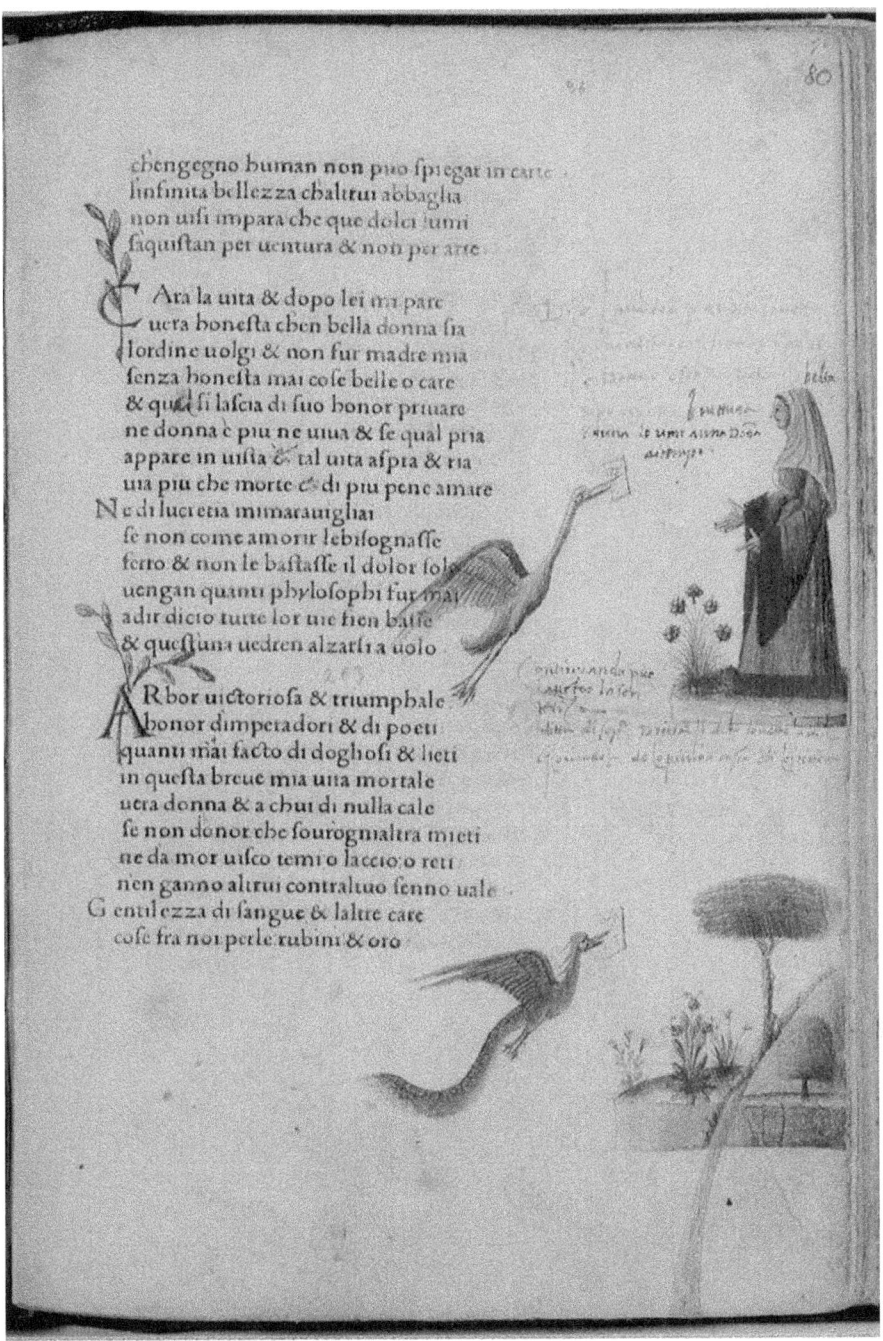

chengegno human non puo spiegar in carte
linfinita bellezza chalirui abbaglia
non uisi impara che que dolci lumi
saquistan per uentura & non per arte.

Ara la uita & dopo lei mi pare
uera honesta chen bella donna sia
lordine uolgi & non fur madre mia
senza honesta mai cose belle o care
& qual si lascia di suo honor priuare
ne donna è piu ne uiua & se qual pria
appare in uista & tal uita aspra & ria
uia piu che morte & di piu pene amare
Ne di lucretia mimarauigliai
se non come amorir lebisognasse
ferro & non le bastasse il dolor sol
uengan quanti phylosophi fur mai
adir dicio tutte lor uie sien basse
& questuna uedren alzarsi a uolo

Arbor uictoriosa & triumphale
honor dimperadori & di poeti
quanti mai facto di doghosi & lieti
in questa breue mia uita mortale
uera donna & a chui di nulla cale
se non donor che sourogni altra mieti
ne da mor uisco temi o laccio o reti
nen ganno altrui contra luo senno uale
Gentilezza di sangue & laltre care
cose fra noi perle rubini & oro

FIG. 5.4. *Brescia, Biblioteca Queriniana, Inc. G.V. 15, f. 96r, Rvf CCLXII-CCLXIII*

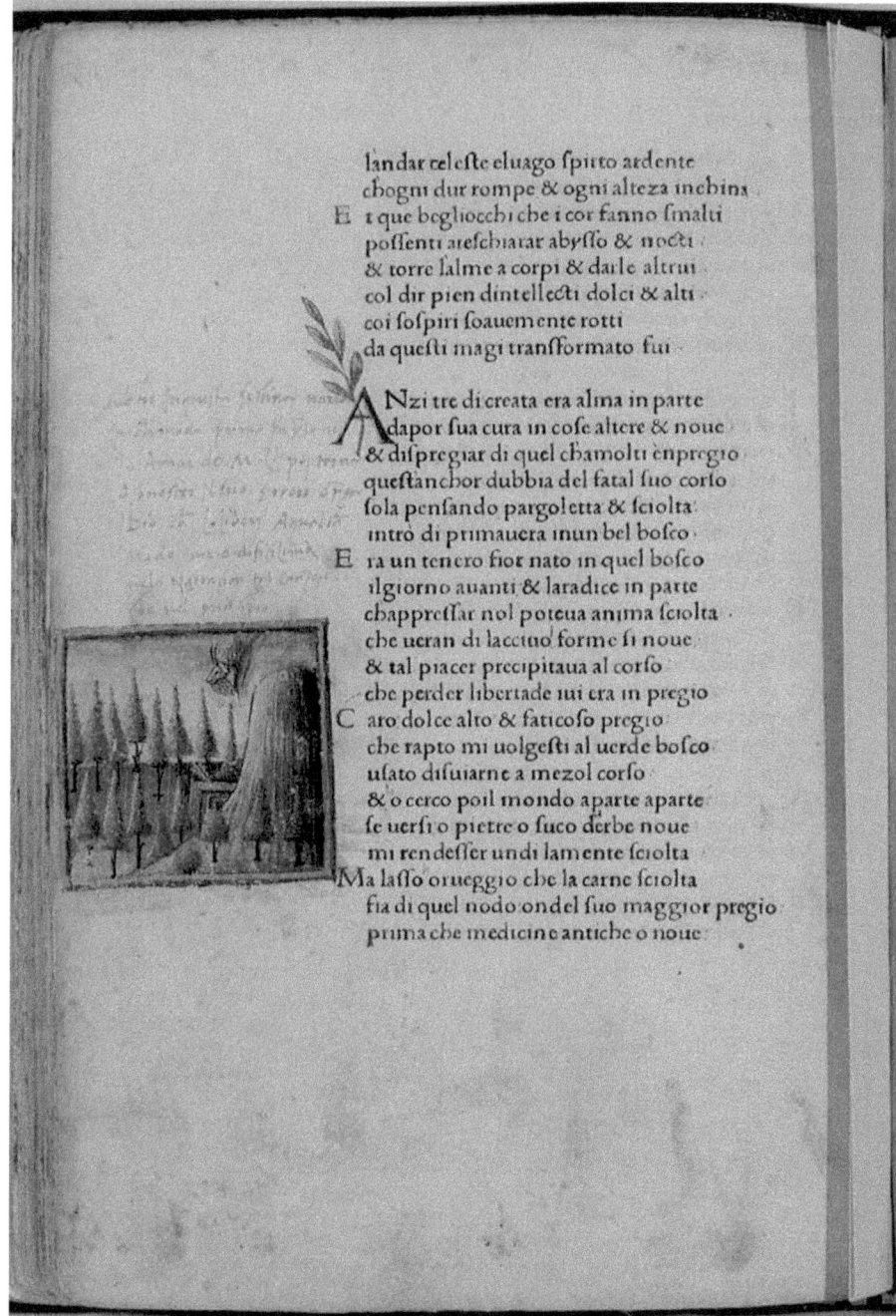

l'andar celeste el uago spirto ardente
chogni dur rompe & ogni alteza inchina
E i que begliocchi che i cor fanno smalti
possenti areschiarar abysso & nocti
& torre l'alme a corpi & dar le altrui
col dir pien dintellecti dolci & alti
coi sospiri soauemente rotti
da questi magi transformato fui·

Anzi tre di creata era alma in parte
da por sua cura in cose altere & noue
& dispregiar di quel chamolti enpregio
questanchor dubbia del fatal suo corso
sola pensando pargoletta & sciolta
intro di primauera inun bel bosco
Era un tenero fior nato in quel bosco
il giorno auanti & la radice in parte
chappressar nol poteua anima sciolta
che ueran di lacciuo forme si noue
& tal piacer precipitaua al corso
che perder libertade iui era in pregio
Caro dolce alto & faticoso pregio
che rapto mi uolgesti al uerde bosco
usato disuiarne a mezol corso
& o cerco poil mondo aparte aparte
se uersi o pietre o suco derbe noue
mi rendesser und i lamente sciolta
Ma lasso or ueggio che la carne sciolta
fia di quel nodo ondel suo maggior pregio
prima che medicine antiche o noue·

FIG. 5.5. *Brescia, Biblioteca Queriniana, Inc. G.V. 15, f. 82v, Rvf CCXIV*

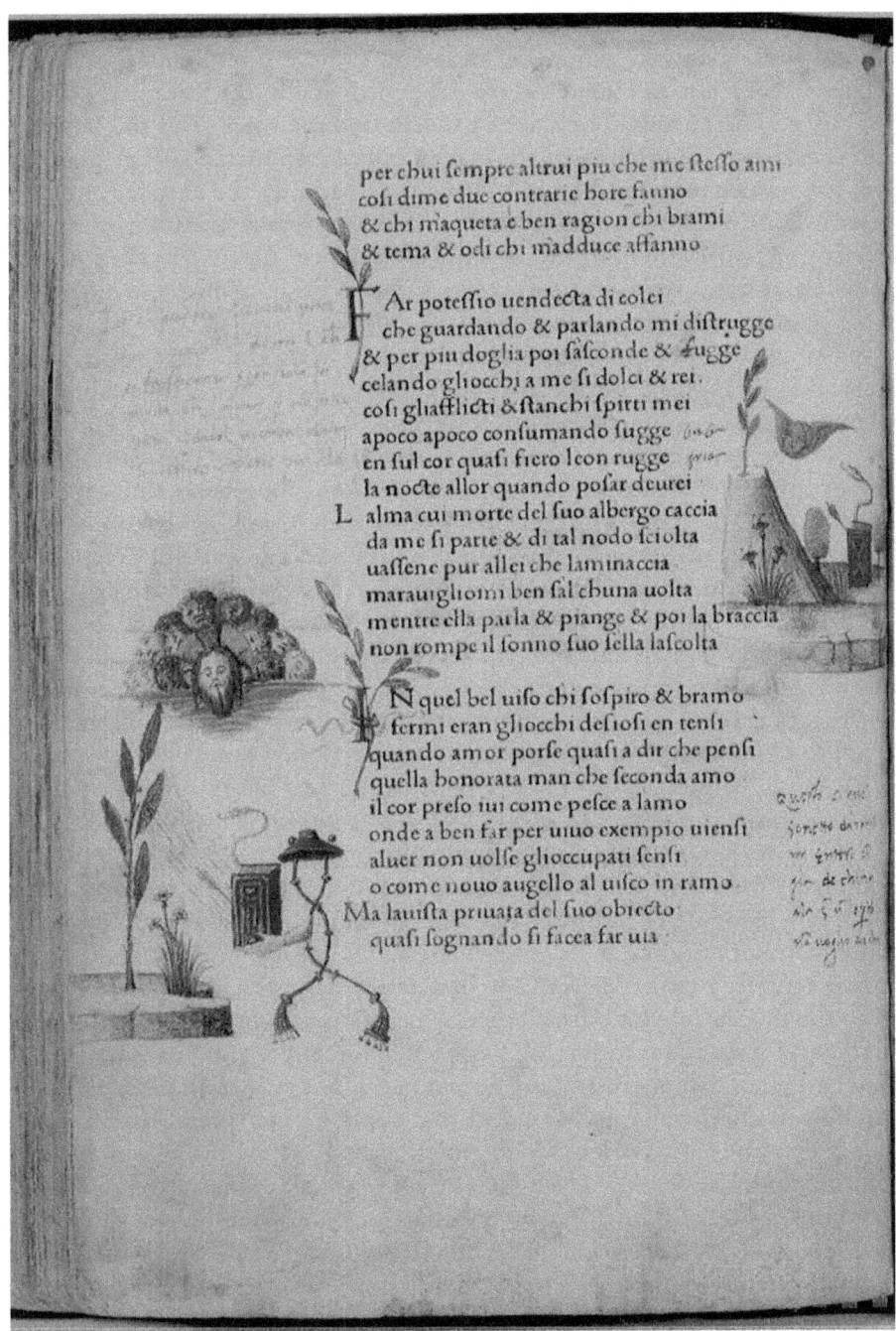

FIG. 5.6. *Brescia, Biblioteca Queriniana, Inc. G.V. 15, f. 94v, Rvf CCLVI-CCLVII*

religious sphere, a sphere that is always conceived through a charitable perspective, far from a sense of sin and judgment. He seems to have interpreted the 'Love' that Petrarch spoke of not as Cupid — the recurring enemy of the poet — but as a helpful *caritas*. The encouraging gaze of Christ and the support of the hat confer a hopeful atmosphere to the image, confirmed once again by the snake's pose: in this picture, it does not torment the book, but rises to admire the laurel.

We have explained how the anonymous illustrator provides a reading that perfectly fits in his time. At the beginning of the Renaissance, the Dilettante Queriniano is able to provide his own original exegesis, based on humanistic care and, at the same time, influenced by courtly style. Some of his icons at first glance appear to have a simply playful aim, but the attention he constantly pays to his audience never lets him forget his critical objective. Let us observe the representations which complement the two sonnets dedicated to Simone Martini (*RVF* 77 and 78). The remarkable painter, praised by Petrarch as more gifted than Polycletus,[16] appears here as a court jester represented with a hook nose, a long beard and an odd, off-balance hat. The Dilettante's real purpose can be understood thanks to the marginal notes; the annotations seem to connect two different moments of creation to the poems.[17] According to this hypothesis, Simone Martini had first been able to portray Laura and her beauty properly, but then made another image — or even a series of pictures — which failed to live up to expectations. From this point of view, the illustrations should be interpreted according to the change in the painter's skill. The first icon, referring to *Per mirar Policleto a prova fiso*, shows the man in everyday guise (while some details of his suit might appear funny, but they are actually not unusual). In my opinion, the annotator conceals his real interpretation under irony. I believe the grotesque representation of *Quando giunse a Simon l'alto concetto* should be read as a kind of sarcastic mockery: empathizing with the poet, the Dilettante is disappointed to see that the picture remains a picture and does not come alive (as in Polycletus's legend). Therefore, he avenges Petrarch by portraying Simone in this particularly ludicrous guise.

Irony is actually a trait typical of the illustrator, and it is a characteristic perfectly suited to the milieu in which he worked. The Milanese court[18] strongly promoted cultural development, encouraging vernacular creation and, in particular, that inspired by Petrarchan poems. The *Canzoniere* was not read as an exemplar that had to be followed uncritically, but as a text that could be interpreted and inspire new creation: Petrarch is not just a model, he is almost a rival against whom to compete. The entirety of his poetry could actually be approached in a narrative and non-rigid way, and this is one of the reasons why Milan welcomed the playful production of Burchiello and of his successors.[19] The Dilettante reserves this very same treatment to the poet's friends too: if he has to blame someone, he often prefers to mock them. This does not mean that he is not able to understand the depth of Petrarch's poetry. On the contrary, in some cases he even seems to harbour bitterness, as it happens near *Italia mia, benché 'l parlar sia indarno* (*RVF* 128, ff. 54r–56r). Here the Dilettante — who also writes two sharp notes[20] — portrays Italy as a mean lady, defaced in her body and surrounded by various beasts. However, it is remarkable that among

FIG. 5.7. *Brescia, Biblioteca Queriniana, Inc. G.V. 15, f. 35r, Rvf LXXVII-LXXVIII*

torna a la mente il loco
el primo di ch'iui di a laura sparsi
i capei d'oro ond'io si subito arsi
A duna aduna annumerar le stelle
en picciol uetro chiuder tutte lacque
forse credea quando in si poca carta
nouo pensier di ricontar m'inacque
in quante parti il fior de laltre belle
stando in se stessa a la sua luce sparta
accio che mai da lei non mi diparta
ne faro io & se pur talor fuggo
in cielo en terra mara chiusi i passi
per ch'agl'occhi miei lassi
sempre è presente ond'io tutto mi struggo
& così meco stassi
ch'altra non ueggio mai ne ueder bramo
nel nome d'altra ne sospir miei chiamo
Ben sai canzon che quant'io parlo è nulla
al celato amoroso mio pensero
che di & nocte nel la mente porto
solo per ch'ui conforto
in cosi lunga guerra anco non pero
che ben m'auria gia morto
la lontananza del mio cor piangendo
ma quinci da la morte indugio prendo

Italia mia benchel parlar sia indarno
a le piaghe mortali
che nel bel corpo tuo sì spesse ueggio
piacemi almen chemiei sospir sien quali

FIG. 5.8. *Brescia, Biblioteca Queriniana, Inc. G.V. 15, f. 54r, Rvf CXXVIII*

these terrific creatures appear a dove and a beaver, known emblems of peace.[21] Moreover, these two animals are the only ones that do not grow from the lady's body, but rather point towards her. In my opinion, even in this dark image, the Dilettante wishes to give a positive reading of the text: Italy is undoubtedly invaded by sin and shame, but there is still hope for her.

The ironic inclination of the anonymous allows him to paint even Sennuccio del Bene — a respectable poet and friend of Petrarch's — as an anthropomorphic creature, with a dragon's body and human hands and face. If we read the *Canzoniere*, or the other works composed by Petrarch, we cannot find an explanation for this particular depiction: Sennuccio is a confidant of the poet, an intermediary between Petrarch, other intellectuals, and Laura.[22] Once again, the Dilettante presents the characters that populate the *Canzoniere* in new and unexpected guises. It is possible he knew the sonnet *Sennuccio, la tua poca personuzza*, a poem possibly misattributed to Dante where the poet is addressed in a very sarcastic tone.[23]

The ironic motif of the sonnet may have been written under this influence: a man of letters at the end of the fifteenth century would have been deeply acquainted with Dante, and the Queriniano's commentator seems to echo the *Commedia* in many passages. For example, in the representation of Fortune as charitable *Dei Ministra* (f. 116v), the concept of the goddess progresses in both Petrarch's and the Dilettante's mind from the idea of a blind enemy to Dante's account: the pictures created by the Dilettante show this change, where the cruel persecutor becomes the sympathetic lady of the poem. The volume's illustrator represents Petrarch's change of mind,[24] but Dante features in the Dilettante's head in the same way he did in the poet's. Let us then return to Sennuccio: knowing the *Commedia* by no means implies knowledge of Dante's other works. However, even without taking into account the uncertain author of the poem, there can be little doubt surrounding the considerable flow of Florentine poetry in Milan, a fact that could have favoured a circulation of this derisory theme.

The Dilettante proposes an innovative interpretation of the *fragmenta*, which combines irony, appeal to courtly audience, knowledge of classical and contemporary poetry and, above all, a deep understanding of the text. The anonymous illustrator interprets Petrarch's poems and introduces them to his listeners through pictures; indeed, we could say that he *translates* Petrarch's sonnets into images. If we look at it from an inclusive point of view, translation is a phenomenon that should not necessarily mean the conversion from one language into another, but may also implicate an intersemiotic transposition, concerning the passage from one semiotic form to another.[25]

Studying the rise of Petrarchism necessarily means analysing the reception of his text through the centuries, in order to understand why and how Petrarch's sonnets were translated. The queriniano volume can be considered a translation. It is certainly an interesting example, capable of representing a particular environment and a particular age, and moreover it certainly bears witness to the desire to adapt the *Canzoniere*. With its images and notes,[26] the incunable tells us about the Milanese court, showing the cultural fervour of a fascinating environment that had started

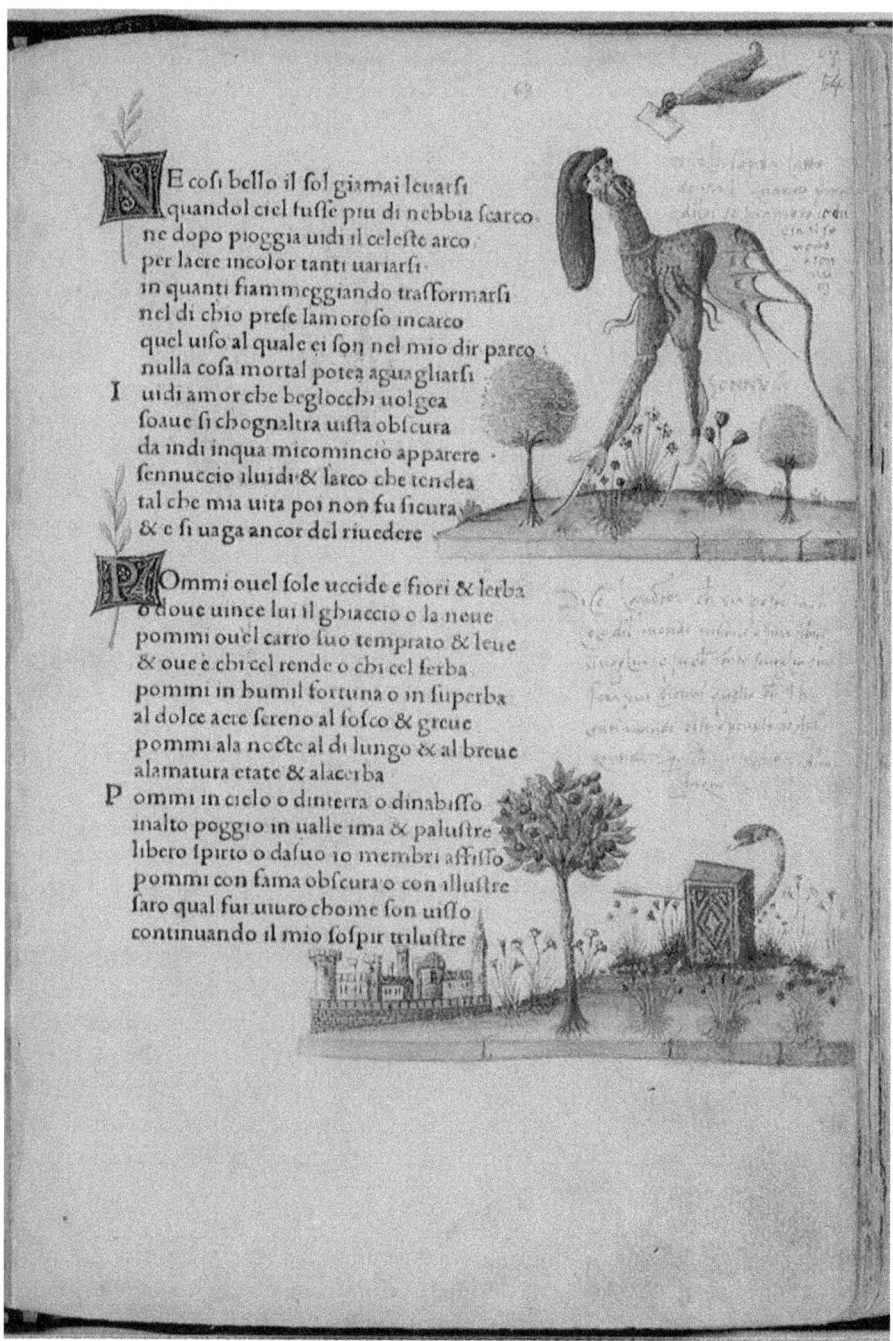

Fig. 5.9. *Brescia, Biblioteca Queriniana, Inc. G.V. 15, f. 63r, Rvf CXLIV-CXLV*

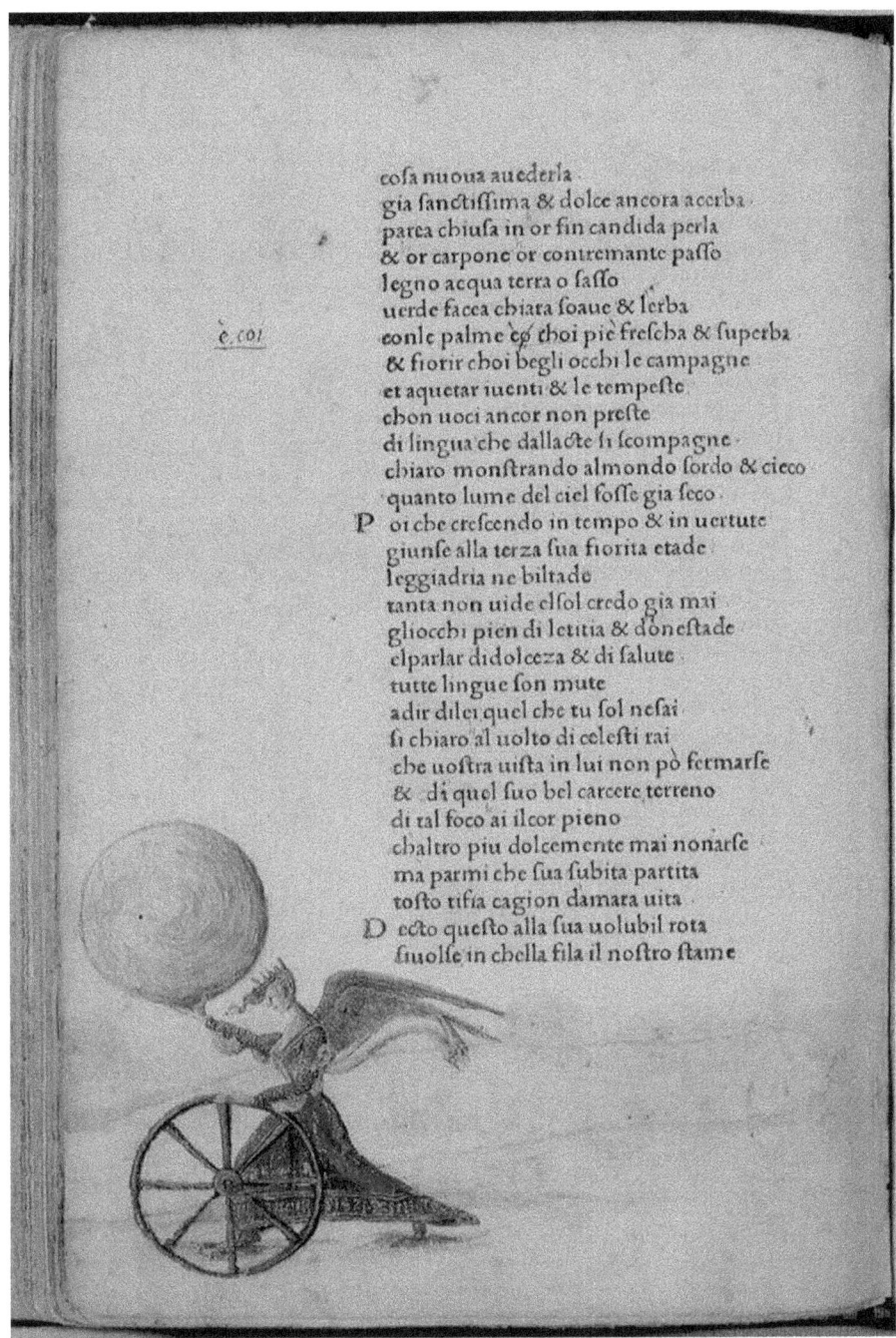

cosa nuoua auederla
gia sanctissima & dolce ancora acerba
parea chiusa in or fin candida perla
& or carpone or contremante passo
legno acqua terra o sasso
uerde facea chiara soaue & lerba
conle palme c̸ choi pie fresca & superba
& fiorir choi begli occhi le campagne
et aquetar iuenti & le tempeste
chon uoci ancor non preste
di lingua che dallacte si scompagne
chiaro monstrando almondo sordo & cieco
quanto lume del ciel fosse gia seco.
P oi che crescendo in tempo & in uertute
giunse alla terza sua fiorita etade
leggiadria ne biltade
tanta non uide elsol credo gia mai
gliocchi pien di letitia & donestade
elparlar di dolceza & di salute
tutte lingue son mute
adir dilei quel che tu sol nesai
si chiaro al uolto di celesti rai
che uostra uista in lui non pò fermarse
& di quel suo bel carcere terreno
di tal foco ai il cor pieno
chaltro piu dolcemente mai nonarse
ma parmi che sua subita partita
tosto tisia cagion damara uita.
D ecto questo alla sua uolubil rota
siuolse in chella fila il nostro stame

FIG. 5.10. *Brescia, Biblioteca Queriniana, Inc. G.V. 15, f. 116v, Rvf CCCXXV*

discovering the *Canzoniere* from an uncommon viewpoint. This perspective had to combine a light narrative with a thorough knowledge of the topic, since it was conceived for a specific courtly audience, which was humanistic in some ways. The Dilettante's interpretation could still have been free from Bembo's rigorous accent and at the same time devoid of fifteenth-century Latin rigour. The anonymous author's translation into images is a far cry from standard conventions, and, even now, can provide us with an innovative and precious commentary. Once again, the *Canzoniere*, the subject of so many different interpretations over the centuries, proves its wealth — of images, translations, and poetry.

Notes to Chapter 5

1. This chapter introduces some reflections I have already presented in other locations. I reckoned that this could be an important opportunity to acquaint non-native Italian speakers with the Petrarca queriniano, a volume which I firmly believe deserves to be valued: this is why I decided to write about images I consider particularly paradigmatic and interesting, whether or not I have already written about them. Cf.: Giulia Zava, 'Interpretazione e ironia nelle immagini del Petrarca queriniano', in *Filologia ed ermeneutica. Studi di letteratura italiana offerti dagli allievi a Pietro Gibellini*, ed. by Marialuigia Sipione and Matteo Vercesi (Brescia: Morcelliana, 2015), pp. 13–28; Zava, 'Dilettante nell'illustrazione, Maestro nell'esegesi. Il disegno interpretativo nelle immagini del Petrarca queriniano', *Quaderni Veneti*, 2 (2015), 201–39; Zava, 'Dalla poesia all'immagine: l'illustrazione interpretativa del Petrarca queriniano', in *Ut pictura poesis. Intersezioni di arte e letteratura* (Trento: Università degli Studi di Trento — Dipartimento di Lettere e Filosofia, 2016), pp. 45–62.
2. Joseph Burney Trapp, 'The Iconography of Petrarch in the Age of Humanism', in *Il Petrarca latino e le origini dell'umanesimo. Atti del Convegno internazionale*, Firenze 19–22 maggio 1991 (Florence: Le Lettere, 1992–93), p. 25.
3. The volume is reproduced in an anastatic copy: Francesco Petrarca, *Il Canzoniere. I Trionfi. Edizione anastatica dell'incunabolo queriniano G. V. 15*. Venezia, Vindelino da Spira, 1470 (Brescia: Grafo, 1995). It can be also consulted online thanks to the joint care of the Biblioteca Queriniana and the Associazione Bibliofili Bresciani Bernardino Misinta: <http://www.misinta.it/biblioteca-digitale-misinta-2/1400-2/1470-petrarca-canzoniere-e-trionfi-miniato/> [accessed 14 November 2017].
4. Cf. Giuseppe Frasso, Giordana Mariani Canova, and Ennio Sandal, *Illustrazione libraria, filologia e esegesi petrarchesca tra Quattrocento e Cinquecento. Antonio Grifo e l'incunabolo queriniano G V 15* (Padua: Antenore, 1990). The book has been recently reprinted: cf. Francesco Petrarca, *Canzoniere, Trionfi. Commentario all'edizione in fac-simile*, ed. by Ennio Sandal, Giuseppe Frasso and Giordana Mariani Canova (Rome: Salerno, 2017).
5. Cf. Gasparo Visconti, *I canzonieri per Beatrice d'Este e per Bianca Maria Sforza*, ed. by Paolo Bongrani (Milan: Fondazione Arnoldo e Alberto Mondadori, Il Saggiatore, 1979), pp. 43–44; Vincenzo Calmeta, 'La vita di Serafino Aquilano', in *Prose e lettere edite e inedite (con due appendici di altri inediti)*, ed. by Cecil Grayson (Bologna: Collezione di opere inedite o rare, 1959), no. 121, p. 71.
6. Recently, this exemplar of the *Commedia* has been published in an anastatic print too: cf. *Comedia di Dante con figure dipinte. Facsimile dell'incunabolo veneziano del 1491 nell'esemplare della casa di Dante a Roma* (Rome: Salerno, 2014).
7. Cf. Pietro Gibellini, 'Il Maestro Queriniano', in F. Petrarca, *Il Canzoniere. I Trionfi. Edizione anastatica dell'incunabolo queriniano G. V. 15* (Venice: Vindelino da Spira, 1470), pp. xi–xviii; Gibellini, 'Il Petrarca per immagini del Dilettante Queriniano', *Annali Queriniani*, (2000), 41–62.
8. A few scholars have already studied the incunable from this point of view: in addition to the papers by Pietro Gibellini already cited, see Fabio Cossutta, 'Il Maestro Queriniano interprete del Petrarca', *Critica letteraria*, 3 (1998), 419–48; Cossutta, 'Tra iconologia ed esegesi petrarchesca:

note sulla Laura Queriniana', *Humanitas*, 1 (2004), 66–82; Maria Teresa Rosa Barezzani, 'Dalla "pastorella" di Francesco Petrarca al Cerf Blanc di Guillaume de Machaut. Alcune brevi annotazioni', *Civiltà bresciana*, 3–4 (2010), 7–61; Giovanna Zaganelli, *Dal 'Canzoniere' del Petrarca al Canzoniere di Antonio Grifo: percorsi metatestuali*, (Perugia: Guerra, 2000); Zaganelli, 'La storia del Petrarca e la favola del Grifo. Costruzioni narrative', *Annali Queriniani*, (2002), 85–127.

9. For this purpose, it is worth citing the theory expressed by Fabio Cossutta around the reason why Laura has been portrayed this way. 'Vengono a mancare gli assilli dello sguardo lussurioso (il codice trafitto con il serpentello c'è, ma è remoto ed ella non lo vede), viene a mancare qualsiasi traccia di appetito incontinente, e quindi non è impensabile che proprio qui il Maestro abbia collocato un ideale e singolare *Triumphus Pudicitiae*' (Fabio Cossutta, *Tra iconologia ed esegesi petrarchesca...*, p. 74) [English trans.: 'There is no such thing as a lush gaze (the code pierced with the snake is there, but it is far away and she does not see it), there is no trace of incontinent appetite, and therefore it is not unthinkable that here the Master has placed an ideal and unique *Triumphus Pudicitiae*]. Laura can appear undressed because Petrarch does not express lascivious feelings (*RVF* 126 is notoriously a poem based on imagination and memory). In support to this hypothesis, I think it can be useful to take a look at the picture near *Nel dolce tempo de la prima etade* (*RVF* 23, f. 9v): Laura, here, appears as a modest lady, who tries to hide herself from Petrarch's gaze ('Io, perché d'altra vista non m'appago, | stetti a mirarla: ond'ella ebbe vergogna; | et per farne vendetta, o per celarse, | l'acqua nel viso co le man' mi sparse', says the poet — vv. 152–55 [English trans.: 'I, because no other sight so pleases me, | stood and gazed: she covered in her shame: | and for revenge or to hide herself, | she splashed water in my face, with her hand]). The Dilettante complies with Petrarch's words in both cases.

10. As already noticed by Fabio Cossutta in *Il Maestro Queriniano*, p. 425, the connection with the *Triumphus Cupidinis*, III, 157 ('So come sta tra' fiori ascoso l'angue') — and consequently with the 'latet anguis in herba' by Virgil (*Eclogues*, III, 93) — is evident.

11. Near *Che debb'io far? che mi consigli, Amore?* (*RVF* 268, f. 98v), the Dilettante draws a lifted bay tree. The poem actually does not present Laura's death under a particular allegoric viewpoint: the image of the anonymous is here captivating, especially if we consider he is going to propose this kind of representation only in three other situations (when the poet will explicitly refer to it). He may have known the tenth eclogue of Petrarch's *Bucolicum Carmen*, where the poet similarly described Laura's death:

> Laurea cognomen tribuit michi, laurea famam,
> Laurea divitias; fueram qui pauper in arvis,
> Dives eram in silvis, nec me felicior alter.
> Sed letum fortuna oculo suspexit iniquo:
> Forte aberam, silvasque ieram spectare vetustas:
> Pestifer hinc eurus, hinc humidus irruit auster;
> Ac, stratis late arboribus, mea gaudia laurum
> Extirpant franguntque truces, terreque cavernis
> Brachia ramorum, frondesque tulere comantes.
>   (Francesco Petrarca, *Bucolicum Carmen*, ed. by
>   Tonino T. Mattucci (Pisa: Giardini, 1971), p. 348, X, vv. 378–86).

> [The laurel gave me my name; my renown was due to the laurel;
> The laurel gave me my wealth for I found myself rich in the forest,
> Having been poor in the fields, and no man was happier than I was.
> But with malevolent glance did Fortune observe my contentment.
> While I had chanced to go off to visit the ancient woodlands
> Pestilent Eurus on one hand swept in, and rain-swollen Auster
> Struck from the other. And felling trees far behind they uprooted
> My joy and delight, my laurel. They buried its savagely shattered
> Boughs and its fair-crested leaves forever under the earth's surface.
>   (*Bucolicum carmen*, trans. Thomas G. Bergin
>   (London: Yale University Press, 1974), pp. 141–84 (p. 183)]

12. For this reason, cf. Marco Santagata, *I frammenti dell'anima. Storia e racconto nel Canzoniere di Petrarca* (Bologna: Il Mulino 2011² [1992]), pp. 169–70:

    Se Avignone è il teatro dell'amore infelice, Valchiusa è quello della felicità amorosa. Niente è mutato nel rapporto con Laura: la donna è sempre irraggiungibile. [...] Eppure, nonostante ciò, il ricordo di Laura in Valchiusa è carico di dolcezza. [...] In Valchiusa tutto parla di Laura: il paesaggio l'ha incorporata e nel paesaggio essa rivive, e con la sua immagine restituita dalla natura riaffiora l'onda dei ricordi [...]. Neppure dopo la morte di Laura Valchiusa perderà queste prerogative: seguiterà a essere il regno dell'amore possibile.

    [While Avignon is the theatre of unhappy love, Valchiusa is the theatre of loving happiness. Nothing has changed in the relationship with Laura: the woman is always unreachable. [...] Nevertheless, the remembering of Laura in Valchiusa is full of sweetness. [...] In Valchiusa everything speaks of Laura: the landscape has incorporated her and in the landscape she relives, and with her image restored by nature the wave of memories reappears [...]. Not even after Laura Valchiusa's death will she lose these prerogatives: she will continue to be the kingdom of possible love].

13. Cf. Francesco Zambon, 'Sulla fenice del Petrarca', in *Miscellanea di studi in onore di Vittore Branca, I: Dal Medioevo al Petrarca* (Florence: Olschki, 1983), pp. 411–25.
14. This kind of suggestion was frequent in the medieval period. See, for example, Dante's and Petrarch's mention of the Gemini and Taurus constellations respectively in the *Commedia* (but even in the poem *Io son venuto al punto de la rota*) and in the *Canzoniere* and the *Triumphi*.
15. I quote Petrarch's verses, here and elsewhere, from Francesco Petrarca, *Canzoniere. Rerum Vulgarium Fragmenta*, ed. by Rosanna Bettarini (Turin: Einaudi, 2005).
16.

    Per mirar Policleto a prova fiso
    con gli altri ch'ebber fama di quell'arte
    mill'anni, non vedrian la minor parte de la beltà che m'ave il cor conquiso.
    Ma certo il mio Simon fu in paradiso
    (onde questa gentil donna si parte),
    ivi la vide, et la ritrasse in carte
    per far fede qua giù del suo bel viso. (*RVF*, 127, vv. 1–8)

    [Polyclitus gazing fixedly a thousand years
    with the others who were famous in his art,
    would not have seen the least part
    of the beauty that has vanquished my heart.
    But Simone must have been in Paradise
    (from where this gentle lady came)
    saw her there, and portrayed her in paint,
    to give us proof here of such loveliness.]

17. Cf. in particular the first one:

    Uno Simon havea retratta madonna Laura e però fa l'auctor tal sonetto. Et è da sapere che questo Simon havea retratta madonna Laura una volta benissimo, dapoi volse ritrarla e mai non poteo farla che stesse bene: e però fece l'auctor questo sonetto, excusando el pictor, come apar.

    [One Simone had portrayed Madonna Laura, and thus the author composes such a sonnet. Also, it is important to know that this Simone had once portrayed Laura very well; later he wanted to portray her again but he could never do it well: and the author of this sonnet thus portrayed her, forgiving the painter, as how it is shown.]

    I quote the Dilettante's annotations from the edition provided by Giuseppe Frasso, *Antonio Grifo postillatore dell'incunabolo queriniano G V 15*, in Giuseppe Frasso, Giordana Mariani Canova and

Ennio Sandal, *Illustrazione libraria, filologia e esegesi petrarchesca tra Quattrocento e Cinquecento*, pp. 85–140.
18. Regardless the identification with Antonio Grifo, I believe we can take for granted that the illustrator was a member of the Milanese entourage.
19. Ludovico il Moro supported the fame of Bernardo Bellincioni and of the so-called Pistoia, Antonio Cammelli.
20. Cf.: 'Essendo, al tempo che l'auctor fece questa canzon, tutta l'Italia in combustione, fece questa moral canzon a l'Italia predita, zoè ali signori italici' [Since, in the time when the author composed this song, the whole of Italy was in disarray, he dedicated this moral song to the mentioned Italy, that is to say to the Italian nobles] and 'e a questo han imparato questi coionaci italici, farsi vanamente partesani atti a morir senza subiecto per chi non si moveria da cacar per ristaurarli; e, di gionta, i mencchionaci han preso el piú bestial habito del mondo per imitar color che piú gli offendeno' [these Italian idiots have learned this: to become useless partisans fit to die for no reason for those who would not move from the toilet to help them; and, moreover, the foolish people have adopted the most bestial habits in the world to imitate those who outrage them]. Giuseppe Frasso, *Antonio Grifo postillatore dell'incunabolo queriniano G V 15*, p. 107.
21. As for the beaver, cf. the *Physiologus. A Medieval Book of Nature Lore*, trans. by Michael J. Curley (Chicago and London: University of Chicago Press, 1979), p. 52:

> There is an animal called the beaver who is extremely inoffensive and quiet. His genitals are helpful as a medicine and he is found in the king's palace. When the beaver sees the hunter hastening to overtake him in the mountains, he bites off his genitals and throws them before the hunter [...]. O, and you who behave in a manly way, O citizen of God, if you have given to the hunter the things which are his, he no longer approaches you. If you have had evil inclinations toward sin, greed, adultery, theft, cut them away from you and give them to the devil.

22. In *RVF* 237 Petrarch entrusts Sennuccio with the task of greeting the poets who dwell in the third sky; in the *Triumphi* the Florentine parades in the poet's procession. For the figure of Sennuccio, cf. at least Giuseppe Billanovich, 'L'altro Stil Nuovo. Da Dante teologo a Petrarca filologo', *Studi petrarcheschi*, (1994), 1–98 and Daniele Piccini, *Un amico del Petrarca: Sennuccio del Bene e le sue rime* (Rome and Padua: Antenore, 2004).
23.
> Sennuccio, la tua poca personuzza
> onde di' che deriva il desiuzzo
> il qual ti fa portare il cappucciuzzo
> così polito in su la assettatuzza
> quando tu ti vestisti d'un'uzzuzza
> ch'era vergata d'uno scaccatuzzo,
> e che n'andavi in sul tuo ronzinuzzo
> spesso ambiando con la pelosuzza,
> io mi pensava di darti copiuzza
> di quella donna che miri fisuzzo,
> credendo avessi alcuna bontaduzza,
> e t'ho trovato memoria scioccuzza,
> sì ch'io non ti vo' più per fedeluzzo.
> Così so far di me mala scusuzza.

[Sennuccio, little fellow, whence comes the desire that makes you wear this little hood so gracefully on your little person? When you wore a cloak decorated with squares and you rode on your little horse ambling with the little hairy woman, then I thought I would give you that woman whom you do nothing but stare at, believing that there was something good in you — instead I found in you a mind so foolish that I no longer want you among my faithful friends. I know this is a poor justification for what I have done.]

The editors would like to thank Professor Philippe Guérin and our copy-editor Dr Nigel Hope for assisting with the English paraphrase of this famously difficult Italian poem.

Cf. Dante Alighieri, *Opere. Rime, Vita Nova, De Vulgari Eloquentia*, ed. by Claudio Giunta, Guglielmo Gorni and Mirko Tavoni (Milan: Mondadori, 2011), pp. 682–85, *Rime dubbie*, IV.

24. As a matter of fact, Petrarch already spoke of Fortune in *Amor, Fortuna et la mia mente schiva* (*RVF* 124) and in *Datemi pace, o duri miei pensieri* (*RVF* 274, f. 101v). These gloomy sonnets present the woman as an enemy: here she allies with Cupid and Death against the poet's heart, there she integrates the pain of Petrarch's codex. Thus, in the first two icons the anonymous depicts a cruel lady, staring in front of her with unconcerned gaze. The woman of *Tacer non posso, et temo non adopre* (*RVF* 325) is instead a regal figure, who has lost her weapon and that can do nothing but move forward.

25. Cf. Roman Jakobson, 'On Linguistic Aspects of Translation', in *On Translation*, ed. by Reuben Arthur Brower (Cambridge, MA: Harvard University Press, 1959), pp. 232–39.

26. Actually, the annotations of the volume are far less interesting than the pictures: they mainly summarise the contents or give information about the addressees of the poems.

CHAPTER 6

Petrarch and the Pastoral Design of Luca Marenzio's *Madrigali a quattro voci* [...] *Libro primo* (1585)

Massimo Ossi

Commonly regarded as repositories of compositions for singing and playing — whether by amateurs or professionals — madrigal books offer glimpses of cultural practices that go beyond music-making for entertainment. The very fact that they present selections of poetic texts set to music leads us to consider the context within which the chosen poetry was known and valued: patrons and their milieu, whether courtly, academic, or informal, very likely influenced not only what texts a composer set to music, but also which pieces might be included in madrigal books published under their auspices. Certainly composers, in dedicating their works to particular patrons, often testify to the dedicatee's role in hosting musical performances, supporting particular musicians, and even in gathering groups of like-minded intellectuals, patricians, and artists. Such influential patrons, or groups of patrons, could easily have determined most aspects of composers' aesthetic choices, from individual poems to the arrangement of pieces within madrigal books.

This is not to suggest that the composer's role in making aesthetic decisions regarding poets, poems, and which of their works to publish was invariably, or even mostly, secondary; undoubtedly composers such as Adrian Willaert, Cipriano de Rore, Luca Marenzio, or Claudio Monteverdi, to name just a few obvious examples, would have enjoyed considerable freedom in choosing what to set, what to include in a publication, and how to organize its contents. Still, the final product conceivably reflects what the composer considered appropriate for a particular dedicatee, his tastes, and his cultural profile. A madrigal book, seen from this perspective, is a witness to the convergence of tastes and interests peculiar to its cultural environment, and is worth reading closely as such.[1]

Luca Marenzio's first book of *Madrigali a quattro voci* (1585) presents a particularly complex poetic and musical profile (see Table 6.1 at the end of each chapter). Its twenty-one madrigals set almost an equal number of texts by Petrarch (nine, all from the *Canzoniere*) and Jacopo Sannazaro (six, all from *L'Arcadia*), plus three by Torquato Tasso (one each from his youthful *Rinaldo* (no. 20) the *Rime* (no. 19) and *La Gerusalemme liberata* (no. 12)), one by Giovanni della Casa (no. 14), one tentatively attributed to Giovanni Battista Moscaglia (no. 2), and one anonymous text (no. 3). The two most important positions in any madrigal book, at its opening and end, are devoted to works by the book's two main poets: Petrarch's 'Non vidi mai dopo notturna pioggia', stanza 5 from the *canzone* 'In quella parte dove Amor mi sprona' (*RVF* 127), opens the book, and Sannazaro's 'Vienne Montan, mentre le nostre tormora', from the ninth eclogue (lines 37–75), closes it.

The entire volume has a distinctly pastoral character, as has long been recognized.[2] This derives not only from the selections from *Arcadia*, but also, perhaps surprisingly, from the texts chosen from *Il Canzoniere*. Unusual among his contemporaries, Marenzio sets three of the four *madrigali* in Petrarch's collection: 'Non al suo amante' (*RVF* 52, no. 5 in the Libro primo); 'Hor vedi Amor' (*RVF* 121, no. 6); and 'Nova angioletta' (*RVF* 106, no. 8). Marenzio does not include the fourth *madrigale*, 'Perch'al viso d'Amor portava insegna' (*RVF* 54), but the omission is easily justified and indeed highlights the purposeful choice of the other texts.[3] 'Perch'al viso d'Amor' plays on a complex reference to Dante's *Divina Commedia*, and although verses 4–7 establish a natural setting ('E lei seguendo su per l'erbe verdi | udì' dir alta voce di lontano: | 'Ahi quanti passi per la selva perdi!' | allor mi strinsi all'ombra d'un bel faggio'), their tone and affect do not suggest a pastoral atmosphere. The inclusion of this text would, in other words, have detracted from the more frankly amorous and mythologizing character of the other three.[4] Marenzio's inclusion of these three *madrigali*, unremarkable as it may seem at first glance, was in fact unique: although he was neither the first nor the only composer to set these texts, only a meagre handful of publications included two of them, and none all three.[5] As a group, the *madrigali* chosen for his Libro primo constitute a linked cycle and share naturalistic themes, focusing on the allure — which often operates through the poet's gaze — of the *pastorella* or *angioletta* situated in a *locus amoenus* and easily accessible (drawing on the age-old topos of the *facilis captus* in a meadow), framed within classical mythological references (Actaeon in 'Non al suo amante', Amor-Cupid in 'Vedi Amor').[6] Marenzio's placement of his settings in a tightly knit group of six pieces that share both poetic and, as we shall see, musical characteristics (nos. 5 through 9) is unlikely to have been accidental.

The other texts from the *Canzoniere* underscore the poetic themes of the *madrigali*. The sonnet 'Apollo, s'ancor vive il bel desio' (*RVF* 34, no. 7), draws on an Ovidian reference to the myth of Apollo and Daphne (vv. 13–14: 'Seder la donna nostra sopra l'erba, | E far de le sue braccia a se stessa ombra'). 'O bella man che mi destringi 'l core' (*RVF* 199, no. 4, the first of the three-part 'ciclo del guanto', devoted to the glove that covers Laura's hand), links to the following text, 'Non al suo amante', with the word 'leggiadretto' ('Candido *leggiadretto* e caro guanto' and 'un *leggiadretto* velo', respectively). The poet's capture by Laura's hand prefigures the snares set by the 'giovinetta donna' in no. 6, and by the 'nova angeletta' of no. 8; in both, he is their willing quarry. 'O bella man' introduces the light-hearted tone, tinged with only occasional darker undercurrents, and pastoral ambience of the five madrigals that follow.

'Non vidi mai dopo notturna pioggia', which opens the volume, introduces a number of recurring verbal elements: the stars ('stelle erranti') as substitutes for Laura, the absent beloved, connect it to the next piece, 'Dissi a l'amata mia, lucida stella', in which the painful 'fiamme, strali e catene' (v. 4) also echo the previous poem's other stand-in for Laura, the flashing light of dawn in the dew and ice crystals ('fiammeggiar fra la rugiada e 'l gielo'). 'Gielo' returns in no. 5 ('gelide acque' and 'amoroso gielo'), as does the image of the veil ('l'ombra d'un bel velo' and 'leggiadretto velo'). In addition, its opening clause, 'Non al suo amante piacque', parallels that of no. 1, 'Non vidi mai'.

Only two of Petrarch's texts depart radically from the lighter, mythologically inspired, tone that pervades the poems just described, dwelling instead on the darker melancholia and grief of such later madrigals as 'Solo e pensoso i più deserti campi vo misurando' and 'Crudele, acerba, inesorabil morte' (both in the ninth book of madrigals of 1599). 'Ahi dispietata morte, ahi crudel vita', excerpted from the *ballata mezzana* 'Amor quando fioria' (*RVF* 324, no. 13), the first of two selections from the second half of the *Canzoniere* (after Laura's death), and 'Tutto il dí piango; e poi la notte', both dwell on life as suffering in which weeping is the absolute primary state of the lover, and he is not so much kept in a state of war ('guerra è il mio stato, d'ira e di duol piena', as it is described in 'Hor che 'l ciel e la terra', *RVF* 164) as away from peace (again, from 'Hor che 'l ciel e la terra': 'et perchè il mio martir non giunga a riva | mille volte il dì moro et mille rinasco | *tanto dalla salute mia son lunge*' [my italics]).[7] The grief of 'Ahi dispietata morte, ahi crudel vita' marks a stark rupture with the preceding madrigal, 'Vezzosi augelli in fra le verdi fronde' (from Tasso's *Gerusalemme liberata*, Canto XVI, ottava 12). The pastoral mood that has dominated to this point is interrupted and, although it returns in later pieces, it does so under the long shadow cast by 'Ahi dispietata morte'. 'Zefiro torna e 'l bel tempo rimena' (*RVF* 310, no. 18), the final text by Petrarch, reflects the innate ambivalence of the pastoral setting, which is riddled with dark myths (Procne and Filomena) and in which the abundance of Spring contrasts with the alienation of the grieving poet.

The Petrarchan texts, in all their variety, are variously complemented by the remaining twelve selections. Sannazaro's *Arcadia* balances *Il Canzoniere*: six madrigals set texts excerpted from it, including a lengthy passage to which Marenzio devotes the closing three-part cycle — as we have seen, a major component of the formal architecture of his *Madrigali a quattro voci*. As I will argue, the heavy reliance on Sannazaro's prosimetrum is not the result of a conventional choice: it provides the literary foundation for Marenzio's commentary on musical style.

Not surprisingly, the first group of texts from *Arcadia* (nos. 9–11) follows the pastoral sequence based on Petrarch (nos. 5–8). But although 'Vedi le valli e i campi che si smaltano' (Eclogue 8, vv. 142–47) extends the lighthearted mood of the preceding madrigals, breaking into the characteristic *terza rima sdrucciola* of the humbler pastoral, the two pieces that follow it, 'Chi vuole udire i miei sospiri in rime' (Eclogue 4, vv. 1–6) and 'Madonna, sua mercè, pur una sera' (Eclogue 7, vv. 25–30), turn to *rime piane* and to longer poetic forms. Both are stanzas from *sestine*, diametrically opposed in both form and tone from the *sdruccioli* of 'Vedi le valli e i campi'. The first is from the opening of the *tenzone* between the shepherds Logisto and Elpino; the second comes from Sestino's monologue, 'Come notturno ucel nemico al sole', which encompasses the entire seventh eclogue. Both dwell on the lover's suffering: 'Chi vuole udire i miei sospiri in rime', recalling Petrarch's 'O voi che ascoltate in rime sparse il suono | di quei sospiri ond'io nutriva il core', the opening verses of *Il Canzoniere*, sets the tone, focusing on the lover's permanent condition, weeping, and prefiguring Petrarch's 'Tutto il dì piango' (no. 17).[8] 'Madonna, sua mercè per una sera' refers to the preceding poem's suffering as the 'antri foschi' that Sestino haunts like a dark bird 'nemico al sole' (v. 1) in the grip of his weeping. In this passage, the weeping is alluded to by the reference to the rain that the sun — a Petrarchan reference to the beloved — dissipates with his (her) return.

'Menando un giorno gli agni presso un fiume' (Eclogue I, vv. 61–67, no. 15) returns to a plainly pastoral subject, the shepherd leading his flock to pasture. However, it does so not in the rougher *terza rima sdrucciola* of 'Vedi le valli e i campi che si smaltano' (no. 9), but in a hendecasyllabic frottola with internal rhymes ('Menando un giorno gli agni presso un *fiume*, | Vidi un bel *lume* in mezzo di *quell'onde*, | Che con due *bionde* trecce allor mi strinse', etc.). Its central image, that of the *pastorella* who captures the shepherd's heart, recalls the similar situation in Petrarch's 'Non al suo amante più Diana piacque'[9] — which in Marenzio's volume opens the explicitly pastoral group of nos. 5–9. It is paired with 'I lieti amanti e le fanciulle tenere' (Eclogue 6, vv. 103–09, no. 16), in which the peasants' strolling and dancing occasions a nostalgic commentary on the modern world's loss of innocence: 'Or conosco ben io che 'l mondo instabile | Tanto peggiora più, quanto più invetera' (vv. 108–09).

To close the book Marenzio chose an extended excerpt from the polymetric *tenzone*, primarily in *terza rima sdrucciola*, between the shepherd Ofelia and the goatherd Elenco, with two brief interjections by Montano, in Eclogue 9 (vv. 37–42 and 46–75). The exchange consists of an introduction, in which Ofelia and Elenco invite Montano to judge their competition (Ofelia's 'Vienne Montan') and which includes his response ('Cantate, acciò che i monti omai conoscano'); this is followed by their comical exchange of insults and taunts ('Corbo malvacchio, ursacco aspro e selvaggio'); their banter is interrupted by Montano, who enjoins them to sing ('Oggi qui non si canta, anzi si prelïa'). Seven strophes of actual song follow, alternating between the two singers without further interruption. The change in mode, from largely narrative in the preceding twenty madrigals to direct speech without narration, sets this group apart from the rest of the book. It also introduces a quasi-theatrical element, a performance-within-the-performance, in which the madrigal singers, in addition to performing Marenzio's music, also perform the Arcadian characters and an imagined re-creation of their songs. This throws into relief both the self-conscious nature of the performance as well as the contrasting styles present in the book itself, from Petrarchan lyric to different shades of the pastoral.

The book's poetic selections reflect what Carlo Vecce, writing about Sannazaro's own poetic style, has called the opposition of the 'rusticale-bucolico-comico' [rustic-bucolic-comic]' and the 'lirico-elegiaco-petrarchista' [lyric-elegiaic-petrarchist]' modes, the contrast between Theocritus and Virgil that preoccupied humanists at the end of the fifteenth century and that shaped the development of Sannazaro's technique and authorial voice.[10] This debate is inscribed throughout *Arcadia*, and is encapsulated in the final selection, in which Ofelia and Elenco represent the two sides — Ofelia, player of a humble wind instrument, the *sampogna*, and Elenco, who plays the humanists' idealized string instrument, the *lira*, who re-enact (symbolically) the mythical contest between the divine Apollo and the earthy faun Marsyas. When Ergasto-Apollo makes reference to the goddess Pale and her sacred nymphs, for example, Ofelia-Marsyas can only match him by turning to Pan and (in a stanza not set by Marenzio) to Priapus. Montano's eventual judgment, also not set by Marenzio, is that the two are equal in merit and that 'Apollo, il qual v'aspira | abbia sol la vittoria' (vv. 148–49) — a barely veiled nod to classicism that conveniently co-opts the lower idiom, just as Sannazaro himself lays claim to both literary traditions.[11] Marenzio's entire volume may be seen, in retrospect, as working out and amplifying the dynamic interaction of the two aesthetic and literary currents, showing both the wide gaps and the significant overlap between them.

As Einstein remarked, 'throughout his career Marenzio's choice of texts bespeaks a fastidious taste'.[12] His approach to both *Il Canzoniere* and *Arcadia* appears to have been carefully selective — the focus on Petrarch's *madrigali* seems a strong indication of this, as does the wide selection of passages from Sannazaro's eclogues — the first, fourth, sixth, seventh, eighth, and ninth are all represented. And although some of the poetry had been highly popular before he set it (for example, 'Or vedi Amor' had been set nearly thirty times by 1585), he was first (and in some cases alone) in setting a number of texts: Petrarch's 'Non vidi mai dopo notturna pioggia' (no. 1); 'Vedi le valli e i campi' (no. 9), 'Menando un giorno' (no. 15) and 'Vienne Montan' (no. 21) from *Arcadia*; nearly all of the texts not by Petrarch or Sannazaro — 'Dissi a l'amata mia lucida stella' (no. 2), 'Vezzosi augelli in fra le verdi fronde' (no. 12), 'Su 'l carro della mente' (no. 19), and 'Lasso dicea, perchè venisti Amore' (no. 20). And in some cases he was only the second composer to make use of a particular poem: 'Tutto il dì piango' (no. 17),[13] 'I lieti amanti e le fanciulle tenere' (no. 16),[14] 'Ahi dispietata morte, ahi crudel vita!' (no. 13)[15], 'Apollo s'ancor vive il bel desio' (no. 7),[16] and 'Chi vuol udire i miei sospiri in rime' (no. 10).[17] As a literary anthology, then, *Madrigali a quattro voci* suggests a subtle and well-developed sensibility attuned to the literary programme of Sannazaro's *Arcadia*, centred on a dialectic of style and genre relative to tradition that was probably honed in formal academic discourse or in the *ridotti* of highly cultured elites. But how is it as a book of madrigals? What does the music add to the literary programme? A great deal, as it turns out. Marenzio grafts onto the book's poetics a musical poetics of his own, in which an exploration of the rhetorical possibilities of style is combined with an object lesson in compositional virtuosity. Text and music coexist on equal footing to create works (both individual madrigals and the book in its entirety) that are larger than the sum of their parts.

From a purely musical standpoint, Marenzio makes use of four basic stylistic models:

(1) a relatively neutral, largely contrapuntal, texture, delivering the text in measured rhythmic motion and in longer phrases that match the poetic syntax, but without exploring either extreme expressive highs or extreme lows;

(2) a light texture marked by faster note values (*note nere*), contrapuntal *intreccio* (consisting of tightly interwoven lines in quick succession), and text delivery in shorter units that display a certain *sprezzatura* in their phrasing, focused almost entirely on unproblematic or festive scenes from Arcadia;

(3) a slow, melancholy, darkly pensive, and often dissonant or chromatic motet-style counterpoint, with heavy emphasis on individual affective words, connected with erotic suffering in general; and

(4) *canzonetta* style, predominantly homorhythmic, syllabic, dance-like, reliant on reduced textures (duets and trios), and heavily rhyme-bound, reserved for the more rustic *tableau* at the end.[18]

The interaction between these musical styles, each of which may be thought of as representing a different rhetorical strategy, parallels the poetic discourse that develops over the course of the *Primo libro*. Table 6.2 charts the pairing of texts and musical styles over the course of the book.

The first four madrigals, which as we have seen are either by Petrarch or in Petrarchan style, are uniformly objective in tone, largely descriptive, and may be regarded as a kind of rhetorical *exordium*, hinting only obliquely at what is to come and establishing a learned, classical, madrigal style. They are highly contrapuntal, and indeed the final lines of 'Non vidi mai dopo notturna pioggia', 'così bagnati ancora | li veggio sfavillar ond'io sempr'ardo', are set in what Einstein called, anachronistically, 'a double fugue', in which the motives for 'così bagnati ancora' and 'li veggio ...' are heard first alone and then in double counterpoint — above and below each other — as well as in close imitation, a kind of *stretto*. Semantics aside, Einstein is correct in suggesting that this passage represents 'a manifesto announcing a new program':[19] not so much because of its compositional virtuosity in and of itself, but as the musical representation of Petrarch's highly refined style, around which the collection's literary theme revolves. Put another way, as Sannazaro sought a new language for the pastoral against the backdrop of Petrarchan classicism, so Marenzio looks to 'reinvent' the musical pastoral in light of the tradition of 'serious' musical *petrarchismo* rooted in high-art counterpoint (for which we may take Adrian Willaert and Cipriano de Rore as paradigmatic examples).

And indeed the next five madrigals, characterized by the Petrarchan pastoral, share faster note values, virtuosic contrapuntal *intreccio* and rhetorical *sprezzatura*, hallmarks of Marenzio's style of the 1580s, but they are not homogeneous. In these pieces, as Einstein put it, 'it is obvious that [Marenzio] is searching for a special type of pastoral expression suited to the four-voiced texture'.[20] But as the *Primo libro* amply illustrates, there is no single solution to the problem of a 'special type of pastoral expression', just as there is no single literary pastoral. Even the Petrarchan pastoral is not all of a piece, and Marenzio's settings underscore the diversity of mood among the four selections from *Il Canzoniere*. 'Non al suo amante' (no. 5) presents a sudden contrast with the preceding four pieces: it is built on the rapid alternation of voice pairings — primarily, at the start, the contrast between soprano and bass against alto and tenor, but shifting pairs throughout the piece — declaiming the text in homorhythm. From this texture emerge occasional points of emphasis, marked either by sudden slowing of the rhythm and by harmonic emphasis ('le gelid'acque'; 'cruda') or by the characteristic nature of individual motives ('il vago e biondo capel'; and at the end 'tutto tremar d'un amoroso gielo').

This rapid repartee is intensified in the next madrigal, 'Or vedi Amor' (no. 6), in which imitation between voice pairings is replaced from the start by complete independence of all four parts. The opening is striking in its rhythmic profile, contrasting slower declamation ('Or vedi Amor') with a sudden reduction in values ('che giovinetta donna'). The impression, after the relatively clear textures of 'Non vide mai', is one of suddenly rushing energy and brilliance. Paired imitation returns at 'et ella in treccie 'n gonna' (bass and tenor followed by alto and soprano), clarifying the texture; similarly, sudden shifts from fast to slower declamation and harmonic emphasis, as in the previous madrigal, mark important moments of the text ('si siede e scalza ...'). Again, the ending is marked by a characteristically madrigalian effect: 'e qualcuna saetta fa di te e di me, signor, vendetta', with its swift scalar passages for 'saetta' and emphatic downbeat emphasis, conveys an almost martial character, parallel to the trembling that ended 'Non al suo amante'. The emphatic 'di te e di me', marked by registral shifts, recalls the 'morirò, si morirai' dialogue of 'Dissi a l'amata mia lucida stella' (no. 2) — in retrospect, the listener is made aware of the continuity of technique between earlier and later madrigals in the collection.

The progressive intensification of bucolic ebulliency of nos. 5 and 6 is momentarily interrupted by the two-part sonnet 'Apollo s'ancor vive il bel desio'. Petrarch's treatment of the Ovidian myth of Apollo and Dafne — which darkens the carefree Arcadian pastoral mood, just as the story of Actaeon and Diana had undermined the superficial playfulness of the *pastorella* scene in 'Non al suo amante più Diana piacque' — as a discursive sonnet poses a double problem for the composer. First, its long poetic form, requiring a two-part musical setting, is matched by its syntax, which is both leisurely and complex in comparison with that of the *madrigali*. And second, its affective mood is diffuse, not easily encapsulated within the broad-brush rendering of the previous pieces. And indeed Marenzio returns to the less punchy tone that had characterized the opening four madrigals: contrapuntal textures dominate, largely articulated according to syntactical units. Moments of rhythmic and harmonic relaxation do occur to emphasize significant passages in the text ('già poste in oblio: dal pigro gielo e dal tempo aspro e rio'), punctuating the dense polyphonic textures. The closing line of the first part ('Ove tu prima, e poi fu' invescato io') picks up the dialogic contrasts in sonority that Marenzio had already used in the previous pair of *madrigali* at 'di te, di me' and 'morirò, si morirai'. The pastoral, in this long piece, moderates its *sprezzatura* and rhythmic energy, leavening it with the complexity and relative restraint of the classical madrigals that open the book.

In response to Petrarch's direct and more succinct style of the *madrigale*, 'Nova angeletta sovra l'ale accorta' returns to fast declamation and contrapuntal *intreccio*, complete with the fast repartee between high and low voices at 'senza compagna mi vide'. The *madrigali*, then, frame the 'classicizing' style of 'Apollo, s'ancor vive il bel desio' and, in a sense, unmask its somewhat more restrained, even reverent, tone as just another face of the new Petrarchan pastoral manner that is at the centre of these four madrigals. Marenzio by this point has established its characteristic traits: contrapuntal wit, rhetorical brilliance, and charm.

This, significantly, carries over to Sannazaro's 'Vedi le valli e i campi che si smaltano' (no. 9), which despite its *terza rima sdrucciola* is treated in the same manner as the Petrarch texts that precede it, setting up a crucial contrast of musical and poetic style that will return in the book's closing *tenzone*.[21] This madrigal's distinctive rhythmic play at 'Intorno ai fonti i pastor lieti saltano', in which 'saltano' becomes dominant has been discussed at some length by both Einstein and Gerbino; I will only add here that the contrasting duets of its opening section bring back the characteristic sonority of 'Non al suo amante più Diana piacque', rounding off the group and underscoring in this, the first Sannazaro text, that the style Marenzio has introduced with the Petrarch texts serves equally well for the rustic dances of shepherds and *pastorelle*.

The change of affect that marks the following pair, 'Chi vuol udir i miei sospiri' and 'Madonna sua mercè' (nos. 10 and 11), affords Marenzio the opportunity to introduce the third character in his stylistic palette, the slower, motet-like, soft (or *mollis*), dissonant or chromatic contrapuntal style. And it is essential to underscore that the first appearance of this, his quintessentially Petrarchan pathos, occurs in combination with Logisto's tale of suffering, told in *endecasillabi piani* — Sannazaro's own self-consciously Petrarchan brand of pastoral eclogue. Nothing in this madrigal steps out of character — not the slow declamation, not the placement of dissonances ('angoscioso pianto'), not the exposed duets: this could be a setting of any dark sonnet from *Il Canzoniere*. In the remainder of the book, Marenzio shifts between these three styles abruptly from madrigal to madrigal, highlighting the cross-over interplay of musical style and poetic types. Just as the first nine madrigals have been characterized by the gradual introduction of an appropriate musical language for the Petrarchan pastoral, the second half of the book revolves around a group of lamenting texts by Sannazaro, Petrarch, and Tasso, set in the most rigorously *molle* pathos: 'Chi vuole udire', Sannazaro's homage to Petrarch (no. 10), Petrarch's 'Ahi dispietata morte' (no. 13), Della Casa's 'Dolci son le quadrella' (no. 14), and 'Tutto il dì piango' (no. 17), again by Petrarch; even 'Lasso dicea, perché venisti Amore', in which the *pastorel*'s indignant complaint is set to an emphatic choral declamation, maintains the serious tone of the others and suggests a nobler spirit than one would expect in a mere hapless rustic.

Although these pensive madrigals dominate the second half of the book, the pastoral mood returns in four pieces on texts drawn from a variety of sources. First among them is 'Vezzosi augelli', which presents a descriptive passage from Tasso's *Gerusalemme liberata* focusing on the sonorous landscape of Alcina's island. 'Menando un giorno', another vision of Arcadia's emblematic object of desire, the alluring *pastorella* at her bath, returns to the breathless *intreccio* of 'Or vedi Amor che giovinetta donna'; and 'I lieti amanti e le fanciulle tenere', another representation of dancing Arcadians in the same vein as 'Vedi le valli e i campi che si smaltano', the only triple-metre madrigal in the entire book, not counting internal passages in 'Vienne Montan'. All three represent scenes of what Gerbino calls 'bucolic carelessness' (notwithstanding the dark background of 'Vedi le valli', Clonico's suicidal love-induced depression).[22]

Petrarch's 'Zefiro torna, e 'l bel tempo rimena', as we have seen, is another matter altogether: the darkest tale of uncontrolled desire and violence, the mutilation and metamorphoses of Procne and Philomel, lurks barely under the surface, and the ultimate focus of the sonnet is the lonely 'widower' bereft of Laura, set against the backdrop of Spring. Marenzio responds to Petrarch's jarring confrontation of appearances and affects by setting against one another, in quick succession, all of the stylistic models with which he has been working. 'Zefiro' opens with the contrapuntal *intreccio* of the earlier pastoral *madrigali*, and at 'e 'l bel tempo rimena' the texture shifts to block declamation by the entire ensemble, a brief almost dance-like homorhythmic passage that dissolves back into a rapid-declamation contrapuntal texture ('e i fiori, e l'erbe'). This once more slips into group declamation ('la sua dolce famiglia'), before focusing on 'garrir Progne' with imitative garrulity (reminiscent of the birds of Alcina's island), and suddenly shifting gears into slow rhythms and a quick circle-of-fifths progression from G minor to A major, D major, G major, and C major to underscore 'e pianger Filomena'. Homorhythmic declamation, paralleling that of 'e 'l bel tempo rimena', returns for 'e Primavera candida e vermiglia', and once again imitative polyphony provides a madrigalistic representation of 'ridon i prati'. This all takes place in the space of fewer than twenty measures, a kaleidoscopic, impressionistic, rendition of the text in which every detail is accounted for and set into musical relief. The overall impression, governed by the G-Dorian mode that lends a slightly melancholy character to the piece, is one of instability, of fleeting surfaces barely registered — a subtle and accurate reading of Petrarch's unstable subjectivity.

Most striking, however, is the shift towards the interiority of the poet's grief: the opening 'Ma per me, lasso' is set to a descending bass tetrachord (D, C, B-flat, A), a classic lamenting figure, and the pathetic motet style of 'Chi vuol udir i miei sospiri in rime' occupies the first fifteen measures, projecting the grief of the sonnet's first tercet. The fleeting return of pastoral character for 'e cantar augelletti …' (again, focusing on the surface of the text to emphasize its underlying contrary affects) only heightens the stark depths of despair of the closing lines, 'E 'n belle donne oneste atti soave | Sono un deserto, e fere aspre e selvaggie', which culminates in the wide triadic falling motive for 'Sono un deserto' (it spans a ninth, from G down to F), a dramatic gesture to which Marenzio will return in his setting of Petrarch's 'Solo e pensoso i più deserti campi' (*RVF* 35) some fourteen years later.[23] In 'Zefiro torna' Marenzio achieves a complete synthesis of his new pastoral style and the pathetic *stile molle* of his most serious motet-like serious compositions.

It is only in the final group, 'Vienne Montan' (no. 21) that he deploys the fourth stylistic model, the *canzonetta*, a lighter genre generally considered of lower aesthetic value than the madrigal and perfectly matched to the apparently rustic style of the *tenzone* between shepherd and goatherd from the ninth eclogue. After the elegantly refined, Petrarchan-Virgilian, pastoral style, and especially coming at the end of the book following the series of dark lovers' laments and complaints, this three-part cycle provides a surprising, even jarring, change of pace. As I noted earlier, the distinction between the aesthetic poles represented by the two herdsmen emerges in part from the different deities to which each refers: Ofelia calls on Pan and other earthy gods, while Elenco refers to Apollo, who flees from Ofelia's 'romore' taking his Delian rites with him, and appeals to the goddess Pale, who adorns his hair with a classical wreath ('Che nessun altro se ne può dar vanto');[24] In Ovid's *Fasti*, Pale protects shepherds and their flocks, and specifically guards them against dangerous encounters with woodland spirits and in particular with Diana at her bath, introducing (at least for audiences familiar with Ovidian mythology) an oblique intertextual reference to Petrarch's 'Non al suo amante più Diana piacque'.[25] At the end of the excerpt set by Marenzio, he eventually calls on 'sacred nymphs' to favour both him and Ofelia in their amatory pursuits, signalling that the two singers, as mocked and scorned lovers, share a common goal — another reference to the convergence in the *Arcadia* of the two poetic traditions.

And indeed poetic style is the actual subject of Sannazaro's eclogue. The invitation to Montan and the exchange of insults, which take up the first and second parts of Marenzio's *canzonetta*, are all set in *terza rima sdrucciola* appropriate to the main speaker, Ofelia, whereas Elenco establishes the tone for the actual *tenzone* (which takes up the entirety of part three, the longest of the group) by switching to his own, more classical *endecasillabi piani*, which the rustic Ofelia will have to master to keep up. Montano's eventual judgement, assigning credit to Apollo for both singers' ability, is not part of Marenzio's musical setting, but it is clear that Ofelia rises to the occasion.

The musical setting deftly brings together different elements to produce a seamlessly flexible blend of high and low sonorities. Marenzio chooses the Lydian mode on F, already in the sixteenth century a marker of pastoral themes, although its earlier use in the *Primo libro* had been for 'Dissi a l'amata mia, lucida stella' (no. 2) and 'O bella man che mi destringi 'l core' (no. 4), neither of which draws on the pastoral. Perhaps in the earlier works, which as I have argued were part of an introductory section, it linked the 'amata' of no. 2 with the *pastorelle* of later madrigals, and in 'O bella man' it underscored, however subtly, the natural element ('tutt'i loro studi | Poser Natura e 'l Ciel'). The open fifth with which Ofelia starts his invitation, 'Vienne ...', immediately evokes the *sampogna*'s drone, for example, and the ponderous declamation in slower rhythms, articulated by both upper and lower duets in succession, also suggests a rough, unsubtle, diction, like an opening fanfare motive. A similar injunction underscores Montano's 'Cantate', again exchanged between low and high sonorities before moving into the characteristic triple metre of rustic dancing (recall 'I lieti amanti'). The coincidence of the lively, cross-accented musical metre, both duple and triple, and poetic form underscores the suggestion that a corrupt century can be restored to vigour through the two singers' revival of ancient traditions, a return to simplicity in an over-sophisticated age.[26]

Ofelia's first insult ('Montan, costui che meco ...') returns to his rougher declamation, but immediately embraces both the imitative counterpoint of the Petrarchan pastoral ('guarda le capre'), and the lamenting style, although in a mocking tone ('misera mandra ...'). Elenco's response, in part two, from the start deploys characteristically complex counterpoint, but switches briefly to the upper–lower duet texture ('cotesta lingua'), quoting both the open fifth and the rhythm of Ofelia's address to Montano. His own use of the *molle* affect ('misera selva') responds to Ofelia's, but adds an element of high rhetoric from the classical madrigal, the simultaneous juxtaposition of two textual elements — 'misera selva' and 'che coi gridi assordila' — the one lamenting, in the lower voices, the other uttered by the soprano in an emphatically indignant outcry. The recollection of the slightly misplaced, similarly assertive, shepherd's accusations in 'Lasso dicea' (no. 20) is unmistakeable. Elenco appropriates the *sdrucciolo* of his antagonist, but does not lose his rhetorical high ground, belting out its accusation, 'assordila', at the top of his lungs. It would be unlike Marenzio to miss the opportunity. His insult closes with a contrapuntal setting of 'getta la lira omai che invano accordila' — a reference to Apollo throwing away his lyre in disgust, its elegant music, represented by the complexity of the texture and the lyrical melismas ('lira', 'accordila'), having become useless against the noise generated by Ofelia's coarse wind instrument.

Once the two begin their duel, spurred on by Montano's admonition at the end of part two, Marenzio presents his audience with a disarmingly plain, almost naïve, exchange. The upper duet (soprano and alto) sing Elenco's lines; the low voices respond with Ofelia's. Both are set in relatively simple note-against-note texture, and primarily in quarter-notes. Neither seems to refer to specific musical markers of the pastoral (other than simplicity), but there are subtle touches in Marenzio's melodic writing: Elenco opens by inverting Ofelia's invitation to Montano, the opening motive of the first part, and as a result each of the four strophes begins with a variation of this melodic idea, as well as with the open fifth sonority. Motivic integration may be less important here than the referentiality made possible by the aural clue, but the result lends the entire cycle a sense of formal coherence and unity.

The two scorned lovers having ended with similar complaints about their lovers (Ofelia's unnamed shepherdess, Elenco's loftier Thyrrenia) and having marked their cadences with very similar melodic contours (both descents from C to F), they join for the next two stanzas — another example of the composer's art trumping the poet's, since the superimposition of texts is only available to a polyphonic ensemble. Their parallel utterances are therefore brought into relief, continuing the alternation of their 'voices' to reinforce the sense that this is now a duet proper, not just a sequence of solos.

The final stanza, 'Fresche ghirlande di novelli fiori', returns to the triple metre of 'I lieti amanti e le fanciulle tenere' as the singers join in pledging rewards to the sacred nymphs (conveniently these may be either Pan's or Pale's) in return for their beloveds' favours. Rightfully, these are Elenco's lines, but here the implication is that they share them in a general devotional offering. Surprisingly, perhaps, the book's final word goes to the canzonetta, the popularizing genre in opposition to the madrigal's cultivated affectation, but let us not forget that the palm in the end goes to Apollo as Pan skulks away scornfully. But Apollo, in Montano's telling, has broad tastes:

> Tacci, coppia gentil, ché ben graditi | son vostri accenti in ciascun sacro bosco | [...] Ma quel facondo Apollo, in qual v'aspira, | abbia sol la vittoria, e tu, bifolco, | prendi i tuo' vasi, e tu, caprar, la lira. | Che 'l ciel v'accresca come erbetta in solco!
>
> [Be silent, gentle duo, for your songs (*accenti*) are most welcome in every sacred grove [...] But let eloquent Apollo, who inspires you, be the only winner, while you, herdsman, take your bowls, and you, goatherd, your lire. May the heavens let you flourish like grass in the furrows!]

As a final consideration stemming from the choice of the canzonetta style, and in particular the dance-like quality of its chorus-like ending, 'Fresche ghirlande', it is worth noting that the overall shape of the book — a multipartite prologue, followed by a sequence of 'chapters' presenting various moods, and a closing quasi-theatrical dialogue resolving in a communal dance — was not uncommon for pastoral social events. Marenzio visited Ferrara, where *feste campestri* were particularly favoured, in 1580–81, and would have heard both the *musica segreta* and the staged and semi-staged dance entertainments of the court. The notion of closing such an entertainment with a dance (and 'Fresche ghirlande' would have lent itself to being both danced and sung, first by the performers themselves, and then by the audience) could well be reminiscent of such events. As Gerbino notes,

> the exceptionally high number of texts on pastoral and naturalistic subjects preserved in Marenzio's output is to be understood within the context of this specific orientation of the Este court culture, promptly relocated in Rome after Luigi's elevation to the Cardinalate.[27]

* * * * *

In 1585, the year of the *Madrigali a quattro voci*, Marenzio's Roman colleague Ruggero Giovannelli also published a madrigal volume focused entirely on Sannazaro's use of *sdruccioli* (indeed, Giovannelli boldly titled his *Gli Sdruccioli: il primo libro de madrigali a quattro voci*). As Giuseppe Gerbino has argued, his and Marenzio's were highly unusual choices that were prompted, most likely, by a circle of patrons who were particularly interested in Sannazaro.[28] It is also probably significant that in 1584–85 Marenzio concentrated much of his activity around lighter genres: the first book of *villanelle* for three voices (1584); the second book of *canzoni napolitane* and the third book of *villanelle* 'nel modo che oggidì si usa cantare a Roma', both for three voices and both published in 1585. Although none of the texts can be attributed to Sannazaro, the focus on *villanelle* and *canzonette*, typically associated with the bucolic, the comedic, and with a rougher musical and literary sensibility, may have prompted him to reflect on the relationship between genres and their stylistic associations — a clue to Marenzio's attitude towards the smaller works perhaps lay in the fact that all three collections were assembled by others on his behalf.[29]

Noting the high productivity of 1584–85, Marco Bizzarini sees Marenzio's particular concentration on the four-voice texture as evidence of a

> sense of noble *gravitas*, an ideal of sober classicism. It is no coincidence that, among the twenty-one compositions that form the first book *a 4*, texts by Petrarch predominate alongside a notable presence of Sannazaro and Tasso. Guarini and the court versifiers are set aside, a fact that reinforces the classical character of the literary choice.[30]

Although an element of classicism is undeniably present, as we have seen, the *gravitas* that Bizzarini finds in the book stems largely from the association of *alla breve* time signatures with the motet-like style of pieces like 'Tutto il dì piango', which as he notes Alfred Einstein had associated with 'the archaic style of Cipriano de Rore'. But as Table 1 underscores, the incidence of *alla breve* signatures, which although as Bizzarini points out is high for Marenzio, is specifically circumscribed (with the anomalous exception of 'Nova angioletta') to the melancholy madrigals, which may be seen as contrasting episodes occurring in the context of the largely optimistic bucolic character that dominates the book. *Gravitas* is to be found, more generally, in the serious literary issues that are explored over the course of the twenty-one madrigals and in the particular curatorial intent that appears to govern their organization.

In 'The Madrigal and its Outcasts', Gerbino charts the rather meagre cultivation of Sannazaro among sixteenth-century madrigalists — so meagre, indeed, that Giovannelli's and Marenzio's collections caused a disproportionate spike in the number of settings in the 1580s. Even thus boosted, his presence in the repertory appears insignificant in comparison with the popularity Petrarch enjoyed during the same period.[31] In fact, Gerbino's table highlights the contrast between composers' interests and Sannazaro's actual significance for the world of letters. What makes Marenzio's *Primo libro* appear even more anomalous, however, is the way Petrarch and Sannazaro are interwoven throughout it: a survey of the Vogel–Sartori catalogue shows that there are only a few books that mix the two in proportions and organization that are approximately similar to Marenzio's, and that they tend to stem from between 1540 and 1565, that is, between twenty and forty years before the *Primo libro*. This is the case with such books as Bernardo Lupacchino's *Secondo libro [...] a quattro voci* (Venice, Gardano 1546), which among its thirty madrigals includes ten on texts by Sannazaro, six by Petrarch, two by Ariosto and one by Luigi Tansillo, along with a number of anonymous texts; Giulio Fiesco's *Il Primo libro [...] a quattro voci* (Venice, Gardano, 1554), which opens with a tightly woven group of cycles by Sannazaro, Petrarch, and Boccaccio, but fills out the remainder of its contents with largely anonymous poetry; or most notably Francesco Menta's *Primo libro [...] a cinque* (Venice: Gardano, 1564), which consists almost entirely of cycles and individual madrigals on Sannazaro and Petrarch texts. Closer to the time of Marenzio's *Primo libro* we find that only his own *Madrigali a quattro, cinque, et sei voci libro primo* (Venice: Vincenzi, 1588) and *Fifth Book a cinque* (also 1585) mix the two authors in similar proportions.

The particular profile of Marenzio's *Primo libro*, then, emerges as an oddity even in comparison with Giovannelli's, which was entirely focused on Sannazaro and his *sdruccioli*. The salient, and particularly striking, characteristic of this volume lies in the apparent awareness of the literary stakes represented by the authors and by the choice of particular texts, an awareness that was then translated into musical stylistic terms. The presence of what Einstein sees as a pastoral style peculiar to these four-voice madrigals strongly suggests that Marenzio himself may have been aware of the subtler points of discussion surrounding Sannazaro and Petrarch, and that he sought to situate music within the literary-aesthetic debate.

Reading a madrigal book as a literary collection — setting madrigals in dialogue with one another, seeking semantic continuities and recurring themes, tracing the deployment of musical styles over the arc of its contents, and analysing its formal architecture — may not seem in keeping with the common perception, which I described at the outset of this essay, that madrigal books are not really books, but only repositories of individual pieces for performance. Their only resemblance to books of literature, in this view, resides in their physical layout but not in the way they are conceived and used. Indeed, their format, as part-books each containing only the music for the individual voices, to be realized as a coherent whole only in performance, ephemeral and not intrinsic to their materiality, seems to confirm their equivocal status in the world of books.

But this is merely one dimension of what is in fact a complex reality suspended between orality and material fixity.[32] As objects, madrigal books contain the fundamental elements of completeness: the poetry is there in its entirety, and the music can be scored, sung through, and the full shape and organization of the contents can be studied and discussed. Moreover, even if not outwardly sung from, the musical notation serves as a mnemonic device, a reminder of performances heard or imagined. This dimension, independent of a public hearing, an immediate presence, may in fact have been essential to the experience of listening and thinking about music in the early modern period. As Andrew Dell'Antonio has argued, much musical culture revolved around the practice of 'musicking', which was 'theorized as a forceful interpretative [...] stance rather than a passive reception of emotion-shifting sound'.[33] This manifested itself in extensive 'discussion about music', based on the ability to collect and recollect musical experiences — particular pieces, particular performances, individual performers — and to articulate one's memories of those experiences not necessarily in technical terms, but rather in terms of one's own apprehension of those experiences. In other words, a musical experience is not only determined by the particular individual piece or performance, but by the aggregate of memories and sensations the individual listener is able to recollect, associate with it, and articulate in the context of a discourse about such an experience. This is not fundamentally different from the ways in which a literary text was approached, and literary criticism from the early modern period preserves ample documentation of such 'discourse about' literary texts and genres — first and foremost among them the poetry of Petrarch himself. Thinking about *Il Canzoniere*, for example, embraced not only individual poems, but the entirety of the work, its structure, narrative continuity, and intertextual connections between its component parts.[34]

A volume like Marenzio's *Primo libro de madrigali a quattro voci*, then, emerges from such a reading as a complex, richly layered, discourse encompassing poetic and musical genres. It explores the styles possible in association with various genres, as well as their expressive potential. The various modes of expression that are available as a result of this exploration also serve as signifiers of class and character; they do this as literary constructs aligned with well-established models of social interaction. It opens a window into a particular approach to 'musicking', to the potential range of experiences, both literary and auditory, of its audience, and even to the nature of gatherings in which such collections of madrigals might have been the focus of performance, listening, and learned, critical discussions, among the participants.

TABLE 6.1. Synoptic Table of Marenzio's *Madrigali a quattro voci* (1585)

No.	Text incipit	Music	Mood and Texture (Music)	Poet	Source
1	Non vidi mai dopo	G-Dorian (1-flat); C mensuration; normal clefs	Neutral.	Petrarch	*Canzoniere* 127 (Canzone in 7 stanzas; stanza 5, lines 57-65)
2	Dissi a l'amata mia	F Lydian (1-flat); C mensuration; normal clefs	Neutral.	[G. B. Moscaglia in Sartori; no attr in Repim]	Unknown
3	Veggo dolce mio bene	D 1-flat; C mensuration; normal clefs	Neutral-pensive.	Anon.	Unknown
4	O bella man	F (1-flat); C mensuration; normal clefs	Light-neutral.	Petrarch	*Canzoniere* 199 (sonnet, in two *parti*)
5	Non al suo amante	C (no signature); C mensuration; g2, c2, c2, f4	Light with moments of pathos. *Intreccio* texture.	Petrarch	*Canzoniere* 52 (madrigale)
6	Hor vedi Amor	G (no signature); C mensuration; g2, cc2, c2, f4	Light.	Petrarch	*Canzoniere* 121 (madrigale)
7	Apollo, s'ancor vive	C (no signature); C mensuration; g2, c2, c3, f4	Light-neutral.	Petrarch	*Canzoniere* 34 (sonnet in two *parti*)
8	Nova angioletta	G Mixolydian (no signature); alla breve mensuration; g2, c2, c3, f4.	Light. Rapid declamation clause by clause. '*Intreccio*' texture.	Petrarch	*Canzoniere* 106 (madrigale)
9	Vedi le valli e i campi	C (no signature); C mensuration; g2, c2, c3, f4	Light. Makes a clear pair with *Nova angioletta*; similar rapid declamation, although with less *intreccio* texture.	Sannazaro	*Arcadia*, eclogue 8

The Pastoral Design of Luca Marenzio 119

10	Chi vuol udir i miei sospiri	D Dorian; alla breve mensuration; chiavette (?): g2, c2, c3, f3	Heavy melancholy. No repetitions until last line.	Sannazaro	*Arcadia* Eclogue 4
11	Madonna sua mercè	A (with regular C#, G#, and F#); C mensuration; normal clefs (c1, c3, c4; f4)		Sannazaro	*Arcadia* Eclogue 7
12	Vezzosi augelli in fra le verdi fronde	A Ionian; C mensuration; normal clefs (c1 etc.)	Light. Links its declamation to *Nova angioletta* and *Vedi le valli*, but more broken up and slower.	Tasso	*GL*, canto 16 ottava 12
13	Ahi dispietata morte	E; alla breve mensuration; normal clefs (c1 ...)	Heavy melancholy. Similar to *Chi vuol...*	Petrarch	*Canzoniere* 324, lines 4-12 (ballata mezzana)
14	Dolci son le quadrella	D; C mensuration; normal clefs (c1, c3, c4; f4)	Melancholy/Pensive. Moments of declamative *sprezzatura*.	Giovanni della Casa	*Rime* 10; in two *parti*
15	Menando un giorno	C Ionian (no signature); C mensuration; normal clefs (c1 ...)	Light. Picks up from *Nova angioletta* and its companions. Rapid declamation, *sprezzatura*.	Sannazaro	*Arcadia* Eclogue 1
16	I lieti amanti,	G Mixolydian (no signature); 3 mensuration; normal clefs (g1 ...)	Light. Continues from *Menando*, with similar *sprezzatura*. More articulated.	Sannazaro	*Arcadia* Eclogue 6 lines 104-109
17	Tutto il dì piango	In two parti; A (?; 1-flat); alla breve mensuration; chiavette (g2, c2, c3, f3)	Heavy melancholy. Returns to the melancholy mood of *Ahi dispietata* and its allies.	Petrarch	*Canzoniere* 216 (sonnet, in two *parti*)

18	Zefiro torna	In two *parti*; G Dorian (1-flat); C mensuration; chiavette (g2, c2, c3, f3)	Mixed. Return to the *sprezzatura* of *Nova angioletta* etc. for the first part, but interrupted at *garrir Progne* ... only a temporary break in mood. Happiness is not fully experienced. Part 2 is like *Ahi dispietata* ... with a break at 'cantar ... fiorir'; 'Sono un deserto' motive.	Petrarch	*Canzoniere* 310 (sonnet, in two *parti*)
19	Su'l carro della mente,	In two *parti*; C (1 flat); C mensuration; chiavette (g2, c2, c3, f4)	Mixed. Recalls the overall neutral/pensive but not melancholy mood of the first 3 madrigals; with occasional bursts of *sprezzatura* from the faster pieces. Discursive syntax makes for awkward musical periodization.	Tasso	*Rime*, sonnet 13 (in two *parti*)
20	Lasso dicea perché venisti Amore,	D Dorian (1 flat); alla breve mensuration; chiavette (g2, c2, c2, f3)		Tasso	*Rinaldo* (GL?) Canto 5 ottava 16
21	Vienne Montan	F Lydian	Canzonetta-like, but largely not complex contrapuntally.	Sannazaro	*Arcadia* eclogue 9 (in three *parti*)

TABLE 6.2. Marenzio's *Madrigali a quattro voci* (1585), grouped by mood and texture

Neutral/pensive:
1. Non vidi mai dopo *Canzoniere* 127
   (Canzone in 7 stanzas; stanza 5, lines 57–65)
2. Dissi a l'amata mia [G. B. Moscaglia in Sartori; no attr in Repim]
3. Veggio dolce mio bene (Anon)
4. O bella man *Canzoniere* 199 (sonnet, in two partes)

Light, *intreccio* texture, *sprezzatura* declamation:
5. Non al suo amante *Canzoniere* 52 (madrigale)
6. Hor vedi Amor *Canzoniere* 121 (madrigale)
7. Apollo, s'ancor vive *Canzoniere* 93 (sonnet in two parti)
8. Nova angioletta *Canzoniere* 106 (madrigale)
9. Vedi le valli e i campi Sannazaro, *Arcadia*, eclogue 8

Melancholy:
10. Chi vuol udir i miei sospiri Sannazaro, *Arcadia* Eclogue 4
11. Madonna sua mercè Sannazaro, *Arcadia* eclogue 7

Light:
12. Vezzosi augelli in fra le verdi fronde Tasso, *GL*, canto 16 ottava 12

Melancholy/pensive:
13. Ahi dispietata morte *Canzoniere* 324, lines 4–12 (ballata mezzana)
14. Dolci son le quadrella Giovanni della Casa, *Rime* 10; in two parti.

Light:
15. Menando un giorno Sannazaro, *Arcadia* Eclogue 1
16. I lieti amanti Sannazaro, *Arcadia* Eclogue 6 lines 104–09

Melancholy/Mixed melancholy/pensive:
17. Tutto il dì piango *Canzoniere* 216 (sonnet, in two parti)
18. Zefiro torna *Canzoniere* 310 (sonnet, in two parti)
19. Su'l carro della mente Tasso, *Rime*, sonnet 13 (in two parts)
20. Lasso dicea perché venisti Amore Tasso, *Rinaldo* Canto 5 ottava 16

Light pastoral, canzonetta-style:
21. Vienne Montan Sannazaro, *Arcadia* eclogue 9 (in three parti)

Notes to Chapter 6

1. For an early study of Marenzio's poetic choices understood in light of their sources, see James Chater and Lorenzo Bianconi, 'Fonti poetiche per i madrigali di Luca Marenzio', *Rivista Italiana di Musicologia*, 13 (1978), 60–103. The pioneering study of a madrigal composer's literary tastes across the entire arc of his career remains Nino Pirrotta's 'Scelte Poetiche di Monteverdi', *Nuova rivista musicale italiana*, 2 (1968), 10–42, 226–54, subsequently translated as 'Monteverdi's Poetic Choices', in *Music and Culture in Italy from the Middle Ages to the Baroque. A Collection of Essays* (Cambridge, MA and London: Harvard University Press, 1984), pp. 271–316. Alfred Einstein, in his pioneering and still unmatched study of the genre, *The Italian Madrigal*, trans. by Alexander H. Krappe, Roger H. Sessions, and Oliver Strunk (Princeton: Princeton University Press, 1949), laid the foundation for a careful analysis of the literary aspect of the genre.
2. See for example Einstein, *The Italian Madrigal*, pp.652–59.
3. Alfred Einstein remarks on the choice in his discussion of this book. See Ibid., p. 653.
4. Francesco Petrarca, *Canzoniere*, ed. by Sabrina Stroppa with an introduction by Paolo Cerchi (Turin: Einaudi, 2011), pp. 110–11, commentary on *RVF* 54.
5. Francesco Manara included both 'Nova angeletta' and 'Hor vedi, Amor' in his first book for four voices (1555), as did Guglielmo Gonzaga in his *Madrigali a cinque voci* (1583); Domenico Magiello set both texts, but published them separately in his first (1567) and second (1568) books of madrigals for five voices. 'Nova angeletta' and 'Non al suo amante' appeared in Lodovico Balbi's second book for four voices (1576).
6. *Canzoniere*, p. 103.
7. For 'Amor quando fioria' (*RVF* 324), see *Canzoniere*, 501; 'Hor che'l ciel e la terra' (*RVF* 164) is discussed on *Canzoniere*, 293; and for 'Tutto il dí piango' (*RVF* 216) see *Canzoniere*, 361.
8. Iacopo Sannazaro, *Arcadia*, with an introduction and commentary by Carlo Vecce (Rome: Carocci, 2013), p. 118 n. 1.
9. Ibid., p. 71.
10. Ibid., p. 219
11. Ibid., pp. 32–33.
12. Einstein, *The Italian Madrigal*, p. 659.
13. First set by Cosimo Bottrigari in his *Canzoni, arie a 1* (1574).
14. Annibale Coma's version appeared contemporaneously with Marenzio's in his *Madrigali libro terzo a 5* (1585).
15. Set by Biagio Pesciolini in his *Libro terzo de madrigali a 6* (1581).
16. Set by Paolo Lagudio in his *Primo libro de madrigali a 5* (1563).
17. The only other setting is by Girolamo Scotto, who included it in his *Primo libro de madrigali a due voci* (1541), which is remarkable for its concentration on texts by Petrarch, Sannazaro, and Boccaccio in a book of two-voice pieces that appears to have had a largely didactic intent, to judge by its explicit assignation of modes to each madrigal.
18. Einstein's assessment of the stylistic variety is not entirely positive ('they are unequal in style and merit'), and he surmises that 'the composition of these twenty-one four-voiced madrigals [...] spreads over a considerable period' (*The Italian Madrigal*, p. 653).
19. Ibid., p. 656.
20. Ibid., p. 653.
21. Giuseppe Gerbino remarks on the stylistic disconnect between music and verse in this madrigal. For his analysis of Marenzio's use of rhythm to highlight the *sdrucciolo* rhymes within a madrigalian style that remains independent of the formal constraints of the *terza rima* metre, see his 'The Madrigal and its Outcasts: Marenzio, Giovannelli, and the Revival of Sannazaro's Arcadia', *The Journal of Musicology*, 21 (2004), 3–45. On this point, see also Einstein, *The Italian Madrigal*, pp. 653–54.
22. 'The Madrigal and its Outcasts', p. 4.
23. Published in his *Nono libro de madrigali a cinque voci* (Venice: Gardano, 1599). On the reuse of this motive by Marenzio and others see Massimo Ossi, 'Monteverdi's "Zefiro torna e 'l bel tempo rimena" as Hypertext', *Early Music*, 45.3 (2017), 393–402.

24. Sannazaro, *Arcadia*, pp. 32–33.
25. 'Goddess, placate for us the springs and fountain spirits | Placate the gods dispersed through every grove. | Keep from our sight the Dryads and Diana's bath, | And Faunus lying in the fields at noon.' Ovid, *Fasti*, trans. and ed. with an introduction and notes by Anthony James Boyle and Roger Dillard Woodard (London: Penguin, 2004), p. 106, no. 4, lines 759–72.
26. As Francesca Bortoletti notes, the pastoral becomes, for humanist poets, both poetic and political. Through the eclogue, with its invocation of oral practices, the modern poet attains a moral, civilizing, role. See Francesca Bortoletti, 'Arcadia, festa e performance alla corte dei Re d'Aragona 1442–1503', *The Italianist*, 36/1 (2016), 1–28 (p. 6).
27. On the Ferrarese pastoral, especially at Belvedere, see Giuseppe Gerbino, *Music and the Myth of Arcadia in Renaissance Italy* (Cambridge: Cambridge University Press, 2009), pp. 304–14.
28. In 'The Madrigal and its Outcasts', p. 9, Gerbino posits a specifically southern context for Giovannelli's work, which is dedicated to Ferrante Penna, the feudal lord of Ailano, a small locale north of Naples.
29. *Il Primo libro delle villanelle a tre voci* [...] *raccolte da Ferrante Franchi* (Venice: Giacomo Vincenzi e Ricciardo Amadino, 1584); *Il secondo libro delle canzonette alla napoletana* [...] *raccolte per Attilio Gualtieri* (Venice, Vincenzi et Amadino, 1585); and *Il Terzo libro delle villanelle a tre voci* [...] *nel modo che hoggidì si usa cantare in Roma. Raccolte da Christoforo Ferrari* (Rome: Gardano, 1585).
30. Marco Bizzarini, *Luca Marenzio: The Career of a Musician between the Renaissance and the Counter-Reformation*, trans. by James Chater (Burlington: Ashgate, 2003), p. 279.
31. Gerbino, 'The Madrigal and its Outcasts', p. 20, Table 1a.
32. This essay draws on my previous work on the idea of madrigal books as curated collections, beginning with Monteverdi's Fifth Book of Madrigals (1605), the organization of which I discussed in *Divining the Oracle: Claudio Monteverdi's seconda prattica* (Chicago: University of Chicago Press, 2003), pp. 59–95. Other essays and presentations on this topic include, 'À la recherche du temps perdu: Il Primo libro di madrigali a tre voci (1575) di Andrea Gabrieli', forthcoming in *La Performance della Memoria*, ed. by Francesca Bortoletti and Annalisa Sacchi (Bologna: Baskerville, 2018), pp. 237–58; 'Petrarchan Discourses and Corporate Authorship in Cipriano de Rore's *Primo libro di Madrigali*, 1542–1544', in *Cipriano de Rore: New Perspectives on his Life and Music*, ed. by Jessie Ann Owens and Katelijne Schiltz (Turnhout: Brepols, 2016), pp. 153–90; 'Heinrich Schütz and Italian Aesthetics in Venice', in *Denn Musik ist der größte Segen... Festschrift Helen Geyer zum 65. Geburtstag* (Weimar, Studio Verlag, 2018), pp. 77–92; 'Wert's Settings of Tasso's *Gerusalemme liberata* in his *Ottavo Libro a Cinque* (1586)', in *International Conference on the Italian Madrigal 1550–1610: 70th Birthday Celebration for Anthony Newcomb*, University of California at Berkeley (November 2011); 'Epic, Pastoral, and Theatrical Cycles in Madrigal Books from the Late Sixteenth Century: Andrea Gabrieli's *Madrigali a tre voci* (1575)', Renaissance Society of America (Washington, DC, 2012); 'Venus, Mars, and Comus: Structure and Interpretation of Claudio Monteverdi's *Madrigali Guerrieri et Amorosi* (1638)', Christopher Newport University, Virginia, February 2014 and Rome, Università degli Studi 'La Sapienza', March 2014.
33. Andrew Dell'Antonio, *Listening as Spiritual Practice in Early Modern Italy* (Berkeley and Los Angeles: University of California Press, 2011), p. 11.
34. On the relevance of Petrarchan criticism to the interpretation of madrigal books, see my 'Petrarchan Discourses and Corporate Authorship in Cipriano de Rore's *Primo libro di Madrigali*, 1542–1544'.

PART II

Claiming Petrarch for Modern Times

CHAPTER 7

Georges and Madeleine de Scudéry: Two Polite Commentators of Petrarch

Dominique Chaigne

Although the influence of Petrarch was more tenuous in the seventeenth than in the sixteenth century,[1] the Scudérys, natives of Apt through their paternal lineage, allowed the Provençal roots of the *Canzoniere* not to disappear. Retracing the main stages in the story of Petrarch and Laura in Provence in twelve sonnets, Georges de Scudéry's 'Description of the Famous Fontaine de Vaucluse'[2] condenses the memory of the *Canzoniere*. As for Madeleine de Scudéry's romance *Mathilde d'Aguilar*,[3] it reports the amorous initiation of the eponymous character in the company of Laura and Petrarch in the gardens of Avignon. Their conversations — a direct line of descent — are based on sonnets from the *Canzoniere* that Mathilde and her friends comment on. In both cases, interpretation makes itself at home in fiction. The choices made by Georges de Scudéry imply hermeneutics in so far as rewriting necessarily has an interpretative dimension. His sisters stage a debate on the reception of Petrarch's sonnets within the framework of gallant conversation. I therefore suggest exploring how fiction — understood as a literary representation that constitutes a world considered as autonomous or at least partly distinct from reality — interprets some aspects of the *Canzoniere*.

In 1649, Georges de Scudéry published the section entitled 'Description of the Fontaine de Vaucluse' as an opening to his collection *Poésies* (p. 1). This title, like that of the romance, suggests the Scudérys' works are concerned with breaking up the matrix of the *Canzoniere*. When Madeleine de Scudéry evokes the amorous initiation of the young Spanish aristocrat Mathilde d'Aguilar, she seems to be borrowing snippets from Petrarch only as a pretext to develop gallant conversations about love as part of the characters' worldly leisure. The 'Fontaine de Vaucluse' is only a brief stop in the *Canzoniere*. Petrarch mentions the landscape of Vaucluse, with which Laura will be associated or even confused, in a sporadic and allusive way. All the examples from the corpus corroborate this idea:

> Valle, che de' lamenti miei se' piena
> fiume, che spesso del moi pianger cresci,
> fere selvestre, vaghi augelli, et pesci,
> l'una et l'altra verde riva affrena.[4]

> Fresco, ombroso, fiorito et verde colle,
> ov'or pensando et or cantando siede, et
> fa qui de ' celesti spiriti fede quella
> ch'a tutto 'l mondo fama tolle. (p. 377)

> [Valley so filled with all my laments,
> river so often swollen with my tears,
> wild beasts, wandering birds and fish,
> reined in by these two green river-banks,
>
> air warmed and calmed by my sighs,
> sweet path that ends in such bitterness,
> hill that pleased me, that now saddens,
> where by habit Love still leads me.]

> Cercato o sempre solitaria vita
> (le rive il sanno et le campagne sordi e i
> boschi) per fuggir questi ingegni sordi et loschi,
> che la strada del Cielo anno smarrita. (p. 393)

> [I've often sought the solitary life
> (river-banks know it, and fields and woods)
> to escape these dull and clouded minds,
> who have lost the road to heaven.]
> (RVF 259)

> Tosto che giunto a l'amorosa reggia vidi onde
> nacque l'aura dolce et pura,
> ch'acqueta l'aere et mette i tuoni in bando (p. 212)

> [As soon as I came to the regions of love
> and saw where the pure, sweet breeze was born
> that clears the air, and banishes the thunder,]
> (RVF 113)

> Cosi sol d'una chiara fonte viva move 'l
> dolce et l'amaro, ond'io mi pasco ; una
> man sola mi risana et punge. (p. 289)

> [So from one pure living fountain
> flow the sweet and bitter which I drink:
> one hand alone heals me and pierces me.]
> (RVF 164)

The two works' synecdochal relation to Petrarch can also be perceived in the choice of the sonnet as the one form emblematizing the *Canzoniere* even though the collection includes many other medieval poetic forms, with twenty-nine songs, nine sestinas, seven ballads and four madrigals. Georges de Scudéry composes twelve sonnets and Madeleine mentions fourteen.[5] Compared to the 366 poems composed by the prolific Tuscan, the two works seem to dismantle the source and ruin its order since they simply rewrite a few sonnets and echo some incipits.[6] Finally, Petrarchism emerges only in very discreet ways: Madeleine cites Petrarch but her selection is debatable. Not only does she exclude the devotion poems, but she also seems to have selected a few anecdotal, occasional sonnets.

As for Georges, he deliberately delays the appearance of the couple by privileging the evocation of the ever-changing theatre of nature in the first five texts. The last seven sonnets occasionally send back a hypotextual echo that can instantly be picked up in the nominal allusion indirectly reminding the reader of a story: proper names are endowed with the power to encapsulate a narrative in a latent form. This is why they are repeated throughout the sequence:

> Pétrarque, belle Laure, admirable Vaucluse
> ['Petrarch, fair Laura, admirable Vaucluse', *Poésies diverses*, l. 12, p. 6]
>
> Tous parlent de Pétrarque, et de sa chère Amante
> ['All converse about Petrarch and his dear Lover', *Poésies diverses*, l. 12, p. 7]
>
> [ces aimables rivages] Ont appris de Pétrarque à si bien soupirer.
> [...] [mille innocents oiseaux/Nous redisent encore [...]] Ce que Laure disait à son Amant fidèle.
> ['[These amiable shores] learnt so well from Petrarch how to sigh. [...] [A thousand innocent birds | Are telling us again] what Laura told her faithful Lover', *Poésies diverses*, ll. 4, 11, p. 8]
>
> Sans doute je le vois, cet Amant si vanté
> [...] lui qui suit de sa Laure, et l'ombre et la figure.
> ['Surely I can see him, this Lover so much praised [...] Him who follows his Laura's shadow and figure', *Poésies diverses*, ll. 5, 7, p. 9]
>
> [Ces rochers] ne font ces ruisseaux, que pour la mort de Laure
> Et les pleurs de Pétrarque arrivent jusqu'à nous.
> ['It is only for Laura's death that [these rocks] are shedding streams | And Petrarch's sobbing reaches us', *Poésies diverses*, ll. 13–14, p. 10]
>
> Et Laure partagea le destin de ses Vers.
> ['And Laura knew the same destiny as his lines', *Poésies diverses*, ll.14, p. 11]

Georges de Scudéry's work is neither really concerned with its lineage nor strictly looking for patronage. The text only shows traces of a few memories concerning the love story: a line from sonnet 7, 'And [...] as Petrarch loved her sovereign beauty' ('Et [...] Pétrarque aimant sa beauté souveraine') starts praising the beloved woman and is completed by a hemistich from sonnet 11, 'this bright Star' ('cet Astre brillant'). He mentions Laura and her lover's despair in sonnet 9, 'Him who follows his Laura's shadow and figure, blaming his destiny for being so cruel' ('Lui qui suit de sa Laure, et l'ombre et la figure, accusant son destin, de trop de cruauté'), sonnet 10, 'Alas, how painful was it for the poor lover to see his Laura touched by one Parca !' ('Hélas quel douleur sentit ce pauvre Amant, | Quand sa Laure sentit l'atteinte de la Parque!') and sonnet 11, 'too soon was [this bright star] extinguished' ('on vit [cet Astre brillant] trop peu durer').

Therefore, in spite of a few direct references to the paragon, the aim of Georges de Scudéry's sonnets is to make room for the memory of Petrarch so that it can grow and stabilize at the same time as the Petrarchan topical resources are discussed.

If allusions are rare and discrete in both works, the Scudérys nevertheless keep relying on devices different from mere quotes in order to situate themselves. Their links with the *Canzoniere* also consist in a structural inheritance: both works display a two-part structure explained by Laura's absence, copying the traditional editorial structure of the collection,[7] 'Rime in vita di laura' and 'In morte di Laura'. *Mathilde d'Aguilar* is based on a return journey as it traces the path of its eponymous character to Avignon and back home: Mathilde d'Aguilar, with her father Dom Rodolphe d'Aguilar and her mother Constance, leave Spain to escape the internecine wars plaguing the kingdom of Castile. The family decide to settle in the Court of Rome in Avignon. Mathilde is entrusted to Laura's aunt. She learns Italian in six months and spends much time with Laura and Petrarch, who nurture and cultivate her mind as if she were their only child. A few months later, Constance dies from a long illness. The King of Spain then orders Dom Rodolphe d'Aguilar to come back, promising him that he will be appointed Governor of Lerma provided Mathilde stays in the Court of Spain or with the Queen. Mathilde and her father therefore leave Avignon for good.

The topical composition is reinforced by a symbolic one: from the start, Mathilde is Laura. The text regularly reminds the readers of their attachment: 'they were always seen together' ('on ne les voyait jamais l'une sans l'autre' (*Poésies diverses*, p. 14)), 'Mathilde could not be separated from Laura' ('Mathilde était inséparable de Laure' (*Poésies diverses*, p. 16)). But above all, Mathilde resembles Laura.[8] Scudéry plays with striking parallelisms between features (fairness, Laura's age when she met Petrarch and Mathilde's age) or emotions aroused by amorous gallantry: when Laura is on the Sorgue, the poem engraved on the boat makes her 'blush' (*Poésies diverses*, p. 56) (*rougir*); being wooed in Burgos, Mathilde also 'blushes' (*Poésies diverses*, p. 84). The twinning is also made clear by the nickname the couple gave to Mathilde, 'little Laure' ('la petite Laure' (*Poésies diverses*, p. 14)). This is how she became, like Laura, the privileged addressee of Petrarch's work, which she 'knew and recited in the most gracious way' ('[qu'elle] savait et récitait avec la meilleure grâce du monde' (*Poésies diverses*, p. 17)).

Even if Mathilde does not follow the path recommended by Laura (she marries Alphonse and has a house built next to Laura and Petrarch's in Vaucluse) the memory of the *Canzoniere* has an impact on the structure of the narrative: Petrarch and Laura's relation vanishes from the second part of the novella, for 'Petrarch had to leave the day Mathilde left' ('Pétrarque fut obligé de partir le jour que Mathilde partit' (*Poésies diverses*, p. 81)). This separation[9] is reminiscent of the *dispositio* of the Italian work split along the line of Laura's presence and absence: the structure leads the lover, whose desires were initially frustrated, to go beyond sensual appetites and, after Laura's death, beyond himself. The spiritualization of profane love, which is absent from Madeleine de Scudéry's work,[10] is replaced by Petrarch's poetic consecration, as related by Laura: 'Petrarch received in Rome the greatest honour a man can receive, for he was publicly crowned, precisely where the Caesars knew the same glorious destiny' ('Pétrarque a reçu à Rome le plus grand honneur qu'un homme de grand mérite puisse recevoir, puisqu'il a été couronné publiquement, au lieu même où les Césars ont tenu à gloire de l'être' (*Mathilde*, p. 180)).

Finally, the 'Description of the Fountain of Vaucluse' displays the same two-part structure: as in the *Canzoniere*, Laura's arrival is postponed to sonnet 5. Verging on hypotyposis, the precision of the visual lexicon ('I can see them' ('je les vois', sonnet 1), 'while everyone would see' ('aux yeux de tout le monde', sonnet 2), 'Hardly can they be seen | As soon as they are seen' ('A peine les voit-on', sonnet 3), 'charming the eyes' ('qui charme les yeux', sonnet 3), 'such a beautiful and ravishing sight' ('nous ravit par un objet si beau', sonnet 5) is combined with a spatial deictization: 'Here' ('ici') is used in sonnet 1 and repeated six times in sonnet 2 and twice in sonnet 5. This emblematizes the author's need to give a setting to the poetic voice by imagining the energy of a triumphant landscape emerging as revelation. Sonnets 6–12, on the other hand, have nostalgic overtones and evoke two ghosts, Laura and Petrarch, erring by the Sorgue as if in the Elysian Fields of the Vaucluse.

Thus, both works show traces of Petrarch's *Canzoniere*, including snippets that are sometimes so diluted in the general economy that readers seem invited to question their function: if the works are fundamentally different from their source, they clearly or indirectly suggest ways to engage in the interpretation of the fiction they include. Studying the fictive dialogues staged in *Mathilde d'Aguilar* as well as the narrative voice, which works as a critical or approving censor, can help identify parameters that determined the attitude of the modern reader or listener.

First of all, most of the time the text calls for a fictional public reading with two or three contributors or a *disputa* to show how polemic discussion matters regarding the reception of the work. Madeleine de Scudéry groups minds together so as favour the exchange of viewpoints, a process through which Petrarch's sonnets are analysed and appropriated. The Petrarch/Laura relationship takes on a social rather than a mystical dimension.

Madeleine de Scudéry portrays Mathilde as an interpreter by giving her two voices: one that matches the ethos of the girl with an adolescent mind and evokes the beauty of her love story, and another displaying a worldly ethos that is distant and amused, addressing the Ladies' wit. It is therefore no accident that the character of Petrarch chooses most of the time to have Mathilde read or sing his sonnets: the soft inflections of the girl's voice render the gentleness of some of his sonnets written in the Corinthian style,[11] an effeminate and voluptuous style which Vitruvius does not hesitate to associate with the image of a young virgin.[12] Petrarch's enthusiasm for her diction can be perceived in some excerpts: '[Mathilde] knew all the lines he had composed for Laura and recited them in the most gracious way; therefore, Petrarch sometimes said that only in Mathilde's voice could he bear to hear his own works' ('[Mathilde] savait tous les vers qu'il avait fait pour Laure, et les récitait de la meilleure grâce du monde ; aussi Pétrarque disait-il quelquefois, qu'il ne trouvait ce qu'il avait fait supportable, que dans la bouche de Mathilde' (*Mathilde*, p. 17)). Further on in the novella, Petrarch 'asks Mathilde to recite [a sonnet] to Laura' ('il pria la jeune Mathilde de réciter [un sonnet] à Laure' (*Mathilde*, p. 20)).

However, little by little, Petrarch becomes the victim of the trust he has placed in Mathilde. She mocks him: the gallant aesthetic claimed by Madeleine de Scudéry relies on jibes as part of the codes of good company and a sign of the Ladies' perfect control of language. The fact that Petrarch's sonnets are gently mocked is not anodyne. While the Abbé de Sade vehemently rejects the glove sequence, arguing that 'one should be [...] astonished to see the most learned man of his century, busy with great matters (as it shall become obvious), write four sonnets on such a frivolous topic' ('On devrait être [...] étonné de voir l'homme le plus savant de son siècle, occupé de grandes affaires (comme on le verra bientôt), faire quatre sonnets sur un sujet aussi frivole'[13]), Mademoiselle de Scudéry exploits it to account for the decontextualized reception of Petrarch in a worldly society. Here is what she says:

> Mathilde asked Petrarch if he was really sure he had never written any gallant line or praise that wasn't for Laura and he answered it was widely known and noted. [...] But still, Mathilde added, who did you write the three glove Sonnets for? Your question baffles me, Petrarch said, I wrote them for the fair person who had dropped the glove. So you wrote them for me, Mathilde concluded, for the glove is mine. [...] Petrarch was so surprised that he felt a bit annoyed and the whole circle was laughing.[14]

Here, banter imposes itself as the tone of good company, a controlled and polite form of laughter and a way for the audience to express its reaction as it questions some of Petrarch's choices.

The humour of banter — completely different from cruel or rude attacks — can be found again in another episode characterised by a pleasant joviality:

> as she spoke, [Laura] pointed to Mathilde who, pleasantly turning towards Petrarch, told him Laura was teasing him [...] and Laura [...] told the whole company that Mathilde had composed the couplet on the spot in order to trick Petrarch.[15]

Banter is an aesthetic of connivance between Ladies and its practice implies the creation of an atmosphere of light-hearted wit. It produces an allusive literature requiring the complicity of an exclusive and cultivated audience.

The jibes targeting Petrarch allow, first of all, the fictive criticism of his work as regards its style or the interpretation of this or that sonnet. Mathilde starts singing the couplet in the moonlight:

> Nul ne sait comme Amour sait blesser et guérir,
> Qui ne sait comme Iris parle, et rit, et soupire:
> Heureux qui vit sous son empire,
> Et bienheureux encore ceux qu'on y voit mourir.

[No one knows how Love can wound and cure, | who does not know how Iris speaks, laughs and sighs: | Happy the ones that live under her spell, | and happier yet the ones that die from it] (*Mathilde*, p. 58)

After a few jibes about who fathered this song, Petrarch admits that

> Half the song is in a sonnet I believe I wrote; judge by yourself; here is what I wrote in my mother tongue,
>
> > Non sa com'amor sana, e come ancide
> > Chi non sa come dolce ella sospira
> > E come dolce parla, e dolce ride.[16]

[he does not know how Love heals, and how he kills, who does not know how sweet her sighs are, and how sweet her speech, and sweet her smile.] (RVF 159)

The fictive fault noted by Petrarch can be confirmed by a reading of the sonnet 'In qual parte del ciel, in quale ydea': excessive emphasis and ornamentation characterized by an extensive rhetoric of *copia* and amplification. Convinced that Laura is an exceptional being, Petrarch pretends first to be wondering about the origin of such beauty. The rhetorical questions are cadenced in a binary rhythm ('In quale parte, in quale ydea [...] qual nimpha [...] qual dea' | From what part of the heavens, from what idea [...] What nymph of the fountain, what goddess), while the contrasting tropes (above/below; virtue vs. guilt) and images give an example of the typical flowery style. However, since Laura is exceptional, the three questions asked in the convoluted quatrains are not answered in the tercets.

Admitting that he used fourteen lines to reveal what Mathilde condenses in four, the Petrarch from *Mathilde d'Aguilar* doesn't seem to claim a simple style yet he considers removing what impedes communication in order to guarantee a form of transparency: while meaning is immediately conveyed in Mathilde's couplet, it is scattered in Petrarch's sonnet, diffracted by the many figures of speech that make the style heavily ornamented and the lines hardly readable. The simplification of Petrarch by French Petrarchists will make up for this, especially with Ronsard's two *Continuations*.[17]

Finally, Mathilde confronts Petrarch with the question of interpretation by deliberately misreading sonnet 46. Here is the first quatrain:

> L'oro et le perle, e i fior vermigli e i bianchi,
> Che'l verno devria far languidi et secchi, son
> per me acerbi et velenosi stecchi, ch'io provo
> per lo petto et per li fianchi. (*Mathilde*, p. 20)
>
> [The gold and pearls and flowers, crimson and white,
> that winter should have made dry and withered,
> are cruel and venomous thorns to me,
> that sting me fiercely in the chest and side.] (*RVF* 46)

This sonnet points out the illusory dimension of the mirror: the poet complains that Laura, looking at herself, turns prouder and prouder and insensitive to his love, to the point that she might forget his love and be content with her own self. Mathilde pretends to take it as a satire against herself, according to a conception of literature that assimilates poetry to performance.[18]

Mademoiselle de Scudéry's work assimilates Petrarch's sonnets to oral literature, in which the text cannot be separated from its context.[19] Thus, not only does Mathilde think that the ornaments she picked and placed on Laura's face are inappropriate to reveal her beauty, but she also believes that Laura is more concerned with artifice than with the poet. Three other sonnets are subjected to a similar counter-authorial reading. In sonnet 146, Petrarch praises Laura's beautiful hand and complains that he should return the glove he took from her. In sonnet 147, Laura's hands are still beautiful, even with gloves. Finally, in sonnet 148, the poet regrets having returned the glove, which was his treasure.

In the romance, the glove scene is rewritten by Madeleine de Scudéry but she changes the setting: sitting on a balcony with Laura, Mathilde drops her glove and Petrarch picks it up without noticing it is the girl's. Without believing the poet is declaring his love for her, Mathilde laughs at decontextualized poems that can now mean everything and nothing. Such misreadings — or mishearings, rather — can be explained by the fact that Petrarch's works are featured in gallant scenes. Born from the art of worldly conversation, the gallant aesthetic is essentially based on the importance given to the reception of speech. It characterizes conversations in which ideas are discretely, loosely and apparently naturally organized. If Mathilde's song is preferred to Petrarch's sonnet it is also because gallantry favours the voice for its qualities, timbre and tone.

Finally, by inserting short forms — a few sonnets by Petrarch — in conversation, mixing prose and verse, Madeleine de Scudéry composes a novella reflecting the flexibility, the variety and the jaunty, artificial spontaneity of gallant speech. However, written texts, fixed and structured by nature, all the more so as they are canonical, regular sonnets, do not easily lend themselves to performance: orality appears as a 'feminine' marker, characterized by openness, whereas writing appears as 'masculine', producing a definite, self-referential meaning that can be missed, even by Laura or her double. Petrarch's collection appears as a saturated system, a horizon of signs that can only be apprehended through the sequence of the poems, their connections and echoes. When Laura and Mathilde, new members of the Republic of Letters, oppose Petrarch, they are playing with a poetics of polite joyfulness and in doing so, ensuring the longevity of the texts, maybe even their fruitfulness.[20]

In Georges de Scudéry's sonnets, the lyric 'I' stands as an expert interpreter. It could be a figure of the poet deciphering his surroundings with his own techniques, relying on the emotions aroused by senses.[21] Indeed, he relies on sight: 'I think I can see her' ('Il me semble la voir'), 'Surely I can see her' ('Sans doute je la vois' (sonnet 9)) and hearing: 'seem to speak' ('semble parler') 'all things seem to be speaking' ('tout semble nous dire') 'tell stories' ('racontent cette histoire') 'all converse' ('tous parlent') 'everything is about him, everything tells us about her' ('tout nous parle de lui, tout nous entretient d'elle') 'And Petrarch's sobbing reaches us' ('Et les pleurs de Pétrarque arrivent jusqu'à nous'(sonnet 7)). This text also builds the *ethos* of an archaeologist driven by a double concern for conservation and renewal. The beginning of sonnet 6 illustrates this:

> Quelles superbes tours, se mirent dans ces eaux ?
> Quel grand et vieux château, s'élève jusqu'aux nues,
> Et semble couronner ces montagnes chenues,
> De ces fameux débris, aussi riches que beaux ?
> Là, ce pan de muraille, est presque sans créneaux ;
> Ici l'on voit ramper, l'hierre aux feuilles menues ;
> Et du temps immortel, les forces trop connues,
> Respectent toutefois, ces précieux lambeaux.
> Ha, je les reconnais ! Sans doute je remarque,
> Le château qu'habitait l'Amante de Pétrarque,
> Je vois de son Amant, la fameuse maison. (p. 6)
>
> [What magnificent towers are mirrored by these waters?
> What old great castle rises to cloudy heavens
> as if to crown the hoary mountains
> with these famous ruins, equally rich and fair?

> Here, what remains from a high wall is nearly without a crenel;
> There the slender ivy leaves can be seen crawling;
> And immortal time's all too familiar forces
> nevertheless respect these precious scraps.
> Ha, I know them! Surely I remark
> The castle where Petrarch's Lover lived,
> I can see her Lover's famous house.]

In this sonnet, the poet presents himself as a specialist on the Fountain of Vaucluse, which he has observed carefully. His field work is defined by the lexical field of ruins ('what remains from a high wall', 'without a crenel', 'scraps'). The importance of his mission — chronicling his discoveries to help reconstituting a place condemned to disappearance — is emphasized by the phrase 'immortal time's all too familiar forces'. As a consequence, the poet must document an absence, that of 'Petrarch's Love' and 'her Lover'.

The duty to preserve goes with the wish to assimilate the knowledge of a cultural work to a public good, as explained in the last tercet of sonnet 12:

> Puissent de temps en temps, cent fameux écrivains,
> Par les doctes labeurs de leurs savantes mains,
> Chanter votre grandeur, et que je sois le moindre. (p. 12)

> [May a hundred famous writers, occasionally,
> through the skilled labour of their erudite hands,
> sing your greatness, and may I be the smaller.]

Thus, the poet and reader invest the Fountain of Vaucluse, a palimpsest-like place. It is the only way they can make up for the disappearance of the object.

One might suggest that the initial image of erring — caused by the absence of the couple in sonnets 1–5 — could be perceived as an image for the reader's arrival into the world of hermeneutics, piecing meaning together from traces. The second part of the collection takes a fruitful turn. Bits and pieces seem to reconstitute a fragmentary domain that is, however, not the past territory of the Fountain of Vaucluse yet. Little by little, personifications reveal the traces of the past that are surfacing in the present. It is the case in sonnet 7:

> Les ombres, les rochers, et les bois d'alentour,
> Les prés, et les vallons, et l'illustre Fontaine,
> Semblent parler encore, de l'agréable peine,
> Qui les fit soupirer, et la nuit et le jour. (p. 7)

> [Shadows, rocks and woods all around,
> Meadows, vales and the illustrious Fountain,
> seem to be still talking about the pleasant woe
> That made them sigh night and day.]

and in sonnet 8:

> Les vents, même les vents, qu'on entend respirer,
> [...]
> Ont appris de Pétrarque à si bien respirer.
> [...]

> Les flots, même les flots qu'on entend murmurer
> [...]
> Imitent une voix, qui charmait les courages,
> [...]
> Au lieu même où je suis, mille innocents oiseaux
> Nous redisent encore, près de ces claires eaux,
> Ce que Laure disait, à son Amant fidèle.

[The winds, even the winds that can be heard breathing, | [...] Learned from Petrarch how to breathe so well. | [...] The waters, even the waters whose murmur can be heard | [...] Are mimicking one voice, that charmed the brave, [...] Precisely where I stand, a thousand innocent birds | Are telling us again, near these clear waters, | What Laura told her faithful Lover' (sonnet 8, p. 8)]

and then:

> Jamais Cygne mourant n'eut la voix si plaintive
> Lorsque du clair Méandre on l'entend sur la rive,
> Finir sa belle vie en des accents si doux :
> Ces rochers en pleuraient, ils pleurent encore ;
> Ils ne font ces ruisseaux, que pour la mort de Laure,
> Et les pleurs de Pétrarque arrivent jusqu'à nous. (sonnet 10, p. 10)

[Never did a dying Swan moan so plaintively,
From the bank of the clear Meander he can be heard
Ending his fair life with the softest inflections:
It made the rocks weep and they are still weeping;
It is only for Laura's death that they are shedding streams,
And Petrarch's sobbing reaches us.]

A retrospective view of the first sonnets will lead the reader to search among the ruins doomed to disappear: far from revealing a merely gratuitous setting, sonnets 1–5 replace the lost object by alliances between nature and the couple's story. Georges de Scudéry partly borrows these analogies from Petrarch: indeed, the poet weaves links between love and nature in the *Canzoniere*. Laura's personal identity is sometimes lost in a cultural identity: the magnetic power of the lover's name attracts a chain of other names obeying rules of metaphoric and musical contiguity. There are phonic symbols for the Dame, the breeze (*l'aura*, the laurel; *l'auro*, gold; *l'aurora*, l'aurore) and metaphorical associations (the angel or the nymph, Daphne, the swan, the sun, the snow). Petrarch is turned into a swan, a stone, a fountain, a flame and an eagle, among other things.

The loss of the original landscape can therefore be made up by these substitutes that still let the tragic love of Laura and Petrarch surface: it is the liquid element that recreates the presence of Laura in a beautiful scattering — the Nymph of Sorgue, crystal liquid, currents (sonnet 1, p. 1), gushes, eternal torrents (sonnet 2, p. 2), the diligent stream, the great silver mirror, her beautiful mirror (sonnet 3, p. 3), rich silver ribbons (sonnet 4, p. 4). Petrarch is animalized as he turns into an immortal swan (sonnets 10 and 12, p. 10, 12), or mineralized, as underlined by the parallelism 'It made these rocks weep and they are still weeping [...] And Petrarch's sobbing reaches us' ('Ces rochers en pleuraient, ils en pleurent encore [...] Et les pleurs de

Pétrarque arrivent jusqu'à nous' (sonnet 10, p. 10)). 'The realm of soundwaves echoes their story: water, birds, shepherds, rocks, meadows and vales 'seem to be still telling [it]' ('semblent [en] parler encore' (sonnet 7, p. 7)).

Thus, even as they borrow significant elements from the *Canzoniere*'s amorous *topoi*, the Scudérys reorder them, moving them around to compose a new plot: a visit of the Fountain of the Vaucluse haunted by ghostly presences or young Mathilde's initiation to love. These references are sometimes perceived as completely integrated into their new cultural context. The surfacing of the memory of the *Canzoniere* in Georges de Scudéry can be seen as an emergence of the residual that stimulates verbal virtuosity and, more generally, style and manner. In a close relationship with her readers, Madeleine de Scudéry makes them discover the joys of banter: referring to Petrarch, the text involves them in the shaping of a place where polite worldly leisure frames free and playful conversations.

Translated by Fanny Quément

Notes to Chapter 7

1. Firstly, there were few translations (Philippe de Maldeghen's in 1600, published again in Douai in 1606, Placide Catanusi's in 1669 and an attempt made by Madame de Grignan). Secondly, Petrarch is criticized in some texts (see for instance Malherbe's comments in the margins of Desportes's works, or Sigogne who was intent on undermining Petrarchan aesthetics). Finally, novels drew more attention than poetry.
2. *Poésies diverses* (Paris: A. Courbé, 1649).
3. Madeleine de Scudéry, *Mathilde d'Aguilar* (Paris: Edme Martin et François Eschart, 1667).
4. Francesco Petrarca, *Canzoniere*, ed. Alberto Chiari (Milan: Mondadori, 1994), sonnet 301, p. 447.
5. Sonnets 38, p. 20; 101, p. 29; 189, p. 56; 66, p. 62; 266, 267, and 268 les 266, p. 67; 136, p. 72; 57 and 58, p. 76; 122, 123, 124, and 125, p. 79.
6. From sonnets 201, 189, 139, 66, 166, 167, 168, 186, 57, 58, 122, 123, 124, 125.
7. Regarding the editorial structure and its effects on reading, see Christoph Niederer, 'La bipartizione *in vita/in morte* del *Canzoniere* di Petrarca', in *Petrarca e i suoi lettori*, ed. by Vittorio Caratozzolo and Georges Güntert (Ravenna: Longo, 2000), pp. 19–41.
8. Eve Duperray notes that 'Petrarch teaches [Mathilde] Italian in six months as if she had been adopted. The resemblance becomes so obvious that one day, Petrarch takes Mathilde for Laura' ('Pétrarque lui [Mathilde] apprend l'italien en six mois comme à une fille adoptive. L'identification devient si forte que Pétrarque, un jour, se méprend sur la personne de Mathilde' (*L'Or des mots: une lecture de Pétrarque et du mythe littéraire de Vaucluse des origines à l'orée du XXe siècle* (Paris: Publications de la Sorbonne, 1997), p. 100).
9. A letter from Laura to Mathilde informs the reader that Petrarch will stay in Rome. *Mathilde*, pp. 180–81.
10. Madeleine de Scudéry obscured another essential dimension: the pain inflicted by love is replaced by the love of happiness.
11. According to Cicero, the soft style can be related to the epideictic genre. See *Orator* XIII.42. Peletier celebrates the great softness of Petrarch's style. See *Art poétique* (1555), in *Traités de poétique et de rhétorique de la Renaissance*, ed. by Francis Goyet (Paris: Librarie générale française, Le Livre de poche classique, 1990), p. 293.
12. Vitruve, *De l'Architecture*, IV, I, ed. by Pierre Gros (Paris: Belles Lettres, 2015).
13. Sade, *Mémoires pour la vie de François Pétrarque, tirés de ses oeuvres et des auteurs contemporains, avec des notes, et les pieces justificatives*, 3 vols (Amsterdam: Arskée and Mercus, 1764–67), II, 88.
14. '[Mathilde] demanda à Pétrarque s'il était bien assuré de n'avoir jamais fait de vers de galanterie et de louanges que pour Laure, il répondit que cela était su et remarqué de tout le monde [...]

Mais encore, reprit Mathilde, pour qui pensez-vous avoir fait les trois Sonnets des gants? Ce que vous me demandez, me surprend, reprit Pétrarque, je les ai faits pour la belle personne qui avait laissé tomber le gant. Vous les avez donc faits pour moi, reprit Mathilde; car le gant est à moi [...] Pétrarque fut si surpris qu'il se trouva un peu embarrassé car toute la compagnie riait.' (*Mathilde*, pp. 68–69).

15. 'en disant cela [Laure] montra Mathilde, qui se tournant agréablement vers Pétrarque, lui dit que Laure raillait [...] ensuite, Laure ayant dit à toute la compagnie que Mathilde avait fait une ce couplet à l'heure même, afin de tromper Pétrarque' (*Mathilde*, p. 64).
16. 'la moitié de [cette] chanson est dans un sonnet que je crois avoir fait ; jugez-en vous même ; voici ce que j'ai dit en ma langue naturelle, Non sa com'amor sana, e come ancide | Chi non sa come dolce ella sospira | E come dolce parla, e dolce ride' (*Mathilde*, p. 59).
17. Ronsard admits it himself: 'Marie, tout ainsi que vous m'avés tourné | Mon sens et ma raison, par vôtre voix subtile, | Ainsi, m'avés tourné mon grave premier stile | Qui pour chanter si bas n'estoit point destiné' [Marie, just as you have turned / my sense and my reason, with your subtle voice,/ so have you turned my grave, early style, /which was not destined to sing so low] (translation: Carole Birkan-Berz), in the last sonnet of *Continuation des Amours*.
18. Influenced by linguists from the anglophone world, Paul Zumthor defines performance as 'the complex action through which a message is simultaneously transmitted and perceived, here and now' ('l'action complexe par laquelle un message est simultanément transmis et perçu, ici et maintenant'). Paul Zumthor, *Introduction à la poésie orale* (Paris: Seuil, 1983), pp. 32–33.
19. See Delphine Denis, 'Conversation et enjouement au XVIIe siècle: l'exemple de Madeleine de Scudéry', in *Du Goût, de la conversation et des femmes*, dir. by Alain Montandon (Clermont-Ferrand: Association des publications de la Faculté des lettres et sciences humaines, 1994), pp. 111–29 (p. 126).
20. Madeleine de Scudéry insists on their humility (pp. 22 and 77), which Myriam Dufour-Maître defines as a 'feminine virtue [that was] key to enter the field of literature discretely' ('[une] vertu féminine [qui] devient le moyen d'une subtile inscription dans le champ littéraire', Myriam Dufour-Maître, *Les Précieuses, naissance des femmes de Lettres en France au XVIIème siècle* (Paris: Champion Classiques, 2008), p. 394). Georges de Scudéry's Laura is similarly qualified in sonnet 7.6.
21. See the last tercet in sonnet 12.

CHAPTER 8

The Untranslatable Laura: Nineteenth-Century French Perspectives

Jennifer Rushworth

New critical attention has been afforded to the concept of the 'untranslatable' in recent years as a result of Barbara Cassin's *Vocabulaire européen des philosophies: dictionnaire des intraduisibles*, first published in 2004 and subsequently translated into English in 2014 as *Dictionary of Untranslatables: A Philosophical Lexicon*.[1] According to Cassin's introductory definition:

> Parler d'*intraduisibles* n'implique nullement que les termes en question, ou les expressions, les tours syntaxiques et grammaticaux, ne soient pas traduits et ne puissent pas l'être — l'intraduisible, c'est plutôt ce qu'on ne cesse pas de (ne pas) traduire.
>
> [To speak of *untranslatables* in no way implies that the terms in question, or the expressions, the syntactical or grammatical turns, are not and cannot be translated: the untranslatable is rather what one keeps on (not) translating.][2]

It is this sense of the untranslatable which I wish to invoke in my title; as this volume amply testifies, Petrarch's poetry, too, is untranslatable not because it is impossible to translate (though it may at times appear to be so), but rather because it forever calls for fresh translations, which can, happily, never be definitive or sufficient.

In this chapter Petrarch's beloved Laura is, more specifically, described as 'untranslatable' in two different ways. In Cassin's sense, Laura's name and the polysemy it generates are explored as 'what one keeps on (not) translating', through the example of various nineteenth-century French translators of Petrarch's *Canzoniere*. Laura's name evokes in turn and at times simultaneously a plethora of signifiers — *l'aura* [the breeze], *l'auro* [the laurel], *l'oro* [gold], *l'ora* [time], or *l'aurora* [dawn], to name but the principal variants — and this type of wordplay poses a constant and thorny challenge to translators of Petrarch's *Canzoniere*. By way of conclusion, however, Laura's untranslatability or resistance to translation is considered from the perspective of a more technical, ecclesiastical meaning of the word 'translation', namely 'the transference of the relics of a saint either from their original place of burial into an altar tomb or shrine, or from one shrine to another'.[3]

Though not a saint, this religious meaning of translation is argued to be relevant to Petrarch's Laura, whose burial site interested readers of the *Canzoniere* in thrall to a wider 'quest' for Laura's historical identity.[4] Before treating these two aspects of Petrarch's 'untranslatable Laura', I begin with an overview of French Petrarchism in the nineteenth century, in order to set the scene and provide some context for what will follow.

Nineteenth-Century French Petrarchism: A Brief Introduction

French Petrarchism has typically been considered to be foundational for sixteenth-century poetry by the likes of Maurice Scève, Pierre de Ronsard, or Joachim du Bellay.[5] As Jean Balsamo in particular has explored, sixteenth-century French poets turned to Petrarch as a way of reinvigorating their own national language; accordingly, the ostensible *italianisme* of these poets also often, paradoxically, masked a form of *anti-italianisme* which proclaimed that the French literary language was equal or superior even to the Italian of Petrarch.[6] Sixteenth-century French Petrarchism, whether through more or less direct translation of the medieval poet or a freer process of poetic imitation (the art of *pétrarquiser*), was fuelled by both ambivalence and rivalry with respect to its chosen model. In contrast, in this chapter I will explore a later manifestation of French Petrarchism, locatable in the nineteenth century. Unlike their sixteenth-century predecessors, nineteenth-century French readers and translators of Petrarch sought not so much to rival as to adopt the medieval poet as, controversially, somehow French.

After the ubiquity of the Petrarchan mode in sixteenth-century poetry, French Petrarchism largely fell silent, a victim of its own success. In the nineteenth century, a recognized period of Romantic medievalism, Dante is thought to be of greater importance and prominence.[7] Yet, as Edoardo Zuccato in particular has argued in relation to English examples, the influence and inspiration of Petrarch at this same time ought not to be overlooked.[8] Indebted to the early work of Lide Bertoli and more recently to Ève Duperray's wide-ranging study of French Petrarchism across the centuries, in *Petrarch and the Literary Culture of Nineteenth-Century France* I have sought to trace comprehensively this more modern French engagement with Petrarch through attention to both translation and rewriting, in and out of the canon.[9]

Nineteenth-century French Petrarchism had two identifiable and distinct types of catalyst, literary and political. Three eighteenth-century authors, Voltaire, Jean-Jacques Rousseau, and the abbé de Sade, were responsible for sowing the seeds of a second wave of French interest in Petrarch.[10] The first, Voltaire, translated the first stanza of *RVF* 126, a celebrated *canzone* which begins 'Chiare, fresche et dolci acque' [Clear, fresh, and sweet waters] and which celebrates Laura's oneness with the Provençal landscape.[11] This translation was to act as a bookmark in the *Canzoniere*, drawing French translators back to this poem time and time again.[12] The second, Rousseau, was instrumental in the fashion for what Duperray has termed 'le roman pétrarquiste' [the Petrarchan novel], through his immensely popular *Julie, ou la*

Nouvelle Héloïse.[13] The third, however, was no doubt the most significant, through his authoring of a lengthy biography of Petrarch, the three-volume *Mémoires pour la vie de François Pétrarque*.[14] The abbé de Sade was himself not only Avignonese but even, as he partly hoped to prove by way of family documents transcribed in his *Mémoires*, a descendent of Petrarch's Laura, née Laure de Noves but by marriage Laure de Sade and mother of eleven children. Such, at any rate, was Sade's thesis.

Besides these literary influences, politics also had a role in the renewal of Petrarchism in the nineteenth century. The unification of Avignon with France at the Revolution, after its prolonged status as a papal annexe, provided new inspiration for claiming the city and its illustrious medieval past as French.[15] Soon thereafter, Napoleon himself founded the Athénée de Vaucluse, an organization with the mission of promoting local culture, including Petrarch; one of the Athénée's early tasks was to organize celebrations in honour of the fifth centenary of Petrarch's birth (1804), at which the Napoleonic column was installed at Fontaine-de-Vaucluse.[16] Two further anniversaries celebrated in France as in Italy were to foment peaks of interest in Petrarch later in the century: 1874, the fifth centenary of Petrarch's death; 1904, the sixth centenary of Petrarch's birth.[17] As Henry Cochin observed on the latter occasion, such celebrations were 'le point de départ de belles périodes de travail' [the starting point for excellent periods of work], which included not only translations but also essays and editorial projects, all Petrarch-centred.[18]

It was against this backdrop, both literary and political, that nineteenth-century French Petrarchism developed. Yet unlike its sixteenth-century predecessor, Petrarchism in this later period was not primarily a result of rivalry in terms of national language, that is, the wish to demonstrate and expand the capabilities of French through recourse to the translation and importation of Italian models, among them most prominently Petrarch.[19] Rather, nineteenth-century Petrarchism functioned through adoption and appropriation, claiming that Petrarch was, indeed, French. The most explicit of such claims came early on, from the abbé de Sade, in a letter at the start of the first volume of his *Mémoires* addressing his potential Italian readers directly:

> Que diriez-vous, si on osoit vous disputer Pétrarque ? Il a reçu le jour dans le sein de votre belle contrée, cela n'est pas douteux ; la Ville d'Arezzo l'a vu naître, on ne peut pas lui contester cet honneur ; mais il a fait ses études à Carpentras, à Avignon, à Montpellier. Ses meilleurs Ouvrages ont été conçus, commencés, plusieurs même achevés sur les bords de la Sorgue ; les rochers de Vaucluse ont répété mille fois les sons harmonieux de sa lyre ; dans ces belles Odes que vous admirez tant, il prend à témoin les sources, les bois, les monts & les prés de cette solitude : enfin, c'est là qu'il a conçu ce Poëme épique auquel il doit la couronne.
>
> Il s'agit à présent de sçavoir, si un homme de Lettres n'appartient pas plus au Pays où il a été élevé, formé, instruit, où il a composé ses meilleurs Ouvrages, qu'à la terre où il a reçu & quitté la vie. C'est un problème que je vous laisse à résoudre. Je me garderois bien de dire sur cela ce que je pense : je craindrois d'exciter votre courroux, en vous enlevant un des plus grands ornemens de votre patrie.[20]

[What would you say if someone dared to dispute your claim to Petrarch? He first saw the light of day in the heart of your beautiful land, of that there can be no doubt; the town of Arezzo witnessed his birth, no other one can compete for this honour; but he studied in Carpentras, Avignon, and Montpellier. His best works were conceived, begun, and many also completed on the banks of the river Sorgue; the rocks of Vaucluse have repeated a thousand times the harmonious sounds of his lyre; in these beautiful *canzoni* which you admire so much, he calls as witness the springs, woods, mountains, and meadows of this solitary place: lastly, it is here that he conceived the epic poem to which he owes his crown.

It is necessary, then, to consider now whether a man of letters does not belong more to the country where he was brought up, formed, and educated, and where he composed his best works, than to the earth where he received life and whence he departed the same. It is a problem that I leave you to resolve among yourselves. I would rather refrain from speaking my mind on this matter; I would fear to incite your wrath, by depriving you of one of the greatest ornaments of your country.]

With this passage, Sade set the tone for French encounters with Petrarch through the following century, by boldly asserting that Petrarch was, in essence, not Italian but French. Sade, and others after him, based such a claim on innovative and idiosyncratic criteria for identity, according to which residence, education, love, and place of writing mean, or ought to mean, more in terms of identity than the traditional importance ascribed to birthplace and place of death.

Translating Petrarch into French in the nineteenth century was, in part, a way of accentuating or voicing this polemically charged claim about identity and belonging. A comprehensive study of translations and translators in nineteenth-century France published in 2012 declared that 'Le XIXe siècle n'est sans doute pas un très grand siècle pour la traduction de Pétrarque en France' [The nineteenth century is doubtless not a very important century for the translation of Petrarch in France].[21] Yet this statement is based upon the few complete French translations of the *Canzoniere* published in the nineteenth century, and neglects the many incomplete translations undertaken in the same time frame, not to mention the translation of other works by Petrarch, whether the *Trionfi* or his various works in Latin. In this period there are some six complete translations of the *Canzoniere*, frequently accompanied by the *Trionfi* and published between 1842 and 1903.[22] There are, however, countless more incomplete translations of the *Canzoniere*, which I have attempted to chart elsewhere.[23] Here I wish to return to a representative selection of these translations, in relation to one central crux of translating Petrarch's *Canzoniere*, that is, the challenge of rendering the polysemy of Laura's name and its constituent syllables.

What's in a Name? The Untranslatable Wordplay on Laura

While nineteenth-century French translators often sought, following Sade, to demonstrate and affirm Petrarch's Frenchness, this claim necessitated a revisionist approach to the poet and his oeuvre. The French adoption of Petrarch was markedly selective, privileging his vernacular love sonnets far above any of his Latin works in either poetry or prose. Yet even as far as Petrarch's sonnets were concerned, one recurrent stylistic feature was consistently denigrated by French readers after Sade: Petrarch's wordplay on the name of Laura. Simonde de Sismondi's assessment from early in the nineteenth century is, in this respect, representative:

> J'aimerais mieux que la pensée, le sentiment, la passion, me rappelassent Laure, que l'éternel jeu de mots de *lauro* (le laurier), ou *l'aura* (l'air, le souffle du matin). Le premier surtout revient sans cesse, non pas dans les poésies seulement, mais dans la vie entière de Pétrarque ; on ne saurait dire si c'est de Laure ou du laurier qu'il est amoureux, tant celui-ci lui donne d'émotion toutes les fois qu'il le rencontre, tant il en parle avec saisissement, tant il consacre de vers à le chanter.[24]

> [I would rather be reminded of Laura by thought, sentiment, and passion, than by the eternal wordplay of *lauro* (laurel) or *l'aura* (air, the morning breeze). The first especially returns incessantly, not only in Petrarch's poetry, but also throughout his entire life; it's hard to tell whether he's in love with Laura or the laurel, so much does the latter fill him with emotion every time he sees it, so vividly does he talk about it, so many verses does he dedicate to singing it.]

French readers around this time often reacted, like Sismondi, with irritation at the ambiguity and confusion that arises from Petrarch's love of puns and polysemy. These readers wanted Petrarch to be French, but only on their own terms, terms which at times necessitated the rejection of essential aspects of Petrarch's art. These same readers also wanted to celebrate Laura's Frenchness, but accompanied by a somewhat reductive reading of poems about Laura which they sought to restrict in meaning to Laura as a specific historical individual.

In such a reading, many texts had to be either expunged from the selection of Petrarch being translated (unless the translation was one of the rarer projects committed to completion) or preserved but edited so as to present to the reader a more restricted range of meanings, which, for instance, would point to Laura explicitly rather than to a laurel (one of the favourite, Ovidian-inspired images of Petrarch for his beloved).[25] As regards the approach of reduction or simplification, a particularly stark example is one translation of *RVF* 126 by A. P. A. Bouvard, in which the first reference to Laura (in the original, 'colei' [she], v. 3) is replaced by the explicit name of Laure:

> Chiare, fresche et dolci acque,
> ove le belle membra
> pose colei che sola a me par donna.

> [Clear, fresh, and sweet waters,
> where her beautiful limbs
> laid she who alone to me seems a lady.]

* * * * *

> Ondes fraîches, claire fontaine,
> Où Laure apparut à mes yeux.[26]
>
> [Fresh waters, clear fountain,
> Where Laura appeared before my eyes.]

In this translation, there is no possible ambiguity about which woman the poet is watching, while the fragmentation of Laura's body into 'belle membra' [beautiful limbs] has also been elided.

Chief among Petrarchan texts considered culpable of excessive onomastic wordplay was *RVF* 5, a sonnet in which the name of Laura (in either a Provençal or a Latin diminutive form, *Lau-re-ta*) is fragmented across and embedded in the poem.[27] Once more setting a trend, Sade had already dismissed *RVF* 5 for its

> jeu de mots puerile sur les syllabes qui composent le nom de Laure ou Laurette qu'il est impossible de rendre en François, & qui est bien au-dessous d'un génie tel que celui de Petrarque.[28]
>
> [childish wordplay on the syllables which make up the name Laure or Laurette which is impossible to render in French and which is very much beneath a genius such as that of Petrarch.]

Pierre-Louis Ginguené reiterated this same criticism in his influential multi-volume *Histoire littéraire d'Italie*, similarly admitting that he would reproach Petrarch for 'des jeux de mots puérils' [childish wordplay] — borrowing liberally from Sade's earlier accusation — 'tels surtout que cette étrange décomposition du nom de Laure, ou plutôt de *Laureta*, en trois parties' [such as in particular that strange decomposition of the name of Laura, or rather of *Laureta*, in three parts].[29] Finally, another translator at the very start of the twentieth century, Ernest Cabadé, similarly judged that:

> C'est un véritable tour de force que ce morceau ; la pensée est, du reste, plus que subtile, elle est obscure, torturée ; somme toute, ce n'est pas ce sonnet qui ajoutera rien à la gloire du poète. C'est une espèce d'acrostiche sans grande saveur.[30]
>
> [This piece is a real *tour de force*; the idea is, besides, more than subtle, it is obscure, contorted; all in all, this sonnet will not add anything to the poet's glory. It is a type of acrostic without great taste.]

These comments suggest the constancy of the low regard in which *RVF* 5 was held by French readers and translators throughout the nineteenth century. Yet in describing the sonnet as an acrostic Cabadé also unwittingly suggests one possible way of translating this particular sonnet, one which, indeed, had already been followed by Emma Mahul in the second volume of her five-part translation of all 317 sonnets from Petrarch's *Canzoniere*. Here is the first stanza of Mahul's necessarily free translation:

> Louer son nom n'est pas petite chose:
> Amour d'un trait l'écrivit dans mon cœur.
> Unissez-vous à la bouche demi-close,

> Redites-le, soupirs, moi je ne l'ose
> Et je craindrais d'altérer sa douceur.³¹
>
> [Love in a flash wrote her name in my heart,
> And praising it is no small matter.
> Unite yourselves to my parted lips,
> Repeat it, sighs, for I dare not
> And would fear to spoil its sweetness.]

In this way, while Sade dismissed the sonnet as untranslatable (in his words, 'impossible de rendre en François' [impossible to render in French]), Mahul demonstrates that — returning to Cassin's definition of the untranslatable — the very difficulty of translating this sonnet invites translation and retranslation, in innovative and even virtuosic, if necessarily imperfect, ways.

Besides *RVF* 5, especially challenging for translators reluctant to engage with onomastic play is a series of four sonnets in the middle of the *Canzoniere* which all open with the word 'L'aura' (*RVF* 194 and 196–98). As we have seen, this type of sonorous, homonymical pun (Laura/laurel) was not popular with Petrarch's late eighteenth- and nineteenth-century readers. Nonetheless, nineteenth-century French translators who tackled these sonnets were still forced to find some sort of solution to this further Petrarchan untranslatable. The most literal solution — 'La brise' [The breeze] — was possible but unsatisfactory in its loss of the pun on Laura's name.³² The most similar in terms of sound — 'L'aure' — preserved Laura's name, but was potentially meaningless, hence, perhaps, the embarrassed italicization of this solution.³³ As Anatole de Montesquiou pointed out in a note to his translation of *RVF* 239 (a *sestina* in which one of the recurrent keywords is also 'l'aura'/Laura), the putative word 'l'aure' is not, alas, French:

> Pour la consonnance et le jeu de mots obligé, j'ai essayé l'emploi de ce mot italien francisé. J'aurais bien voulu trouver pour cela quelque autorisation dans notre vieux langage : mais toutes mes recherches ont été vaines ; le mot *aure*, qui, s'il existait, signifierait *brise*, et justifierait, par la langue italienne et par la langue latine, une assez illustre origine, a toujours été étranger à la France.³⁴
>
> [For the sake of consonance and the necessary wordplay, I have experimented with using this Frenchified Italian word. I would have liked very much to find for this some authorization in our old language, but my investigation has been to no avail; the word *aure*, which, if it were to exist, would mean *breeze*, and would prove, through the Italian and Latin languages, quite an illustrious origin, has always been foreign to France.]

Petrarch's play on 'l'aura'/Laura has since been traced back to the Provençal troubadour Arnaut Daniel.³⁵ Seemingly unaware of this Occitan model, however, Montesquiou suggests that the creation of a new word, 'l'aure', on the model of the Italian, lacks the sanction of historical precedent but is nonetheless too appealing a solution to be discarded. Here we see in miniature how translation can directly enrich and expand a language, by introducing new words and encouraging recourse to neologisms.

For the four 'L'aura' sonnets, however, Montesquiou opted not for 'l'aure', but rather for other similar sounding, suitably Petrarchan words. Thus, in Montesquiou's translation *RVF* 194 begins with the phrase 'L'*o*rageux air' [The stormy air], retaining the allusion to Laura's name ('L'or'/Laure) through premodification of the noun 'air' (where the reference to 'L'aura' as breeze is retained).[36] In contrast, it is precisely the word 'L'air' which is chosen by Joseph Poulenc to introduce his translation of all four of these sonnets, in a compromise between sense and sound.[37] Then, to start *RVF* 196 Montesquiou opts for 'L'*au*rore' [The dawn], accompanied by a rather defensive footnote:

> Je sais fort bien que, dans le texte, il n'est pas question d'*aurore* ; mais j'ai voulu, par un son, donner l'idée d'un jeu de mots qui plaisait à la tendresse du poète.[38]
>
> [I know well that the original has nothing to do with *aurore* [dawn]; but I wanted, through a sound, to give the idea of a play on words which pleased the tenderness of the poet.]

This choice is sympathetic to the *Canzoniere*, since Laura is, after all, assimilated to Aurora elsewhere (see, for instance, *RVF* 291), although clearly Montesquiou remains uneasy with this solution.

It would be interesting to look at solutions to the opening homonymy of these four 'L'aura' sonnets across a wider time period and between different target languages, as well as important to widen the survey to other sonnets in the *Canzoniere* with similar forms of onomastic wordplay. For the present, however, the nineteenth-century French examples cited above amply demonstrate that Laura is, through her very name, 'what one keeps on (not) translating'. In the absence of any wholly satisfactory solution, translators repeatedly returned to Petrarch's sonnets as a space of experimentation and compromise. Petrarchan wordplay was, in short, not merely unpopular but also challenging and intriguing for nineteenth-century French translators.

Translating the Body: Gravesites and the 1874 Petrarchan Celebrations

As noted at the start of this chapter, translation in an ecclesiastical sphere can refer to the movement of a saint's relics (whether whole body or fragmented remains) from one resting place to another, the latter usually chosen as a place of greater honour or the centre of particular devotion to the saint in question. The day on which such a translation takes place is often commemorated in liturgical calendars. To take one example, Benezet of Avignon lived in the twelfth century and built a bridge over the Rhone, the famous *pont d'Avignon*, where he was interred in a chapel. In 1669 Benezet's grave was disturbed by a flood and his body found to be incorrupt. The saint was then translated to Avignon cathedral, though he was moved again in the nineteenth century to the church of Saint Didier.[39] Neither Laura nor Petrarch have any claims to such sanctity, yet their gravesites bear witness to a similar process of veneration and even a desire for translation, as I will suggest in the final part of this chapter.

Interest in Laura's grave is an important strand of French Petrarchism, from the sixteenth century on. The story begins in 1533, when Maurice Scève claimed to have found Laura's grave in a church in Avignon; authenticating evidence included a poem purportedly by Petrarch, as well as a medal depicting a lady with the inscription M.L.M.I., which Scève interpreted as 'Madonna Laura Morta Iace' [Here lies the dead lady Laura].[40] This exciting discovery might eventually have been dismissed as a hoax, but for the royal *placet* from François I who visited the site and composed a poem in honour of the find.[41] Following Scève (though not all were convinced by his claim), nineteenth-century French Petrarchism did not require the translation of Laura, since her remains were already present in the city where her cult was particularly fervent. Instead, the presence of Laura's body in Avignon on newly French soil, after the city's unification with France at the Revolution, in a certain sense preceded and laid the foundation for the translation of Petrarch's poetry into French, and certainly aided the claim that Petrarch was French, as discussed above.

Petrarch's body, however, lay far from Avignon in the small hilltop village of Arquà. On the occasion of the 1874 celebrations marking 500 years since Petrarch's death, the translator Edmond Lafond lamented Petrarch's distance from Avignon in the following sonnet:

> De saint Pierre le Rhône avait reçu la barque,
> Et les papes français se faisaient provençaux,
> Lorsqu'un vendredi saint tu vis Laure, ô Pétrarque ;
> Cinq siècles ont, depuis, passé sur vos tombeaux.
> Trop loin d'elle, tu dors sur la colline d'Arque ;
> Vaucluse te rappelle au milieu de ses eaux ;
> Les sonneurs de sonnets t'y nomment leur monarque,
> Viens compter tes sujets dans ces chanteurs nouveaux.
> Au bruit de nos concerts, dont elle semble fière,
> Ta dame, secouant son antique poussière,
> Se lève du cercueil que lui garde Avignon.
> Triomphe du sonnet qui la rend immortelle !
> La voici, grâce aux vers qui célèbrent son nom,
> Vieille de cinq cents ans, mais toujours jeune et belle.[42]

[Of Saint Peter the Rhône had received the ship,
And the French popes were making themselves Provençal,
When one Good Friday you saw Laura, O Petrarch;
Five centuries have, since, passed over your graves.

Too far from her, you sleep on the hill of Arquà;
Vaucluse is calling you back in the middle of her waters;
There the sonnet-ringers name you their monarch,
Come count your subjects in these new singers.

At the sound of our concerts, of which she seems proud,
Your lady, shaking off the ancient dust,
Gets up from the grave which Avignon has kept for her.

Triumph of the sonnet which makes her beautiful!
There she is, thanks to the verses which celebrate her name,
Five hundred years old, but still young and beautiful.]

In this sonnet by a translator of Petrarch, published in an appendix to the work of another translator of the same, the two meanings of translation explored in this chapter rub shoulders.[43] Translation of Petrarch's sonnets from Italian into French is accompanied by a desire to transport Petrarch's body from northern Italy to join Laura in Avignon. This translator-poet laments that Petrarch sleeps 'Trop loin' [Too far] from Laura, and seeks to unsettle the cosiness otherwise suggested by the rhyme of 'Pétrarque' and 'Arque' by expounding the greater claims of Avignon on the poet. Laura, meanwhile, is imbued in this sonnet with an odour of sanctity, since she shares with saints such as the aforementioned Benezet the holy attribute of being physically incorrupt. She is, as Lafond declares, 'Vieille de cinq cents ans, mais toujours jeune et belle' [Five hundred years old, but still young and beautiful]. Laura's incorruptibility is, however, thanks not to saintliness but to poetry, and more specifically the sonnet.

In this case Laura does not need translating because she is already in Avignon, whence she joins her voice to the clamour of Petrarch's nineteenth-century French admirers who desire the translation (in both senses of the word) of his corporeal and poetical remains.[44] Despite concerns about aspects of Petrarch's poetics (in particular the play on Laura's name, deemed, as we have seen, excessive and puerile), nineteenth-century French readers of the poet were keen to bring Petrarch home to Avignon. Yet it was perhaps Petrarch's resistance to this translation that kept both himself and Laura ripe for retranslation. Returning to Cassin, the untranslatability of Laura — Petrarch's beloved and a symbol of his poetry — is precisely that which ensures that the *Canzoniere* 'keeps on (not) being translated', in different languages across the centuries, in a rich tapestry of reception history of which this chapter has followed but one shimmering thread.

Notes to Chapter 8

1. *Vocabulaire européen des philosophies: dictionnaire des intraduisibles*, ed. by Barbara Cassin (Paris: Seuil/Le Robert, 2004); *Dictionary of Untranslatables: A Philosophical Lexicon*, ed. by Barbara Cassin, Emily Apter, Jacques Lezra, and Michael Wood (Princeton: Princeton University Press, 2014). For a useful range of recent critical responses to this volume, see *Translation and the Untranslatable*, ed. by Michael Syrotinski (= *Paragraph*, 38.2 (July 2015)).
2. Cassin, 'Présentation', in *Vocabulaire européen des philosophies*, pp. xvii–xxii (p. xvii); Cassin, 'Introduction', trans. by Michael Wood, in *Dictionary of Untranslatables*, pp. xvii–xx (p. xvii).
3. Definition of 'translation' cited from *The Oxford Dictionary of the Christian Church*, ed. by F. L. Cross and E. A. Livingstone, 3rd edn (Oxford: Oxford University Press, 1997), p. 1637.
4. This phrase borrows from 'The Quest for the Historical Beatrice' in Alison Milbank, *Dante and the Victorians* (Manchester: Manchester University Press, 1998), pp. 102–16.
5. See, for instance, Sara Sturm-Maddox, 'The French Petrarch', in *Petrarch and the European Lyric Tradition: Annali d'Italianistica*, 22 (2004), ed. by Dino S. Cervigni, 171–87; Sara Sturm-Maddox, *Ronsard, Petrarch and the 'Amours'* (Gainesville: University Press of Florida, 1999); *Les Poètes français de la Renaissance et Pétrarque*, ed. by Jean Balsamo (Geneva: Droz, 2004). For a broader European perspective, see Leonard Forster, *The Icy Fire: Five Studies in Petrarchism* (Cambridge: Cambridge University Press, 1969) and William J. Kennedy, *The Site of Petrarchism: Early Modern National Sentiment in Italy, France, and England* (Baltimore: Johns Hopkins University Press, 2003).
6. See Jean Balsamo, *Les Rencontres des Muses: italianisme et anti-italianisme dans les Lettres françaises de la fin du XVIe siècle* (Geneva: Éditions Slatkine, 1992), especially chapter 5 on 'Le "*Pétrarque français*"', pp. 217–54.

7. For a general overview of French medievalism in this period, see *La Fabrique du Moyen Âge au XIXe siècle: représentations du moyen âge dans la culture et la littérature françaises du XIXe siècle*, ed. by Simone Bernard-Griffiths, Pierre Glaudes, and Bertrand Vibert (Paris: Honoré Champion, 2006). On the nineteenth-century obsession with Dante, see: *Dante in the Nineteenth Century: Reception, Canonicity, Popularization*, ed. by Nick Havely (Oxford: Peter Lang, 2011); *Dante in the Long Nineteenth Century: Nationality, Identity, and Appropriation*, ed. by Aida Audeh and Nick Havely (Oxford: Oxford University Press, 2012); Michael Pitwood, *Dante and the French Romantics* (Geneva: Droz, 1985).
8. Edoardo Zuccato, *Petrarch in Romantic England* (Houndsmill: Palgrave Macmillan, 2008). See also Gerhart Hoffmeister, 'The Petrarchan Mode in European Romanticism', in *European Romanticism: Literary Cross-Currents, Modes, and Models*, ed. by Gerhart Hoffmeister (Detroit: Wayne State University Press, 1990), pp. 97–111.
9. See: Lide Bertoli, *La Fortuna del Petrarca in Francia nella prima metà del secolo XIX: note ed appunti* (Livorno: Raffaello Giusti, 1916) and 'I traduttori francesi del Petrarca nel secolo XIX', in *Raccolta di studi di storia e critica letteraria dedicata a Francesco Flamini da' suoi discepoli* (Pisa: Mariotti, 1918), pp. 653–79; Ève Duperray, *L'Or des mots: une lecture de Pétrarque et du mythe littéraire de Vaucluse des origines à l'orée du XXe siècle: histoire du pétrarquisme en France* (Paris: Publications de la Sorbonne, 1997); Jennifer Rushworth, *Petrarch and the Literary Culture of Nineteenth-Century France: Translation, Appropriation, Transformation* (Woodbridge: The Boydell Press, 2017).
10. On the wider French interest in medieval matters in the eighteenth century, see Alicia C. Montoya, *Medievalist Enlightenment from Charles Perrault to Jean-Jacques Rousseau* (Cambridge: Brewer, 2013).
11. See Voltaire, *Essai sur les mœurs et l'esprit des nations* (1756), ed. by Bruno Bernard, John Renwick, Nicholas Cronk, and Janet Godden, 9 vols (Oxford: Voltaire Foundation, 2009–), IV (2011), 274. All quotations of the original Italian text are from Francesco Petrarca, *Canzoniere*, ed. by Marco Santagata, 4th edn (Milan: Mondadori, 2010).
12. French translations of the first stanza of *RVF* 126 published between 1756 and 1903 are listed in Appendix 2 of Rushworth, *Petrarch and the Literary Culture of Nineteenth-Century France*.
13. See Ève Duperray, 'Le mythe littéraire de Vaucluse dans le roman pétrarquiste de *L'Astrée* (1607–1628) à *Adriani* (1853)', in *Dynamique d'une expansion culturelle: Pétrarque en Europe XIVe–XXe siècle: actes du XXVIe congrès international du CEFI, Turin et Chambéry, 11–15 décembre 1995: à la mémoire de Franco Simone*, ed. by Pierre Blanc (Paris: Honoré Champion, 2001), pp. 417–27, as well as Duperray, *L'Or des mots*, pp. 109–23.
14. Jacques F. P. A. de Sade, abbé, *Mémoires pour la vie de François Pétrarque, tirés de ses œuvres et des auteurs contemporains, avec des notes ou dissertations, & les pieces justificatives*, 3 vols (Amsterdam: Arskée et Mercus, 1764–67).
15. See René Moulinas, *Histoire de la Révolution d'Avignon* (Avignon: Aubanel, 1986).
16. Materials relating to the early days of this organization are gathered in *Mémoires de l'Athénée de Vaucluse, contenant le compte rendu des travaux de cette Société depuis son institution, et le recueil des ouvrages en prose et en vers, lus à sa séance publique* (Avignon: De l'Imprimerie d'Alph. Berenguier, An XII/1804).
17. On these anniversaries see Duperray, *L'Or des mots*, pp. 222–57, as well as Harald Hendrix, 'Petrarch 1804–1904: Nation-Building and Glocal Identities' and Francesca Zantedeschi, 'Petrarch 1874: Pan-National Celebrations and Provençal Regionalism', both in *Commemorating Writers in Nineteenth-Century Europe: Nation-Building and Centenary Fever*, ed. by Joseph Leerssen and Ann Rigney (Basingstoke: Palgrave Macmillan, 2014), pp. 117–33 and pp. 134–51 respectively.
18. Henry Cochin, *Le Jubilé de Pétrarque (extrait du 'Correspondant')* (Paris: De Soye et fils, 1904), p. 7.
19. See Balsamo, *Les Rencontres des Muses*.
20. Sade, *Mémoires*, I, pp. lxxi–lxxii.
21. Christine Lombez and others, 'Poésie', in *Histoire des traductions en langue française: XIXe siècle: 1815–1914*, ed. by Yves Chevrel, Lieven D'Hulst, and Christine Lombez (Lagrasse: Éditions Verdier, 2012), pp. 345–442 (p. 378).
22. Ferdinand de Gramont, *Poésies de Pétrarque: traduction complète: sonnets, canzones, triomphes* (Paris:

Paul Masgana, 1842); Anatole de Montesquiou, *Sonnets, canzones, ballades et sextines de Pétrarque traduits en vers*, 2 vols (Paris: Leroy, 1842); Joseph Poulenc, *Rimes de Pétrarque, traduites en vers, texte en regard*, 4 vols (Paris: A. Lacroix, 1865), of which a second edition was also published in 1887: *Rimes de Pétrarque: traduction complète en vers des sonnets, canzones, sextines, ballades, madrigaux et triomphes, par Joseph Poulenc: deuxième édition, revue et corrigée*, 2 vols (Paris: Librairie des Bibliophiles, 1887); Francisque Reynard, *Les Rimes de François Pétrarque: traduction nouvelle* (Paris: G. Charpentier, 1883); Fernand Brisset, *Les Sonnets de Pétrarque à Laure: traduction nouvelle avec introduction et notes* (Paris: Perrin et Cie, 1899) and idem, *Canzones, triomphes et poésies diverses: traduction nouvelle avec introduction et notes* (Paris: Perrin et Cie, 1903); Hippolyte Godefroy, *Poésies complètes de Francesco Petrarca* (Montluçon: Imprimerie A. Herbin, 1900). Note that in fact the last, Godefroy's translation, is not complete, despite its titular claims, but omits seven poems: *RVF* 55, 59, 63, 99, 149, 314, and 324.

23. See Appendix 1 in Rushworth, *Petrarch and the Literary Culture of Nineteenth-Century France*.
24. 'Chapitre X : Influence du Dante sur son siècle ; Pétrarque', in J. C. L. Simonde de Sismondi, *De la littérature du Midi de l'Europe*, 4 vols (Paris and Strasbourg: Treuttel et Würtz, 1813), I, 386–425 (pp. 408–09).
25. On the Ovidian laurel in Petrarch see Peter Hainsworth, 'The Myth of Daphne in the *Rerum vulgarium fragmenta*', *Italian Studies*, 34.1 (1979), 28–44.
26. A. P. A. Bouvard, *Fables nouvelles et poésies diverses* (Auxerre: Imprimerie de Gallot-Fournier, 1835), p. 183.
27. On this poem, see Fredi Chiappelli, 'L'esegesi petrarchesca e l'elezione del "sermo lauranus" per il linguaggio dei *Rerum vulgarium fragmenta*', *Studi petrarcheschi*, n.s., 4 (1987), 47–85.
28. Sade, *Mémoires*, I, 177.
29. Pierre-Louis Ginguené, *Histoire littéraire de l'Italie*, 9 vols (Paris: Chez Michaud frères, 1811–35), II, 564.
30. Ernest Cabadé, *Les Sonnets de Pétrarque traduits en sonnets français avec une préface de M. de Trèverret* (Paris: Alphonse Lemerre, 1902), p. 5.
31. *Choix de sonnets de Pétrarque traduits par Madame S. Emma Mahul des comtes Dejean: seconde édition revue, corrigée et augmentée de la traduction de différentes poésies de Pétrarque* (Florence: Héritiers Botta, 1867), p. 125.
32. In the translation of Francisque Reynard, *Les Rimes de François Pétrarque: traduction nouvelle* (Paris: G. Charpentier, 1883), pp. 130–33, all four sonnets start with 'La brise'. See also Emma Mahul, *Sonnets inédits traduits de Pétrarque, cinquième publication complétant la totalité des sonnets* (Rome: Héritiers Botta, 1877), p. 73, where the translation of *RVF* 197 likewise begins with 'La brise'.
33. See, for instance, Gramont, *Poésies de Pétrarque*, pp. 134–36, as well as Philibert Le Duc, *Les Sonnets de Pétrarque: traduction complète en sonnets réguliers, avec introduction et commentaire*, 2 vols (Paris: Leon Willem, 1877–79), II, 12, 16, 18, and 20. 'L'aure' and 'L'Aure', albeit not in italics, is also the translation chosen by Godefroy, *Poésies complètes de Francesco Petrarca*, pp. 181–84.
34. Montesquiou, *Sonnets, canzones, ballades et sextines de Pétrarque*, II, 112.
35. Arnaut Daniel described himself in one poem as 'Ieu sui Arnaut qu'amas l'aura' [I am Arnaut who gathers the breeze], as noted by Gianfranco Contini, 'Préhistoire de l'*aura* de Pétrarque', in his *Varianti e altra linguistica: una raccolta di saggi 1938–1968* (Turin: Einaudi, 1970), pp. 193–99 (first published in *Actes et mémoires du premier congrès international de langue et littérature du Midi de la France* (Avignon: Palais du Roure, 1957), pp. 113–18).
36. Montesquiou, *Sonnets, canzones, ballades et sextines de Pétrarque*, II, 45.
37. Poulenc, *Rimes de Pétrarque* (1877), I, 234 and 236–38.
38. Montesquiou, *Sonnets, canzones, ballades et sextines de Pétrarque*, II, 48.
39. Details from *The Oxford Dictionary of Saints*, ed. by David Hugh Farmer, 5th edn (Oxford: Oxford University Press, 2004), pp. 52–53.
40. On this discovery, see Olivier Millet, 'Le tombeau de la morte et la voix du poète: la mémoire de Pétrarque en France autour de 1533', in *Regards sur le passé dans l'Europe des XVIe et XVIIe siècles: actes du colloque organisé par l'Université de Nancy II (14 au 16 décembre 1995)*, ed. by Francine Wild (Berne: Peter Lang, 1997), pp. 183–95, and Enzo Giudici, 'Bilancio di un'annosa questione: Maurice Scève e "la scoperta" della tomba di Laura', *Quaderni di filologia e lingue romanze*, 2 (1980), 3–70.

41. The poem found in the grave and supposedly by Petrarch is reproduced in Sade, *Mémoires*, II, 41 ('Notes justificatives'), with the poetic epitaph by François I on p. 42.
42. Edmond Lafond, 'Le centenaire de Pétrarque', cited from 'Appendice: fêtes de Vaucluse et d'Avignon: sonnets à Pétrarque et à Laure', in Le Duc, *Les Sonnets de Pétrarque*, II, 351–82 (pp. 375–76). On the occasion of the 1874 Petrarchan celebrations Lafond's sonnet, as Le Duc notes in a footnote, was awarded third prize and a silver medal under the category *Sonnet sur Pétrarque* [*Sonnet about Petrarch*].
43. For Edmond Lafond's earlier project of translating Petrarch, undertaken with his uncle, see Ernest Lafond and Edmond Lafond, *Dante, Pétrarque, Michel-Ange, Tasse: sonnets choisis traduits en vers et précédés d'une étude sur chaque poëte* (Paris: Comptoir des Imprimeurs-Unis, 1848), especially pp. 91–326 for the section on Petrarch, which includes translations of 192 sonnets from the *Canzoniere*.
44. For the pun on 'remains' and an analysis of a wider interest in the graves of poets in the period, see Samantha Matthews, *Poetical Remains: Poets' Graves, Bodies, and Books in the Nineteenth Century* (Oxford: Oxford University Press, 2004).

CHAPTER 9

❖

Orpheus versus Hermes: On a Few Twentieth-Century French Translators of the *Canzoniere*

Riccardo Raimondo

Introduction: The Imaginary of the Translator

A synchronic and diachronic study of translations can help us explore the complex dynamics of the reception of a literary work through history and examine the traces made by its reception on the strata of time. Some translations prove to be most significant as they show a particularly fortunate — or incredibly unfortunate — dialogue between the author and his translator. Not only can they become literary landmarks acknowledged as equal to the source texts, they also become historical artefacts revealing the traces left by a translational tradition, leaving a permanent tinge on the literary complexion of nations. It seems many translations of Petrarch's *Canzoniere* belong in this category and I wish to take their 'numinous power' as an opportunity to explore a few notions that are central in contemporary translation studies, especially what I wish to call the 'imaginary of translation'.

How can the main features of a translation and its translator be identified and described? What part do imagination and interpretation play in the choices made by the translator? These questions can be answered by means of a synthetic perspective on translation opposing two mythical figures, Hermes and Orpheus. Relying on mythology, I will identify several types of translators and profile their various imaginaries and hermeneutic approaches.[1]

Indeed, it is crucial to examine the processes through which the imaginary and imagination feed the dynamics of translation practices. As a matter of fact, many choices originate in the translator's creative imagination, which is embodied in his or her linguistic or even poetic choices, whether the translator is aware of the process or not.[2] I will therefore deal with translation from the angle of *genetics* in a broad sense, rethinking its nature in the light of imagination and hermeneutics. For it is thanks to such interdisciplinarity[3] that one can hope to organize the many intertwined factors which are at play in literary translation in a consistent system embracing both the linguistic dimension and the socio-cultural background.[4]

The creative imagination from which the translator's choices derive could be considered, from a Jungian point of view, as an 'active imagination'[5] which is embodied in the words chosen: in this respect, the translating imagination can be said to have a 'germinal disposition'.[6] Such a conception of imagination echoes Giambattista Vico, who in *Scienza nova* (1744)[7] develops his theory of the 'fantastic universals', relating imagination to poetry (*poiesis*, ποίησις, 'creation') and to the way societies produce and transform knowledge through history. In this context, my goal is obviously not to reinvent a 'theory of imagination' as Paul Ricœur intended,[8] but rather to envision a 'poetics of the will',[9] examining a certain amount of phenomena and experiences that 'combine theory and practice'.[10] Carrying out this inquiry is a way to offer a few thoughts on this 'mental entity', this 'fabric with which our abstract ideas or concepts are tailored', this 'ingredient in an inscrutable, enigmatic mental alchemy'[11] called imagination.

The first metaphor bears the name of Hermes, the messenger of the gods and the one who lives in a place of transit located between Mount Olympus and the human world. It is a mythological metaphor for a translation that is somehow servile in its literalism, taken hostage by the signified and subdued by signifiers. Hermes is in fact — according to Charles Le Blanc — 'enchained and enslaved by the content of the message (Hermes cannot tell what he wants), but also by its form since it completely overshadows him as an individual (he cannot deliver his message as he would like to)'.[12] Hermes is deprived of any freedom regarding the delivery of his message — translations of the Hermes kind will often be a sort of semantic transposition.

On the other hand, Orpheus stands for the unease that has been typical of translators since Cicero and Saint Jerome, that is to say the difficulty to remedy the *dissidio* going on between meaning and form — that is where the translator's freedom lies. Thus, Orpheus looks for ways to produce a consistent and satisfying adaptation, one that does not simply communicate the content but also recreates a seductive literary form. In this perspective, conveying the meaning is still the main imperative and the form becomes an *effect* (according to a definition by Jean-René Ladmiral)[13] to be rendered in an effort to 'leave on the reader, through translation, the same impression [...] as if he were reading the work in the original', as Schleiermacher famously wrote.[14] In other words, this approach considers the *formal* aspect of translation as a 'dynamic equivalent' according to Eugene A. Nida.[15] Disciples of Orpheus will thus favour *contrast* in their practice. According to an 'Orpheist' such as Jean-Charles Vegliante, — the figure of Orpheus 'groping around in the dark better mirrors the literary translator who is confronted with forms that "can hold" thanks to their particular web of signification, the elusive and fragile *vis formans* (Dante) which is to be *revived* without being *lost*'.[16]

Let us draft some useful equations to clarify these categories, retracing the evolution of a few translations of Petrarch's *Canzoniere*.[17]

Hermes the Prisoner

Gérard Genot's *Chansonnier* can be considered as an example of a translation worked under the aegis of Hermes:

> (1) Voi ch'ascoltate in **rime sparse** il suono
> Di quei sospiri ond'io nudriva 'l core
> In sul mio primo **giovenile errore**
> Quand'era in parte altr'uom da quel ch'i' sono,
>
> Del **vario stile** in ch'io piango et ragiono
> Fra le **vane speranze**, e 'l **van dolore**,
> Ove sia chi per prova intenda amore,
> Spero trovar pietà, non che perdono.
>
> Ma ben veggio or sì come al popol tutto
> Favola fui gran tempo, onde sovente,
> Di me medesmo meco mi **vergogno**;
>
> Et del mio **vaneggiar** vergogna è 'l frutto,
> E 'l pentersi, e 'l conoscer chiaramente
> Che quanto piace al mondo è breve sogno.
>
> *hendecasyllables*
> **ABBA ABBA CDE CDE**

[Petrarch, *Rerum vulgarium fragmenta*, ed. by Giuseppe Savoca (Florence: Olschki, 2008)]

> (2) Vous écoutez en **rimes éparses** le son
> De ces soupirs dont j'ai nourri mon cœur
> En ma première et **juvénile erreur**,
> Quand j'étais en partie autre homme que ne suis,
>
> Pour le **style variable** où je pleure et devise
> Entre les **vains espoirs** et la **vaine douleur**,
> Près de qui entendît par épreuve l'amour
> J'espère de trouver pitié voire pardon.
>
> Mais je vois maintenant comment du peuple entier
> Je fus grand temps la fable, en sorte que souvent
> De moi-même à part moi je sens **vergogne**.
>
> Et d'avoir **divagué** la vergogne est le fruit,
> Et repentir, et connaissance claire
> Que ce qui plaît au monde est, sans durée, un songe.
>
> *Heterometry (mostly alexandrines, a few decasyllables).*
> *Some slight irregularities. No rhyme scheme.*

[© Petrarch, *Chansonnier, Rerum vulgarium fragmenta*, ed. by Giuseppe Savoca, trans. by Gérard Genot (Paris: Les Belles Lettres, 2009), reproduced by permission]

You are listening, in scattered rhymes, to the sound
Of these sighs on which I fed my heart
In my first erring youth,
When I was partly another man than I am,

For my variable style when I weep and converse
Between vain hopes and vain pain,
Among those who knew the ordeal of love
I hope to find pity, or even pardon.

But now I see how of all the people
I was for long the fable, so that often
I myself of myself feel ashamed.

And of raving, shame is the fruit,
And repent and clear knowledge
That what delights the world is fleeting, a dream.

[English translation by Fanny Quément, previously unpublished]

The translation seems almost transparent as regards the rules of direct visibility and shows an extreme attention to the transposition of each term (*vergogna* > *vergogne*; *giovenile* > *juvénile*; etc.). Indeed, Gérard Genot refers to Giuseppe Savoca's critical edition to complete his translation. Savoca's research on the manuscripts (2008)[18] and his edition of the *Canzoniere* (2008)[19] are based on an analysis of textual concordances. For Genot, translating the *Canzoniere* thus consisted in conducting lexicographic and semantic research, with a specific attempt to contextualize. Genot was intent on reproducing structures, geometries and sonorities via direct transpositions and transparent re-textualizations.

According to Genot himself, his translation actually pays very little attention to style, though it is obviously not due to any kind of laziness. For him, style is generally one of these things that cannot be translated,[20] even if he reveals to the reader some of the elements he took into account when transposing, such as lexical archaisms. In his notes to the translation (pp. xcv–cix), he also explains how he dealt with metrics:

> Traduire vers par vers, en allant à la ligne pour l'œil, et si possible en respectant l'ordre des mots, sauf lorsque les deux langues présentent des automatismes différents, et que calquer ceux de l'une dans l'autre reviendrait à donner l'impression fausse d'un procédé intentionnel là où il n'y a que la manifestation d'une constante générale.
>
> [Translating line by line, spacing the lines properly for the eye, and respecting word order as much as possible, unless the two languages work so differently that imitating what is automatic in one of them would eventually give the misleading impression that there was an intentional design when there was only something standard.] (introd., p. xcvi)

It is impossible for him to translate rhythm by coining a metric which 'would hold only at the cost of modifications that would impoverish the text and which, even more than a translation in prose, would betray Petrarch's metrics' (introd., p. xcvi). Genot therefore goes for a poetic prose following the progression of the Italian text, hoping not to lose 'cadence effects'. No doubt, this solution is not flawless. For instance, as Genot says himself, 'what is irreversibly lost is harmony, the vocalic flow' (introd., p. xcvi).

This is why Genot is more concentrated on a semantic translation. He translated for example 'avoir divagué' for 'vaneggiar' in a sort of semantic transposition that would save the etymology of the word. In the same vein, Clément Marot (*c.* 1541–44)[21] translated this as 'vain exercice' cutting the Italian word into two parts — the adjectival root (*vano*) and the verbal suffix (*-eggiare*) meaning an action, an 'exercise'. In a similar way, Vasquin Philieul (1548–55)[22] translated it as 'vaine entreprise' and Jerôme d'Alvost (1584)[23] as 'vain labeur'.

His experience as a translator therefore illustrates a choice between two opposite incentives, conciliating the desire to achieve a purely semantic translation, and the necessity to limit the damage inevitably inflicted on form. In other words, Genot's translation is not *segmental*; he does not aim at 'transcoding' according to the definition by Maurice Pergnier.[24] He is hoping, however, 'to give a global equivalent of what is stated',[25] without brutally neglecting the poetic dimension. The utopian views supported by the disciples of Hermes can thus be summed up by the following motto: *quality of exegesis through transparency of form and vice versa.*

Translating with Orpheus

Style, 'an extremely complex crossroads in the structure of language',[26] is crucially at stake in translation. It is present throughout the text — in the macrocosmic forms of speech and syntax as much as in the microcosm of morphology, punctuation and typography. It involves literary genres, diction, the way ideas and poetic images are threaded, the use of figures of speech, and so on.

According to Taber, the question of how to translate style can be answered in two different ways. He draws perfectly[27] a common polarity, two tendencies that seem irresistible: (*a*) on the one hand, there is always a will to recreate, more or less analogically, the stylistic features of the source text in the target text, which could be called an 'attempt at familiarization'; (*b*) on the other, there can be an attempt at recreation, a drastic re-textualization, a practice of *contrast* aiming, for instance, to modernize the source text or to give a specific interpretation of it. In order to illustrate this polarity, let us read more translations of the first sonnet in the *Canzoniere*, a first one by Yves Bonnefoy and another by Jean-Yves Masson.[28] While both translators do share the same desire to preserve the sonnet form, all their stylistic choices can be contrasted.

(1) Voi ch'ascoltate in **rime sparse** il suono
di quei sospiri ond'io nudriva 'l core
in su'l mio primo giovenile errore
quand'era in parte altr'uom da quel ch'i' sono,

del vario stile in ch'io piango et ragiono,
fra le vane speranze e 'l van dolore,
ove sia chi per prova intenda amore,
spero trovar pietà, nonché perdono.

Ma ben veggio or sì come al popol tutto
favola fui gran tempo, onde sovente,
di me medesmo meco mi vergogno;

et del mio **vaneggiar** vergogna è 'l frutto,
e 'l pentérsi, e 'l conoscer chiaramente
che quanto piace al mondo è breve sogno.

hendecasyllables
ABBA ABBA CDE CDE

[Petrarch, *Opere italiane*, ed. by Marco Santagata
(Milan: Mondadori, 1996)]

(2) Pour ces écrits, plaintes, ressassements
Ballottés[29]
Heterometry (mostly alexandrines, a few decasyllables).
Some loose lines. No rhyme scheme.

From you who can hear, in my scattered rhymes,
All this whimpering with which I watered my heart
In the wanderings of my early youth,
When I was other [*autre*] than now, at least a little.

For these writings, complaints, repetitions
Tossed between vain hopes and vain pain,
I expect compassion, if not forgiveness:
Haven't you suffered the ordeal of love?

But now I plainly see that I was
Everyman's long fable, and often I feel
Shameful, when I meditate on myself.

And of my frenzy, it is the fruit, this shame,
And so are repent, and knowing, clearly,
That earthly delights are brief, nothing but dreams.

[English translation by Fanny Quément,
previously unpublished]

Bonnefoy's heterometry and the global aesthetic in which he works clearly show his determination to interpret the text. But this is neither an interpretation grasping the main features of the source text nor a mere poetic recreation of the work. The translator allows himself to be carried away by a will to expand and alter the text, by 'a necessity to transpose' it.[30] As Fabio Scotto[31] remarks, Bonnefoy's is a 'project to modernize through translation'[32] which could be considered as a translation achieved through a 'living form'.[33] As a translator, Yves Bonnefoy is therefore looking for a 'fortunate difference' as Michela Landi[34] puts it. He values difference, *contrast*, and distance. Concretely speaking, his careful analogical transposition of sonorities[35] goes along with a radical change in speech form and concept ordering (see for instance the last two lines in the second quatrain). But Bonnefoy doesn't stop there. Interpreting style is for him a way to interpret meaning, and one can notice how the imaginary of the translator impacts his linguistic choices. His goal — as he explains it — is to emphasize 'the yet unexplored erotic drives'[36] in Petrarch's poetry, 'a more carnal thought',[37] but in the end, this is a personal re-reading of Petrarch's poetry. As Scotto remarks, 'Yves Bonnefoy's Petrarch therefore appears to be closer to the earth and to his desires than to Platonic dualism'[38] — whereas this dualism is characteristic of the poet of Laura.

It is necessary to stop for a while here. The use of the word 'frénésie' (v. 12) can be seen as an example of the striking signs that an *erotic imaginary*[39] influences Bonnefoy's translation practice in so far as he lowers the register of the word *vaneggiar* down to a bodily and pathological interpretation, the French word *frénésie* being derived from imperial Latin *phrenesis* and from ancient Greek φρένησις ('frenzy, frantic delirium'). The bodily dimension is confirmed by the etymology of the Greek word φρήν which means at once spirit, soul, thought and diaphragm, for in ancient physiology, the diaphragm was the seat of passions, instinct and thought (*Vocabolario Etimologico Pianigiani*). Other words like 'gémissements' for '*sospiri*' (v. 2), also confirm the intention of the translator to explain a sort of 'carnal poetics'. In fact, the words *vaneggiar* and *sospiri* imply a more contemplative state of mind than do *frénésie* and *gémissements*.

According to Fabio Scotto, on the one hand, Bonnefoy hopes to preserve 'his entire autonomy from the strictly linguistic tendencies of structuralist *formalism* and from the socio-linguistic *functionalism* of communication'.[40] On the other, he refuses to take sides between source-oriented and target-oriented translators [*sourciers et ciblistes*] 'due to the impossibility of reducing a text to its meaning, and to the necessity of recreating a modern and personal sound and rhythm, resisting all temptations to give an archaic ring'.[41] In doing so, he shows the value of loose metrics and 'revives' the text in contemporary French, all the while showcasing his own 'writing subjectivity'[42] as a poet and translator. Obviously, the legitimate eclecticism of his theory does not protect him from the risk of a Promethean drift, a risk to which all translators are exposed.

Bonnefoy's approach strikingly shows that the translation of meaning and that of form both spring from a hermeneutic movement of thought as well as from a *motus* of imagination. Pergnier's work proves again to be decisive: 'What any translation — whatever its qualities are — delivers is not the meaning of the poem (nor of its segments) but the exegesis and the interpretation made by a privileged reader (the translator).'[43]

Interpretation and imagination are therefore at play in all translations, and the best ones are precisely grounded on this thought. Not only is it crucial for translators to acknowledge the imaginary and hermeneutic foundations of their work, it is also dangerous to neglect them. Like any repression, that of hermeneutics causes, sooner or later, the return of the monsters to the surface of conscience. In the case of translation, the translator's psyche projects its own shadow onto the text, giving it a new destiny. When recommending, though rightly so, a 'radical replacement of the stylistic specificities of the original text',[44] the translation might end up taking over and destroying the source text, which would become, metatextually, food for another poetic. However, the translator's style can yield a completely different kind of result and rely on an entirely different form of inspiration. Jean-Yves Masson's translation of Petrarch's *Canzoniere* (2004)[45] illustrates this.

> (1) Voi ch'ascoltate in **rime sparse** il suono
> di quei sospiri ond'io nudriva 'l core
> in su'l mio primo giovenile errore
> quand'era in parte altr'uom da quel ch'i' sono,
>
> del vario stile in ch'io piango et ragiono,
> fra le vane speranze e 'l van dolore,
> ove sia chi per prova intenda **amore**,
> spero trovar pietà, nonché perdono.
>
> Ma ben veggio or sì come al popol tutto
> favola fui gran tempo, onde sovente,
> di me medesmo meco mi vergogno;
>
> et del mio **vaneggiar** vergogna è 'l frutto,
> e 'l pentérsi, e 'l **conoscer chiaramente**
> che quanto piace al mondo è breve sogno.
>
> *hendecasyllabe*
> ABBA ABBA CDE CDE
>
> [Petrarca, *Opere italiane*, ed. by Marco Santagata
> (Milan: Mondadori, 1996)]
>
> (2) Vous, auditeurs en mes **rimes éparses**   → folies
> De ces soupirs dont j'ai repu mon cœur   [Catanusi 1669]
> Quand j'étais jeune, en ma première erreur,   → folies
> Et que j'étais pour part autre que suis,   [Ginguené 1875]
>   → fous délires
>   [Godefroy 1900]
>
> Pour mes discours et mes pleurs si divers   → que ce qui
> Sur mes douleurs et mes souffrances vaines,   plaît au monde
> J'attends **pitié**, sinon pardon, de ceux   n'est que songe.
> Qui par preuve ont connu ce qu'est **amour**.   [C. Marot *c.* 1541–1544]
>
> Mais je vois bien à présent que de tous
> Je fus longtemps la fable, et il m'en vient
> Tout à part moi grand'honte de moi-même;
>
> De mes **folies** les fruits sont à honte,
> Le repentir, et la **claire science**
> Que ce qui plaît au monde n'est qu'un songe.
>
> *decasyllables*
> *aBBa (a being an assonance) in the first quatrain.*
> *No rhyme scheme in the rest of the sonnet.*
>
> [Copyright 'Pétrarque, *Le Chansonnier*:
> extraits trad. par Jean-Yves Masson', *Europe*, 82 (2004), 902–03.
> Reproduced by permission]

> You, hearing amongst my scattered rhymes
> The sighs with which I relished my heart
> When I was in my prime, erring,
> And partly other than I am,
>
> For my so diverse words and cries
> About my vain pains and sufferings
> I expect pity, if not pardon, from those
> Who, through trial, knew love.
>
> But now I plainly see that of all men
> I was for long the fable, and there ensues
> From me a great shame of myself;
>
> Of my follies the fruits are shame,
> Repentance and clear knowledge
> That what delights the world is but a dream.
>
> [English translation by Fanny Quément, previously unpublished]

This work and others[46] immediately testify to Jean-Yves Masson's sensitivity to a translational tradition: he quotes other translators and follows their path. According to Masson, only 'the pulsing beat of the lines [...] can support and bring forth their profuse meanings, and help the reader accept passages based on enumeration':[47] in his view, using the alexandrine is 'betrayal'.[48] He considered that the alexandrine (often used in the translations of Petrarch) could not properly convey the 'nervous rhythm of the Italian hendecasyllable', whereas the decasyllable enabled him to inscribe his translation within the French lyric tradition. Indeed, it is through the decasyllable that the French poets from the sixteenth century first integrated Petrarchan influences, and 'adapted Petrarchan rhetoric to French'.[49] Finally, in order to make the readers hear the *distance* that necessarily separates them from the text, Masson indulges in quite a few syntactic archaisms, but above all, he endeavours to respect French classical prosody (all vowels being pronounced) and invites his readers to heed it.

> En choisissant la métrique la plus stricte, c'est à l'intuition d'une parenté d'esprit (évidente) avec nos poètes de la Pléiade, mais aussi, par-delà le temps, avec Mallarmé (intuition que je dois surtout aux réflexions théoriques de Mario Luzi, et sur laquelle ce n'est pas ici le lieu de s'expliquer), que j'ai obéi.
>
> [When I chose the strictest metric, I was guided by the intuition that there was an (obvious) spiritual affinity with our poets from the Pleiades, but also, beyond time, with Mallarmé (an intuition I mostly owe to Mario Luzi's theoretical reflections, but this shall not be further explained here).][50]

The solution proves to be particularly efficient. These reading recommendations will help a watchful and conscientious reader to enjoy the text more deeply, while another kind of reader — much more naive or unaware — might at any rate notice the rhythm of the text and appreciate its archaisms. This multiplies the ways in which the text can possibly be read — which is, besides, one of the distinctive features of the mystical and Platonic-Christian imagery at the core of the *Canzoniere*.[51]

The extreme attention Masson pays to *form* and *effect* could nevertheless imply that his translation neglects meaning — and it is true the use of the alexandrine might have spared the translation many a semantic sacrifice. But in his case, as Masson says, the reflection on rhythm does not simply result from a scholarly, literary, historical and philological preoccupation. It is aimed at grasping the imaginary of Petrarch which is indirectly communicated through style.

> Je crois qu'il est bon, malgré tout, que cet effort de rapprochement ne soit pas excessif et que le texte lu en français fasse entendre une distance avec la langue courante — ne serait-ce que parce que le lexique de Pétrarque est un lexique aristocratique, contrairement à celui de Dante; Pétrarque est un poète que son refus de la foule, son dédain du vulgaire, rapprochent de Mallarmé. Il est bon aussi de faire entendre que pour lui, la poésie est une langue séparée, un instrument adapté à un regard poétique fondamentalement tourné vers la saisie de l'Idée. Langue suspecte, d'ailleurs, à bien des égards, car en vrai platonicien Pétrarque se méfie de sa propre poésie [...] qui ne s'accomplit que dans le silence. Côtoyer ce silence de Pétrarque — silence intérieur à l'œuvre, non le silence du renoncement à l'œuvre — est aussi une raison plus secrète de le traduire. En prendre conscience est en tout cas une manière de saisir ce que pourrait être pour nous [...] la 'modernité' de Pétrarque.

> [I think, nevertheless, that it is good to set limits to this attempt at acculturation and to make sure that a certain distance from the current idiom can be heard — if only because Petrarch's diction is an aristocratic diction, unlike Dante's; Petrarch is a poet whose rejection of the multitude and contempt of the vulgar are similar to Mallarmé's views. It is also a good thing to make the reader understand through sound that for him, poetry is a language apart, an appropriate instrument for a poetic look that is fundamentally turned bent on grasping the Idea. Besides, this language is suspicious in many ways, for Petrarch, as a real Platonician, is wary of his own poetry [...] which comes to pass in silence only. Becoming acquainted with Petrarch's silence — a silence *within* his work, not the silence of the renunciation of the work — is also a more tacit reason to translate it. Growing conscious of it is at any rate a way to grasp what [...] Petrarch's 'modernity' could be for us.[52]

All the principles of familiarization as a translation practice can be found in these lines. If Petrarch considers poetry as a language 'apart', contemplating 'the grasping of the Idea', a practice of familiarization should therefore look for a way to translate this strangeness, to make today's reader feel the difference. One could make out in this reflection what Meschonnic would call a *forme-sens* (single entity encompassing meaning with form). But what matters is not to give a proper form to the content, or a precise signification to form. The issue raised by Masson in these remarkable lines is about grasping another level of content (poetical, philosophical and symbolical) which style can only express transtextually, that is to say through the elusive connections between its components and everything that is within the text or outside it. This is very different from a reflection on form as the reality on which the text (and therefore the translation) is based: form is the *forma* of a harmony, of a much wider organic and transtextual whole. Finally, as a 'moderate target-oriented translator', Masson envisages not only the reading of the target text but also that of the source text by a foreign reader who would not be a specialist of the source language. He admits that even if he aimed at working a translation that would be 'pleasant to read', he also tried to turn it into a tool that would be useful to read the text in its original tongue, for 'the legitimate function of a translation is *also* to help read the original text'.[53] Incidentally, the decasyllable 'Que ce qui plaît au monde n'est qu'un songe' has its caesura right between the verb 'plaît' and its indirect object 'au monde': syntax and metrics are at odds, and the word 'monde' seems to be set apart. Given the derogatory connotations of this word in evangelical texts, Masson could be thought to have wilfully shown, with a prosodic translational gesture, a feeling of contempt for the multitude. Clément Marot probably shared in the same contempt and his translation seems to borrow from the Bible.[54] An inner caesura can also be noticed in line 12 ('foli/e'): being the only infringement of classical rules, it significantly emphasizes the word 'folie'. Finally, the translation 'folies' is a good example showing the way in which Masson followed a translational tradition and maybe also the most widespread interpretation of the word 'vaneggiar': 'folies' (Catanusi, 1669),[55] 'folies' (Ginguené, 1875),[56] 'fous délires' (Godefroy, 1900).[57]

These are some of the implications in Bonnefoy's *translating recreation* and Masson's scholarly translation — two ways of translating style, two imaginaries taking different positions on one form of poetic writing. Moreover, even though these two kinds of inspiration testify to the existence of a polarity, it is also true that they only partially correspond to Taber's dichotomy and the opposite poles we deduced from it.

Indeed, all reflections on translation often remain similar to an object with vague, elusive and mysterious contours. It even seems to be the fundamental characteristic of translation studies, as of any recent field of studies: there is an inevitable discrepancy between the limited system of thought and the wideness of the world around us, between the slow geometries of language and the nuances of reality, between ideas and phenomena.

Translating the Mind

The previous remarks suggest that no discussion of translation can do without a study of *meaning* and *form*, two notions that are at once distinct, dialogical and complementary. However, another path will be taken here, with a few general thoughts on the history of translation.

As an inner function of language and a metaphor of its hermeneutic powers, translation has been, for many writers, something more important than a mere transposition from one language to another. For Charles Baudelaire or Gérard de Nerval, among others, linguistic transposition is only something accessory in a much deeper quest. For these writers, the moment of translation corresponds to an expansion of the translator's language and imaginary, a real hatching.[58] It is an evolution of their linguistic abilities, a doorway to a treasure, a legacy of images, fascinations and symbols and not simply the inheritance of a linguistic system. Thus, the target language is considered as *a sound-box* for the source language instead of being merely seen as the final result of a linguistic process. This sound-box is full of *foreign* mechanisms giving a new space for expression, a new semantic and rhetorical germination of the target language.[59]

The translator opens his text up to a whole series of new signifieds which were already integrated, included, well-known in *both* the source language *and* the target language: translation is a hatching process. It can therefore be considered as a verbal space to explore conscience. In Giorgio Caproni's words, it 'broadens the field of one's own existence and conscience',[60] a broadening which characterizes both translation and imitation.[61] In this view, the idea of 'handing the text over' is too narrow to define what the text undergoes. There is something alchemical in this movement which could be described, as Antonio Prete puts it, as 'a *transmutation* through which the first text, listened and listened to again, worked and reworked, takes the shape of another language, puts on another voice'.[62]

For example, Albert Béguin notes that translating German poets is for Nerval a way to 'liken himself to a form of knowledge and to coincide with [other] poet[s]' spiritual adventure'.[63] Translation is where minds can meet and not simply a linguistic place of transit: 'the affinities that make great minds akin matter far more than the transmission mode for ideas and themes'.[64]

So it is not surprising that many writers and translators have claimed that they found, in literary texts, marks left by something that transcends language and which, as a consequence, also transcends *meaning* and *form* at the same time as it imprints them. As a result, this *spiritual quality*[65] of the text rightly becomes another object for translation studies.

In this perspective, modern or contemporary definitions of translation are no longer valid, and translators no longer have to make a radical choice between form and meaning, source-oriented or target-oriented translations. Translation is reimagined and another *translational gesture* is possible.

This issue was tackled by the German romantics, who questioned the necessity to translate the spirit, the *genius* of the text. For theorists such as Schlegel or poets like Novalis, translation should translate a whole unit, rebuild a global poetics.[66]

This is why a third figure, that of Apollo, joins Hermes and Orpheus. With Apollo, translation indulges in mysterious, *transitive* speech, a speech which, according to the literal meaning of *transitive*, 'expands from subject to object',[67] 'an oblique speech, similar to Apollo's oracles, the oblique god, *loxias*'.[68] Here, translation can be considered as an act of knowledge, in the purest meaning of the Greek word for *sapienta*, gnosis (γνῶσις 'knowledge through memory'). One can in fact assume that there exists in this world an archetypal representation of reality, an imaginary through which human beings can shape images and be shaped by them: 'everything shapes and is shaped by everything [...] and one might feel urged to find, sound, judge, argue, remember everything in everything',[69] explains Giordano Bruno. As it has already been suggested, translation can therefore be used as a tool 'to link conscience with this archetypal imaginary awakening a function of memory which is at once linguistic, symbolic and metaphysical'.[70] Thus, translation becomes 'a true knowledge of reality, a philosophical and spiritual act'.[71]

Indeed, like any work on words, translation implies a work on/through imagination, and on/through all the faculties which lay beyond and below the linguistic aspect of the process. François Vezin goes as far as to speak of a 'translinguistic function of imagination' which becomes apparent when translating turns into 'an eminently philosophical activity', when 'a form of transcendence is at stake'.[72]

The translator's relation to the text thus becomes very intimate and deep, a work of interiorization and appropriation. The translator is neither looking for an immediate transposition (Hermes) nor for a familiarization or an over-interpretation through *contrast* (Orpheus). He follows the flow of *empathy*: through the Other and thanks to him, he returns to himself. Aragon's translation of Petrarch's *Canzoniere* will serve as a last example to conclude our inquiries on theory and practice.

(1) **Voi ch'ascoltate in rime** ~~sparse~~ **il suono**
di quei sospiri ond'io nudriva 'l core
in su'l mio primo giovenile errore
quand'era in parte altr'uom da quel ch'i' sono,

del vario stile in ch'io **piango et** ~~ragiono~~,
fra le vane speranze e 'l van dolore,
ove sia chi per prova intenda amore,
spero trovar pietà, **nonché perdono**.

Ma ben veggio or sì come al popol tutto
favola fui gran tempo, onde sovente,
di me medesmo meco mi vergogno;

et del mio **vaneggiar** vergogna è 'l frutto,
e 'l pentérsi, e 'l conoscer chiaramente
che quanto piace al mondo è breve sogno.

hendecasyllabe
ABBA ABBA CDE CDE

[Edition employed in the 'Pleiade' of Aragon:
Petrarca, *Opere italiane*, ed. by Marco Santagata
(Milan: Mondadori, 1996)]

(2) **Vous qui surprenez dans mes vers le bruit**

   je plains mes ennuis

Decasyllables, 'variously imitated'
(Louis Aragon, preface, 1947)
ABBA ABBA CDE CDE[73]

[*Cinq sonnets de Pétrarque* (1947), in Louis Aragon,   → *ronge*: *songe*
Œuvres poétiques completes, 2 vols,   [C. Marot, *c.* 1541–44]
Bibliothèque de la Pléiade, ed. by   → égarements
Olivier Barbarant (Paris: Gallimard, 2007), II.]   [J. de Sade, 1764]

You who overhear in my lines the noise
Of these sighs on which I fed my heart
In my first erring youth
When I was another man than I am.

> To various tones I moan my worries
> Vain hope following vain pain
> If one knows love in its calamity
> I will expect pity, not pardon, from him.
>
> But I plainly see how I was the fable
> Of all the people for long, and the torment,
> Within me, of shame is thus gnawing me.
>
> Days gone astray, from which I kept only
> This repentance and clear understanding
> All that delights the world is but a dream.
>
> [English translation by Fanny Quément, previously unpublished]

Aragon's translation illustrates the movement of empathy more than any linguistic reflection, as the author explains himself in his *Explications du traducteur*.

> Traduire n'est rien, vain remue-ménage: l'inimitable même, il faut l'imiter. Si peu qu'on le puisse et qui sait? comme l'ombre sur le mur, amplifiant les gestes de l'homme, tant pis qu'il n'y ait que la marionnette du chanteur, elle vaut mieux que sa photographie. L'inexactitude, l'interprétation, l'à-peu-près, tout ce qui sera reproché au copiste, importe moins que ce ton de voix essayé, retrouvé peut-être. On ne manquera point d'observer que de l'original n'est passée que la grimace: éloge inespéré, car seule peut grimacer la vie.
>
> [Translation is an empty, vain commotion: what is inimitable must be imitated. As scarcely possible as it is and, who knows? as with the shadow on the wall, magnifying the gestures of the man, never mind if one only gets the puppet-figure of the singer, it is still better than a photograph of him. Inexactness, interpretation, approximation, everything the copyist will be reproached with, matters less than the vocal tone that is tried out and perhaps even recovered. It will of course be noticed that only a grin remains from the original: unhoped-for praise, for only life can grin.[74]]

As he reads the *Canzoniere*, Aragon looks for the way to find his own lyricism, making his own words and poetics resound in Petrarch's words. His is a *poeticizing thought*,[75] operating as a process throughout the translation, and resulting from a (conscious or unconscious) work in which the imagination and the imaginary of the translator play a major part.

Jean-Baptiste Para remarks[76] that Aragon no longer describes Petrarch's nightingale or his Laura. His translation looks for the birdsongs of his own nightingales and, as he confesses indirectly in the sonic watermark that can be found in *Explications du traducteur*, he celebrates his beloved Elsa Triolet through Laura. Besides, the sentence used as an epigraph to the first edition of his translations from the *Canzoniere*[77] ('They said Laura was somebody ELSE') is obviously a pun masking the first name of his wife Elsa, as Franck Merger noticed.[78] Para therefore states that 'if Petrarch sometimes seems to function as a mirror in Aragon's work, it is also because he prefigures in his way a kind of 'mentir-vrai' [truthful lying].[79] Incidentally, one could rightly wonder whether the contraction on line 8 ('non point pardon de lui' for 'nonché perdono' or 'non che perdono'[80]) is due to Aragon's limited knowledge of Italian or if it is another way for him to *lie*, to project his own imaginary onto Petrarch's text.

At any rate, Aragon's dexterous style can be admired as it oscillates vertiginously between tradition and innovation: he shows that it is perfectly possible for a translation to meet the double requirement of line regularity and rhyming scheme and to renew language at the same time. On the one hand, the decasyllables he 'variously imitated'[81] give a real impression of modernization. On the other, Aragon explicitly quotes from C. Marot's first translation (*c.* 1541–44) and seems to have been inspired by J. de Sade (1764), which suggests he wants to inscribe himself within a translational tradition.

Aragon translated 'vaneggiar', for example, with 'jours égarés', a word describing a sort of 'existential geography' (if we think when Jacques de Sade translated 'égarements' or when he talked about the 'égarements de la jeunesse'[82]). In fact, we can consider 'vaneggiar' here also like a variation of the theme of the *peregrinatio amoris*, as Paolo Rigo argued.[83] In this way, Aragon and de Sade show here an intimate interpretation of Petrarch's poetry.

Moreover, he carefully preserves Petrarch's rhyming scheme. Actually, it might be argued that rhymes are more than a stylistic effect in this sonnet: they can also express a movement of the mind, of its reasoning and thought. The *dissidio*, described in the quatrains, is solved in the tercets, and it is the rhyming scheme that has the power to mark this change. It seems Aragon is trying to imitate a 'thought form'[84] as much as a poetic form. Again, as with Masson, what matters is not only to see that the meaning results from the microcosmic units of the text, but also to rebuild it from the angle of its macrocosmic features. Aragon uses all the tools at his disposal: relying on an original process, he works a translation that gives birth to a new personal imaginary at the same time as he modernizes Petrarchan poetics.

Conclusions: Hermeneutics, Imagination and Translation

A study of some translations of the first sonnet in the *Canzoniere* shows that despite the variety of approaches, a translator is always influenced by one of these three tutelary figures: Hermes, Orpheus, and Apollo. I have relied on these figures to present three types of translational imaginaries and approaches. The interpretative implications that have been pinpointed appear to be most interesting insofar as translation can be considered as a 'hermeneutic model'.[85]

Nevertheless, I didn't go so far as to build a new theory of interpretation the way Danica Seleskovitch, Marianne Lederer and Fortunato Israël have done.[86] My work simply offers a few practical tools which can help to solve some of the problems raised by the theory and practice of interpretation. These tools might of course be useful to translators, but they have also been conceived more precisely for critics, researchers and students or any other readers interested in the question of interpretation as part of the translation process.

Presenting them as sketches seemed to be the best and most honest option. The goal was to coin a few conceptual phrases as a contribution to translation studies, without claiming that a full-fledged methodology is born. For dealing with translation is indeed about bringing help, offering theory as a lifeboat in the tempest of practice.[87]

Translated by Fanny Quément

Notes to Chapter 9

1. For a more detailed description of the theory of translation imaginaries, of which this article represents the first prototype, see Christina Bezari, Riccardo Raimondo and Thomas Vuong (ed.), *The imaginaries of translation – Les imaginaires de la traduction, Itinéraires*, special issue of the journal *Itinéraires*, n°2018/2-3 (2019) [online: journals.openedition.org/itineraires].
2. See: Linda Collinge, *Beckett traduit Beckett: de 'Malone meurt' à 'Malone Dies', l'imaginaire en traduction* (Geneva: Droz, 2000); Mathias Verger, 'Antonin Artaud et l'imaginaire de la traduction', *Carnets de Chaminadour*, 4 (2015), 61–85.
3. See Susan Bassnett and André Lefevere, *Constructing Cultures: Essays on Literary Translation* (Clevedon: Multilingual Matters, 1998), pp. 109–25.
4. Ibid., p. 10:

    We need to learn more about the acculturation process between cultures, or rather, about the symbiotic working together of different kinds of rewritings within that process, about the ways in which translation, together with criticism, anthologisation, historiography, and the production of reference works, constructs the image of writers and/or their works, and then watches those images become reality.

5. Carl Gustav Jung, 'Réflexions théoriques sur la nature du psychisme', in *La réalité de l'âme*, ed. by Michel Cazenave (Paris: Librairies Générale Française, 1998), p. 1046.
6. Carl Gustav Jung, *Énergétique psychique*, trans. by Yves Le Lay (Genève, Georg, 1956); reissued in 'L'énergétique psychique', in *La réalité de l'âme*, p. 330.
7. See Giambattista Vico, *Scienza nuova. Libro primo (Dello stabilimento de' principi)*, §XLIX; *Libro secondo, (Della sapienza poetica)*, §V; *Libro quarto (Del corso che fanno le nazioni)* §VI: '*universali fantastici.*' New edition: *La scienza nuova* (three editions: 1725, 1730 and 1744), ed. by Manuela Sanna and Vincenzo Vitiello (Milan: Bompiani, 2012).
8. Paul Ricœur, *Du texte à l'action. Essais d'herméneutique II* (Paris: Éditions du Seuil, 1986), p. 237.
9. Ibid.
10. Ibid., p. 238.
11. Ibid., p. 241.
12. Charles Le Blanc, *Le complexe d'Hermès* (Presses Universitaires d'Ottawa, 2009), p. 19. See also *Odyssey* 5.102.
13. Jean-René Ladmiral, *Sourcier ou cibliste* (Paris: Les Belles Lettres, 2014), p. 200–07.
14. Friedrich Schleiermacher, *Des différentes méthodes du traduire*, trans. by Antoine Berman and Christian Berner, ed. by Alain Badiou et Barbara Cassin (Paris: Éditions du Seuil, 1999), p. 53.
15. Eugène A. Nida, *Toward a Science of Translation. With special reference to principles and procedures involved in Bible translating* (Leiden: Brill, 1964), p. 159ff. and *passim*.
16. Jean-Charles Vegliante, *D'écrire la traduction* (Paris: Presses de la Sorbonne Nouvelle, 1996), p. 90.
17. Two different editions of the *Canzoniere* will be referred to, depending on the translation under study: Giuseppe Savoca's edition, chosen by Gérard Genot for his translation (2005), and Marco Santagata's (1996) chosen by Olivier Barbarant for the Pléiade edition of Aragon's poetic works. The latter will be used for comparison with the other translations. The editions of Petrarch's *Canzoniere* differ in minor details only, the text having remained quite stable through time, notably thanks to the author's manuscripts. The reader might notice a few small differences such as 'ragiono' (Santagata) and 'ragiono' (Savoca), 'nonché' (Santagata) and 'non che' (Savoca). Yet these changes do not impact the meaning. The very few textual variants are well indexed in Santagata's critical edition (1996). For a close analysis of the history of the *Canzoniere* and

its edition, see Marco Santagata, *I frammenti dell'anima. Storia e racconto nel Canzoniere di Petrarca* (Bologna: Il Mulino, 1992).
18. Giuseppe Savoca, *Il Canzoniere di Petrarca tra codicologia ed ecdotica* (Florence: Olschki, 2008).
19. Petrarch, *Rerum vulgarium fragmenta*, ed. by Giuseppe Savoca (Florence: Olschki, 2008).
20. See Riccardo Raimondo, 'Les lieux de la perte: esquisses pour une taxonomie de l'intraduisible', *Atelier de traduction*, 24 (2015), 61–77.
21. Clément Marot, *Six sonnetz de Pétrarque sur la mort de sa dame Laure, traduictz d'italien en françois* (Paris: G. Corrozet, c. 1541–44), *RVF* 1.
22. Vasquin Philieul, *Laure d'Avignon, mis en françoys par Vaisquin Philieul* (Paris: J. Gazeau, 1548); *Toutes les œuvres vulgaires de François Pétrarque, contenans quatre livres de M. D. Laure d'Avignon, sa maistresse, jadis par luy composez en langage thuscan et mis en françoys par Vasquin Philieul, avecques briefz sommaires ou argumens requis pour plus facile intelligence du tout* (Avignon: de B. Bonhomme, 1555).
23. *Essais de Jerôme d'Alvost sur les sonnets du divin Pétrarque avec quelques Pöesies de son invention* (Paris: l'Angelier, 1584).
24. Maurice Pergnier, *Les fondements socio-linguistiques de la traduction* (Paris: Honoré Champion, 1978), 2nd edn (Geneva: Slaktine, 1980), 3rd edn (Presses Universitaires de Lille, 1993), p. 24.
25. Ibid., p. 57.
26. Charles R. Taber, 'Traduire le sens, traduire le style', *Langages*, 28 (1972), 55–63 (p. 61).
27. Ibid., p. 62.
28. For a more detailed comparison between these two translators, see: Riccardo Raimondo, 'Corps mystique et corps sensuel: Jean-Yves Masson et Yves Bonnefoy traducteurs du *Canzoniere* de Pétrarque', in Michel Collet, Margaret Gillespie and Nanta Novello Paglianti (ed.), *Métamorphoses: corps, arts visuels et littérature. La traversée des genres*, Binges, Orbis Tertius, 2019, p. 77-92.
29. Petrarch, *Je vois sans yeux et sans bouche, je crie: vingt-quatre sonnets traduits par Yves Bonnefoy, accompagnés de dessins originaux de Gérard Titus-Carmel* (Paris: Galilée, 2011).
30. Yves Bonnefoy, 'Le *Canzoniere* en sa traduction', *Conférence*, 20 (2005), 361–77 (p. 361).
31. Fabio Scotto, 'Yves Bonnefoy traducteur de Leopardi et de Pétrarque', *Littérature*, 150 (2008), 70–82.
32. Ibid., p. 80.
33. Bonnefoy, 'Le *Canzoniere* en sa traduction', p. 370.
34. Michela Landi, 'Yves Bonnefoy et la traduction: l'enseignement et l'exemple de l'Italie', *Littérature*, 150 (2008), 56–69.
35. See for instance the way Bonnefoy renders the alliteration in the second tercet, 'E del mio vaneggiar vergogna è 'l frutto' being translated by 'Et de ma frénésie, c'est le fruit, cette honte'.
36. Bonnefoy, 'Le *Canzoniere* en sa traduction', p. 372.
37. Ibid., p. 375.
38. For an extensive study on the first exponent of this erotic imaginary, see: Riccardo Raimondo, 'Jacques Peletier traducteur du Canzoniere de Pétrarque', *Canadian Review of Comparative Literature/ Revue Canadienne de Littérature Comparée*, 46.2 (2019), 235–51.
39. Scotto, 'Yves Bonnefoy traducteur de Leopardi et de Pétrarque', p. 82.
40. Ibid., p. 70.
41. Ibid.
42. Ibid., p. 71.
43. Maurice Pergnier, 'La traduction comme exégèse: le cas de la poésie', *TTR: traduction, terminologie, redaction*, 12.2 (1999), 159–71 (p. 161).
44. Taber, 'Traduire le sens, traduire le style', p. 62.
45. Jean-Yves Masson, 'Poèmes du *Canzoniere* et *Triomphe de l'Amour*', *Europe*, 82, (2004), 74–95.
46. See Yves Chevrel et Jean-Yves Masson, eds, *L'Histoire des traductions en langue française (XVe–XXe siècles)*, 4 vols (Lagrasse: Verdier, 2012-17).
47. Masson, 'Poèmes du *Canzoniere* et *Triomphe de l'Amour*', p. 69.
48. Ibid., p. 70.
49. Ibid.
50. Ibid., p. 72.

51. See Luca Marcozzi, *Petrarca platonico. Studi sull'immaginario filosofico del Canzoniere* (Rome: Aracne, 2011), *passim*; Silvia Finazzi, *Fusca claritatis, La metafora nei Rerum vulgarium fragmenta di Francesco Petrarca* (Rome: Aracne, 2011), pp. 97–134 and *passim*.
52. Ibid., pp. 70–71.
53. Ibid., p. 72.
54. Clément Marot is perhaps the initiator of this spiritual imaginary of the *Canzoniere* in French literature. To retrace the phases of his evangelical inspiration, see: Riccardo Raimondo, 'Clément Marot, traducteur évangélique du Canzoniere de Pétrarque', *Renaissance and Reformation / Renaissance et Réforme*, forthcoming 2019.
55. Placide Catanusi, *Œuvres amoureuses de Pétrarque* (Paris: Estienne Loyson, 1669).
56. Pierre-Louis Ginguené, *Les Œuvres amoureuses de Pétrarque, sonnets, triomphes, traduites en français, avec le texte en regard et précédées d'une notice sur la vie de Pétrarque* (Paris: Garnier Frères, 1875).
57. Hippolyte Godefroy, *Poésies complètes de Francesco Petrarca, traduction nouvelle par Hippolyte Godefroy: sonnets, canzones, sestines, triomphes* (Montluçon: A. Herbin, 1900).
58. Riccardo Raimondo, 'Le *démon fugitif* de l'imagination: propositions pour une traductologie comparée: Nerval et Baudelaire', *Nouvelle Fribourg*, 2 (2016), <nouvellefribourg.com>.
59. Ibid.
60. Giorgio Caproni, 'Divagazioni sul tradurre', in *La Scatola Nera* (Milan: Garzanti, 1996), pp. 57–71 (p. 62): 'un allargamento nel campo della propria esperienza e della propria coscienza' (trans. by Riccardo Raimondo and Fanny Quément).
61. See the chapter on Giorgio Caproni in Antonio Prete, *All'ombra dell'altra lingua: per una poetica della traduzione* (Milan: Bollati Boringhieri, 2011), p. 106.
62. Antonio Prete, 'Traduzione come ospitalità', *Revista de Italianística*, 14 (2006), 115–20 (p. 118): 'una *trasmutazione*, per la quale il primo testo, ascolto dopo ascolto, esercizio dopo esercizio, prende un'altra lingua, un'altra voce' (trans. by Riccardo Raimondo and Fanny Quément).
63. Albert Béguin, *L'Âme romantique et le rêve* (Paris: José Corti, 1991), p. xv.
64. Ibid.
65. This spiritual quality could also be called 'the language of the soul': cf. *Un linguaggio dell'anima. Atti della giornata di studio su Tommaso Landolfi*, ed. by Antonio Prete and Idolina Landolfi (Lecce: Manni, 2006).
66. Le Blanc, *Le complexe d'Hermès*, pp. 82–83.
67. Riccardo Raimondo, 'Territori di Babele. Aforismi sulla traduzione di Jean-Yves Masson', *Ticontre*, 3 (2015^a), 171–80 (p. 173).
68. Jean-Yves Masson, 'Territoire de Babel (notes sur la théorie de la traduction)', *Corps Ecrit*, 36 (1990), 157–60 (p. 158).
69. Giordano Bruno, *Sigillus sigillorum, liber secundum* [1583], §II: 'tutto forma ed è formato da tutto... e noi possiamo essere portati a trovare, indagare, judicare, argomentare, ricordarci d'ogni cosa attraverso ogni altra' (trans. by R. Raimondo and F. Quément), in *Opere mnemotecniche II*, ed. by Marco Matteoli, Rita Sturlese and Nicoletta Tirinnanzi (Milan: Adelphi, 2009).
70. Raimondo, 'Le *démon fugitif* de l'imagination'.
71. Ibid.
72. François Vezin, 'Philosophie et pédagogie de la traduction', *Revue philosophique de la France et de l'étranger*, 130 (2005), 496.
73. Petrarch, *Je vois sans yeux et sans bouche, je crie*.
74. Louis Aragon, 'Explications du traducteur, introduction aux *Cinq sonnets de Pétrarque*' (1947), in Louis Aragon, *Œuvres poétiques completes*, 2 vols, Bibliothèque de la Pléiade, pref. by Jean Ristat, ed. by Olivier Barbarant (Paris: Gallimard, 2007), I, 1036.
75. See Antonio Prete, *Il pensiero poetante. Saggi su Leopardi* (Milan: Feltrinelli, 2006), p. 80.
76. It is noted by Jean-Baptiste Para in his 'Notice aux Cinq sonnets de Pétrarque', in Aragon, *Œuvres poétiques completes*, I, 1571.
77. This is a very peculiar edition. It shows a very long title without any mention of the translator and editor: '*Cinq Sonnets de Pétrarque avec une eau-forte de Picasso et les explications du traducteur, à La Fontaine de Vaucluse, MCMXLVII*'.
78. Franck Merger, 'La réception de Pétrarque en France au XXème siècle: l'exemple d'Aragon', *Les*

annales de la société des amis de Louis Aragon et Elsa Triolet, 10 (2008), <louisaragon-elsatriolet.org>.
79. Jean-Baptiste Para in his 'Notice aux Cinq sonnets de Pétrarque', in Louis Aragon, *Œuvres poétiques completes*, t. I, p. 1572.
80. This is a textual variant arising in the edition by Petracci (1601), Catanusi (1669) and Ginguené (1875), probably consulted by Aragon.
81. Louis Aragon, 'Explications du traducteur, introduction aux *Cinq sonnets de Pétrarque*' (1947), in Aragon, *Œuvres poétiques completes*, t. I, p. 1036.
82. Jacques de Sade, *Œuvres choisies de François Pétrarque, traduites de l'italien et du latin en français*, 3 vols (Amsterdam: Arskée & Mercus, 1764), I, 115.
83. Paolo Rigo, 'Peregrinatio', in *Lessico critico petrarchesco*, ed. by Luca Marcozzi and Romana Brovia (Rome: Carocci, 2016), pp. 240–41.
84. François Jost wrote extensively about the historical and literary crossings between the sonnet form and its spiritual qualities, which derive from 'the mystic of numbers', especially regarding the use of the number seven. Yet the fact that the sonnet has been interpreted from a mystic-symbolic angle at some points in history does not account for its birth or its nature. These interpretations can, however, 'suggest that such number symbolism is likely to have guaranteed the success of the sonnet' among authors and translators (François Jost, *Le sonnet de Pétrarque à Baudelaire* (Berne: Peter Lang, 1989), pp. 32–39).
85. See Paul Ricœur, 'Le paradigme de la traduction', *Esprit*, 253 (1999), 8–19; Domenico Jervolino, *Ricoeur: Herméneutique et traduction* (Paris: Ellipses, 2007); Richard Kearney, 'Vers une herméneutique de la traduction', in *Paul Ricoeur. De l'homme faillible à l'homme capable*, ed. by Gaëlle Fiasse (Paris: PUF, 2008), pp. 157–78.
86. See Marianne Lederer et Danica Seleskovitch, *Interpréter pour traduire* (Paris: Didier, 1984); Fortunato Israël et Marianne Lederer, *La théorie interprétative de la traduction*, 3 vols (Paris/Caen: Minard, 2005).
87. The most part of the contents of this article is translated and improved from Riccardo Raimondo, 'Orphée contre Hermès: herméneutique, imaginaire et traduction (esquisses)', *Meta*, 61 (2016), 650–74.

CHAPTER 10

Echoes of the Petrarchan *Innamoramento* in Tim Atkins's *Petrarch Collected* and Emmanuel Hocquard's *Un Test de solitude*: Two Poets between Subversion and Dialogue

Thomas Vuong

'Tout sonnet est un sonnet de Pétrarque'[1]

'Every sonnet is a sonnet by Petrarch', says Jacques Roubaud, himself a prolific sonnet-writer, acute theoretician, and erudite reader of modern and contemporary sonnets. Still, in an age of destructured poetry, it is somewhat difficult to consider that poems called sonnets might still be closely related to Petrarch's *Canzoniere* to the extent that the Father of Humanism could claim partial authorship. Emmanuel Hocquard's *Un test de solitude*, published in 1998, is subtitled 'Sonnets' but these poems have apparently very little to do with the canonical form. The very mention of the form appears as quite a paradox, coming from a poet who rejected most of the lyrical options taken by post-war French poetry. His work is indeed characterized by the refusal of *chantage lyrique*[2] — a French pun on lyric 'song' as lyric 'blackmail' — and by the search for a straight syntax to represent the world most truthfully and logically. Jacques Roubaud, who ends his 2012 sonnet anthology *Quasi-cristaux* on Hocquard's work, signals the importance of a major *littéraliste* poet's use of the form as proof of the sonnet's overarching ductility, bearing in mind that with Hocquard it does stray quite far from what is usually considered a sonnet in France.[3]

On the other side of the Channel, Tim Atkins, who defines himself as one of the few English poets who refuse to fall within a lyric, post-Ted Hughes lineage, published *Petrarch Collected Atkins* in 2014, a collection of 366 supposed translations, transpositions, and pseudo-translations of the 366 pieces of the *Rerum Vulgarium Fragmenta* that maintain a weak, episodic, though persistent and primeval, bond with the Tuscan model. Atkins thus sets himself in a line of experimental adaptations stemming from Oskar Pastior's *33 Gedichte*. Unknowingly corroborating Roubaud's statement, in the introduction to his twenty-first-century anthology *The Reality Street Book of Sonnets*, Jeff Hilson rightly underlines that Atkins's poems and to a certain extent all contemporary sonnets 'are translations. And some of the poems are not sonnets at all.'[4]

Whatever the definition of the sonnet could be, both poets claim the form in order to place themselves paradoxically against a certain European tradition. Both also claim links with American concrete poetry and Objectivism (which Hocquard helped publish in France) and with Apollinaire.[5] Yet, both of them chose to rewrite and refer to the *Canzoniere*, especially with the theme of the *innamoramento* — the topical moment of falling in love that has been adapted and imitated by Petrarchan poets throughout the centuries. Each in his own way, these two poets typically appropriate the *'vulgarium'* part of the *RVF* and adapt the *innamoramento* to make it even more prosaic, triggering two very different courses of deconstruction, subversion, and dialogue. The present chapter proposes a comparative perspective on how two extreme contemporary approaches of the *innamoramento* can still be linked to Petrarch's emotion-focused, abstract, metaphysical stance, not least through the form of the sonnet.

The Importance of being *Innamorato*

Tim Atkins's *Petrarch Collected* often refers to the *innamoramento*, as the English contemporary poet roughly follows the pattern of the *Canzoniere* in which the Tuscan poet frequently returns to this crucial event of his life. The first instance of a direct rewriting of this fabled encounter shows the poet not only wishes to revisit the *topos* but also initiates a reflection about it. The *innamoramento* is initially reduced to a movie producer's pitch ('Boy meets girl') and clichés about passion, before being evoked under the light of retrospect and quotation (starting with Johnson's line) until the starting premise gets turned upside-down in an apparently naive rephrasing of Petrarch's decades-long, consuming obsession.

> 5.2
>
> Boy meets girl   on the left-hand side
> Traditionally that of desire and irrationality
> Mathematicians are not immune
> One day in the future Dr Johnson will say
> Remarriage is a triumph of hope over experience
> In a concert-goers' life
> Love of books is more unhappy
> The beloved   Selected Writings Of
> Guillaume Apollinaire
> Between the legs on a breezy day in April
> Is where I long to be   where
> My story is strong   where
> My life went wrong   boy meets girl
> Girl eats boy[6]

Among the references summoned by this postmodern rewriting of an *innamoramento* comes Apollinaire, one of the European fathers of concrete, or rather visual, poetry, mostly known in the English-speaking world for his *Calligrammes*. Be it through the multi-polarized, retrospective light shed on the Ur-event of lyric poetry or through the inclusion of images and drawings, early on Tim Atkins's *Petrarch* announces its intention to reshuffle most of the lyrical conventions — and indeed the project constitutes a reflection on translating, rewriting, and being inspired by a distant poetic ancestor, rather than an actual rewriting of his work.[7]

Thus, the end of his response to Petrarch's sonnet 190, '*Una candida cerva sopra l'erba ...*' (famously adapted by Wyatt as 'Whoso list to hunt, I know where is an hind ...') rewrites the allegorical depiction of the *innamoramento* with the loved one as a doe: in Atkins's 190, the lover falling into a streamlet fascinated by the apparition of his beloved becomes

> Falling into the old pond
> Instead of love[8]

The preceding syntax is not clear enough to assert that the poet himself is the one falling in the pond — it could be autumn leaves, or the colourful lights they convey — but the transformation of clear, running water into a stagnating pond (distinct from 'love') clearly asserts the need to get away from a long-standing tradition of lyric *innamoramento*. As shall be seen throughout this chapter, the very fact that this poem does not depict an explicit encounter — only a rather imprecise but '[i]mminent | [u]nyielding' glimpse of someone — and that the only reference to Petrarch and Wyatt is this fall into the stagnating water of an undecidable subject both testify to this project of revisiting without rewriting a source-text.

Similarly, Hocquard's recourse to typographical poems and his rewriting of the initial encounter demonstrate how contemporary poets can position themselves against the Petrarchan archetype while still referring to it. Thus, the first so-called sonnet of *Un test de solitude* clearly constitutes an *innamoramento*, which may be read as a rewriting of the most famous of all, the Petrarchan one:[9]

> I
>
> Jolie
> Des yeux rieurs, une vague tristesse dans l'expression du visage.
> — Comment épelez-vous ce prénom?
> Tout ce qui pourrait être dit serait brouillé par la rumeur des voitures sur la route, devant la boulangerie.
> Piero della Francesca.
> Contente-toi, pour aujourd'hui, d'acheter un demi-pain.
> Bonjour Viviane Vendeuse.
> «Dénoncez tout courrier obscène au régisseur des postes.»
> Depuis le début de l'été ou le naufrage du Titanic.
>
> I
>
> Pretty.
> Laughing eyes, a touch of melancholy in her face.
> — How do you spell your first name?
> All that could be said would be drowned out by the noise from the cars on the road in front of the bakery.

> Piero della Francesca.
> Make do, for today, with just buying half a loaf
> of bread.
> Hello Salesgirl Viviane.
> 'Please report any obscene mail to the Post-
> master.'
> Since early summer or the wreck of the Titanic.[10]

Here, the blurring of sounds by the passing road prevents the reader from linking this work with the lyric tradition: both poets refer to Petrarch while distancing themselves from this very reference in the same breath. Moreover, Hocquard's rewriting of the *innamoramento* becomes, if not straight parody, at least a poem loaded with reminders of cultural or scopic changes: a man's love declaration becomes transmuted into a legal warning against harassment, which should be signalled. Even the characteristics of the beloved contribute to that sense of detachment,[11] from the first word of the book ('*jolie*' alone is stranger than the nobler '*belle*', which would be the archetypal adjective of love poetry) to her sociological characterization (she works as a sales assistant at a baker's) or her very name ('*Bonjour Viviane Vendeuse*', as one must understand her identifying pin). It is as if Hocquard consistently undermined every aspect of the noble, Petrarchan-inspired *innamoramento* in order to launch a grammatical reflection on being in the world, in which the woman will be an addressee rather than the object of desire as the book unfolds.

Besides, in his mock-newspaper-journal 'Les Nouvelles de ma cabane' — in fact letters sent to friends and gathered in the miscellaneous volume *ma haie* — Hocquard himself directly links the writing of sonnets to feeling in love, albeit ironically:

> Comme je le disais l'autre soir à Oscarine, j'écris des sonnets. J'ai toujours écrit énormément de sonnets. Mais pas toujours. [...] C'est plus un penchant (cf. saint-Augustin) qu'un trait de caractère. J'ai dû écrire presque autant de sonnets que Ronsard et bien davantage que Du Bellay. Si j'ai écrit un nombre si élevé de sonnets, c'est que j'ai été amoureux un nombre très élevé de fois. Comme Ronsard. Si écrire des sonnets était un trait de caractère, j'aurais écrit, j'écrirais des sonnets chaque fois que j'ai été, je suis amoureux. Eh bien, non, justement. C'est comme ça que j'ai compris qu'écrire des sonnets est un penchant. Un penchant qui se réveille chaque fois que je tombe dans cette sorte d'état amoureux qui fait écrire des sonnets [...] quand je suis tombé amoureux de Bonjour Viviane Vendeuse, je n'ai pas du tout pensé à écrire une élégie. Ni une ode, ni une ballade. C'est le sonnet qui s'est imposé dans toute son évidence. C'est comme ça que j'ai compris que l'amour que je lui porte est un amour à sonnets. Ce genre d'amour précis qui m'a fait écrire, quand j'étais amoureux de la moitié des filles du lycée Saint-Aulaire à Tanger, toutes classes confondues de la sixième à la terminale, un nombre incalculable de sonnets. C'est pourquoi écrire des sonnets est aussi l'indication évidente que je rajeunis.[12]

Of course, not only is this letter obviously staged as a window onto the poet's supposed intimacy, whose very notion of disclosing Hocquard plays with throughout his work and interviews, but the love evoked here sounds distinctly like a mocking version of the eternal, mystical love of the *Canzoniere*: while Ronsard's sonnets of *Les Amours* do constitute a reference in French literary culture, his 'Amours' are rather different from Petrarch's, being at times quite carnal while their very plural runs contrary to Petrarch's lifelong obsession.[13] Here the casual love for 'half the girls of the Saint-Aulaire high school in Tangiers' should probably not be considered on the same ethical level as Petrarch's love for Laura in his *Canzoniere*.

Moreover, both the automatic link between love and the sonnet on the one hand and the association of the form with *juvenilia* give a mock-poetic shade to this text, although it is impossible to dismiss the poet's assertions completely. Hocquard's regular insistence on humour rather than irony — for irony would imply a distortion of the signifying link Hocquard reveres — must lead us to take these poetics of the love sonnet as both serious and pleasantly exaggerated, just as his evocation in sonnets I–XXI of Russell's and Wittgenstein's famous rhinoceros leads both to a philosophical inquiry and to the pleasant incongruity of the animal.

Linguistics are of importance, as Hocquard states having fallen in love not with a woman called Viviane but with an utterance that is both an apostrophe and a simultaneous designation of the woman's name and function: 'Hello Salesgirl Viviane'. Here the aesthetics and ethics of denomination, parataxis, and transitivity will all play a crucial role throughout the collection, arguably about more than infatuation itself, which seems to serve as a basis for a meditation on these topics, with love as a recurring event. Indeed, while the introductory poem functions as an explicit, if deconstructed, *innamoramento*, it must be stated that the analysis of the rest of the collection through the lens of Petrarch's influence is but a hypothesis, which is substantial since the rest of the book stems from this initial encounter, but which remains nevertheless only one of a handful of themes and influences. Most of the following poems do not refer directly to Petrarch or Petrarchan themes. However, Hocquard's hostile stance against lyricism, combined with his paradoxical recourse to the sonnet, make it necessary to scrutinize how the echoes of the *innamoramento* sound and reappear throughout the eponymous 'test of solitude'.

Finding truthful words for the world: circumstantial poems

While Petrarch mentions biographical details only sparsely, both contemporary poets rely on topical reference: for instance, Tim Atkins writes a sonnet on the death of Margaret Thatcher, triggering a process of remembrance of past eras that recalls the popular music of the 1980s as much as the shrill voice of the late Prime Minister. He summons this voice in a paradoxical device, regretting that her death allows this voice to ring through tributes and archive broadcasts. Needless to say this poem of circumstances deviates fully from its Trecento counterpart: almost nothing in Atkins's poem can be compared to sonnet 93 of the *Canzoniere*, 'Più volte Amor m'avea gia detto: Scrivi', save maybe for the ninth line, which has a vague Petrarchan look, only to be syntactically and thematically deflated by the following one:

> Is it possible to ever give up on love or on hope
> The way food does[14]

Tim Atkins deals more gravely and intimately with death in sonnets 268 and 269. The former is dedicated to Stacy Doris, a writer, translator, and friend of the poet, and written after her death. Stacy Doris also happens to be one of the bridging figures between Atkins and Hocquard, as the latter collaborated with her on the anthology *Violence of the White Page*. French translations of her book have also been published by P.O.L., as has *Un test de solitude*. Situated one sonnet after the famous 'In vita/In morte' divide, this sequence both places the poems within the continuity of the Petrarchan tradition — keeping the departed one somehow alive through words — and at a distance from the celestial beliefs of Christianity, with the longer poem 269 answering Petrarch's meditations on remaining on Earth after Laura's death, such as that following *ballate* 270's 'quella che fu mia donna al ciel è gita':[15]

> I am waving this hankie
> She is dead now really dead so
> Not like in books
> Where the dead are
> But in life where the dead aren't[16]

In Atkins's rewriting of Petrarch, the reference to personal circumstances does not constitute a mere shift in poetics but also helps to sketch an ethical map: the poet gives literary relevance to actual beings, whereas the Italian poet, centred on Laura, fails to mention either his own wife or his son, dead in 1361 — an instance of neglect which the English poet rephrases in 26:

> Absence of autobiography is an ambiguous sign
> Is it any wonder that as a wandering semi-holy
> Horny mendicant one from time to time
> Forgets to pay one's national insurance &
> Fathers invisible children[17]

From his own admission, Tim Atkins, who does not seem too fond of the man Petrarch may have been, protests against this obliteration of family circumstances in Petrarch's *Canzoniere*, by writing a sonnet meant to celebrate all at once parenthood, the meeting of autobiographical circumstances, and the 'small poem' (that is to say, the sonnet):

> Let it be said it is enough to be in love
> With a daughter light   of whom there is but one   in this small poem
> Of which there was but one   & to hold it all going
>   in this small room & yet remarkable[18]

Both Atkins and Hocquard mention family or friends' names in their work, without much explanation about who they are. Significantly, Atkins poses with his children in one of the images of the back cover of his collection, encompassing these crucial facts of life that could be dismissed as trivial by a focus on the mystical and love-lyrical aspects of the *Canzoniere*. Even more overtly, Hocquard devotes an entire sonnet to a resolution to write from circumstances, after seeing Viviane turning her back on a map of Reykjavik, a city reminiscent of the poet's former work. The titular 'test of solitude' occurs as the poet shows his experimental, never commercialized[19] movie *Le Voyage à Reykjavik*, shot with Alexandre Delay and

Juliette Valéry, in performances around the area.

VII

Sa voix de Viviane est Viviane.
Avouant son incompréhension souriante dans la lumière qui vient mourir sur son visage et sur ses mains, la jeune femme tourne le dos à la carte blanche de Reykjavik.
J'ai pris la décision.
Ce livre — j'entreprends de l'écrire pour *vous* — sera le plus simple qui soit. Prenez-le pour ce qu'il se propose d'être: un vrai livre d'images directement puisées aux circonstances. Et s'il se mêle aux sentiments discrets de celui qui l'écrit quelques échos de philosophie c'est que, pour l'auteur de ces pages, la, philosophie se peut aussi montrer par des images.

VII

Her Viviane-voice is Viviane.
Admitting with a smile her incomprehension in the light that comes to die on her face and her hands, the young woman turns her back on the white map of Reykjavik.
I've made the decision.
This book — I undertake to write it for *you* — will be the simplest possible. Take it for what it means to be: a real picture book drawn directly from circumstance. And if there are some echoes of philosophy mixed in with the discreet sentiments of the writer it is because, for the author of these pages, philosophy can also be done in pictures.[20]

This conjuring of a 'true book of images | directly drawn from circumstances' linked with Reykjavik refers both to the rooting of the collection in the poet's present and an attempt to use writing as a form of tracing as faithful to reality as film or photography. If Viviane turns her back on a map that we see, the reader then pictures her from the front: her truthful presence stands in front of the symbol of signification that is a map — which is literally the writing of *topoi*. This pre-eminence of the reality of beings, under the guise of circumstantial poetry, sets Hocquard's depiction of life apart from Petrarch's idealization of Laura; while both write in order to show images of the loved one, Hocquard's is attached to the building of present images rather than idealized and topical ones.

Besides, the mention of the specific word 'circumstances' puts Hocquard's work within the lineage of Goethe's famous remark to Eckermann, that poetry is always poetry of circumstances.[21] Only the French poet does not write in a prosaic, down-to-earth manner, as Jacques Réda does with his *Sonnets dublinois*. On the contrary, Hocquard proceeds by removing many biographical or contextual references, thus leaving the reader in front of cryptic allusions to an unknown reality from which a feeling of strangeness derives, rather than obscuring the link between well-known signified and a topical signifier.

The evocation of Viviane in daily life appears as the driving force of an inquiry into the ability of words to convey meaning. Under the influence of Stein's famous 'Rose is a rose is a rose is a rose'[22] and transposing into poetry Wittgenstein's probes at a logical clarification of thought,[23] Hocquard uses the poem as a way to bypass language's inability to tell the truth about the world:

XX

Viviane est Viviane. *Évidente, seule.*
Qui parle?
La phrase est sans auteur. La phrase est sans sujet. La phrase est sans verbe.
Dans la phrase, *est* n'est pas un verbe dont la première Viviane serait le sujet et la seconde l'attribut.
Il n'y a qu'une seule Viviane. *Seule, évidente.*
Quels verbes Viviane enveloppe-t-elle?
Lever les yeux, sourire, dire « Bonjour », se tourner, se pencher, prendre le pain, se retourner, peser, tendre le pain, dire «Au revoir»...
Je promène ma pensée du *canale* à la souche brûlée. C'est un jardin qui marche

XX

Viviane is Viviane. *Evident, alone.*
Who is speaking?
The sentence is without author. The sentence is without subject. The sentence is without verb.
In the sentence, *is* is not a verb with the first Viviane for subject and the second for predicate.
There is but one Viviane. *Alone, evident.*
Which verbs does Viviane involve?
To look up, smile, say 'Good morning', turn, bend over, pick up the bread, turn around, weigh, hold the bread, say 'Goodbye'...
I am walking my thoughts from the *canale* to the burnt stump. This is a walking garden.[24]

Here the figure of the woman is linked to a concern about both elocution and signification, where the utterance of the name erases the grammatical links between words, thus loading the initial tautology with a deeper meaning — one that could be deemed as the characteristic of poetic language — until the name triggers the final list of verbs that actually depict what Viviane is, what Viviane does, beyond the apparent dead-end tautology.

Finding Truthful Words for the World: Tautology over Analogy

As Viviane is both the most frequent tautologized word of the collection and the recipient of the quest of truth it contains, the Lady — or, as the poet questions the linguistic process of signification, her name — appears to be the most, if not the only, established correspondence, in a world of many irreconcilables. Referring regularly to Viviane anchors the poet's speech even deeper in an unquestionable relation of signification, both through the litany of tautology — and the variations on the same Viviane-themed tautology — and thanks to the vocative mode. In terms of rhetoric, the *donna* therefore becomes not a literary device based on an over-fantasized woman and designed to lead closer to transcendence, but a figure of certainty that functions only because it designates with the utmost transitivity of proper nouns a real human being; while still remaining in the domain of speech, Hocquard's Viviane is as real and material as Petrarch's Laura is conceptual and celestial.

This reflection on the way poetry can transitively tell the essence of its objects appears in another of Hocquard's sonnets:

XV

La règle dit que voir est un verbe d'action.
Je change la règle et je dis que voir est un verbe
d'état (ou de changement d'état).
Ce qui est évident quand on y réfléchit.
Je vois une feuille. Je ramasse une feuille.
Les deux phrases ne sont pas équivalentes.
Je dessine une feuille est encore autre chose.
Giacometti voit un chien. Ce chien qu'il voit ce
jour-là.
Il dit: «Je suis ce chien».
Il fait la sculpture de ce chien. Autoportrait.
Je vois Viviane.
Viviane est Viviane.
J'écris les sonnets de Viviane.[25]

XV

The rule says *to see* is an active verb.
I change the rule and say *to see* is a stative verb
(expressing state or change of state).
Which is obvious when one thinks about it.
I see a leaf. I pick up a leaf.
The two sentences are not equivalent.
I draw a leaf is something else again.
Giacometti sees a dog. The dog that he sees on
this particular day.
He says: 'I am this dog.'
He makes a sculpture of this dog. Selfportrait.
I see Viviane.
Viviane is Viviane.
I write the sonnets of Viviane.[25]

The tautology of the penultimate line is more than just a spanner in the works of logic or a hypothetical stalling in the progression of both look and poetical discourse; it may be read as a secret key to the dialogue with the *Canzoniere*. The poet's final reluctance, both to imitate Giacometti's statement, as it appears in sonnets I–V, of becoming what one sees in order to depict it under the lights of one's interiority, and to project a male's fantasies and social definitions onto a woman he barely knows, unlike what historical Petrarch must have done at his *innamoramento*, speaks in favour of a true, unconceding quest for the truth of beings. Thus, Hocquard's aborted evocation of a painting of the Italian Renaissance at the first meeting between Lady and Poet ('Piero della Francesca. | Contente-toi, pour aujourd'hui, d'acheter un | demi-pain') appears as the first sign of an actual fight against the dynamics of estrangement that underlie the classical *innamoramento*, as the poet does the opposite of what Swann famously does with Odette:[26] he rejects the prism of past beauty, and generally of culture, in order to see the world as it is.

Indeed, for all Hocquard's estrangement with the lyric tradition — one that has Petrarch among its main source — the poet's aim is probably less to satirize a centuries-long lineage of poets, the last of whom are according to him like dogs chewing on a meatless bone[27] and thus tasting nothing but their own blood, than to search for the truth of things with the imperfect tools of language. Thus, he states in an interview about that precise tautology:

> La tautologie m'est apparue comme l'énoncé par excellence. Elle est un modèle logique de vérité. Elle est «inconditionnellement vraie pour la totalité des possibilités de vérité.» (Wittgenstein.) Mais [...] la tautologie n'a aucun pouvoir descriptif ou explicatif.
>
> Or la relation entre l'énoncé «*Viviane est Viviane*» n'est pas simplement une relation logique, abstraite, générale. C'est une relation bien réelle [...] Viviane existe aussi *pour de vrai*, comme disent les enfants. Écrire «*Viviane est Viviane*», ce n'est pas échouer à représenter Viviane. C'est la seule *image* claire possible. Mais cette image n'est pas une *représentation*. Le recours à la tautologie est la seule façon de *tout* dire de Viviane, n'importe quel autre commentaire ne pouvant qu'être métaphorique, réducteur ou défaillant.[28]

The poet thus dismisses the metaphorical relationship to reality — which stems from Petrarch, finds its more impressive deformations in surrealism, and against which the entirety of post-war twentieth-century French poetry reacts[29] — as much as he dismisses narrative, which explains why his paradoxical prose-*canzoniere* will not tell the story of a poet and a saleswoman at a bakery. Tautology — and possibly metonymy, as in sonnet V's liminal 'Sa voix de Viviane est Viviane' — constitutes Hocquard's way to reach for the *donna* through words rather than representation.

On the other hand, in his rewritings of the *innamoramento*, Tim Atkins consistently resorts to these comparisons that Hocquard rejects — although to such a grotesque extent that it only undermines the cliché of transfiguring the world through tropes:

> 60
>
> Somewhere in Folklore
> 1. She grew on him like she was a colony of E. Coli and he was room-temperature Canadian beef.
> 2. She had a deep, throaty, genuine laugh, like the sound a dog makes before it throws up.
> 3. Her vocabulary was bad as, like, whatever.
> 4. Her face was a perfect oval, like a circle that had had its two sides compressed by a Thigh Master.
> 5. Her hair glistened in the rain like a nose hair after a sneeze.
> 6. He fell for her like his heart was a mob informant, and she was the East River.

It
Was
Easy
To
Mistake
A
Woman[30]

Here, the enumeration of six ridiculous comparisons functions as a list of different tropes traditionally presiding over representations of love:
— medicine, with *innamoramento* as contamination the way Petrarchan poets see it, only more prosaic;
— sexual insults, with the item rather unsubtly calling the woman's laugh one of a sick bitch;
— poetic, and even meta-poetic since one of the annoying punctuations the woman uses is 'like', precisely the word for *simile*;
— aesthetics drawn from painting, where the face, supposedly shrine of the soul, is called back to its status as part of the body, being here force-worked as a muscle;
— this equivalence of the different parts the body is then extended by the subversion of the erotics of hair, where the musical or Hollywood-overused (or Bollywood, or Cairo, or…) cliché of wet hair is turned into another, much less noble part of bodily hairiness ;
— deadly love, turned into a *film noir* casual execution.

These components of Renaissance definitions of love are reduced by the initial line as 'Folklore', and the end of the sonnet sees the definite condemnation of tropes in order to flesh out a woman, as old-fashioned depiction becomes a 'mistake'. A common suspicion towards metaphor joins Atkins and Hocquard here, and expands into defiance against a traditional view of love as a mystical rather than material union:

> 70
> Like a sign of ecstatic union
> Dr Johnson said
> I turned towards her
> And said
> Although we met
> Only once
> We were like
> Two hummingbirds
> Who had met
> Only once
> Wits who had writ
> 'The autobiography of my organs'
> Or something about[31]

It should be noted that once again simile is ridiculed here, becoming a tautology: rather than expressing the truth of one's self, this iteration merely shows the impotency of comparing, as it involves 'like' and not 'to be' as the tautological hinge.

Other rewritings of Petrarchan metaphors need not be as directly subversive, but can be mere actualizing of the original as in the first line of a rather faithful adaptation such as 223, which opens on

When the sun's car's done gone into the sea[32]

The classical chariot of the sun becomes a rather modern, and mundane, undefined car, although the sonnet roughly sticks to the themes and progression of Petrarch's 223, 'Quando 'l sol bagna in mar l'aurato carro...'. Atkins's version ends up by rephrasing Petrarch's 'doglia' as 'art-brut laments', thus giving a clue to the kind of adaptation he proceeds to, turning the noble casual or vulgar and drawing from everyday life in order to actualize the *vulgarium* in terms of both subject and rhetoric, incidentally accomplishing the plurality of *vario stile* Petrarch announced he was seeking in his programmatic sonnet. Metaphor as a poetic device thus keeps on being discussed by these two poets under the shade of Petrarch, with Hocquard dismissing it and Atkins mostly inflating it until it reaches a comical, grotesque, ironic, and simultaneously quite poetic outburst. However, it is not the only classical tool these two poets scrutinize, among those poetry has at its disposal in order to convey the true nature of the world: the other Western archetypal figure of speech, the list, plays a central role in their rewriting of Petrarch.

Vertigine della lista:[33] Enumeration as an Alternative to Lyric Seriousness

Being confronted with the unsuitability of traditional poetic language, both poets resort to other means, such as enumeration, in order to create poetry out of everyday life. In the second part of his book, Hocquard finds himself facing the ridicule of claiming tautology as a work of poetry, less in terms of signification — for in 'Viviane is Viviane' the second name is not necessarily the same as the first, one being a designation *per se* and the other the designation of a specific woman — than of pretence of actually being the source of existence. The idea that a tautology may give a disdainful idea of the actual work of the poet is only suggested and is replaced by an evocation of the list as something that could be claimed by a poet:

XX

On ne devrait attribuer que les propositions incertaines. Un nom propre par incertitude.
Quel sens y aurait-il à signer une tautologie?
Viviane est Viviane signé Emmanuel Hocquard serait proprement insensé.
Mais cela peut aussi donner une indication du type sur *l'étiquette il est écrit*: « Don de E. H. à Viviane ».
La liste noire des corbeaux disposés par ordre de grandeur croissante ou décroissante dans les vitrines du musée d'Histoire naturelle,
la culture d'étiquettes du Jardin botanique en hiver,
la liste des courses et des musées...

XX
Only uncertain propositions should be attributed.
One proper name per uncertainty.
What sense would it have to sign a tautology?
Viviane is Viviane signed Emmanuel Hocquard
would be really insane.
But it can also furnish information of the type
on the label there is written: 'Gift of E. H. to
Viviane.'
The black list of ravens arranged by increasing
or decreasing size in the cases of the Museum of
Natural History,
the cultivation of labels in the Botanical Garden
in winter,
the list of errands and museums...[34]

Here Hocquard dismisses the idea of tautology as claimable work, suggesting maybe another modality of clear utterance — the simple enumeration of names being possibly as close to reality as tautology can be, without the latter's pretention to be an image of reality. It is remarkable that in this poem Hocquard separates each component of the final enumeration as if it were a verse rather than for reasons of syntax or enunciation. The old poetic device of the list makes the poem draw into poetry's first resources, both fuelling Hocquard's project with poetic power from its original spring and maintaining a strict adhesion to his austere stance on language — it is the litany of the Greek ships that is faintly convoked here, rather than the Homeric epithet. It is even possible that this very list of separate enunciations, located in the last poems of the second section, constitutes the titular test of solitude: an attempt to find a linguistic modality of truth outside tautology. Even more noteworthy is the fact that this enumeration itself lists potential enumerations.[35] It is also quite ironic that in sonnets II–XX, this reflection on the impossibility for a poet to claim anything truthful ends on a shopping list, in another adhesion to Hocquard's prosaic stance.

The rewriting of the list also functions as a triggering device in Atkins, where the poet uses the initial enumeration of streams in Petrarch's sonnet 148 to start his own sonnet 148:

Non Tesin, Po, Varo, Arno, Adige et Tebro,	Not Tessin, Tiber, Varo, Arno,
Eufrate, Tigre, Nilo, Hermo, Indo et Gange,	Adige, Po, Euphrates, Ganges, Tigris,
Tana, Histro, Alpheo, Garona,	Nile, Erno, Indo, Don, Danube,
e 'l mar che frange,	Alpheus, Garonne, the sea-breaker
Rodano, Hibero, Ren, Sena, Albia,	Rhône, Rhine, Iber, Seine, Elbe,
Era, Hebro;	Loire, Ebro;
[...]	[...]
Cosí cresca il bel lauro in fresca riva,	Let this fair laurel grow on the fresh bank,
et chi 'l piantò pensier' leggiadri et alti	and he who planted it, in its sweet shade
ne la dolce ombra al suon de l'acque scriva.	to watery sounds, write high and happy thoughts.[36]

This initial list of rivers from Italy, Asia, and then the entirety of Europe — from

Spain's Ebra to Ukraine's Don, and from Germany's Rhine to Peloponnese's Alpheus — gets reduced to an initial, condensed allegory, before being lightly expanded:

> 148
>
> Rivers of men   the university of life & the school of etcetera
> Are my rivers   cholesterol reducing juice drinks
> Severn Wandle Thames Seine Llobregat Hudson
> Aldi   Lidl or Besos
> Neither wood chipwallpaper off the holy cross
> Fragment of a shopping list from Nazareth
> Or blood spilled by a blood donors drive in a
> Portacabin   or free blow-jobs van in the Castro   can convince me   After 40 days in the wilderness
> Awaiting the plaster-casters
> Vision transcribed out of some ancient language
> Or best-selling book about tantra
> Trouble my singing   When a lover loves or dreams of another
> & finds themselves walking over the fields at 4AM in tuxedo & patent leather
>   shoes it is true
> The Writer's Voice   comes apart at what cost?[37]
> [...]

Atkins's sonnet drifts from Petrarch's source after having enumerated some of the rivers the poet has been by, and the drift operates within the enumeration itself: the foreign-sounding names turn into brands from discount, foreign supermarkets, as if the immensity of the world was reduced to a succession of aisles among which one could pick up whichever choices of life one wishes to acquire. Far from Petrarch's long and dangerous travels, this sonnet would be one of the low-cost carriers.

The mention of the 'shopping list from Nazareth', as the poem turns from enumeration to evocation of different contemporary, prosaic avatars of religion and mysticism, not only recalls Hocquard's 'liste des courses et des musées' with its list of religious themes juxtaposed as items on the shelves of a shop, but also blends the trivial and the sublime into the final visions where corporality (Californian 'free blow-jobs van in the Castro' as much as the mystic, Vedic 'tantra') gives way to half-phantasmagorical, half-grotesque hallucinations.

The form of the sonnet itself should include triviality, as sonnet 302 starts, with a play upon the comparison between the little piece of poetry and a little room where the poet can sparsely talk — and in Italian *stanza* designates both a room and a poetic stanza:

> 302
>
> If the sonnet is a room   which is a room
> For all life to perform in —
> Then it is preferable to have one with a window desk and toilet[38]

Indeed, both Atkins and Hocquard comment on their appropriation, and considerable distortion, of the form of the sonnet, in moves that reveal how they relate to tradition.

The Form of a Sonnet: An Ironic Relation with Tradition

When it comes to form, Hocquard actually maintains this ambiguity between a strong, logical destructuration of the sonnet and the preservation of an ironic link that can be interpreted on many levels.

Thus, Hocquard appears to be reducing the definition of the sonnet to its fourteen lines — the confusion between rhymed sonnet and unrhymed fourteener being less frequent in French than in English poetry — while taking 'line' literally, by refusing to distinguish verse and prose, as seen in earlier examples. He justifies this by the need for continuity in a pseudo-demonstration that neglects his own equating of a finite line with a prose line going the full width of the page:

> J'écris des sonnets de quatorze lignes. Tous les sonnets ont, direz-vous, quatorze lignes. Ce n'est pas si simple que ça. [...] Par exemple dans un sonnet découpé en quatre strophes, que faire des trois lignes blanches? Faut-il les compter comme lignes ou les compter comme non-lignes? [...] j'écris des sonnets de quatorze lignes qui se suivent. J'évite ainsi le problème posé par les quatre strophes et les lignes blanches qui les séparent.[39]

Moreover, this stance does not prevent him from writing a poem[40] made of three quatrains, amounting to fourteen lines only if the white lines in-between stanzas are included in the count. Similarly, Atkins composes sonnet 121 as a quatrain followed by five pairs of a blank line and a written line, amounting to fourteen when counting the blanks.

Hocquard's experimental and on many levels paradoxical use of the sonnet, or so-called sonnet, and of its ironic denomination, can be understood both as a laughing nod towards the signifying link as processed throughout the collection which would fit into a form that is ironic and paradoxical too, and as a sincere reshaping of the form.

However, Hocquard's poetics have included constraint before this collection. When evoking the works of his small publishing house, Orange Export Ltd, where during the 1970s he would manufacture booklets from authors as diverse as Pascal Quignard, Georges Perec, Claude Esteban, Denis Roche, Jacques Roubaud, Bernard Noël, Michel Deguy or fellow *littéralistes* Anne-Marie Albiach and Claude Royet-Journoud, Hocquard mentions being proud of a particular size of booklet that he links to a constraint, a fixed form:

> Sur le plan formel, notre grande fierté est l'invention de la collection *Chutes*, [...] C'est une forme fixe, à contraintes souples: cinq pages de texte (vers ou prose) à raison de cinq ou six lignes maximum par page. À l'inverse du sonnet, par exemple, l'unité formelle n'est pas constituée par le poème, mais par le volume.[41]

His pride at a formal find tells as much about the nature of the latter, made of an external and material, rather than internal, definition. Denominational irony notwithstanding, *Un test de solitude* extends a former formal meditation on the shaping of the poem by its format: the sonnet, essentially reduced to a rectangle, appears as a way to unify different types of poems. Thus the sonnet appears for what it is under a concrete poetry perspective: a *Form* that can visually order perception as well as the lyric *Gestalt*'s inner dynamics are supposed to do, becoming under Hocquard the visual equivalent of the lyric, rhyming pattern of Petrarch.

The irony therefore becomes an assertion of superiority: by undermining the lyrical expectations linked to the form by multiplying or ridiculing them, Hocquard gives strength to his own radical definition of the sonnet. For a sonnet it is still; as Dominique Moncond'huy has shown,[42] one of the essential qualities of the twentieth-century sonnet is its shape on the page. Hocquard states that what defines the form is that it is a rectangle above all;[43] in *Un test de solitude*, he describes an empty basin much as his pseudo-sonnets look like, under the shape of an exact and clear rectangle for the eyes ('Pour les yeux, exactement un rectangle clair'[44]).

Atkins's liminal invocation of Apollinaire sets both poets under the patronage of the *Calligrammes*: poems for the eyes — except that this great monument of lyricism, the sonnet, becomes a visual form above all. The precedence of the reader's gaze allows the sonnet to take various forms, as one can literally see here, without even reading the poem:

XXIII

Arbres et oiseaux se croisent au hasard dans le ciel
les ifs   les pies
l'herbe   les grives
les pins   les merles
les saules   les huppes
l'antéfixe   les coucous
la glycine   les fauvettes
les acacias   les mésanges
la charmille   les corneilles
les bambous   les bouvreuils
les peupliers   les étourneaux
les eucalyptus   le héron cendré
le séquoia géant   les rouges-gorges
les mûriers platanes   les bergeronnettes[45]

The importance of the central void, from a philosophical perspective, has already been addressed; nevertheless, one should not conclude that Hocquard's poetry is purely philosophical. Indeed, this concrete poem has more links with the sonnet and the lyrical tradition than could be thought: the shape left blank by the enumeration is one of a V for Viviane thus making this proto-sonnet the exact reverse of acrostic tours-de-forces, among which sonnets feature regularly as a dedicatory piece.

Moreover, Moncond'huy proposes[46] that this blank can also be read as a feminine vulva — yet another V-word — thus turning a concrete pseudo-sonnet into a modern, visual reinterpretation of the lyrical tradition of the blazon. It is worth developing this interpretation into an anti-Petrarchan or rather anti-lyrical stance, by suggesting the visual V refers only to the visual aspect of Petrarch's puns on the name Laura, which are both sonorous and graphic; moreover, the void rather than the hard initial wall of the first letters of the verse makes this anti-blazon rather feminine; ultimately, the missing word rather than the obscenity of its deciphering turn the allusion into some etymological porno-a-graphy, some non-writing of an obvious sex.

The French critic also remarks[47] that even Hocquard's macrostructural project constitutes an ironical nod towards the sonnet: the two sections of 33 and 25 sonnets form an arithmetical equivalent of the proportions of the sonnet: $33/25 = 1.32$, while 8/6 = 1.3333 — thus taking an opposite stance to the classical, lyrical sonnet's use of evenness by giving odd proportions to these graphic, logical, quite odd sonnets. Besides, it should be added to D. Moncond'huy's remarks that this numeral relation is also linked to the V of Viviane, that Hocquard, in his paradoxical anti-traditionalist stance, answers Petrarch more faithfully than many of his translators in one point, which is that his poems are numerated with Roman numbers in the way any person of letters of Petrarch's era would have done.

On the other hand, Atkins obviously uses the contemporary, Arabic numeral system; his position is more transgressive than Hocquard's since he also rejects numeration as composed solely of integers and integrates translations of his poems or variations on a similar theme corresponding to his poems' numbers. His project being less meticulous than Hocquard's demanding, restrained quest, Atkins goes for the wider scale in adapting the entirety of the *Canzoniere* — and even surpassing its original number of 366 poems, thanks to his use of non-integers. His use of the form shows also how he may be more transgressive of Petrarch-bound rules of the sonnet, as he frequently goes over the sacrosanct number 14. Of course his adaptations of *ballate*, *canzone*, or *madrigali* do not count fourteen lines — without being formally constrained as the originals — but he also exceeds the 14-line limit in some of his adaptations of Petrarchan sonnets.

His inscription in a visual tradition is made more obvious by the presence of drawings and even of a sonnet that is actually a page of comic book: rather than subverting the lyric tradition of the sonnet, Atkins inscribes his work in a counter-tradition which, although quite young on the surface (the Oulipian Étienne Lecroart delivered the first rigorous comic-book sonnets in 2007), can be linked to an entire lineage of visual readings of the sonnet, into which a critical eye could fit Roubaud, Cendrars, Rimbaud, the Modern Age acrostics, and even certain *incunabula* of Petrarch.[48]

However, the use of a wide line space and the absence of stanzas (most of his sonnets are made of successive lines) blur the visual impression of the sonnet: it is only the break at the end of each line that helps to define the poem as fourteener, although to complicate identification even more, the many blanks within the line hinder the end-of-line audibility that ought to define an unrhymed sonnet. For instance, in the aforementioned lines

> Let it be said it is enough to be in love
> With a daughter light   of whom there is but one   in this small poem[49]

it is impossible to decide by hearing only whether the line ends after 'light', 'one', or 'poem'. This process of fragmenting the poem within the very frame of the line is not new either: Jacques Roubaud uses it as early as 1967 in his inaugural sonnet collection, ∈. Once again, being experimental does not exclude inserting oneself into a lineage, and although Atkins's sonnets may not look or sound like sonnets, they should not be excluded from the field of the form, whose definition they help to question: it is partly through the inscription within sonnetic sub-traditions — variations on Petrarch, experimental redefinings of the sonnet — that they get their status as sonnets.

Conclusion

Thus, these two poets' connection with Petrarch appears as a crucial, defining one, however much they oppose or stray from their supposed model, which at times arguably functions as a pretext in both senses of the word. Hocquard is clearer in his opposition to lyric poetry and his irony towards this Ur-example, the *Canzoniere*, while Atkins, who refers more directly to Petrarch, adopts a more nuanced stance.

This very discussion of what tradition and a contemporary poet's relation towards it should be stands at the core of these two poetic projects: rather than Petrarch himself, it is the present that they address.

As Yves Bonnefoy puts it beautifully when explaining why he translated some sonnets of the *Canzoniere*, 'how could one not believe that poetry as a whole, though chained to its original speech, wishes to open itself to other languages and cultures?'[50] It certainly is through an undoubtedly distorting adaptation process that Petrarch resonates in these two poets' work, set in a time when culture has a very different definition; it is nonetheless the echoes of his *innamoramento* that are discussed for the contemporary reader's sake.

Notes to Chapter 10

1. Jacques Roubaud, '*le grand incendie de Londres*' (Paris: Seuil, 2009), p. 1424.
2. Emmanuel Hocquard, *Tout le monde se ressemble: une anthologie de poésie contemporaine* (Paris: P.O.L., 1995), pp. 24–25:

   En poésie, il y a toujours une menace de chantage dans l'air. Les poètes sont, par tradition, de grands maîtres chanteurs. Ils ne font d'ailleurs pas seulement chanter la langue ou les mots de la langue, ils font aussi chanter leurs lecteurs. Ils les tiennent sous le charme.

   [In poetry, there's always a threat of blackmail hanging around. Poets are, according to tradition, great masters of song and blackmail. They actually not only have language or words singing, they also blackmail their readers. They hold them under their spell. (my translation)]

3. Jacques Roubaud, *Quasi-cristaux: un choix de sonnets en langue française de Lazare Carnot (1820) à Emmanuel Hocquard (1998)* (Paris: Yvon Lambert et Martine Aboucaya, 2013), unnumbered pages. The chapter devoted to Hocquard can be accessed in the online version as well: <http://blogs.oulipo.net/qc/description-du-sonnet-francais/chapitre-6-%e2%80%94-breves-notes-sur-l%e2%80%99evolution-de-la-forme/> [accessed 31 July 2018].
4. Jeff Hilson, *The Reality Street Book of Sonnets* (Hastings: Reality Street, 2008), p. 17.
5. Hocquard says he follows Apollinaire's dynamics of blurring of verse and prose in *ma haie* (Paris: P.O.L., 2001) and he has translated Reznikoff's *The Manner music* and writes eloquent pages about his *Testimony* in *La Bibliothèque de Trieste* (Luzarches: Royaumont, 1988, pp. 32–34) where he also quotes Zukofsky. As the next quoted poem shows, Apollinaire is one of Atkins's references throughout *Petrarch Collected Atkins*.
6. Tim Atkins, *Petrarch Collected Atkins* (London: Crater, 2014), p. 9.
7. Tim Atkins's frequent, delighted public reminders that he does not read or speak Italian can be interpreted as an acknowledgement of the absurdity of any unidirectional rewriting and of the need to feed one's work from older works rather than bowing in deference before their altar.
8. Atkins, p. 126.
9. This interpretation is one that Jacques Roubaud has told me he shared, when we discussed Hocquard's poems.

10. Emmanuel Hocquard, *Un test de solitude* (Paris, P.O.L., 1998) [un-paginated — Livre I, sonnet I], translation Rosemarie Waldrop, *A Test of Solitude* (Providence: Burning Desk, 2000), p. 11.
11. For which the German *Verfremdungseffekt*, meaning 'effect of estrangement' and designating, according to Brecht, a voluntary and ostentatious distancing from *mimesis* would be more precise.
12. As I was telling Oscarine the other night, I'm writing sonnets. I have always written loads of sonnets. But not always. [...] It is more an inclination (cf. St Augustine) than a personality trait. I must have written as many sonnets as Ronsard and many more than Du Bellay. If I have written such a massive number of sonnets, it is that I have been in love a massive number of times. As Ronsard had. If writing sonnets was a character trait, I would have written, I would write, sonnets each time I have been, each time I am, in love. Well, as it happens, I haven't. That is how I understood that writing sonnets is an inclination. An inclination that stirs each time I fall into this kind of loving state that has me writing sonnets [...] when I fell in love with Hello Salesgirl Viviane, I did not think the least of writing an elegy. Nor an ode or a ballad. It is the sonnet that has imposed itself like a foregone conclusion. This is how I understood that the love I bear her is a sonnet kind of love. That very kind of love that had me writing, when I was in love with half the girls of the Saint-Aulaire high school in Tangiers (regardless of their class), an uncountable number of sonnets. This is also why writing sonnets is an obvious indication that I am getting younger. (Hocquard, *ma haie*, pp. 426–27; my translation)
13. In French, referring to somebody's 'amours' can mean both a single relationship in the entirety of its history and details, or the whole range of various affairs, infatuations, and sustained relations the subject gets involved in; as the recurring title of Ronsard's different collections, the word connotes a succession of affairs, in a quite un-Petrarchan way.
14. Atkins, p. 126.
15. Francesco Petrarca, *Canzoniere,* trans. by Mark Musa (Bloomington: Indiana University Press, 1996 [1363–74]), p. 390.
16. Atkins, *Petrarch Collected*, p. 400.
17. Ibid., p. 42.
18. Ibid., pp. 290–91.
19. See Alexandre Delay and Emmanuel Hocquard, *Voyage à Reykjavik*, <http://www.pol-editeur.com/pdf/502.pdf> [accessed 31 July 2018].
20. Hocquard, *Un test de solitude*, [unpaginated — Livre I, sonnet VII], trans. by Rosemarie Waldrop, p. 17.
21.
    Die Welt ist so groß und reich und das Leben so mannigfaltig, daß es an Anlässen zu Gedichten nie fehlen wird. Aber es müssen alles Gelegenheitsgedichte seyn, das heißt, die Wirklichkeit muß die Veranlassung und den Stoff dazu hergeben. [...] Von Gedichten, aus der Luft gegriffen, halte ich nichts. (conversation of 18 September 1823, in Johan Peter Eckerman, *Gespräche mit Goethe, in den letzten Jarhen seines Leben* (Frankfurt: Insel, 1992 [1836]), p.44)

    [The world is so great and rich, and life so full of variety, that you can never want occasions for poems. But they must all be occasional poems; that is to say, reality must give both impulse and material for their production. A particular case becomes universal and poetic by the very circumstance that it is treated by a poet. [...] I attach no value to poems snatched out of the air.(translation John Oxenford, 1906, (2006), <http://www.hxa.name/books/ecog/Eckermann-ConversationsOfGoethe-1823.html> [accessed 30 July 2018])]

22. Gertrude Stein, *Geography and Plays* (Madison, and London: The University of Wisconsin Press, 1993 [1922]), p. 187.
23. Hocquard, *ma haie*, p. 22.
24. Hocquard, *Un test de solitude*, Livre I, sonnet XX, trans. Waldrop, p. 30.
25. Hocquard, *Un test de solitude*, Livre I, sonnet XV, trans. Waldrop, p. 25.
26. Marcel Proust, *Du côté de chez Swann* (1913), in *À la recherche du temps perdu*, I (Paris: Robert Laffont, 1987), pp. 194–95.

27. Hocquard, *ma haie*, p. 25.
28. Emmanuel Hocquard and Éric Audinet, 'Entretien avec Emmanuel Hocquard', *Cahier Critique de Poésie*, Marseille, 3.1 (2001), 9–10:

    > Tautology has appeared to me as the utterance *per se*. It is a logical model for truth. It is 'unconditionally true for the entire range of potential truths' (Wittgenstein). But [...] the tautology has no power of description or explanation whatsoever.

    > Yet, the relation between the utterance '*Viviane is Viviane*' isn't only logical, abstract, general, but quite a real one. [...] Viviane also exists *for real*, as children say. Writing '*Viviane is Viviane*' isn't failing to represent Viviane. It is the only possible clear *image*, although this image is not a *representation*. Resorting to the tautology is the only way of saying *everything* of Viviane, any other commentary inescapably being only metaphorical, reductive or inadequate. (my translation)

29. Tim Atkins confirmed to me that he could be seen as one of his sonnet 212's 'men who struggle with the violence in surrealism' (p. 287), especially violence he considers that surrealism inflicts on women's autonomy.
30. Atkins, p. 85.
31. Atkins, *Petrarch Collected*, p. 97.
32. Ibid., p. 302.
33. Umberto Eco, *Vertigine della lista* (Milan: Bompiani, 2009).
34. Hocquard, *Un test de solitude*, Livre II, sonnet XX, trans. Waldrop, p. 66.
35. Thus a link between Perec, whom Hocquard has edited in his Orange Export Ltd. artisanal print, is apparent, for the Oulipian writer has composed not only numerous enumerations such as *Je me souviens...*, but also an essay on enumeration, *Penser Classer* (1985), which itself constitutes a meta-list, as it arranges different ways of arranging books, for instance.
36. Petrarca, trans. Musa, pp. 366–67.
37. Atkins, p. 97.
38. Ibid., p. 438.
39. Hocquard, *ma haie*, pp. 427–28 ('I write fourteen-lines sonnets. Every sonnet has, you'll say, fourteen lines. This is not so simple [...] For instance, in a sonnet cut in four stanzas, what do we make of the three white lines? Must we count them as lines or as non-lines? [...] I write sonnets of fourteen following lines. I avoid thus the issue of the four stanzas and the three white dividing lines', my translation).
40. Hocquard, *Un test de solitude*, Livre I, sonnet XXVIII.
41. Emmanuel Hocquard, [entretien avec Claude Esteban, 1986], in Emmanuel Hocquard, Raquel, *Orange Export Ltd* (Paris: Flammarion, 1986), p. 8:

    > On a formal level, our great pride is the invention of our collection *Falls*, [...] It is a fixed form, with supple constraints: five pages of text (prose or verse) with up to five or six lines per page. Unlike the sonnet, for instance, formal unity is not set by the poem but rather by the volume. It is the ideal volume; minimal, to be sure, but allowing nearly everything. Even the novel. (my translation)

42. Dominique Moncond'huy, 'D'Aragon à Roubaud et Hocquard: le sonnet comme espace', *Formules*, 12 (2008), pp. 11–21.
43. 'Un sonnet, c'est d'abord un rectangle', quoted by Moncond'huy, p. 19.
44. Hocquard, *Un test de solitude*, Livre I, sonnet X.
45. Ibid., Livre II, sonnet XXIII.
46. Moncond'huy, pp. 19–20.
47. Ibid., p. 20.
48. Such as the one analysed by Giulia Zava in this book.
49. Atkins, p. 290.
50. Yves Bonnefoy, *Je vois sans yeux et sans bouche je crie* (Paris: Galilée, 2011) [marginal 'please insert', unpaginated].

CHAPTER 11

'Petrarch's Love Clangs her Triumphal Car': Following Petrarch in Geoffrey Hill's Mid- to Later Work

Carole Birkan-Berz

'[E] vidi il Tempo rimenar tal prede | de' nostri nomi ch'io gli ebbi per nulla.' One translation of these lines from Petrarch's *Triumph of Time* might be: 'I saw Time take so many of our names as prey that I saw them as nothing'.[1] In this epigraph to his last published volume of verse, *Al Tempo de' Tremuoti*, Geoffrey Hill places his literary legacy under the aegis of a Poet Laureate who says his name might not endure. Whether false modesty or lucid *memento mori* on the part of either poet, the paradox remains, reinforced by the archaic, elliptical, somewhat untranslatable nature of these lines. This chapter will examine the importance of Petrarch in Hill's poetic project as it unfolds in his mid-to later work. I argue that Geoffrey Hill struggles with the inheritance of Petrarchism in the Western lyric by engaging with some lesser-known aspects of Petrarch.[2] Following the traces of this wide-ranging Petrarchan intertext, I wish to show that Petrarch is a strong presence in Hill's work, which one can better gauge by examining Hill's mode of translation and adaptation, as well as his attraction to untranslatability. I begin with contextual considerations about translation and Petrarch within Hill's work before looking at two core Petrarchan images in Hill — those of the triumph and the Virgin Mary — and finally examine the Petrarchan intertext as a space of exchange with other poet-translators.

Hill's entire oeuvre displays a strong link with foreign literature and translation. Having written versions of Spanish poetry from the Golden Age or placed himself in the footsteps of the French poetry of Charles Péguy using the interlanguage of French and English, Hill is concerned with what one might call the 'value' of translation. In her pioneering study, Sara d'Orazio shows that Hill's interaction with foreign sources began in the wake of a politically charged translation wave in the 1960s and 1970s, in which translation was a response to aesthetic, ethical and historical concerns.[3] Since the publication of Hill's *Collected Critical Writings* (hereafter CCW) in 2008 and collected poems *Broken Hierarchies* in 2012, it has become possible to map out the various meanings of translation according to the poet and critic. In the essays 'The Eloquence of Sober Truth' and 'Translating

Value', translation is variously defined as a task 'that sustainedly [...] require[s] vigilance' in matters of language, an activity fostering the 'recognition' of the profound meaning of words, the act of 'working justly in words; of working justice into and through and out of language'.[4] Hill says that these moments of recognition may take the shape of puns, or playful or weighty ambiguity (or equivocation) or even become 'traducement', 'defaming' or betrayal[5] — an extreme form of *traduttore traditore*. Much of Hill's criticism is concerned with extensive glossing of particular words and phrases — so much so that this has yielded secondary criticism on the value of words.[6] In the CCW, such words as are glossed and extensively interpreted include 'reasonableness' (of Robert Southwell), 'value' (intrinsic or otherwise), 'tone' as opposed to 'pitch', Hopkins's hapax 'unchancelling' and many others, including indeed 'translation'. In fact, one might say that Hill's translative attention focuses on the words themselves, though he is interested in their context in the original writer (or what he terms 'contexture') as well as in their reception (by a sometimes careless readership). Perhaps because of his particular cautiousness, Hill often does *not* translate the source text but leaves it in its original language, either without any English rendering or with a number of glosses. In contrast to the rigour he seems to require of the translator, his 'translations' *per se* are often called 'free imitations' of foreign poems, with the source text often being termed a mere 'point of departure' for his poem.[7] In reality, Hill's translations are often glosses on important words, exegeses of important concepts, 'parsing' of phrases or multilingual play on etymology; more rarely are they the simple 'carrying over' of source texts or outright metamorphoses of source materials — all this contributes to a sense of the untranslatability at the heart of Hill's aesthetic.[8]

One word the critic could gloss in Hill's work might be 'Petrarchism'. As has often been noted, many of Hill's renowned early sonnets are strictly Petrarchan with regard to rhyme scheme, diction and use of conceits.[9] Much has been written about Hill's revisiting of the Petrarchan sonnet form and his struggle to use it in radical ways in poems such as 'September Song'. In these works, the Petrarchan current flows strongly through some typical sonnet imagery. But though many stock images from Petrarchism appear — e.g. the fire–ice oxymoron, the images of the rose or of the laurel tree — Hill's early work is also strongly critical of Petrarchism. The aptly titled poem 'The Laurel Axe' typically questions the values of this kind of lyric; another poem speaks of 'wired laurels'.[10] This radical, anti-Petrarchist strain can be found in Hill's critical writings as well. An essay on Jonson mocks one character's Petrarchan 'sexual reverence' contrasted with his promiscuousness, and the same character wears a 'gaudy', 'Petrarchan' mask (CCW 49); another piece on Spenser calls the last sonnets of *Amoretti* full of 'Petrarchan cadences' associated with 'clichés of loss, absence, mortality' (CCW 153).[11] A central paradox thus appears continually in Hill's oeuvre, as in that of other authors: can poets continue writing in a form of poetry that may have become hackneyed? As Adorno asked, what is the relevance of the Western personal lyric mode in a world saturated with public atrocities?[12] In the early work, the answer seems to lie in both managing to retain the formal perfection of the sonnet and heightening the mode of trobar clus.[13]

In the 1990s, Hill's response began to change: trobar clus was kept but classical formal perfection gave way to a movement towards free verse. Beginning with *Canaan* (1996) and *The Triumph of Love* (1998),[14] Hill's works most notably include some volume-long modernist style poems and sequences and the flooding of poetry with vernacular elements, with much space given to contemporary discourse. Yet in *The Triumph of Love*, Hill also achieves an unparalleled lyric fluency precisely against those unlyrical odds. As Sara d'Orazio has observed, every time Hill's poetry appears more lyrical, more intimate, his poetics become multilingual, veering closer to foreign languages — usually Romance ones.[15]

One significant aspect of this new poetics is the overwhelming presence of the Italian material within the foreign intertext of the mid- to later work. Hill translates Montale and adapts Pavese, as well as Carducci and Leopardi. Because the struggle with the Petrarchan inheritance is one that runs deep in the Italian tradition, the questions these writers pose is relevant to Hill's own. Many of the writers mentioned above wrestled with Petrarchism to create their own style of lyrical or unlyrical poetry. Laureates for modern times, Carducci and Montale both ended up as Nobel Prize winners; Leopardi and Carducci renewed lyricism in their own ways. All in all, the number of references to a Petrarch-indebted modern Italian poetry in Hill's work may be read as a rebuttal of Ezra Pound's theory that there had been no Italian poetry after Dante — Petrarch being all 'fustian and ornament', unnecessary *bric-à-brac*, a position that helped Pound formulate his aesthetic of Imagism.[16] Outside Leopardi — relegated to a mere imitator of Shakespeare — the only Italian poet Pound cites after Dante is the Fascist sympathizer Gabriele D'Annunzio, who wrote in what critics, including Montale, called 'embellished language'.[17] In a contradictory move, Hill revisits the Poet Laureate and his translators and inheritors to enact his own renewed struggle with Petrarch. Hence, beginning with *The Triumph of Love*, Petrarch is still a central focus for Hill — just as he was with the early sonnets — but he is historicized and used as a more multifaceted reference.

In Hill's work as an older poet, the theme of poetic consecration begins to be seen, and the appeal to the Laureate's authority becomes significant, particularly when set against that of a Pound. When Hill writes: 'the struggle for a noble vernacular: this | did not end with Petrarch' (TL LXX, BH 259), he is comparing his own poetic project with no less than an enterprise in turning a 'vernacular' work into a classic. Hence it should be no surprise that Hill looks at his poetry from a wider angle than Petrarchism, using the *Triumphi* as a basis and including references to the Latin works — some of which, like the *Africa*, earned Petrarch his Laureateship and his enduring renown in the late medieval and early modern era, while his vernacular works only began to be recognized as 'classics' by Bembo over a century after his death.[18] In so doing, he seems to suggest that emotions — the *sospiri* that open both the Canzoniere and the *Triumphi* — might still be valid on a higher plane, with a wider sense of Petrarch's oeuvre, or with 'Petrarch Made New'. Like Petrarch's *Triumphi*, Hill's verse blends classical and vernacular references, attempting to heighten the English lyric to a form of poetry that might capture the dilemmas of the age. However, with Hill, this is always a movement in both directions: from the first sections of *The Triumph of Love*, 'Petrarch' is paired with 'Petronius' (TL III, BH 239): lyric is coupled with satire, high culture can also be brought low. In any case, Petrarch remains a significant, if paradoxical, presence within Hill's mid-to later work, which deserves investigating.

Bearing in mind these considerations, this study now unfolds into three parts, first examining the Hillian versioning or adaptation of two specific Petrarchan topoi from the *Triumphi* and *RVF canzoni* — the topos of the 'triumphal car', then the representation of the Virgin Mary — and finally looking at the wider Petrarchan intertext as a locus for poetic engagement and exchange with other poet-translators.

Hill's *Triumph*: a revisited Petrarchan motif for a new kind of lyric

Like many of Hill's works, *The Triumph of Love* borrows its title from a classic work of literature. But this is no simple adaptation: like Petrarch, the English poet likes to use a plethora of other references.[19] Still, Hill's *Triumph* shares many thematic and formal features with its Petrarchan predecessor. Appropriating the title of the first of Petrarch's *Triumphi*, the volume marks a shift from the taut sonnet sequences of the early work towards longer sequences of poems of sometimes equal, sometimes variable lengths. In this work, Hill negotiates the space for a private lyric poetry in a more public, political arena, and claims the requirement for a '*canzone* of some substance' (TL LV, BH 254). A survey of the themes of Petrarch's *Triumphi* helps throw light on further parallels between Hill and his poetic forebear. Like Petrarch, Hill openly refers to his own poetic career — though his poetic triumph is somewhat mitigated, unlike Petrarch, he has not quite defeated all his critics 'Croker, McSikker, O'Shem' (TL CXLVIII, BH 285). Hill shares many of Petrarch's concerns, as outlined by Zygmunt Barański:

> 'tempo' (v. 1: 'time'), 'memoria' (v. 2: 'memory'), love, existential anguish, glory (v. 15), death (obsessively), friendship, learning, the relationship between the human and the divine, [...] and, of course, the self.[20]

One of the most salient symbols of these concerns is the image of the Roman-style triumphs. In an underlying narrative at once reminiscent of Petrarch's successive triumphs and of the medieval concept of *translatio imperii* — the transfer of power from one empire to the next — Hill's triumphs and defeats are localized in twentieth-century Europe. Narrating his vision of the Second World War as a child then as an old man, Hill's partly autobiographical sequence begins, like Petrarch's, in a personal 'sun-blazed' landscape (TL I). Romsley is Hill's Vaucluse, a place where visions might appear. The consecutive triumphs and downfalls are often deadly sightings, the first ones being of Dunkirk (TL V) and of Coventry 'ablaze' (TL VII): the implied 'triumph' of the Nazi enemy and impending defeat for Britain. But the 'triumph' of the Allied forces is to occur later in the poem, though in subdued form or as '[s]tunned words of victory' (TL LXXXIX).

In Hill, these images are given a contemporary, democratic twist, verging on the burlesque — the 'march', 'procession' or 'pavane' turns into a 'kermesse', 'carnival' or 'street-pageant'. These images are coupled with a classic Senecan sense of moral derision. Seneca is mentioned in section XI of *The Triumph of Love* (BH 241), harking back to his famous dictum that 'Petty sacrilege is punished; sacrilege on a grand scale is the stuff of triumphs.'[21] At first glance, the Petrarchan-Roman triumph is invoked at once to be modernized, internalized — as autobiography — and satirized.

Yet, in a number of ways, Petrarch's poetry goes against the concept of *translatio imperii*. As Karlheinz Stierle and many others point out, Petrarch wished for a Renaissance of ancient Rome in his own Italy.[22] Suffice to say that in his *Triumphi*, the emphasis is not laid on temporal powers but on what transcendent entity will ultimately triumph over the immanent: Chastity triumphs over Love and is vanquished by Death, itself vanquished by Fame, brought down by Time, ultimately triumphed over by Eternity. In a similar vein, the triumphal images that abound in Hill's work are not solely of Roman or Western triumphs but of biblical ones too, further emphasizing the moral dimension of the image: leaders might be revered but ought to be humble — Hill calls this culture 'Judaeo-Christian-Senecan Europe' (TL XI BH 241).[23] This motif is incipient in the volume *Canaan* with the poems 'Ezekiel's Wheel' and 'Respublica' and is developed throughout the three volumes that follow and, according to Hill, form a single work.[24] In the *Orchards of Syon*, section XXIII, Elijah's Chariot is mentioned in the same section as Petrarch. This merging of sources allows Hill to link representations of triumphs with images of Jubilees: a celebration associated with the freeing of the slaves in the Bible and with grace and absolution in Catholic theology. But these images are quickly negated by the poet: the Jubilo is 'hapless' in *Canaan*, or 'not on [his] program' in *The Orchards of Syon* (section L BH 400). In Hill's work, triumphs — and with them the sense of impending doom — are also imperial: the reference to the British empire often lurks in the poems, with the reference to Indian chariots and 'Juggernaut's lovers' — the devotees of Jagganath famously throwing themselves under the vehicle. This reference is taken up later in *Speech! Speech!* where the poet tries to 'reverse-tango' a juggernaut in an Apocalyptic scene.[25] These portentous images are used in Hill's work in a way that is also reminiscent of those used in progressive or left-wing politics: the British charwomen in section 35 of *Speech! Speech!* march 'jovial' to Edwardian and Georgian musical versions of Jove's Temple, 'to Holst's JUPITER as to JERUSALEM' (BH 306). Thus, on top of autobiography, political satire and a modernized Senecan critique of the media circus and triumphant political culture, Hill combines these Petrarchan images with a strong Biblical intertext, superimposing on them an Apocalyptic dimension with a progressive political twist.

Hill's modernizing of the triumph, its modern imperial dimension as well as the depiction of the crowd, are themes that owe much to Shelley's *The Triumph of Life*. Shelley's rewriting predates Hill's by some 176 years but dramatizes the tension between an overarching power and the lives and embodied feelings of individuals.[26] Shelley's captives embody a modern crowd out of control, in thrall to a 'savage music [...] tortured by their agonizing pleasure/convulsed and on the rapid whirlwinds spun' (142–44) 'with impotence of will' (170). Only some individuals, 'the sacred few [...] of Athens and Jerusalem' (128–34) survive the crushing course of

'Life'. Some, like Rousseau, are liminal figures, only lucid enough to tell the tale. In Hill, the emphasis is likewise laid on individual lives, but with a more moral and civic outlook. Section XCI of Hill's *The Triumph of Love* sees the British 'walking wounded', their lives spent in the service of empire or industry (BH 265). Their leaders' discourses of victory are 'less memorable | than those urged from defeat' (TL LXXXIX, BH 264). Hill seems to ask whether the new victors, with their 'parades of strength' (CIII), are able to sustain their victory. Despite the repeated trumpet blows ('Ta-Rah...', TL CXXIX–CXXXIII, BH 279–80), the triumphant British, or even Western powers, appear to be bereft of their values. The emphasis on individuals, the tension between democracy and demagoguery, as well as the depth of reference that accompanies the image of the triumphs, owes much to Shelley's rewriting of Petrarch's *Triumphi*, which strikingly yields 'Jubilee' (111) and 'triumphal chair' (252), and which Harold Bloom has called a juggernaut.[27] But where Petrarch typically has one great power triumphing over another in succession, what emerges in Shelley's poem is the individual voices surviving, not merely the great power coming full force on others. Shelley's late rewriting (before his untimely death), charting the collapse of Rousseauistic ideals, allows Hill to modernize *The Triumph of Love* as well as paint a picture of the overarching triumph — of ideas, of poetry — with some nuance. This emphasizes the doubt Hill expressed in his essay probing Pound's ethics vis-à-vis his poetics and questioning the Poundian-Shelleyan pronouncement that 'poets are the unacknowledged legislators of the age'.[28]

Ultimately, all that is left is for the poet viewing this cataclysmic world is to appeal to a higher power — also depicted in the guise of a single individual — this time a female figure. In Shelley, the mysterious 'Shape all light' (352) embodies a feminine ideal of fair, radiant beauty but her diaphanous figure is elusive and disappears to let 'a new vision' appear (411). Though there is no equivalent of 'Laura' in any of Hill's works, the figure of the Virgin Mary appears in the context of the triumph as a salutary presence crystallizing the feminine with quasi-divine attributes.

The *Vergine Bella*, a Catholic-Petrarchan figure at the heart of Hill's moral and aural landscape

In Petrarch, as in late medieval style, the figure of 'the Lady' is traced by Spiller to the *Stilnovisti*: one glance from the *Donna* means at once salutation and salvation.[29] So it comes as no surprise that Laura could blend with the *Vergine Bella* at the end of the *RVF*. Hill's *Vergine Bella* thus descends from a long line of *Donnas* and *Madonnas*, Queens, Intercessors, and Poetic Muses. While the Lady and the Virgin Mary greet the poet in silence, this silence becomes converted into pure poetry. Yet for Hill, the process is never quite that simple: Mary Mediatrix is herself mediated via a number of historical images and through the mediation of music. She also appears as an embodiment of the process of translation.

At the heart of Hill's Petrarch-inspired *The Triumph of Love* is the figure of a 'Vergine Bella' — taken directly from the ultimate poem of the *RVF*. Like Petrarch,

Hill composes a 'canzone' but instead of conjuring the Virgin's presence at the end of his sequence, he resorts to invoking her in Canto LV (whose Roman numerals incidentally spell the consonants of the word 'Love') as well as in four subsequent cantos (LXXV, LXXXVII, CIX, CXXV). The poet does not translate the phrase from Italian, but gives an oblique replication of the structure of *RVF* 366, where each stanza begins with 'Vergine' and one of her attributes: 'Vergine bella', 'Vergine saggia', 'umana', etc. In Hill, the appeal to Mary is a call for intercession amid desperate times where humanity has become powerless despite certain heroic acts of bravery. In Hill's last published volume *Al Tempo de' Tremuoti*, the Virgin Mary is seen interceding in favour of the city of Siena at a time of earthquakes (section 94): the source for the volume's title being a fifteenth-century painted book-cover by Francesco di Giorgio (BH 939), while the epigraph is the *memento mori* quoted at the beginning of this chapter. This reference also blends with a line in the *Orchards of Syon* where Hill alludes to Dante's 'trope of Justice' as the Virgin in *De Monarchia*.

Appearing at such symbolical junctures in the poet's work, the Hillian figure of the Virgin Mary owes an important debt to her place in Petrarch's poetics, where she appears in Apocalyptic light. As Peter Hainsworth notes, the image of the Virgin 'clothed with light' in *RVF* 366 is taken from Revelation 12.1: 'a woman clothed with the sun, with the moon under her feet and on her head a crown of twelve stars'.[30] Like Petrarch's, Hill's poetry is one of vision: some beautiful epiphanies occur in Hill's Midlands — the 'English light' thus sets the stage for a 'revelation' (section LIII) that prepares us for the 'Vergine Bella' passages a few cantos later. However, these visions are sometimes horrific; the Virgin's face appears 'blast-scarred' in 1945 (TL LV). In Hill's poems, the Virgin has a dual dimension: she is both the intercessor helping bring about humankind's salvation ('forgive us', CXXV) and a very 'umana' ('human') figure able to have direct interaction with the poet himself ('I ask that you ...' TL LV). Although for Petrarch, the figure of the Virgin Mary is a reconciliatory one (*RVF* 366 ends on the word 'pace', the peace which the enamoured Petrarch could not previously 'find'), in Hill there is more scepticism as to the 'peace' or 'justice' a Mary might bring to a disenchanted world. The end of canto LV expresses such doubt: 'even if no-one else shall be reconciled | to a final understanding of it in that light'. Thus, though Mary is seen with her divine attributes, she is also brought down to earth, fractured both by history and by contemporary, agnostic eyes.

In Hill's work, as in Petrarch, the figure of the Virgin also embodies *conversion*, enabling the conversion of Cupiditas into Caritas — of love for Laura into spiritual love for the divine — thus helping the forlorn poet find 'peace'. This interpretation originates in the Church Fathers: Mary is the female figure bringing about the conversion of Eve and of her original sin into grace: 'Vergine benedetta, /che 'l pianto d'Eva in allegrezza torni' (*RVF* 366). With the English Reformation, the image of Mary all but disappeared from liturgy and popular religion, as from English verse, where new images were soon to be invented (as witnesses George Herbert's *The Temple*). The cult of the Virgin Queen quickly replaced Marian devotion. However, the image persists subterraneously in poets like Sidney[31] and literally in recusant poets, to whom Hill is very much drawn. Mary then resurfaces later in the work of Catholic poets linked to the Oxford Movement, such as Gerard Manley Hopkins. In the recusant Robert Southwell, the theme of conversion is expressed in a particular baroque form of *trobar clus*:

> Spell Eua backe, and Aue shall you finde,
> The first began, the last reuerst our harmes,
> An Angels Aue disinchants the charmes,
> Death first by womans weaknes entred in,
> In womans vertue life doth now begin.
>   ('The Virgin's Salutation')[32]

In Hill's work, Mary is likewise a figure of conversion but the tone is more ironic than irenic — 'Oculos tuos ad nos converte' says Hill, quoting Latin liturgy at the beginning of section CIX, then quipping 'you gave us | a bit of a turn here' (BH 270).[33] If the turn of conversion is satirized, one that remains is the turn offered by verse — for example that of the sonnet's *volta*[34] — and by translation. Hill's practice of leaving a number of references in their Italian or Latin original, sometimes appending a translation in the next verse, is reminiscent of the religious meaning of 'translation': 'the moving of a saint's relics from one place to another' or (as in Mary's case) 'the assumption to Heaven without dying'. This is aligned with a source-oriented view of translation treating the original as a sacred entity that should not be tampered with. Yet, Hill's translation can also offer a different kind of 'turn' — a felicitous metamorphosis of the original, such as his modernized versions of the triumph, which served to modernize and satirize. Another felicitous type of 'turn' is intersemiotic translation, where words or ideas are translated into images or music, paradoxically yielding a 'pure' aesthetic experience.

The fact that Hill does not translate 'Vergine Bella' indeed makes an indexical reference to the Petrarchan canzone's musical settings by late medieval or early modern composers such as Guillaume Dufay, Walter Frye or Cipriano de Rore — especially when Hill's appeal to Mary is so often paired with the word 'canzone'. The reference to music is particularly pregnant here as 'Vergine Bella' was one of the few poems from the Canzoniere that was not translated into English until the eighteenth century.[35] Indeed, while there is a striking absence of Marian figures from the canon of English poetry, it is possible that the inheritance of Marian devotion arrived in Hill's verse through a musical channel: as Hill puns 'there are *sound* precedents for this' (TL LV, my italics).[36] It is relevant here that, as Thomas P. Roche points out, Milton should have retained only the 'music' of 'Vergine Bella' — its rhyme scheme — for his poem 'Upon the Circumcision', much as he reintroduced an Italian rhyme scheme into the sonnet. This link with music is consistent with the topos of conversion since the canzone (like the motet) allowed composers to 'convert' secular songs into sacred pieces. Thus, the images of musical 'conversions' at the heart of Hill's verse on the Virgin Mary help to underscore the idea of translatability, of commonality between cultures and religions, rather than the sense of untranslatability at the core of certain words.

For Hill, issues of politics and religion are formal ones too so one might wonder why the poet chose to use the form of the canzone in *The Triumph of Love*, instead of terza rima, used by Petrarch in the *Triumphi* and Shelley in the *Triumph of Time*. Jeffrey Wainwright's reading suggests that this may have been a way for Hill to disengage from an over-arching epic tradition (terza rima being primarily associated with Dante's *Commedia*) and retreat to a more 'scattered', private lyrical mode.[37] Likewise, Peter McDonald has suggested Hill's 'distancing' from the T. S. Eliot of *Four Quartets* (written in unrhymed tercets and highly indebted to Dante).[38] It is interesting that for Petrarch, as for Hill, the canzone could also be used in politics, as witnesses the canzone 'Italia mia' (*RVF* 128), set to music by Verdelot and rewritten by Leopardi as the Romantic 'All'Italia'. One cannot stress enough how central the canzone — or ode — form is in Hill's later work: most of the volumes published after *The Triumph of Love* feature these longer sequential poems comprising one rhymed or unrhymed stanza repeated a number of times, sometimes followed by an *envoi*. As Hugh Haughton observes, music in Hill is 'not only as sensuously immediate but also historically mediated'.[39] This is true of Petrarchan poetry, whose images and cadences are mediated through its various translators.

The Petrarchan intertext as a locus for poetic-political engagement with the poet-translators of the past

As Georges Mounin put it in *Les Belles Infidèles*, three levels of distance separate the translator from the translated material — those of language, history and culture.[40] With Petrarch, the linguistic-historical gap is seven-centuries wide; the translator has to plough through Petrarch's occasional archaism and encyclopaedic knowledge. One substantial bridge over the cultural gap, however, is Petrarch's sonnet form with its formal and thematic devices. Another bridge is the number of poet-translators and inheritors who have helped pass down Petrarch's heritage from century to century. When Hill 'translates', that is to say adapts or borrows from Petrarch, he occasionally uses deliberate source-based strategies which move to close the gap between the present day reader and the fourteenth-century original all the while highlighting its existence. Oftentimes, Hill quotes a fragment of the original text and follows it with a gloss, as in 'Vergine Bella' where he expounds 'here I follow Petrarch | a sinner devoted to your service' (TL LV, BH 254). In other places, he uses homophonic translation. The title *Al Tempo de' Tremuoti* for instance is a homophonic pun on time, musical tempo, and the 'tremors' of ageing. The other example is 'Love's triumphal car', which appears to be replicated from the Italian of *The Triumph of Love*'s 'triumphal carro' (v. 15) possibly via Shelley, where other translators might have used 'Chariot' or 'carriage'.[41] Associated with the verb 'clangs', the effect is burlesque — contrasting with a serious rendition of Petrarch — but it is coherent with the Senecan critique developed above. Another homophonic 'translation' is

> The glory of poetry is that it is solemn,
> Racked with anarchic laughter. Genius
> Thriving on various expediences,
> Like Petrarch's shattered and sustaining column,
> Transforms bare reflex into rhapsody

from *Al Tempo de' Tremuoti*, where reference is made to Petrarch's patron Stefano Colonna as a 'column' with the same pun made by Petrarch in *RVF* 269 ('Rotta è l'alta colonna e 'l verde lauro') and elsewhere in the *Canzoniere*. Petrarch's patron was indeed both 'sustaining' for his art and 'shattered', like Laura, dying from the plague and commemorated in that poem. Here, the effect — like the pun — is a little laboured, a kind of verbal conundrum, but the (possibly) erotic line following it widens the frame of reference by linking the image with that of Love being tied to a column by Chastity in the *Triumphi* (Triumphus Pudicitie, 120). Hill's poetry thus attempts to capture the importance of the original all the while letting us acknowledge the distance that separates us from it — which is another way to frame the problematics of untranslatability.

This distance is partly filled by previous translators and rewriters or adaptors that are now conduits for Petrarch. Hill's poetry makes us retrace our steps in literary history via these inheritors. We have looked at the example of Shelley in the previous pages. Some even more removed inheritors of Petrarch are his first translators into English — Thomas Wyatt and Lord Morley. Hill cites Wyatt in 'Parallel Lives' and refers to *The Quiet of Mind* (translated via Guillaume Budé's French translation of Plutarch). This was originally meant to be a translation of Petrarch's *Remedies against Good and Evil Fortune*, commissioned by Queen Catherine of Aragon, but Wyatt refused to translate the work for fear of offending the King. There is also strong visual emphasis on the first English translator of the *Triumphi*, Henry Parker, Lord Morley. The original edition of *The Triumph of Love* based its cover design on the frontispiece of Morley's *Tryumphs*. Also, at the beginning of *Speech! Speech!* (2000), the early modern translator is represented semi-parodically as 'LORD MORLEY with POMEGRANATE'.[42] This is a reference to a Dürer engraving, which incidentally serves as a frontispiece for Marie Axton and James P. Carley's substantial collection of essays of the same year devoted to the translator-courtier. Entitled *Triumphs of English*, the book surveys in detail how English became a national vernacular language with its own literature partly thanks to the figure of Morley who travelled and translated extensively (often Italian works from their French translators). As Axton contends, Morley was the instigator of the Petrarchan fashion even prior to Wyatt and Surrey.[43] Juxtaposed to Wyatt in the *Collected Critical Writings*, however, Morley appears as a more subdued courtier, able to please in turn Mary Tudor or Henry VIII. Wyatt on the other hand is the one for whom diplomacy could be dangerous. For a court-poet like Wyatt, activities of translation could go hand in hand with 'traducement' or 'defaming' (the other senses given by Hill from the OED). The bringing together of Wyatt with Morley helps sustain Hill's later assertion that 'questions of value' — the value of the written word — 'are inseparable from matters of translation' (CCW 383).[44]

Questions of value are also seen in relation to Petrarch and translation in section XXIII of *The Orchards of Syon*, where after a vision of autumnal gold, seen in parallel with Elijah's Chariot, Petrarch is invoked as 'revived by CHAR [...] | though not | in so many words' (BH 373). Here, Hill may well have chosen to cite the French poet René Char for his name's sonic and semantic proximity with the word 'chariot'. The allusion may also be to René Char as a poet born in L'Isle-sur-la-Sorgue, a place that was as significant in his formative years as it was for Petrarch ('J'avais dix ans. La Sorgue m'enchâssait' ['I was ten. The Sorgue enfolded me', my translation]).[45] Hill may be pointing as well to the poet as the reviver of the Musée Pétrarque in L'Isle in the mid-1980s, curated by the scholar Eve Duperray. Or yet to Char the editor — with his lover the polyglot sociologist Tina Jolas — of *La Planche de vivre*, an anthology of poems in translation, including two poems by Petrarch together with one by the Provençal troubadour Raimbaut de Vacqueiras.[46] One of the Char poems referred to in Hill's verse is a sonnet-like fourteen-line stanza entitled 'Le jugement d'octobre', a symbolic meditation on two forlorn roses, compared to 'la flamme sous l'abri' in a simile signifying literally 'the flame under the shelter': just as one rose is bound to hurt the other with its thorns, so does the live flame in the shelter threaten to betray its occupants. By intimating the idea of a Petrarchan 'revival', Hill points to such a poem as being a bleak rewriting of *RVF* 245. 'Due rose fresche, et colte in paradiso' ('Two fresh roses, gathered in paradise'). Translating Char's 'la flamme sous l'abri' as 'the *curfew*-flame' and putting the poet in conjunction with André Frenaud, Hill elaborates a commentary on Char's poem as possibly being about the experience of the Résistance, a political kind of trobar clus, where encoding becomes a matter of life and death, translation as 'traducement'.

Finally, it is the value of Petrarch's poetry itself which is probed in the reference to twentieth-century Italian poets. At first glance, Cesare Pavese, one of the modern and contemporary Italian poets most represented in Hill's verse (especially in the sequence 'Pindarics', written after Pavese's diaries), is the one who expresses the most distance vis-à-vis Petrarchan lyricism.[47] But another poet with whom Hill has a strong affinity is Eugenio Montale, who negotiates with the legacy of Petrarchism. Famous for his sense of condensation and difficulty, Montale is known for using the forms of the canzone and the motet and is one of the few poets actually translated by Hill: the volume *Without Title* includes a translation of 'La Bufera' and *Al Tempo de' Tremuoti* shows six 'variants' of the poem 'Il gallo cedrone' ('The Capercaillie'). Hill's work also shows Montale as a poet engaging with Petrarch. Indeed, Sara d'Orazio has suggested that the figure of Montale's otherworldly Muse ties in with Hill's elusive female figures, such as his Petrarchan 'Vergine Bella'. Montale's work has been shown to subtly subvert some Petrarchan tropes as well. Recalling his collection *Finisterre* as 'esperienza [...] petrarchesca', Diego Bertelli shows how Montale wrestles with the difficulty of matching the word with the world, enjoining his reader to 'listen to [him]' ('Ascoltami') and at the same time refusing to provide the right words: 'Non chiederci la parola' ('Do not ask us for the word to frame...').[48] In a poem that sets itself against 'poet laureates', Bertelli identifies a quasi-Petrarchan conceit of the lemons ('I Limone') which replace the laurel as part of the volume *Ossi de Seppia* — the dried-up cuttlefish bones of inspiration being subliminally replaced by the lemon's invisible ink.[49] In that vein, it is striking that the titles *Orchards of Syon* and *Ossi de Seppia* share the same initials and that both Montale and Hill's poem are revisited one last time in *Al Tempo de' Tremuoti* in a canzone dedicated to Montale's muse and lover Irma Brandeis recapturing many of the key elements mentioned above: 'Always new trees astonish — carob, aloe, | Blue-wenned fig, the trim and proper lemon, | The wild laurel rendering things trans-human' (BH 911).

As part of his Italian canon, Hill also goes back to two figures of poetry and learning: Giosuè Carducci and Giacomo Leopardi. These last two share the same type of humanistic erudition and scholarship embodied by Hill and are in that respect heirs to Petrarch. In 1899, Carducci (with Ferrarri) was responsible for producing an authoritative edition of the *Canzoniere* which called attention to the 'secular' (that is to say centuries-long) tradition of Petrarchan commentary. One notable instance of this tradition is the commentary of the *RVF* which Leopardi published in 1826, and which Margaret Brose calls a great instance of 'lyric translatio'.[50] In Hill's work, Carducci is not outwardly celebrated for his Petrarchan scholarship but rather for his *Odi Barbare*, a title Hill adapts for his own volume. Carducci's title reflects on what might happen if Italy (and other European cultures) once again became 'barbaric', that is to say truly vernacular or 'non-Greek'. This question was shared by Giacomo Leopardi,[51] the poet most associated with Italian lyricism in Hill and referenced four times in *The Triumph of Love*. At the end of this sequence is an excerpt from Leopardi's letters translated by James Thomson that reads 'A sad and angry consolation' (repeated and parsed by Hill in two or three different ways, reflecting different interpretations).[52] Both *The Triumph* and *Al Tempo* refer to Leopardi's famous poem 'A se stesso' (To Himself), most probably a rewriting of Catullus's eponymous piece but also possibly pointing to Petrarch's 'Che fai? Che pensi?' (*RVF* 273) and to his *epistola metrica* 'Ad se ipsum' (I, 14), a '*meditatio mortis*' probably written at the time of Laura and Colonna's deaths.[53] The penultimate section of *Al Tempo* begins with an injunction ('*Be mindful how much good derives from her* | *Da lei*, from her, from Justice') that sounds as if it could have been an aphorism — albeit a little too optimistic — from Leopardi's *Zibaldone*, an encyclopaedic nineteenth-century version of a commonplace book, in which the poet expounds on philosophical and literary concerns as well as philological ones.[54] Incidentally, the publication of the unabridged English translation of the *Zibaldone*, of which Hill owned a copy, coincides with that of Hill's equally encyclopaedic collected poems *Broken Hierarchies*. The poet-cum-savant Leopardi is known to have shifted from valuing erudition above all to favouring the beautiful, concentrating on lyric poetry rather than scholarship in the later part of his short life. In this respect, Leopardi is known for rewriting canzoni 126 and 129 of the *RVF* as 'Alla Sua Donna' and the patriotic 'Italia Mia' as 'All'Italia'.[55] Interestingly, it was for these poems, as well as 'A se stesso', that Leopardi was most known to the progressive nineteenth-century British expatriates who had fled to Italy. Hill's portrait of Leopardi, however, also includes an anti-Petrarchan line referring to an Italian poet: 'Not Petrarch | *le viscere dell'Amore*', a reference to Leopardi's journaling of his first love, in which he justifies using prose instead of verse. Thus, down to the last details, Hill's relation to Petrarch's heirs is paradoxical.

In conclusion, this chapter has attempted to show the multi-dimensional and multi-faceted expression of Petrarchan elements in Hill's work. Far from being confined to the formal perfection of the Canzoniere, Hill's work deploys a vast range of Petrarchan references, from the *Triumphi* to the Latin works. One such work is the *Itinerarium*, identified by René Gallet in the following lines from *The Triumph of Love*:

> Corner to corner, the careful
> fabric of our lives ripped through
> by the steel claws of contingency.

These lines rephrase the incipit of the *Itinerarium to the Holy Sepulchre*, a fantastic narrative describing a voyage that Petrarch should have embarked on but never did. From the start, Petrarch says that Fortune often 'undoes the great web that was carefully spun by Reason'.[56] Likewise, in Hill, the voyage of sources is sometimes virtual — one to be completed by the reader. Petrarchan sources enjoy vastly different fortunes: some are carefully and resourcefully carried over, many are broken, while others fray out and become very fragmented, leaving only the trace of their reference or allusion. All of Hill's rewritings of Petrarch display a complex, paradoxical attitude, a struggle with the canonical untranslatable source. Despite this, I hope to have shown that Petrarch's influence runs deep in Hill's poetry, informs much of the pictorial, interlinguistic and intertextual material found in it, and reflects on his place within European poetry, both in the lyric tradition and as part of a Modernist line.

Notes to Chapter 11

1. Francesco Petrarca, *Triumphi, Triumphus Temporis* II, 130–31. I would like to thank my fellow editors as well as my colleagues Susan Ang and Kenneth Haynes for their helpful advice and suggestions on earlier drafts of this chapter. Thank you also to Philippe Guérin and Riccardo Raimondo for lending their expertise in Italian language and literature.
2. For discussions of how ambiguity, equivocity, and paradox characterize Hill's poetics, see for example Merle Brown, *Double Lyric: Divisiveness and Communal Creativity in Recent English Poetry* (London: Routledge and Kegan Paul, 1980) and Patrick Hersant, 'La Voix médiane: statut de la parole poétique dans l'œuvre de Geoffrey Hill' (unpublished thesis, Université d'Amiens, 1997).
3. Sara D'Orazio, 'Dialogues with Europe: A Study of Multilingual Intertextuality in the Poetry of Geoffrey Hill' (unpublished thesis, Manchester Metropolitan University, 2009), p. 67.
4. Geoffrey Hill, *Collected Critical Writings* (Oxford: Oxford University Press, 2008), pp. 384–91
5. Ibid., p. 366.
6. Matthew Sperling, *Visionary Philology: Geoffrey Hill and the Study of Words* (Oxford: Oxford University Press, 2014).
7. See for example the 'Acknowledgements' section in Geoffrey Hill, *Broken Hierarchies: Poems 1952–2012*, ed. by Kenneth Haynes (Oxford: Oxford University Press, 2013), pp. 937–39.
8. 'Untranslatability' is used here in the wide sense of what cannot be translated and paradoxically keeps on being translated, as identified by Barbara Cassin. See *Vocabulaire européen des philosophies: dictionnaire des intraduisibles*, ed. by Barbara Cassin (Paris: Seuil/Le Robert, 2004), p. xvii. Also cited by Jennifer Rushworth in this volume.
9. Most use the abba/abba/cdc/dcd rhyme scheme from the *RVF*, albeit with slant rhymes. For discussion of Hill and the sonnet see my own pieces: 'Public or Private Nation: Poetic Form and National Consciousness in the Poetry of Tony Harrison and Geoffrey Hill', *The Public/Private Divide in British Poetry since 1950*, ed. by in Emily Taylor Merriman and Adrian Grafe (Jefferson, NC: McFarland, 2009) pp. 174–90, and 'Retail the Coda: le retour au sonnet dans l'œuvre récente de

Geoffrey Hill', *Revue LISA/LISA e-journal*, 7.3 (2009), <http://journals.openedition.org/lisa/81 ; DOI: 10.4000/lisa.81> [accessed 19 July 2018].
10. Hill, *Broken Hierarchies*, pp. 129 and 484.
11. In an uncollected critical article, Geoffrey Hill also references F. T. Prince's *The Italian Element in Milton's Verse*, whose main theme is how Milton imitated later Italian sonneteers — like Bembo and Della Casa — in reforming the debased Petrarchan clichés of the day. Geoffrey Hill 'Il Cortegiano: F. T. Prince's Poems (1938)', *PN Review*, 147.29 (2002), <https://www.pnreview.co.uk/cgi-bin/scribe?item_id=1300> [accessed 1 August 2018].
12. Theodor Adorno, 'Cultural Criticism and Society', in *Prisms*, trans by Samuel Weber and Shierry Weber (Cambridge, MA: MIT Press, 1981), p. 34.
13. Anne Larue finds trobar clus (or 'closed verse' as practised by the Troubadours, and which is characterized by great complexity and obscurity) in the essence of the Petrarchan sonnet and other complex forms. The term is applied loosely here to encompass other poetic ages too. See Anne Larue, *Poètes de l'Amour: Ovide, Pétrarque, Shakespeare, Goethe* (Paris: Editions du Temps, 2004), pp. 8–9.
14. These volumes are reproduced in *Broken Hierarchies*, pp. 169–286. *The Triumph of Love* is referenced by section number (in roman numerals) and page number in *Broken Hierarchies* (e.g. TL VIII, BH 240).
15. Sara D'Orazio, 'Dialogues with Europe', p. 25.
16. Ezra Pound, 'Partial Explanation' (1928) and 'Guido's Relations' (1929) reprinted in David Anderson, *Pound's Cavalcanti* (Princeton, NJ: Princeton University Press, 1983), pp. 209–14 and 241–51 (pp. xiv, 214, 242).
17. Eugenio Montale, *Life and Work*, ed. by Luca Sereni (Oxford: Mask Press, 2017), p. 32.
18. Hill refers to such works as the *Itinerarium* and the Penitential Psalms (adapted by Petrarch in Latin).
19. Working within a classical model of 'apian' imitation, Petrarch refused to follow any single source (*Rerum Familiarum* XXIII, 19)
20. Zygmunt G. Baranski, 'The Triumphi', in *The Cambridge Companion to Petrarch*, ed. by Albert Russell Ascoli and Unn Falkeid (Cambridge: Cambridge University Press, 2015), p. 78. The only concern in the list that is not shared by Hill is 'Laura'.
21. Seneca, *Epistles*, 87.23, cited in Mary Beard, *The Roman Triumph* (Cambridge, MA: Belknap Press of Harvard University Press, 2007), p. 1.
22. Stierle sees Petrarch as a marking figure in the shift away from a vertical and one-directional *translatio imperii et studii*, arguing also that the (horizontal) exchange between cultures also begins with Petrarch. See Karlheinz Stierle, 'Translatio Studii and Renaissance: From Vertical to Horizontal Translation', in *The Translatability of Cultures: Figurations of the Space Between*, ed. by Sanford Budick and Wolfgang Iser (Stanford: Stanford University Press, 1996), pp. 55–67.
23. On top of the allegorical and satirical dimensions, there is also a tragic side to the triumph, one in which the victims are being paraded. Hill's inclusion of the Holocaust in sections XVIII to XXII is reminiscent of this, recalling for instance, Titus' triumph on returning from the sack of Jerusalem carrying the Jewish Temple's menorah on his chariot (see Beard, p. 43).
24. Jan Harris, 'Geoffrey Hill', Literature Online biography, *Literature Online* [accessed 19 July 2018].
25. This is possibly a reference to Petrarch's *Africa* urging the reader to reverse the march of Time as cited by George Steiner in *After Babel: Aspects of Language and Translation*, 3rd edn (New York: Open Road, 1991), p. 269.
26. For in-depth discussion of Shelley's Italian sources in *The Triumph of Life* and elsewhere, see Alan M. Weinberg, *Shelley's Italian Experience* (New York: Palgrave Macmillan, 1991), especially pp. 244–51 for a discussion of the 'shape all light'.
27. Harold Bloom, *Shelley's Mythmaking* (Ithaca, NY: Cornell University Press, 1969), p.244, cited by Weinberg, *Shelley's Italian Experience*, p. 220.
28. P. B. Shelley, 'A Defense of Poetry', composed in 1821 and alluded to in Hill's essay 'Our Word is our Bond' (CCW, p. 169).
29. Michael R. G. Spiller, *The Development of the Sonnet* (London and New York: Routledge, 1992), p. 30.

30. Francesco Petrarca, *The Essential Petrarch*, ed. and trans. with an introduction by Peter Hainsworth (Indianapolis, IN: Hackett, 2010), p. 147n.
31. See Thomas Rist, 'Astrophil and Stella Maris: Poetic Ladies, the Virgin Mary and the Culture of Love in Reformation England', *Sidney Journal*, 32 (2014), 69–92.
32. Robert Southwell, *Moeoniæ* (London: Printed by Valentine Sims, for Iohn Busbie, 1595), p. 4.
33. In contrast, the even more satirical volume *Speech! Speech!* converts Eve back to the yet more radical figure of 'Lilith' *Speech! Speech!* is referenced by section number (in Arabic numerals) and page number in *Broken Hierarchies* (e.g. SS 88, BH 292). (SS 8, BH 292).
34. For a theological discussion of conversion in Hill's work, see Kathryn Murphy, 'Hill's Conversions', in *Geoffrey Hill and his Contexts*, ed. by Matthew Sperling and Piers Pennington (Oxford: Peter Lang, 2011), pp. 61–80.
35. See Thomas P. Roche, *Petrarch in English* (London: Penguin, 2005) for a brief analysis of Hill's work in relation to Milton, who used the canzone's intricate rhyme scheme in 'Upon the Circumcision' (pp. 188 and 304–05).
36. On medieval and early modern musical versions of Mary see David J. Rothenberg, *The Flower of Paradise: Marian Devotion and Secular Song in Medieval and Renaissance Music* (Oxford: Oxford University Press, 2011).
37. Jeffrey Wainwright, *Acceptable Words: Essays on the Poetry of Geoffrey Hill* (Manchester: Manchester University Press, 2005), p. 94.
38. Peter McDonald, *Serious Poetry: Form and Authority from Yeats to Hill* (Oxford: Oxford University Press, 2002), pp. 206, 216.
39. Hugh Haughton, 'Music's Invocation: Music and History in Geoffrey Hill', in *Geoffrey Hill and his Contexts*, pp. 187–211 (pp. 188–90).
40. Georges Mounin, *Les Problèmes théoriques de la traduction* (Paris, Gallimard, 1963).
41. Lord Morley uses 'Chayre', Anna Hume 'Chariot'. Francesco Petrarca, *The Tryumphes of Fraunces Petrarcke*, trans. by Henry Parker, Lord Morley (London, In Powles church-yarde at the sygne of the holy Ghost, by Iohn Cawood, prynter to the Quenes hyghnes, 1555); Francesco Petrarca, *The Triumphs of Love: Chastity: Death*, trans. by Anna Hume (Edinburgh: Evan Tyler, 1644).
42. Ann Hassan, *Annotations to Geoffrey Hill's Speech! Speech!* (New York: Glossator Editions, 2012), p. 86.
43. Marie Axton, 'Lord Morley's Tryumphes of Petrarcke: Reading Spectacles', in *Triumphs of English: Henry Parker Lord Morley, Translator To The Tudor Court*, ed. by Marie Axton and James P. Carley (London: The British Library, 2000), pp. 171–200 (p. 192).
44. On Wyatt the translator and diplomat, see William T. Rossiter, *Wyatt Abroad: Tudor Diplomacy and the Translation of Power* (Cambridge: D. S. Brewer, 2014).
45. René Char, *Commune présence* (Paris: Gallimard, 1964) p. 3.
46. René Char and Tina Jolas, *La Planche de vivre* (Paris: Gallimard, 1981).
47. For an in-depth study of Hill and Pavese, see Susan Ang, 'The "Pindarics" as *Enigma Variations*: Pavese and Hill in Formal Conversation', in *European Voices in the Poetry of W. B. Yeats and Geoffrey Hill*, ed. by Ineke Bockting, Jennifer Kilgore-Caradec, and Elizabeth Muller (Berne: Peter Lang, 2015), pp. 123–52.
48. Diego Bertelli, 'From Lexicon to Symbol', *MLN* 124.1 (2009), 195–212.
49. Eugenio Montale, *Collected Poems 1920–1954*, trans. Jonathan Galassi (New York: Farrar, Strauss and Giroux, 1998), pp. 2–145 (p. 47). There is affinity with Hill's 'no manner of address will do' ('Metamorphoses', in *Broken Hierarchies*, p. 17).
50. Margaret Brose, 'Mixing Memory and Desire: Leopardi Reading Petrarch', *Annali d'Italianistica*, 22, *Francis Petrarch and the European Lyric Tradition*, ed. by Dino S. Cervigni (2004), 303–19.
51. See Adam Kirsch, 'Giacomo Leopardi's "Zibaldone," the Least Known Masterpiece of European Literature', *The New Republic*, 9 November 2013, <https://newrepublic.com/article/115276/giacomo-leopardis-zibaldone-reviewed-adam-kirsch> [accessed 12 July 2018].
52. Giacomo Leopardi, *Essays, Dialogues and Thoughts (Operette Morali and Pensieri) of Giacomo Leopardi*, trans. by James Thomason (B.V.) (London: Routledge, 1905), p. 29.
53. On Petrarchan sources of 'A se stesso', see Stefano Carrai, 'Leopardi Ad se Ipsum', in Pier Vincenzo Mengaldo, and Società Internazionale per Lo Studio Del Medioevo Latino, *Studi in*

Onore Di Pier Vincenzo Mengaldo per I Suoi Settant'anni, a Cura Degli Allievi Padovani (Florence: SISMEL, Edizioni Del Galluzzo, 2007), pp. 879–85. I am grateful to Jennifer Rushworth for pointing me to this article. On the notion of 'Ad se ipsum' as *meditatio mortis* solely intended for the author (rather than as an elegy for the dead) see Isabelle Abrame-Battesti, 'Parler de soi à soi seul: l'*épître métrique* I, 14 *Ad se ipsum* et la *canzone* 264 de Pétrarque', *Arzanà* 12 (2007), 153–70, <https://doi.org/10.3406/arzan.2007.964>. 'Ad se ipsum' was written concomitantly with Petrarch's paraphrase of the Penitential Psalms, also referenced many times in Hill's work.

54. The use of the feminine pronoun 'Da lei'/'From her' also ties in with Dante's trope of Justice as a Virgin, as previously mentioned.

55. On 'Alla Sua Donna', see Pamela Williams, 'Leopardi and Petrarch', in *Petrarch in Britain: Interpreters, Imitators, and Translators*, ed. by Martin McLaughlin and Letizia Panizza with Peter Hainsworth (Oxford: Published for the British Academy by Oxford University Press, 2007), pp. 277–99 (p. 282). On 'All'Italia' see Daniela Cerimonia, *Leopardi and Shelley: Discovery, Translation and Reception* (Oxford: Legenda, 2015), pp. 59–76.

56. René Gallet (1944–2012) was a Professor of English Literature at the University of Caen and a personal friend of Geoffrey Hill's. His translation of *The Triumph of Love* was published with the help of Christophe Carraud, a great French specialist of Petrarch who published a translation of the *Itinerarium* in his review *Conference* in 1998. See Geoffrey Hill, *Le Triomphe de l'Amour*, trans. by René Gallet (Le Chambon sur Lignon: Le Cheyne, 2002), notes on pp. 153–70 (p.163; note to poem LXXV) and Francesco Petrarca, *Itinerarium ad Sepulcrum Domini Nostri Ihesu Cristi*, reprinted in *Itinéraire de Gênes à Jérusalem*, ed. and trans. by Christophe Carraud and Rebecca Lenoir (Grenoble: Jérôme Millon, 2002), p. 21.

PART III

Practice-Based Criticism and Original Texts

CHAPTER 12

How Petrarch Can Speak to Contemporary Poetry: Yves Bonnefoy as Petrarch Translator and Critic

Thomas Vuong

Yves Bonnefoy (1923–2016) was one of the foremost writers in France throughout the second half of the twentieth century. Stemming from late surrealism, his work covers poetry, art criticism, poetics, and translation. He is best known for having translated many plays by Shakespeare and his entire non-dramatic verse, as well as works by Yeats, Keats, and Leopardi. His last work of translation covers twenty-four sonnets by Petrarch, which — coming from such a passionate figure and master of unrhymed verse or poetry in prose — was received with some surprise at the time (a first publication appeared in the quarterly *Conférence* in 2005, before a hardcover edition in 2012). In his theoretical writings, the poet and translator justifies these choices. It is helpful to sum up briefly a few of these to highlight the continuing interest in Petrarch within the higher circles of the French modern poetic scene. The aim of this chapter is therefore to present in Bonnefoy's own words the reasons why a contemporary master of French poetry would translate Petrarch's sonnets.

According to Yves Bonnefoy, Petrarch remains an important poet for the twenty-first century, one who 'tries to come closer to us',[1] as he describes him in the 2011 presentation of his translation of twenty-four sonnets from the *Canzoniere*. Yet, in a retrospective 2009 lecture, where he discusses the posterity of literature, he mentions Petrarch among other canonical texts, such as the *Odyssey*, the *Aeneid*, and the *Flowers of Evil*, stating that '[e]very book gets old'.[2] Besides, Yves Bonnefoy considers that Petrarch is linked to a certain orthodoxy, be it in a religious or in a broader intellectual sense:

> Un livre aussi célèbre que peu pratiqué aujourd'hui en France parce que c'est vrai qu'il a vieilli, de plusieurs façons, le *Canzoniere* de Pétrarque. Ce poète est souvent la proie d'une orthodoxie qui lui impose des catégories de la pensée et du sentiment, des notions, des relations entre ces dernières, cadres et propositions d'une théologie catholique remarquablement close sur soi auxquels s'ajoutent certaines problématiques de la pensée morale et civique de l'humanisme latin. Quand Pétrarque se veut poète, il est donc étroitement surveillé, sa liberté ne peut être que durement réprimée.[3]

[A book as famous as it is rarely read today in France because it is true that it has not aged well in several ways, Petrarch's *Canzoniere*. The poet is often the prey of an orthodoxy which imposes on it categories of thought and feeling, notions, relations between the two, frames, and propositions of a brand of Catholic theology remarkably closed to the outside world to which you could add certain strands of moral and civic thought deriving from Latin humanism. When Petrarch decides to be a poet, his movements are closely controlled, his freedom is necessarily severely restricted.]

This radically contemporary perspective on Petrarch is then directly linked to the rigid form of the sonnet. Nevertheless, the inheritor of the Surrealists' passionate quest for freedom chose to translate twenty-four sonnets by Petrarch, in the early 2000s. How relevant can such a poet be? Not only does he represent the religious orthodoxy of his time — his *Canzoniere* ends on a renunciation of earthly love and a hymn to Mary — but he also contributed to setting up an influential poetic orthodoxy (Petrarchism) and expanded and grounded the formal one — that of the sonnet.

Towards the end of his poetic career, the poet and translator became openly attached to 'atoms of poetry' which he identified even in remote classics — remote in terms of ideological background as much as time:

> Intéressons-nous à ce que je pourrais appeler des atomes de poésie, ces moments où le texte et la pensée qui mènent le texte sont transgressés, oui, gardons ce mot, sont mis en question, par une intuition qui ne se satisfaisait pas de la représentation du monde que le livre tentait de mettre en place, et trouve à un moment, toujours bref, le moyen de se faire entendre. [...] Eh bien, prenons conscience de la façon dont nous lisons ces poèmes et les gardons à l'esprit. Que fait le souvenir, dans ces cas ? Il préserve des fragments, le plus souvent ce que nous nommons des beaux vers [...] ces beaux vers peuvent être de ces instants où la forme a délivré les mots des stéréotypes qui ankylosent et enténèbrent l'être au monde de leur époque, ce sont des instants de résurrection.[4]

> [Let's concentrate on what I might call atoms of poetry, the moments when the text and thought which govern the text are transgressed, yes, let's keep the word, are questioned, by an intuition which is not happy with the representation of the world which the book was trying to develop, and finds the way to make itself heard at a certain moment which is always brief. [...] Well, let's become conscious of the way we read these poems and bear them in mind. What's the part played by memory in such cases? It preserves fragments, most often what we call beautiful lines [...] These beautiful lines may be these moments when form sets words free from the stereotypes which paralyse and darken the being-in-the-world of their period, these are moments of resurrection.]

Yves Bonnefoy states his core definition of poetry once again: namely, that it begins when the poet frees himself from the conceptual thinking that structures everyday language. In Petrarch's case, this is explicitly what allows him, a contemporary poet who rejects Christian transcendence, to set his sights on his sonnets:

> Traduire, c'est traduire pour nous, hommes et femmes d'une époque tout autre, notamment en ce qui concerne les choses de la religion ou même et plus radicalement la simple pratique du transcendant dans l'existence et le monde.[5]

[To translate means to translate for us, men and women from a totally different age, notably concerning religious matters or even and more radically still the simple practice of the transcendent in the world's being.]

Therefore, in this target-oriented translation, the contemporary poet, translator, and reader must focus on his personal reactions to the Italian poet's verse, leaving aside historical inquiries into its theological significance:

> Je ne m'inquiéterai pas trop de ma science, hélas, bien minime, de Pétrarque et du *Canzoniere*, et prendrai même au sérieux mes impressions immédiates, celles que j'ai éprouvées aux moments de ma vie où je me suis approché, non sans quelque fascination, de ce livre qui aura tant compté dans la poésie de l'Europe.[6]
>
> [I would not bother too much about my knowledge of Petrarch and the *Canzoniere*, which, unfortunately, is rather limited, and would even take my immediate impressions quite seriously, those which I have felt in the moments of my life when, with a tinge of fascination, I have approached this book which has mattered so much in European poetry.]

Besides, Yves Bonnefoy gradually came to change his mind about the form of the sonnet.

> La première partie du sonnet est un piège et la seconde un ressaisissement. La première ce que suggère la rhétorique, cette gestion conceptuelle des pensées et des sentiments si aisément et souvent confondue avec la poésie, et la seconde une occasion de lucidité. Et tout cela à la fois, dans ces quatorze vers, se présentant comme un abrégé du mouvement le plus intérieur de la poésie et de ce qu'elle est en pratique, jamais une visée droite mais un conflit à son plus intime, et jamais une pleine réussite mais l'obstination à vouloir celle-ci [...] Le sonnet est à la fois clôture et brèche, dévoiement de la poésie — vers le discours, vers la rhétorique — et offre d'y revenir. Ce qui explique, à mon sens, la fascination qu'il a exercée, depuis ses premiers jours en Sicile, et son extraordinaire capacité de survie à travers toutes les révolutions qu'a connues au cours de l'histoire de l'Occident l'expérimentation poétique. Il a reparu à l'époque romantique, plus profond et inventif que jamais, il a repris aujourd'hui.[7]
>
> [The first part of the sonnet is a trap and the second a turnaround. The first part is what rhetoric suggests, the conceptual management of thoughts and feelings which is so easily confused with poetry, and the second the occasion for lucidity. And all this at the same time, in these fourteen lines, presents itself like a summary of poetry's innermost movement and of what it is in practice, never a straightforward goal but a most intimate conflict, and never a full success but the stubborn will to achieve it [...] The sonnet is at the same time a fence and a gap, pulling poetry off the track towards oratory and rhetoric, and offering to go back to it. Which explains, as far as I can tell, the fascination it has exerted, from its first days in Sicily, and its extraordinary ability to survive through all the revolutions poetic experimentation has been through in Western history. It has reappeared during the Romantic era, more profound and creative than ever, it has resumed nowadays.]

It is noteworthy that in his own poetry, Yves Bonnefoy started to use the sonnet in sequences around the mid-2000s: his own translations of Shakespeare's *Sonnets* led him both to translate Petrarch and to adopt this canonical form.

Finally, when reading Petrarch, the poet sees the apparition of a modern relation to the body in the writings of this pioneer of the early modern age. Commenting on Sonnet 90, he underlines how stereotypical Petrarch's comparisons of Laura's hair to an angel, to gold, and a godly sun may appear. Paradoxically enough, the Vaucluse poet still manages to breathe life into it.

> Mais ce soleil est «en vie», «un vivo sole», et surtout il y a ce premier vers: «Erano i capei d'oro a l'aura sparsi», où une transgression du symbolique s'ébauche — l'or étant pris dans l'agitation de la brise. Ce qui dans l'ordre naturel est le plus retiré en soi [the gratuitous play upon words, according to Bonnefoy — note of the editors] [...] c'est maintenant ce qui a consenti, en ce jour de printemps, au plus simplement agréable d'un instant des plus ordinaires, ici, maintenant, dans le lieu humain. La transcendance du nimbe médiéval se dissipe dans une lumière qui change de nature, sans rien perdre pourtant ni de son éclat ni de son mystère. C'est déjà la chevelure de la Vénus de Botticelli, cet or où la même brise a le même effet.
>
> Et je remarque aussi que simplement prêter attention à une chevelure de femme, et qui plus est décoiffée, dont le désordre est si aisément interprétable, c'est toujours ce que les orthodoxies morales ou religieuses surveillent jalousement, les contraignant de mille façons jusqu'à les cacher sous des voiles.[8]
>
> [But this sun is 'alive' ('un vivo sole'), and above all there is the first line: 'Erano i capei d'oro a l'aura sparsi', where a transgression of the symbol seems to take form, the gold being caught in the trembling breeze. In the natural order, what is most buried in one's self [. . .] is now on this spring day what has consented to the most simply agreeable part of a most ordinary moment, here and now, in the human world. The transcendence of the medieval halo vanishes in a light whose nature changes without losing either its lustre or its mystery. This is already Botticelli's Venus's hair, the gold where the same breeze has the same effect.
>
> And I also note that simply paying attention to a woman's hair, especially dishevelled hair, [...] whose disorder is so easily interpreted, is always what moral and religious orthodoxies watch over very closely, constraining in a thousand ways, going as far as concealing it under veils.]

Quite clearly, the poet born in the twentieth century sees in Petrarch a pioneer of modernity with the contemporary eye of both an art historian — having extensively written about art, from Giotto and Mantegna to Alechinsky and Giacometti — and of an outsider regarding religious matters.

There might still be a paradox lingering in the simultaneous defence of the sonnet form, and the need for poetry to get rid of every kind of rigidity brought by intellectual orthodoxies.

As a sonnet writer, Yves Bonnefoy therefore asserts the poet's freedom: under his pen, sonnets can count up to sixteen lines, as he tries to loosen the formal constraints and refresh poetic language cast in the same old moulds. While acknowledging the need for form, he insists on how crucial it is for poets to breathe a new idiosyncratic life into it, in a middle-of-the-road position on modernity:

> La forme: ce qui resserre sur soi le réseau des correspondances. [...] La forme est évidemment aussi importante dans ces sonnets que dans les tableaux [...] puisque ces quatorze vers en ces quatre strophes sont un schème au moins aussi

tangible et prégnant que dans le cadre d'une peinture. Mais peut-être n'y est-elle pas manifeste d'une façon aussi évidente, et en tout cas c'est complètement qu'elle s'efface dans le travail de beaucoup de traducteurs, qui ne savent pas la revivre de l'intérieur, et dans des vers réguliers mais de mirliton ou dans un vers libre sans consistance n'en font qu'une imitation par simplement le dehors, sans capacité de retendre quoi que ce soit.

Conséquence, et principe directeur pour la traduction des sonnets: donner priorité à la recréation de la forme et le faire assez hardiment pour que celle-ci, coûte que coûte, se retrouve forme vivante et prenne ainsi un texte aujourd'hui trop peu parlant dans un resserrement qui pourra peut-être, en accentuant la netteté de chaque figure, en raviver les couleurs.[9]

[Form: what tightens on itself the net of correspondences. [...] Form is evidently as important in the sonnets as it is in paintings [...] since these fourteen lines encased in these four stanzas constitute a scheme as tangible and significant as in the case of a painting. But perhaps it does not appear as evidently. In any case, it leaves no traces whatsoever in most translators' works, who fail to experience it from within, in the regular lines of a sorry rhymer or in inconsistent free verse, and produce nothing more than a merely superficial imitation, without being able to draw together anything at all.

The consequence and guiding principle for the translation of sonnets — to give priority to recreating the form and to do it bravely enough for it to become again, at all costs, a living form, thus taking a text which no longer resonates among us today in a tightening which will perhaps allow it, by sharpening the lines of every figure, to refresh its colours.]

Thus fourteen lines by Petrarch can become sixteen in his translation, as the poet expands and refashions the canonical verse into what he sees as a more dynamic rhythm:

126
vidi in una barchetta allegre et sole,

126
I have seen them going, merry
On their light boat, of which I do not know

It is remarkable that, although they have undoubtedly aged, these poems are reshaped by translation. Yves Bonnefoy sees the translating process as a never-ending one, faithfulness consisting in truthful rewriting rather than bland copying — the sincerity of the translator being the main component of a noteworthy translation:

La traduction doit collaborer au poème. Grande responsabilité qu'il va falloir prendre ! Mais pas plus lourde que celle de fidélités plus passives. Et que le traducteur peut bien assumer puisqu'il sera bientôt remplacé par d'autres, s'il apparaît qu'il n'a pas été véridique.[10]

[The translation must collaborate with the poem. What a great responsibility to take! But not more serious than more passive faithfulness. And the translator may very well endorse it since he will soon be replaced by others, if it appears that he has not been truthful enough.]

As an uninterrupted process, translation becomes a lasting bridge between languages — and Petrarch is a nodal point of this relation. Remarking how the Trecento poet writes in Italian about situations he had probably experienced in French, Bonnefoy considers the natural fate of his work to 'open, as this witness of two cultures and two eras, to other languages, other cultures'.[11] He thus concludes that in spite of the irreducible differences between languages, 'When talking about the difficulty of translating poems, one must bear in mind that, under their many guises, whether great ships or thin canoes, these vessels all seek the same harbour.'[12]

Notes to Chapter 12

1. Yves Bonnefoy, 'Prière d'insérer', in Pétrarque, *Je vois sans yeux et sans bouche je crie, vingt-quatre sonnets traduits par Yves Bonnefoy* (Paris: Galilée, 2012), unpaginated ('qui tente de s'approcher de nous'). Translations of Bonnefoy's work in the present chapter are by Guillaume Coatalen and Carole Birkan-Berz.
2. Yves Bonnefoy, 'Vieillir, ne pas vieillir', in *L'Autre langue à portée de voix* (Paris: Seuil, 2013), pp. 173–87 (p. 173) ('Tous les livres vieillissent').
3. Bonnefoy, 'Vieillir, ne pas vieillir' p. 175.
4. Ibid., pp. 174–75.
5. Yves Bonnefoy, 'Le *Canzoniere* en sa traduction', *Conférence*, 20 (2005), pp. 361–77 (p. 365).
6. Bonnefoy, 'Le *Canzoniere* en sa traduction', p. 362.
7. Bonnefoy, 'Vieillir, ne pas vieillir', pp. 177–78.
8. Ibid., p. 183.
9. Bonnefoy, 'Le *Canzoniere* en sa traduction', pp. 369–70.
10. Ibid., p. 377.
11. Bonnefoy, 'Prière d'insérer', [marginal 'Please insert', unpaginated], ('s'ouvrir comme ce témoin de deux pays et deux époques à d'autres langues, d'autres cultures?').
12. Ibid. [marginal 'Please insert', unpaginated], ('On parle de la difficulté de la traduction des poèmes, on doit tout autant se dire que sous leurs guises les plus marquées ces grands vaisseaux ou minces pirogues n'en cherchent pas moins le même port').

CHAPTER 13

Elements of the History of the Sonnet from its Italian Sources: Formal Aspects

Jacques Roubaud

The French poet and mathematician Jacques Roubaud, a first-generation member of the Oulipo and author of a prolific work in verse and prose, is also a self-styled Petrarch scholar. Vast parts of his work include a focus on the sonnet, whose form he studies and anthologizes in his encyclopaedic work Quasi-cristaux. *The title 'Quasi-crystals' is the metaphor he coins for this particular poetic form.[1]*

In this short excerpt from Quasi-cristaux *(taken from chapter 3: 'Elements of the History of the Sonnet from its Italian Sources'), Roubaud studies what he deems to be the third phase of the invention of the sonnet: its use by Petrarch. Having analysed the various aspects of the form in the RVF, he offers his conclusions in his trademark style — a blend of erudition, polemic theorization, and cheekiness. He derives from his study of these sonnets both a meditation on the form's variability — especially as seen through translations — and an assessment of Petrarch's influence on the genre's rise throughout Europe.*

§4 Formal Aspects

4.17 Quantitative results
4.18 There are 317 sonnets
4.19 Quatrains
abba abba: abab abab: abab baab: abab baba
4.20 Tercets
cde (cde cde): 121 cd (cdc dcd): 110 dce (cde dce): 69 cdc (cdc cdc): 10 cdd dcc: 4 dec (cde dec): 2 edc (cde edc): 1

4.21 Hence the following quantitative results:
Guittone–Calvacanti-style quatrains are overwhelmingly present. Sicilian octaves figure very little, they serve as a memory of when the sonnet was formed. Prior to the sonnet, the Sicilian *cobla* is divisible in two: 8 + 6. It can only reasonably be divided in two. The fundamental innovation of the quatrains in enclosed rhymes allows the octave to be divisible and also allows the sestet to be divisible. The

division imposed by the *cde* formula is reinforced by the *dce* variation, which is so present in Petrarch's sonnets. The *cd* form, which is not divisible into two parts, is already in constant play with the other interpretations of the sestet — this play will then continue and become more complex.

4.22 From the Sicilians to Petrarch, a profound change occurred, which gave rise to the sonnet-form. Not to understand this fundamental fact means not to understand anything about what a poetic form is, to say the least.

§5 Petrarch's Influence on the History of the Sonnet Form is Tremendous

5.1 Petrarch's influence on the history of the sonnet form is tremendous. It is felt throughout the centuries and in various languages to the point that I will allow myself to set forth an axiom that states it. This is inspired by the well-known assertion that between two individuals A and B from the same community, one can establish a path of small finite length joining them, using the relation 'A knows B'

5.2 AXIOM (P): EVERY SONNET 'IS' A SONNET BY PETRARCH

5.3 I define the following relation of equivalence between two sonnets A and B: A is equivalent to B if there is a short finite sequence of sonnets $C(1)$, $C(2)$, ... $C(i)$, ... $C(n)$ such that $C(1)=A$, $C(n)=B$ and that for every i, $C(i+1)$ is imitated from or inspired by or translated from $C(i)$. Axiom (P) says there is only one class of equivalence for this relation.

5.4 The universal field of sonnets (from all eras, in all languages) may be divided into sub-fields (which often overlap: $S(1)$ contains the sonnets that are imitations, translations, ... of a given $S(0)$ sonnet from the *RVF*; $S(2)$ are the sonnets that are linked to $S(0)$ by a path of length 2 ...).

5.5 After Petrarch, history in return 'organizes' the *RVF*: some of its sonnets have much more — and/or greater — descendants than others.

5.6 One might attribute a distinct 'weight' to individual sonnets, which might give a 'measure' of the texts, giving an account of their importance understood in this way. I will not attempt this here.

§6 A few sonnets from the *RVF* with great descendants 61 E70

RVF 132
S'amor non è, che dunque è quel ch'io sento?
Ma s'egli è amor, perdio, che cosa et quale?
Se bona, onde l'effecto aspro mortale?
Se ria, onde sí dolce ogni tormento?
S'a mia voglia ardo, onde 'l pianto e lamento?
S'a mal mio grado, il lamentar che vale?
O viva morte, o dilectoso male,
come puoi tanto in me, s'io no 'l consento?
Et s'io 'l consento, a gran torto mi doglio.
Fra sí contrari vènti in frale barca
mi trovo in alto mar senza governo,
sí lieve di saver, d'error sí carca

> ch'i' medesmo non so quel ch'io mi voglio,
> et tremo a mezza state, ardendo il verno.

Hekatompathia
by Thomas Watson
All this Passion (two verses only excepted) is wholly translated out of Petrarch, where he writeth,

> S' amor non e, che dunque e quel ch'i sento? . . Part prima}
> Ma s egli e amor, per Dio che cosa, e quale? . . Sonnet 103}
> Se buona, ond'e l'effetto aspro e mortale?
> Se ria, ond' e si dolce ogni tormento?

Herein certain contrarieties, which are incident to him that loveth extremely, are lively expressed by a Metaphor. And it may be noted that the Author in his first half verse of this translation varieth from that sense which Chaucer useth in translating the selfsame; which he doth upon no other warrant than his own simple private opinion, which yet he will not greatly stand upon.

> If't be not love I feel, what is it then?
> If love it be, what kind a thing is love?
> If good, how chance he hurts so many men?
> If bad, how haps that none his hurts disprove?
> If willingly I burn, how chance I wail?
> If gainst my will, what sorrow will avail?
> livesome death, O sweet and pleasant ill,
> Against my mind how can thy might prevail?
> If I bend back, and but refrain my will,
> If I consent, I do not well to wail;
> {And touching him, whom will hath made a slave,
> The Proverb say'th of old, *Self do, self have*.}   [1]
> Thus being toss'd with winds of sundry sort
> Through dang'rous Seas but in a slender Boat,
> With error stuff'd, and driv'n beside the port,
> Where void of wisdom's freight it lies afloat.
> I wave in doubt what help I shall require,
> In Summer freeze, in winter burn like fire.

[1] Adduntur Tuscano hij duo versus.

RVF 134
> Pace non trovo, et non ò da far guerra;
> e temo, et spero; et ardo, et son un ghiaccio;
> et volo sopra 'l cielo, et giaccio in terra;
> et nulla stringo, et tutto 'l mondo abbraccio.
> Tal m'à in pregion, che non m'apre né serra,
> né per suo mi riten né scioglie il laccio;
> et non m'ancide Amore, et non mi sferra,
> né mi vuol vivo, né mi trae d'impaccio.
> Veggio senza occhi, et non ò lingua et grido;
> et bramo di perir, et cheggio aita;
> et ò in odio me stesso, et amo altrui.

Pascomi di dolor, piangendo rido;
egualmente mi spiace morte et vita:
in questo stato son, donna, per voi.

Vasquin Philieul
Paix je ne trouve, & n'ay dont faire guerre,
J'espère et crains, et bruslant suis en glasse,
Rien je n'estreins, & tout le monde embrasse,
Je vole au ciel, & suis croupant en terre.
En prison m'ha tel, qui n'ouvre ny serre,
Ne me retient pour sien, ne me delasse,
D'amour je vis, & point ne me faict grace,
Et ne me tue, encores moins desserre.
Sans yeulx je voys, & sans langue je crie,
Je quiers secours, & de mourir je prie,
Un aultre j'aime, & à moy je veulx mal.
Je ris en pleurs, & dueil repaist mon ame,
Et vie & mort me faschent par esgal:
Voyla l'estat, ou suis pour vous, ma dame.

Philippe de Maldeghem
Je n'ai dont faire guerre, en vain paix je pourchasse,
Et je crains et j'espère et j'ards de glace étant,
Et je m'envole aux cieux sur la terre couchant,
Je n'étreins rien, pourtant tout le monde j'embrasse.
Tel ne m'ouvre ni serre, et en prison me lace,
Ni pour sien me retient, en ses lacs me tenant,
Et Amour ne me tue, et des fers ne me prend,
Vif aussi ne me veut, et mon ennui ne casse.
Sans langue avoir je crie, aussi je vois sans yeux,
Et je voudrais périr, de secours désireux,
J'aime autrui, et je porte une haine à moi-même,
De douleur je me pais, et en plaignant je ris,
Ennemi à la vie et à la mort je suis,
Pour vous dame je vis en cet état extrême.

§7 Retroaction

7.1 The next part of the sonnet adventure according to that a retroactive reading of the *RVF* also implies that the poems of the Sicilian school, and of its inheritors — Guinizelli, Cavalcanti, Dante, its followers and enemies before Petrarch — have become sonnets. They were not sonnets previously, they *became* sonnets. I do not deny it: I do not deny their being called sonnets. But they earn that term by being Petrarch's 'Plagiarists by Anticipation'.

7.1.1 On Plagiarism by Anticipation (PLANT)

7.2 A historical enquiry into the invention of a poetic form — whichever one it may be — must, before it presents events from the vantage point of the present time, take into account Michael Oakeshott's words warning in *On History*:

7.3 '*By an historical event I mean an occurrence or situation, inferred from surviving record, alleged to be what was actually happening, in a certain respect, then and there, and understood in terms of the mediation of its emergence; that is, understood as an* eventus *or outcome of what went before.'* From which it stems that *'historical events are immune to the criticism of the future: an earlier event cannot be made more historically intelligible in terms of later events.'*[2]

§8 Form and Language

8.1 The description I have just made of the *RVF* is purely abstract. The sonnets are almost empty frames. Nothing is said of what is said [in them].
8.2 Consider for instance poem C, a sonnet
RVF 100
8.3

> *RVF* 100
> Quella fenestra ove l'un sol si vede
> quando a lui piace, et l'altro in su la nona,
> et quella dove l'aere freddo suona
> ne' brevi giorni, quando borrea 'l fiede;
> e 'l sasso, ove a' gran dí pensosa siede
> madonna, et sola seco si ragiona;
> con quanti luoghi sua bella persona
> coprí mai d'ombra, o disegnò col piede;
> e 'l fiero passo ove m'agiunse Amore,
> e lla nova stagion che d'anno in anno
> mi rinfresca in quel dí l'antiche piaghe;
> e 'l volto, et le parole che mi stanno
> altamente confitte in mezzo 'l core,
> fanno le luci mie di pianger vaghe.

> That window where one sun is seen
> when she pleases, and the other sun at noon:
> window that the cold wind rattles
> when days are brief, when winds are northerly:
> and the stone, where on long days my lady
> sits thinking, and reasoning with herself,
> when many places are covered by the shadow
> of her lovely self, or trodden by her foot:
> and the lovely pass where Love caught me:
> and the fresh season that, from year to year,
> renews my former wound, on that day:
> and the face, and the words that remain
> fixed deep in the centre of my heart,
> make my eyes dim with tears.[3]

8 4 I extract from this data a formal 'mould'. Each metrical position is marked with an 'x'. The rhyme scheme is: abba abba cdc dcd.

8.5 Deprived of its words, and taking into account the modern presentation in separate stanzas in which the lines are numbered, the text becomes:

```
             C
1      x x x x x x x x x a
2      x x x x x x x x x b
3      x x x x x x x x x b
4      x x x x x x x x x a
5      x x x x x x x x x a
6      x x x x x x x x x b
7      x x x x x x x x x b
8      x x x x x x x x x a
9      x x x x x x x x x c
10     x x x x x x x x x d
11     x x x x x x x x x c
12     x x x x x x x x x d
13     x x x x x x x x x c
14     x x x x x x x x x d
```

8.5.1 A 'literal' sonnet, pointing to a famous nineteenth century French sonnet.
8.5.2 By Georges Fourest
A pseudo-sonnet which those with a taste for facile jokes will proclaim to be the best in the collection:

Nemo (*Nihil*, cap oo)

X x x x x x x x x x x x x x x x x x x x x x x
x x x x x x x x x x x x x x x x x x x x x x x
x x x x x x x x x x x x x x x x x x x x x x x
x x x x x x x x x x x x x x x x x x x x x x x
x x x x x x x x x x x x x x x x x x x x x x x
x x x x x x x x x x x x x x x x x x x x x x x
x x x x x x x x x x x x x x x x x x x x x x x
x x x x x x x x x x x x x x x x x x x x x x x★
x x x x x x x x x x x x x x x x x x x x x x x
x x x x x x x x x x x x x x x x x x x x x x x
x x x x x x x x x x x x x x x x x x x x x x x
x x x x x x x x x x x x x x x x x x x x x x x
x x x x x x x x x x x x x x x x x x x x x x x
x x x x x x x x x x x x x x x x x x x x x x x

★ If I dare so speak (Author's note)

8.6 It is well known however that sonnets are usually composed in a vernacular language — here 'Trecento' Italian. The question therefore arises: is there a formal relation that occurs with enough regularity and which may be described between the words of a sonnet and its abstract 'mould'?

8.7 This is no easy question. It ought to be pondered, however. Critical 'readings' of sonnets, from which I will generally abstain, often attempt to describe the unfolding of the lines by comparing it to the stanzaic structure of the text. It has been said for instance that *RVF* 100 (examined here) shows a certain conformity between syntax and form. In other cases, critics have noted a clash between form and meaning. Various attempts have been made to describe these relations in general terms. It has been said for instance that a sonnet is a sort of reasoning, a syllogism, where hypotheses are presented in the quatrains and the tercets offer a conclusion. I will not examine these questions.

Translated by Carole Birkan-Berz

Notes to Chapter 13

1. Jacques Roubaud, *Quasi-cristaux: un choix de sonnets en langue française de Lazare Carnot (1820) à Emmanuel Hocquard (1998)* (Paris: Yvon Lambert et Martine Aboucaya, 2013). This work is also freely available online at <http://blogs.oulipo.net/qc/description/chapitre-3-rerum-vulgarum-fragmenta/> [accessed 25 July 2018] from which this excerpt is reproduced. The editors would like to thank Jacques Roubaud for granting permission to reproduce this work here and to Marina Ville, Researcher in Mathematics, for her kind reading of this translation. Roubaud's other works on the sonnet include: Jacques Roubaud, 'La Forme du sonnet français de Marot à Malherbe. Recherche de seconde rhétorique' (unpublished dissertation, Université de Paris IV-Sorbonne, 1990) and *Poétique. Remarques. Poésie, mémoire, nombre, temps, rythme, contraintes, etc.* (Paris: Seuil, 2016).
2. Michael Oakeshott, 'Historical Events', in *On History and Other Essays* (Oxford: Basil Blackwell, 1983), pp. 45–96 (p. 62).
3. Translation by A. S. Kline, *The Complete Canzoniere*, Poetry in Translation, Digital edition 2002, <https://www.poetryintranslation.com/klineascanzoniere.php> [accessed 20 December 2018].

CHAPTER 14

❖

Seven Types of Translation: An Overview and Arrangement of Avant-Garde Translation Practice with Reference to Tim Atkins's *Petrarch Collected Atkins*

Tim Atkins

Introduction

> I ate in the morning what I would digest in the evening; I swallowed as a boy what I would ruminate upon as a man. These writings I have so thoroughly absorbed and fixed, not only in my memory but in my very marrow, these have become so much a part of myself, that even though I should never read them again they would cling in my spirit, deep-rooted in its inmost recesses. But meanwhile I may well forget the author, since by long usage and possession I may adopt them and regard them as my own, bewildered by their mass, I may forget who they are and even that they are others' work.
>
> — Petrarch, *Rerum Familiarum Libri*, XXII, 2[1]

Of all forms of writing, poetry concerns itself with the 'how it is said' more than any other. In the translation of poetry the translator is faced with the task of deciding what to carry over, be it meaning, rhyme, sound, form, or style. Given that it is impossible to translate all of these things, from the outset all translators of poetry have to make individual, intellectual, and aesthetic choices concerning the areas of the text upon which they wish to focus. It is the very impossibility of ever producing a 'complete' translation of any other poem that is translation's greatest excitement and its greatest challenge.

Eliot Weinberger is one of the twentieth century's most distinguished translators of poetry. He comments upon nineteen different translations of the same poem by the Chinese poet Wang Wei in his *19 Ways of Looking at Wang Wei*:

> Translation is more than a leap from dictionary to dictionary; it is a reimagining of the poem. As such, every reading of every poem, regardless of the language, is an act of translation: translation from the reader's intellectual and emotional life. As no individual reader remains the same, each reading becomes a different — not merely another — reading. The same poem cannot be read twice.[2]

My definition of 'poetic translation' is as follows: poetic translation is a form of translation, usually of poetry, in which the aesthetic and execution of the translator is as important as that of the perceived intention of the original writer, and may concern itself with recasting the poem with attention to sound, shape, energy, form, and the translator's creative imperatives as much as to the equivalence of content. This is the method (with many subsets) that I have used exclusively for my translations and versions.

The idea of a translation not needing to be faithful to the original is playfully stated in the French saying 'Translations are like women; if they are faithful, they are not beautiful, if they are beautiful they are not faithful.'[3] Perhaps a more useful and less faithful translation, these days, would be to change the word 'partner' for 'women'. In all of my translations of Petrarch's *Canzoniere*, I have, in various ways, been demonstrably unfaithful to the traditional and impossible idea of equivalence. I have never, in any of my poems, been unfaithful to the creative and generative ideas and methods of poetic translation.

I have divided the practice of creative translation into seven areas. My concern is to outline the variety of strategies used by contemporary poets, and to show how I have used (some of) those strategies in my own translations. That creative combinations continue to be made across (what I present, in a sense, as rigid) boundaries is evidence of their fluidity: as Louis Zukofsky writes at the end of 'Catullus 70', it is, in a sense, 'a scribble reported in water'.[4] The general movement is one in which the translator has increasing choice with the particulars of the poem in question, and the direction in which it is taken. These creative methods of translation were inspired by Bernadette Mayer's writing exercises at The Poetry Project in New York in the 1970s (widely accessible online), and by Stephen Rodefer's translations of Francois Villon. To them both — the highest praise!

1. Constraint Translation

A translation which involves the application of a previously planned procedure to the source text.

In *Constraint Translation* the result of the procedure can be left as is or adjusted according to the requirements of the translator. *Constraint Translation* methods generally attend to original poems on a single word basis. This relates them to Dryden's first translation type, that of metaphrase (metaphrase: 'turning an Author word by word and line by line, from one language into another').[5] *Constraint Translation* methods (usually) use single words and replace or rearrange them using (as will be seen) a single method which is applied throughout to the original poem.

Canadians Douglas Barbour and Stephen Scobie use a variety of constraints in their 1981 collection *The Pirates of Pen's Chance*. In their afterword to this text, Barbour and Scobie set out their poetic concerns, which they state to be 'homolinguistic' — a translation from English to English. Of their translation methods, they state: 'some are closed formal systems, which allow very little leeway to the translator, and some are wide-open, free-association processes which allow the translator unlimited freedom. What remains constant is that there is an original text, a system of translation, and a new text'.[6] Scobie and Barbour further claim that their translations take them 'in directions we would never have gone without the stimulus of this process. The poems are unlike any we would ever write in our own voices; they free us from the expressive demands of the lyric ego.'[7] This is a key point. Writing and translation no longer need be only about the generation and projection of an internal emotional or intellectual essence. Through the use of *Constraint Translation* the poet produces and engages with language in a way which extends the ways of both deriving and producing meaning.

Some of Barbour and Scobie's translation methods fall squarely into the field of *Constraint Translation*. They divide the 'Acrostic Translation' method in two, as follows:

> The traditional acrostic is content to use the first letter of every line to spell out the 'hidden' name. We use two more radical types of acrostic:
>
> (a) Letter/word acrostics, in which the first *letter* of every *word* spells out the original text:
> (b) Word/line acrostics, in which the first *word* of every *line* spells out the original text.[8]

An example of letter/word acrostics is the poem 'A Jesuitical Sonnet for James Joyce', which takes the opening words of Joyce's *Ulysses* ('Stately, plump Buck Mulligan came from [...]') and uses the first letter of each word to create a new text, word by word. In the case of their 'Acrostic Translations' it is not stated which texts Barbour and Scobie use to source the new words in the poem; it is merely stated for this method that the new words are 'of our choosing'. It is, however, possible to guess at the type of text used. In the case of the following poem, the text includes biblical references, perhaps in keeping with its ironic title. The 'Jesuitical Sonnet' begins:

> Seasons turn and turn: early, late,
> Years pass.[9]

Barbour and Scobie's second method is the 'word/line acrostic'. Using Oliver Goldsmith's 'Song' from *The Vicar of Wakefield* ('When lovely woman stoops to folly and finds too late that men betray [...]') a new translation (using each of Goldsmith's words to start a new line) results:

> **When** everything meshes perfectly, it's
> **lovely** interaction, soft generation of liquid vowels, consonance:
> **woman** & man together. Together. She
> **stoops**, he stoops
> **to** enter or she rises in pride over him. It would be
> **folly** to turn away from such pleasure
> [...].[10]

In their third category, 'Structural Translation', Barbour and Scobie restrict themselves further:

> In this category, *all* the words we use are drawn from the original texts, without alteration. Our choice is limited to the methods by which we select words from

the original text, and these methods are often arbitrary or chance-generated. For instance, dealing with a page of prose, we may read down the right or left hand margins, choosing only the words which appear by topographical chance, and observing the order in which they appear ...[...] The reader's urge to *create* meaning is both encouraged and frustrated.[11]

A subset of 'Structural Translation' is the 'One Word Per Line' or 'Reader's Digest Condensed Poem' method, in which Barbour and Scobie choose only 'one word per line from the original (thus a sonnet becomes a 14-word poem), again observing strictly the order in which the words appear'.[12] This method allows them enough choice to write poems 'which make syntactic sense, and which comment, ironically or otherwise, on the sense of the originals'.[13] Milton's 'Sonnet XIX' provides an example of this method:

> WHEN I consider how my light is spent,
> Ere half my days in this dark world and wide,
> And that one talent which is death to hide
> Lodged with me useless, though my soul more bent
> To serve therewith my Maker, and present
> My true account, lest He returning chide,
> 'Doth God exact day-labour, light denied?'.[14]

Barbour and Scobie use the 'Reader's Digest Condensed Poem' method to reduce Milton's poem:

> Anger Song No. 3
> Light dark
> hide
>
> useless Maker
> he denied.[15]

Barbour and Scobie's choice of words take the passive, stoic, and resigned tone of Milton's sonnet and render it in a way that both modernizes and streamlines the original. Although this method is discussed here as a *Constraint Translation* poem, it also falls under the trope of *Editing Translation*. This is an example of translation methods being wider and more varied than a simple 'Seven Categories' list allows.

2.1. Editing Translation

A re-presentation or rearrangement of the original text which highlights a particular aspect of the original. This includes the adding of commentary. Domestication Translation (Type 2.2) is a subset of Editing Translation.

'Commentary Editing Translation' is the incorporation of additional texts or translators' comments into the translated poem. This is the method used by Jack Spicer in *After Lorca* (1957). In what is a series of generally faithful/traditional translations of Lorca's poems, Spicer frames these pieces with a series of letters. In these letters he comments on the process of translation, and muses upon the nature of poetry and his poetics. In one letter he comments 'These paragraphs could be translated, transformed by a chain of fifty poets in fifty languages, and they still would be temporary, untrue, unable to yield the substance of a single image'.[16] In the second letter, he states:

> When I translate one of your poems and I come across words I do not understand, I always guess at their meanings. I am inevitably right. A really perfect poem (no one yet has written one) could be perfectly translated by a person who did not know one word of the language it was written in. A really perfect poem has an infinitely small vocabulary.[17]

Spicer reminds the reader that a translation (because it is made up of words) is a provisional product of the imagination. His insistence upon the inadequacy of words means that Spicer does not see the meaning of a poem as resting primarily with its vocabulary — either his own or that of the poet whom he is translating. His conviction that he is 'invariably right' also reinforces Spicer's (and my) idea that the translator is both empowered and entitled to do whatever they want to do with their chosen poem. Spicer states, in his second letter; 'Words are what sticks to the real. We use them to push the real, to drag the real into the poem. They are what we hold on with, nothing else. They are as valuable in themselves as rope with nothing to be tied to.'[18] Spicer foregrounds the idea that poets use words as tools to carry meaning, although they contain no value in themselves. By freeing particular words from the idea that they contain the essence of a poem and seeing them as merely pointing to it, Spicer is able to circumvent the importance of any particular fidelity to a poet's words; instead, Spicer attempts to free himself to connect with something far more intangible:

> Tradition [...] means generations of different poets in different countries patiently telling the same story, writing the same poem, gaining and losing something with each transformation — but, of course, never really losing anything. This has nothing to do with calmness, classicism, temperament, or anything else.[19]

Spicer uses the title *After Lorca* to flag up the fact that his writing is 'after' Lorca in that it is chasing the spirit of Lorca, written at a later date, and written in imitation. It must at this point be stressed that my definition of translation included ideas of imitation in collections that present themselves as translations. *After Lorca* is a volume in which twenty-three translations of Lorca mix with eleven poems which (although not indicated as such) are written by Spicer. The letters that also make up *After Lorca* can be seen as a commentary and as a type of *Editing Translation* alongside Spicer's assumption of Lorca's persona.

In many poems I have (as has Spicer) written new poems which (although occupying a position to suggest that they are poems by Petrarch) bear no resemblance to the particular content of the poem in the *Canzoniere*. The poems, however, always exist within the concept (again from Spicer) of the translator imagining, writing and expanding the original authorial essence which exists on a larger scale than particular poems. We are invariably right, whatever we decide to do with our source text. My translations, in these cases, use (to mangle Spicer) new words which I stick to the 'original' and imagined Petrarchian 'real'; an author (in my reading of his life and the *Canzoniere*) whose major themes include intertextuality, unfulfilled desire, self-obsession, the position and power of the author, artifice, and exaggeration. I use contemporary metaphors, language, and syntax to express Petrarch's concerns, in order to enable Petrarch's themes and engagements to live as twenty-first-century poems, as opposed to the museum pieces which they often appear to be.

Examples of Commentary/Editing Translation strategies occur throughout *Petrarch Collected Atkins*. 'Poem 159' comments on and plays with some lines by Petrarch:

> Who seeks for divine beauty seeks in vain
> If he has not used his eyes to look then
> & seen her using them & making them move
> He does not know how love can do things
> Such as sighing speaking smiling etc
> Petrarch wrote that The sap
> I wrote that.[20]

In 'Poem 162', Petrarch addresses his domestic landscape with love by describing the countryside and landscape around Vaucluse. I have taken this activity and reimagined the author's overwrought exploration ('By now there cannot be among you even one stone that is not learning to burn with my flame')[21] thus:

> The hoot-owl turning
> In the dusk may well turn
> Into the last light but will not
> Turn into a churn-owl
> There were times when
> It is good to be a mother
> Of any stripe or colour
> Back when you had hair
> And Worcestershire's alders were poppers[22]

A further way which I have engaged with Editing Translation and Commentary is simply to make a poem using endnotes from a number of translators. My 'Poem 58' consists entirely of endnotes from the Durling and Nichols translations, indicated in my text by asterisks. My first lines run:

> The recipient of this poem has not been identified
> One of these presumably a pillow that cruel one
> *one of the remedies for love was thought to be repose & meditation
> Love the second perhaps *the second gift, perhaps a book
> A book of moral reflections road on the left (the left side: where the heart is)
> *reminiscent of Horace's 'Ars longa, vita brevis'[23]

By using these endnotes my aim is to show how words and translators (again, mirroring Spicer) are able to point to meaning but never pin it down. All poems are subject to interpretation and variant readings. Through replacing the poem with endnotes, the reader is free to imagine what constituted Petrarch's original poem and reflect upon the fact that all reading is an interpretation.

Editing Translation can entail adding or subtracting or extracting words to a poem. My impulse to edit poems and use/suggest fragments came from reading Sappho (particularly in the translation by Suzy Q. Groden), from taking pleasure in misheard conversations, from having partial knowledge of several languages, and from listening to dub reggae. Dub reggae originated in Jamaica in the early 1970s. The result of producers such as Lee Perry and King Tubby taking popular reggae songs originally with vocals and remixing them so that vocals dropped out or appeared only in fragments, this otherworldly, disjunctive-yet-melodic music was an important strand of the musical counter-culture in the UK in the mid to late 1970s. From reading and not understanding Shakespeare in school to attempting to read widely in the Romance languages (with far from perfect language skills), my understanding has often felt partial. I often have the feeling that I encounter poems or worlds which I am unable to grasp perfectly or completely. This experience was initially frustrating but slowly changed — in part through my reading of Sappho and listening to dub — to become a pleasing and creative engagement. The partial and fragmentary nature of many of my poems is therefore deliberate; in my translation method called *Fragmentary Editing Translation*, I have created a method which depends upon lack of understanding. It is similar to the method used by Spicer in that it addresses issues of ignorance, but where he inserts words to fill a lack of knowledge of the original language, I have left gaps. The method is as follows: I have only translated words that I know (or think I know). The first four lines of my translation of 'Poem 353' run:

>..singing....
>...time passing
>.............the night...
>..month [24]

Petrarch's Italian is 'Vago augelletto, che cantando vai | o ver piangendo it tuo tempo passato | vedendoti la note e 'l verno a lato | e 'l di dopo le spalle e I mesi gai:'.[25]

2.2. Domestication Translation

A subset of Editing Translation in which the original poem is presented, explicitly, within a different physical, cultural, or linguistic setting.

The first subset of *Domestication Translation* is 'Geographic Domestication Translation'. This is a recasting of a poem so that its geographic location is changed. This type of translation happens in George Bowering's *Kerrisdale Elegies* and it is also a major trope in many of my translations. In *Kerrisdale Elegies*, Rilke's *Duino Elegies* is transposed to Kerrisdale, British Columbia. Rilke's first elegy, as translated by Stephen Mitchell, runs:

> Perhaps there remains for us some tree on a hillside, which every day we can take into our vision;
>> there remains for us yesterday's street and the loyalty of a habit so much at ease
>>> when it stayed with us that it moved in and never left.[26]

This, in part, in Bowering, becomes: 'Maybe I should walk along 41st Avenue where mothers in velvet jogging suits push prams.'[27]

Bowering takes Rilke's floating and general meditations and makes them geographically ('41st Avenue') and culturally ('velvet jogging suits') specific. This form of translation, 'Geographic Domestication Translation', moving as it does from Rilke's universal and transpersonal meditations to Bowering's suburban twentieth-century west coast Canada constitutes the core and key thrust of Bowering's book. This method of translation is similar to that of Italian Renaissance painters whose canvases relocate the Christian myths to a pastoral Italian landscape. In Bowering's case, the aesthetic, geographic location, and execution of the translator is as important as that of the perceived intention of the original writer. This is what qualifies this work as a translation (it is a *poetic* translation) within my range of definitions. Rilke's tree of life image which opens his fourth elegy becomes in Bowering, 'These high chestnut branches along Larch Street'.[28] Bowering mentions Yankee Stadium, cop cars, and bars full of smoke. He writes 'through' as 'thru' and throughout his translation locates Rilke in a recognizable, and far from rarefied, suburban geographic and linguistic suburban Vancouver.

This method is important to my translations. My domesticated/relocated Petrarch speaks in several types of contemporary English and addresses a twentieth-century geographic, linguistic, political, and literary reality. In terms of 'Geographic Domestication Translation' I have relocated many of the poems to places where I have lived. My intention is straightforward: I want my world, be it (primarily) London, Barcelona, or Worcestershire, to be the place where the themes and ideas explored by Petrarch are played out, using methods similar to those of the aforementioned Renaissance painters. My impulse, here, stems partly from the belief that my poems do 'what my authors might have done if they were writing their poems now'[29] but also from a love of the writing of New York School poets, especially Frank O'Hara and Ted Berrigan. Both of these poets peppered their writings with references to their city and to their friends. In a word search of my translations, Tooting appears ten times, Colliers Wood comes up four times, and there are many references to other London locations, from New Cross ('Your breasts in New Cross on | April 21st 2003 | Smeared with news print')[30] to Green Park ('Green plant of such greenness that it is greener! | Than the greenness in Green Park itself!')[31] to mentions of Tottenham Court Road ('The catfish star over the Tottenham Court Road')[32] and Piccadilly Circus ('Standing in Piccadilly Circus seeking satisfaction from a large Chinese').[33] Worcestershire and Malvern (symbols for me of both youth and restriction) are also mentioned:

> & once I wrote 15 haiku   in a day
> On my back beneath a hedge on the Malvern Hills
> & the fawns & small rabbits licked every bump of my body   then
> Before I had hair & which now grows abundant off   my every ledge & shelf
> It is 18 years in this poem   of combing[34]

The second type of *Domestication Translation* is linguistic. Although it rarely exists separately from 'Geographic Domestication Translation', it is useful to consider

Donny O'Rourke's translations in his and Richard Price's 1996 volume *Eftirs/Afters* as it provides such a clear example of 'Linguistic Domestication Translation'. O'Rourke's translations take milder forms of 'Linguistic Domestication Translation' (such as Bowering's use of 'thru') and, both for the specificity of the language and for the number used, relocate their French originals firmly and strongly in Scotland. In *Eftirs/Afters*, O'Rourke takes poems by Blaise Cendrars, Robert Desnos, Philippe Soupault, and Valery Larbaud, and renders them in the spoken Scottish that was used most famously by Robert Burns, Hugh MacDiarmid, and Tom Leonard. The language that O'Rourke uses is almost as far from English as the original French is. A brief excerpt from 'Non, L'Amour N'est Pas Mort' portrays Robert Desnos as a lover who 'Disnae want tae be mindit fur oniethin ense oan this sneistsome scruffin.'[35]

'Sneistsome scruffin' is translated by William Kulik, in *The Voice of Robert Desnos*, as 'love of you'.

3. Misreading Translation

A partial representation or distortion of the original text.

Misreading Translation differs from *Allusive Referential Translation* in that it decides upon a particular way of refracting a poem before the act of translation begins (*Allusive Referential Translation* allows for spontaneity and a variety of responses in a single translation) and it differs from *Constraint Translation* as it does not insist on a previously planned procedure. Several of bpNichol's 'Translating Translating Apollinaire' poems provide examples of *Misreading Translation* strategies. He writes in *Translating Translating Apollinaire* that he decided to put a section of Apollinaire's 'ZONE':

> thru as many translation/transformation processes as i & other people could think of. I conceived of it as an openended, probably unpublishable in its entirety, piece. As of this date (August 29, 1978) i have elaborated 55 different systems & or results [...] The pieces included here begin with the three memory translations written over the atlantic ocean on May 27th [1975]. TTA 4 is the original poem as published in 1964 & all the pieces that follow are based on TTA 4.[36]

The three poems which come before 'TTA 4' come about not through *Constraint Translation* processes (which are discussed above) but through methods of *Misreading Translation*. 'TTA 1' is described by Nichol as 'memory translation (order of recall)'. He writes down his fleeting memory of the original (1964) translation 'flat on my back on the floor'.[37] In his next translation ('TTA 2') Nichol takes this poem ('TTA 1') and restructures it: 'according to recalled order'.[38] In 'TTA 3', Nichol again takes his remembered version ('TTA 1') of his original ('TTA 4') and, treating it as a new poem, revises it.

Barbara Godard's machine-based translations of Apollinaire's 'Les Fenêtres'

Godard makes plain her debit to and development from bpNichol. Writing on her machine translations of 'Les Fenêtres', all of which are unable to deal with combinations of words and which, instead, translate word for word, Godard states that:

> Language is thus divorced from any social or communicative function, pure matter not reified commodity [...] Reading for the letter rather than the spirit or meaning, the machine translations accentuate the undecipherability of Apollinaire's poem and underscore the infinite combinatory potential of language [...] In their focus on the letter of the word, the systems I have used in this instance highlight the difference in any act of repetition, taking language to the limits of intelligibility in the strange combinations they produce.[39]

Godard's translations are not the end product but the start of the translation process. This new material simply provides additional material which can be worked up to produce a linguistically engaging version.

Steven Vincent is explicit in his use of Misreading Translation. In his *Sleeping with Sappho* (2009) he takes Anne Carson's translations of Sappho as the text to misread. Vincent states: 'I took Anne Carson's translations of Sappho and I went through and translated them all from the English. Essentially, I turned words or phrases over into their opposites.'[40]

It is interesting to compare Vincent's method with that of Nichol. In 'TTA 49: replacing words with their antonyms using THE NEW AMERICAN ROGET'S COLLEGE THESAURUS', Nichol uses a word-by-word constraint to produce a new poem. Here, Vincent applies the idea in a more impressionistic and less programmatic manner. It is useful to note that in general, contemporary translation strategies will be applied differently and produce very different results depending upon how the translator chooses to use them. Vincent translates poems from Anne Carson's *If not, Winter: Fragments of Sappho* (2002). Carson's translation of 'Poem 52' ('I would not think to touch the sky with two arms')[41] is turned by Vincent into its antithesis: 'Shameless, I embrace the tree | Thick woven, fuzzy, red bark'.[42] 'Antithetical Translation' requires creative judgement. Vincent's 'Shameless' overturns Carson's humble and chaste refusal of union, and his tree returns the focus of desire to the earth, making the pristine, blue sky a rough, messy, red object. This is his method throughout his translations. They are interesting because, as can be seen from the example cited, they engage with the earlier poem in a way which encourages either a pleasing independent reading of the new translation, or a deeper reading of the poem from which it comes. This can be seen, further, in Carson's and then Vincent's versions of Sappho's 'Poem 162'. Carson's entire poem is one line long: 'with what eyes?'.[43] In contrast, Vincent takes the materiality of the eyes and both relocates them and energizes them: 'Right in the throat, night or day, | this white ball, luminous, spinning'.[44] Carson's plural 'eyes' becomes singular and, possibly, not an eye at all. Instead of being calm and abstract, Vincent's 'white ball' is a 'luminous', 'spinning' thing which is present, active and crackling with an energy that is entirely absent from Carson.

I have used 'Antithetical Translation' in my translations of Petrarch in a manner which takes Vincent's poem-by-poem approach and applies it to a particular aspect of Petrarch's biography. Petrarch does not mention his two children in the *Canzoniere*. Petrarch exists in the text as a solitary lover, as a writer, as a spiritual seeker, and as a friend, but not as a father. I have written the opposite of this aspect of his life by writing quite extensively about children. This type of translation can be seen as antithetical if the impulse stems from the poems alone, but it could be seen, also, as a type of Editing Translation, if knowledge of the author's biographical details and a desire to present a fuller authorial picture were the cause of the incorporation of such material. This approach occurs in my 'Poem 95', with the line '2 children run around the outskirts of this story'[45] and in 'Poem 25' which ends with the three lines: 'However many angels you pass over in Kwik-e-Mart | With your cart | Why is there no mention of children?'[46] Children are repeatedly mentioned in my poems: the word 'daughter' appears in twelve poems. My daughter Koto is the subject of 'Poem 215', which ends as follows: 'Let it be said it is enough to be in love | With a daughter light of whom there is but one in this small poem | Of which there was but one & to hold it all going in this small room & yet remarkable'.[47] Again, invoking my definition of poetic translation, 'the aesthetic and execution of the translator is as important as that of the perceived intention of the original writer'.

4. Allusive Referential Translation

A translation (inter-lingual, intra-lingual, or inter-semiotic) which involves the creation of a new poem as a result of a (detailed or cursory) reading of the source text.

In *Allusive Referential Translation* (the same as homolinguistic translation) the unit of meaning translated may be word, phrase, or larger (often general) inferred meaning. At its widest point, the translator may attend less to particular words or phrases than to themes, tone, and/or the representation of personae. Dick Higgins and Steve McCaffery developed the idea of *Allusive Referential Translation* (also called 'Homolinguistic Translation' by McCaffery) in a series of articles written in the mid-1970s. In 'Towards an Allusive Referential' (1982) Higgins writes that he hopes for an intuitive displacement from 'the expected over the threshold into the unexpected, not for the sake of novelty, but in order to refer to some additional and relevant element'.[48] For Higgins, 'in a piece of verbal art, any symbol is in some degree an allusive referential'[49] and there is no right or wrong. Noting Mac Low's and Cage's use of the word as a language unit, Higgins states that his interest is in larger semantic units, his aim being 'to work with transforms (phrases)'.[50] He concludes that 'All artistic language is, then, a metaphor for experience and an allusive referential for it'.[51] This is an expansion of *Allusive Referential Translation* because Higgins' interest in phrases opens up an even wider range of translation reference. Higgins' importance to the contemporary translation of poetry is enormous: he makes explicit the key ideas that: (1) intuition and interpretation are both valid and important; (2) writing is an 'assemblage' and; (3) the word is less important than the phrase. Higgins' ideas are developed by McCaffery in his discussion of his *Allusive Referential Translations* of Gertrude Stein's *Tender Buttons* (1914). In his introduction to *Every Way Oakly* (1976), McCaffery writes that his poems 'generate contentually new texts that, nonetheless, obey certain of the basic tenets of translation (the passage from a source to a target language and the preservation, in that passage, of some trace of the source elements)'.[52] McCaffery notes that Stein's *Tender Buttons* utilized peripheralities of her own viewpoint and cubist techniques of fracturing still lives to produce her pieces. His aim is the same.

McCaffery gives an example of his method for translating Stein in a 2009 interview in *The Danforth Review*. (It should be noted here that McCaffrey is speaking about his practice of intralingual translation.) He explains: 'One follows the trajectories of one of several allusions. For instance, 'the dog growls' might yield 'a noun is very angry', or via the allusive track of 'dog' = 'Fido' and 'Fido equals faith' arrive at 'Faith makes canine noises.'[53] McCaffery also makes use of 'functional reversals' (e.g. nouns for verse forms). Stein's sentence 'The difference is spreading' became 'No one same article unlike a wide' where 'The difference' yielded the first five words and 'is spreading' became 'a wide'.[54]

'Poem 63' in *Petrarch Collected Atkins*, in which Petrarch declares his weakness before Laura and his willingness 'to set sail [...] for everything' (Durling 140)[55] becomes, in my version, a poem about love and adventure. The opening line '*On The Road* opens in Worcestershire'[56] domesticates Petrarch's aim and replicates its absurdity (he can never escape Laura) by juxtaposing a work of bohemian male comradeship upon a conservative and displaced (and autobiographical) English backwater. The final lines of my poem, continuing Petrarch's theme, are as follows:

> There is no anchor
> Tied to this art see you have no way out of it
> Ready to set sail with every wind or just
> Sit here with everything
> Breathing [57]

The poem takes the themes of transcendence, opportunity, relationships, and travel and brings in references to other texts (Roland Barthes's *A Lover's Discourse*) and contemporary and personal references. Although a very different poem is produced, the method and the result fall squarely within Higgins's and McCaffery's definition of Allusive Referential Translation as a 'preservation [of] some trace of the source elements'[58] and Barbour and Scobie's 'often deliberately perverse or whimsical'[59] 'Metonymic Translation' strategies. A further example of my use of this method occurs in my translation of 'Poem 353'. Petrarch (in Musa's translation) opens: 'O lovely little bird singing away'.[60] It is this line which provides the inspiration for the whole of my poem. In the same way that Petrarch and the nightingale sing in celebration of (and, Petrarch suggests, mourn for) life, my list, which is an alphabetical list of invented birds, intends (through the varieties and playfulness of the names) to suggest the glories of singing, which is a metaphor, in Petrarch, for writing. This is set alongside the absurdity of the act of both talking to a bird (in this poem) and, throughout the *Canzoniere*, devoting one's life to an idealized (and possibly imaginary) woman. My unpublished draft translation of 'Poem 353' begins:

> Agnosticbird, Asprinbird, Buttonbird, Batbird, Blondebird, bissettbird, Bongwaterbird, Bingeorpurgebird, Cloudbird, Canarywharfbird, Charlieyardbird, Cornbird, Dervishbird, Dornbird, Eggmeatbird, Frenchbird, Fourteenbird, Guppybird

This litany of collaged references continues from A through to Z and ends with the line 'Zaumbird, Zincbird, Zionbird, Zframedomesticbird, ZZZZZZZ-wordbird.'

Collage is similar to Allusive Referential Translation because the source texts are — in the case of my translations — selected for their creative relationships. The difference is that Allusive Referential Translation tends to draw its words from the poet's imagination, whereas collaged texts already exist.

It is here useful to return to parts of Barbour and Scobie's definition of Allusive Referential Translation, in which they state: 'In these poems, the words of the original text are replaced by words which we associate with them, through synonyms, comparison, paraphrase, analysis, expansion, contraction, puns, allusions both literary and personal.'[61] Barbour and Scobie's focus on 'the words of the original text' is just the start. They see translation as: 'a form of metonymy, "substitute naming," in view of Robert Kroetsch's theory that the use of metonymy rather than metaphor is a key to post-modern writing. This is the loosest, most open-form method of translation.'[62] Petrarch collages lines by his contemporaries at the end of each stanza in his 'Poem 70'. He adds lines by Arnaut Daniel (or, possibly, William of St Gregory), Guido Cavalcanti, Dante, Cino Pistoia, and he alludes to Virgil ('What am I saying?' mirrors a line from *Aeneid* 6). He also ends the final stanza by quoting the first lines of his own 'Poem 23' from this collection. Commenting on Petrarch's method, Mark Musa states that: 'He identifies his own mental processes with that of each poet, creating a cumulative effect.'[63]

I make extensive use of Allusive Referential Translation and 'Collage Translation' in 'Poem 186'. Here, Petrarch states how immortal Laura is and how he imagines her effect on the classical heroes. My poem places her in dialogue with, and imagines her through, the use of historical and contemporary writers by using a collage of famous first lines from a variety of texts which I found by surfing the internet and by pulling random books from my bookshelf. Laura is, hopefully, brought to contemporary readers as a vibrant, artificial, literary creation, similar (in these aspects at least) to the Laura who appears in Petrarch's original poem. Again, the game of recognition (for readers) of sources and the element of surprise in their combination, along with the overarching theme of literary love, makes up the key elements of my Allusive Referential Translation.

There are many other uses of collage in my poems, and pop culture is represented as heavily as literary culture. 'Poem 68' ends with a line by the soul singer Al Green: 'It's you that I want but it's him that I need.'[64] Krazy Kat (the cartoon character written and drawn by George Herriman) is an important figure as Petrarch (for his constant, ridiculous, comedic and touching faithfulness for Laura) is beautifully mirrored by the eternally lovestruck, optimistic, deluded, and tormented Krazy Kat, and both their torments are caused by the endlessly inventive 'other' in the form of either Laura or Ignatz mouse. I have taken dialogue in 'Poem 134' and 'Poem 135' straight from two Krazy Kat comic strips. 'Poem 134' comes from Herriman's strips, dated 6 September 1938, and 'Poem 135', dated 30 March 1919. ('Poem 135' ends with Krazy Kat speaking: 'Li'l ainjul | I dreamt he | Kissed | Me.')[65] 'Poem 204' uses a Krazy Kat comic strip as the template for my poem, and the Crater Press edition of a selection of my translations has a picture of Krazy Kat being hit by a brick (hurled, out of frame, by Ignatz) upon the cover. In this case, the pictorial association of Krazy Kat with Petrarch can be seen as an Intersemiotic Translation as well as (in the use of lines from Krazy Kat in 'Poem 134' and 'Poem 135') an Allusive Referential Translation | 'Collage Translation'. The effect in many of my translations is 'cumulative' because a poem may be created out of a variety of methods and contains a multitude of tones, references, and sources. My interest as always is to engage with Ezra Pound's dictum; to make it new! To conclude this section with a metaphor, the Petrarch text which leads to the new poem comes from the process of looking into a mirror — invoking Gertrude Stein's idea of a translation being 'a true reflection' — and seeing something for the first time, as opposed to the more mechanistic and less-creative idea of a translator simply making a copy of a painting.

5. Derangement of the Senses Translation

A translation based upon a foregrounding (and often misunderstanding) of either the visual or acoustic elements of the original poem.

The *Derangement of the Senses Translation* methods detailed in this section all involve ways in which the translator attends to the sonic or visual aspect of a poem more than the content or meaning. The title of this translation type comes from Arthur Rimbaud's phrase 'dérèglement méthodique de tous les sens',[66] and his view that powerful poetry is produced as a result of such disorder/derangement. *Derangement of the Senses Translations* utilize methods which involve the production of poems through the filter of one or more of the senses, rather than through a Rimbaudian shift of being.

There are many examples of 'Homophonic Translation'. Steve McCaffery distinguishes between what he calls 'Homolinguistic' and 'Homophonic' translation. In an interview in *The Danforth Review*, he states that 'Homolinguistic translation is the application of the rules of orthodox translation to a text to be translated in the identical source language.'[67] On the other hand, 'Homophonic Translation' is a method whereby 'one tries to preserve the sounds of the source words in the language of the target text (e.g. 'germ appeal' for 'Je m'appelle' or 'a creature' for 'écriture').[68] The way I use 'Homophonic Translation' does not differentiate between foreign-language translation and same-language translation. 'On the Road' can be translated homophonically as 'Honda Ode' (the title of a volume from Oystercatcher Press of my shorter poems) in the same way as other-language lines or poems can and so there is no reason to differentiate. Marcel Benabou provides a fine example of Homophonic translation from English into French. Benabou, quoted in the *Oulipo Compendium*, takes Keats' 'A thing of beauty is a joy forever' and translates it as: 'Ah, singe debotte | Hisse un jouet fort et vert'.[69] There is also a Japanese author, mentioned in the same section of the *Compendium*, who goes under the pseudonym of Edogawa Rampo: a Japanese Homophonic translation of Edgar Allen Poe.

'Homophonic Translation' depends upon the interpretive ear of the translator. Although there are a limited number of possibilities that any line can offer, it is interesting to note that the same method can produce texts which reflect the interests or approach of the listener-translator. David Melnick's translations of books one and two of *The Iliad* in his *Men in Aida* turn a (generally, in translation) robust, plainspoken, and militaristic poem into a highly charged gay epic. Melnick's translation opens with the following lines: 'Men in Aida, they appeal, eh? A day, O Achilles! | Allow men in, emery Archaians! All gay ethic, eh?'.[70] It is clear that Melnick's ear, interests and agenda all influence his choice of words. It is interesting to note that even the act of hearing depends so much on the aesthetic and lexical shape of the poet's ear, as opposed to the vibrations that enter it.

I produced approximately fifteen 'Homophonic Translations' for *The Canzoniere*, only a few of which finally made it into the final manuscript. 'Poem 234' is an example. I have arranged the poem on the page so that the Italian lines follow mine. It runs:

> O Comrade check here first importance
> O camaretta che gia fosti un porto
> All the gravy tempest my journey
> a le gravi tempeste mie diurne
> Fond to say or the lack re: my knock turn or
> fonte se' or di lagrime nocturne,
> Shell desolate pervert gonna pour toe
> che 'l dí celate per vergogna porto.
> Or let a keyhole Cherokee airy intercom photo
> O letticciuol che requie eri et conforto[71]

'Homophonic Translation' helped to develop my ear, stretch my imagination, make me more conscious of my lexicon, and produce several lines which could be worked into other, looser, translations. As a method upon which to base an entire volume, however, I found it too limiting a method. 'Homophonic Translation', as with many constraint methods, is most useful in the generation of either ways of looking at a poem or producing lines which can then be knit into a poem which is not slave to a single method. This is the way that I have used the 'Homophonic' method for my Petrarch translations.

A full and varied engagement with *Derangement of the Senses Translation* methods comes in the 'Translucinacion' issue of *Chain* (2003) magazine. Poets Allison Cobb and Jen Coleman take Burton Watson's translation of Chuang Tzu's text 'Supreme Happiness (Section 18)' and subject it to a variety of distortions. Cobb and Coleman write:

> Translation is obscured through the boundaries of our senses. We heard the poem through the noise of a shower, challenged our vision with smeared glasses, challenged our physical abilities as draftspeople by translating into pictographs, and in other ways 'translated' Chuang Tzu's lessons through the fog of the physical world [...] If, as Lao Tzu says, the Tao is incommensurable, a doubtful text is the best interpretation.[72]

The first part of Watson's translation runs as follows:

> Once a sea bird alighted in the suburbs of the Lu capital. The marquis of Lu escorted it to the ancestral temple, where he entertained it, performing the Nine Shao music for it to listen to and presenting it with the meat of the T'ai-lao sacrifice to feast on.[73]

This opening, in Cobb and Coleman, changes into 'Haven't you heard of the suburb seabird | that capitals and temples entertains | with its meat and listing?'.[74] This method is described as 'Translation of Chuang Tzu with the Noise of the Shower Running'. The method called 'Translation of Chuang Tzu from Behind Smeared Glasses' produces 'Hiving you heaved toward the sea. A capital | three. Canned meat lists towards fists. Eat |' is.[75] Cobb and Coleman follow this with the method entitled 'Translation of Hearing Chuang Tzu While Not Looking at the Writing Page.' The result is: 'Living you hewed toward the sea | Three lists to feast | Dazed three days'.[76] (The final three methods are 'Translation of Hearing Chuang Tzu from a Cell Phone on Street', 'Translation of Hearing Chuang Tzu from a Cell Phone in a Check-Cashing Office' and 'Translation Chang Tzu from Pictographs'. The three openings run 'Near-living hewed to the feed. | Birds suffer free and inert. | A bird look day',[77] 'Lying never hued | to the bird look. | Days, voices in | the summer food | fingerlet',[78] and 'Nesting to keep from flood | leads the sun to be buried, not swallowed | sun flooded to love bleeding seed-sun'.[79])

Cobb and Coleman's methods produce many pleasing variations. The aspect of their translations which is most interesting, however, is the variety of methods which they use. Given the variety of results that are achieved by a single 'Derangement' method ('Homophonic') the expansion of possibilities is a significant development of poetic translation.

Derangement methods are an exciting expansion of translation possibilities. All poetry, I believe (and as I have discussed briefly above) contains a mixture of constraint (be it method or form) and individual influence (be it vocabulary, content, rhythm, or influences). In my writing, *Derangement of the Senses Translation* is more about ways of reading a poem in order to generate material than producing a final poem. As I have shown, however, this is not always the case.

6. Intersemiotic Translation

An interpretation of one sign system by means of another

Intersemiotic Translation (also known as 'transmutation') is defined by Roman Jakobson as 'an interpretation of verbal signs by means of nonverbal sign systems'.[80] This type of translation, the most usual form of which, in poetry, is the relationship between painting and poetry, does not, as Jakobson has it, need to start with words: it may be the case that a poem is a translation ('interpretation') of a painting, or, indeed, any other form of art.

Gary Barwin and Derek Beaulieu's *frogments from the frag pool* (2005) and McCaffery's *The Basho Variations* (2007) provide multiple translations of Japanese poet Matsuo Basho's celebrated 'Frog' poem. McCaffery provides thirty-seven different translations, three of which can be considered as intersemiotic versions, and Barwin and Beaulieu's collection contains sixteen poems in which the visual aspect of the poem is at least as important as the words. Their translation titled 'Aquarium' (57) — see below — of Basho's haiku, translated by Dom Sylvester Houédard (and which appears in *Rational Geomancy*) as 'frog | pond | plop',[81] is rendered in a manner which visually enacts the frog jumping into a pond.

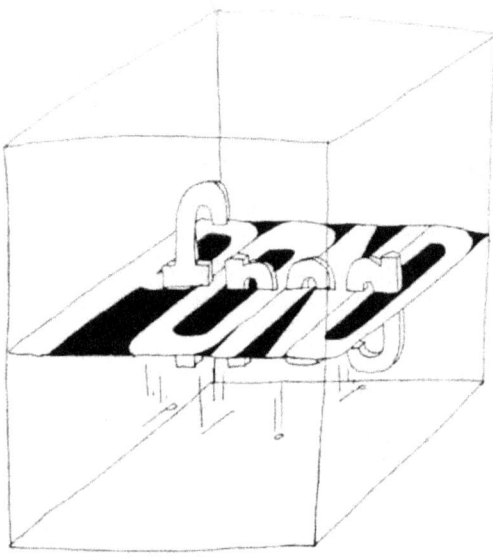

FIG. 14.1. Gary Barwin and Derek Beaulieu, 'frog pond plop', *Frogments from the Frag Pool* (n.p., 2005).

In 'Ponderous' (see image below) Barwin and Beaulieu suggest a Zen-like serenity and mindless/contemplative state by laying their three words across the page in a manner which leads the reader through the frog's action to a silent full stop inside a rising thought bubble. By translating their poem thus, the words are able to point to a meaning which the words themselves, if they were not presented in this manner, would be unable to suggest.

McCaffery's poem entitled 'The ghost or bouma shaped Basho' takes the 'frog | pond | plop' basic translation and over three pages (or four, if the blank page which follows is also considered part of the sequence) does a similar job to that of Barwin and Beaulieu's 'Ponderous'.

On the second page, McCaffery draws an outline around the three basic words and, on the third/final page, erases the words to leave empty space where they once were. In the same way that the frog leaves ripples and then silence, McCaffery leaves a ripple around his three words. Using this method, he suggests that the pond and the mind of the reader return to their original (in Buddhist thinking) pure, concept-free state with the conclusion of the poem — an idea that is sympathetic to Basho's zen-based work. By presenting his poem in this manner, McCaffery makes

Fig. 14.2. Gary Barwin and Derek Beaulieu, 'frog pond plop', *Frogments from the Frag Pool* (n.p., 2005).

explicit an aspect of the poem which (when it is free from the visual translation) is much more subtle in its purely linguistic form.

There is one Intersemiotic Translation in my Petrarch poems. 'Poem 52' uses the method employed by Christian Bok in his translation of Rimbaud's poem 'Voyelles' (see image below). Rimbaud's poem ascribes colours to each of the vowels; Bok has taken this idea and replaced each letter of Rimbaud's poem with the colours that Rimbaud himself suggested. All consonants are grey. Bok, in the poem which appears on the cover of *Sulphur*, 44 (Spring 1999), thus intersemiotically translates Rimbaud's poem into a visual piece. I have used Bok's method to translate Petrarch's 'Poem 52'.

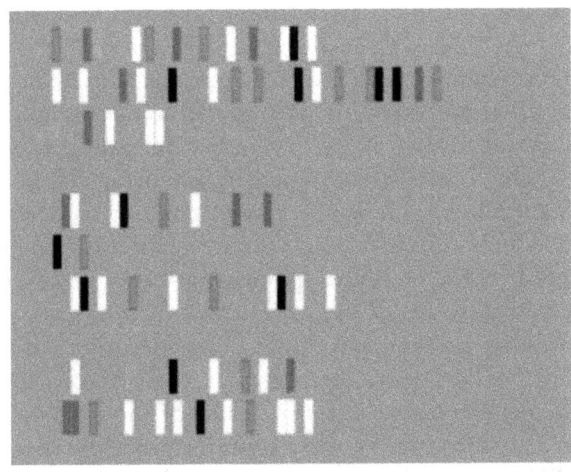

Fig. 14.3. Tim Atkins, 'Poem 52'.

7. Hoax, Parody, and Persona Translation

An original text which is presented as a translation, for purposes of either deceit or play.

If *Allusive Referential Translation* is the area of translation which offers the greatest freedom for a translator to engage with a poem or poet, *Hoax, Parody, and Persona Translation* modifies source texts to be translated in a manner which disqualifies them as translations. *Hoax, Parody, and Persona Translations* are, finally, *about* translation (and other matters unconnected with translation) rather than being a translation itself.

In 1997, American poet Kent Johnson authored a series of poems entitled *Doubled Flowering*. This volume was purportedly by an obscure Japanese poet called Araki Yasusada (of whose work Johnson presented himself as editor). Yasusada's poems were imagistic, tender, disjunctive pieces in which the poet appeared as a survivor of the Hiroshima bombing. These poems were greeted with excitement in America by both the poetry mainstream and the avant-garde. *The American Poetry Review* (July/August 1996) featured a special supplement and Ron Silliman pronounced the poems to be vital works of great interest. It was only slowly that it trickled out that the poems contained references which were clearly out of place, and the enthusiasts sought to reposition themselves and respond to their initial readings. In poetry terms, the scandal was tremendous. The editor of *The American Poetry Review*, Arthur Vogelsgang, in *Lingua Franca* (and, importantly, quoted on the back cover of *Doubled Flowering*) stated: 'This is essentially a criminal act.'[82]

Doubled Flowering includes a scholarly introduction, a list of three Japanese editors, letters from Yasusada, endnotes, appendices, an attack (on the back cover, by Vogelsgang), and an afterword by Marjorie Perloff. The volume's reception raises the question of the importance of a final poem and its existence and value when read without knowledge of the author. That Yasusada's poems were praised when read as the product of a Japanese A-bomb survivor, and dismissed when read as parodies by an American poet, raises important and enduring questions about reading and value.

In his essay on poetic imposters, 'Fraud's Phantoms: a brief yet unreliable account of fighting fraud with fraud (no pun on Freud intended) with special reference to the poetics of Ressentiment' (2008),[83] Charles Bernstein notes various types of literary hoax, all of which are differentiated by intention. Bernstein lists one type as 'Spoof or Personae' hoax.[84] Here, the purpose is not to deceive the reader but to create a persona which allows the poet to write in a different voice. Bernstein lists Robert Sheppard's 'Wayne Pratt' poems and also places Fernando Pessoa's heteronyms and Jack Spicer's Lorca poems in the same category. Johnson/Yasusada appears in Bernstein's list as 'literary frauds' alongside others, including Australian modernist/fraud Ern Malley. Here, Bernstein sees the intention of the poets as: 'ridiculing what the perpetrators see as the fraud of modernism, poststructualism, or multiculturalism'.[85] In Bernstein's eyes, it 'undermines the rhetoric of sincerity'.[86] Bernstein ascribes 'white male rage'[87] to (among others) Johnson, and backs up his assertion by quoting the collective response by Juliana Chang, Walter K. Lew, Tan

Lin, Eileen Tabios, and John Yau that appeared in the Summer 1997 issue of *Boston Review*. Their criticism suggested that Johnson was reprising 'the stereotype of the deferential Asian' and diminishing contemporary Japanese poetic achievement.[88] Bernstein concludes his critique of Johnson/Yasusada by suggesting that this hoax (defined as a 'Trap Hoax') exists, primarily, to catch out editors, to mock perceived injustices, misreadings, and political correctness, and to prick the bubble of conceit within which such powerful editors and critics float.

Bernstein states: 'The idea that it doesn't matter who actually wrote the poem is a tried but not so true shibboleth from New Criticism. Of course it matters, it always matters.'[89] I agree with this statement. I also believe that the Johnson/Yasusada poems and accompanying literature around them (the responses, the counter-responses, and the follow-up volume of Yasusada's correspondence) have done what is often cited as being the key task of art: to ask important questions, as opposed to providing answers. These questions matter. I believe *Doubled Flowering*, and its follow-up, *Also, With My Throat I Shall Swallow Ten Thousand Swords: Araki Yasusada's Letters in English*, to be important engagements with issues of identity (the role and location of an author), of cultural imperialism (here manifesting as orientalism), of (if this is viewed as a translated text) Domestication Translation and historical accuracy, and of the way that poetic communities view authenticity and perceived threats. I hope that I am not being naïve in reading the Yasusada poems as sincere and creative engagements with these issues.

Johnson wrote an extended review of *Horace*, my previous volume of 'translations' in *The Chicago Review*, in which he expanded on, and expressed sympathy with, the translation poetics which *Horace* enacted. In lines which Kent Johnson wrote — and ascribed to me — issues of translation are discussed. After meeting in a pub in Cambridge (England) and proceeding to roam around the city discussing translation poetics — none of which happened — Johnson has me say in a hoax interview:

> I'd say that even though the spectrum might have unrecognized regions is not to suggest, in any way, that there is something lacking in standard forms of translation, or that these are waiting to be superseded. To the contrary, actually. But I wonder, and I guess this is what you in a way are asking, too: If we can have the works of, say, both Brahms and Cage understood as music, the art of both Watteau and Duchamp understood as painting, the writing of both Tennyson and Mac Low understood as Poetry, why can't we imagine that the task of Translation might extend, for the sake of certain purposes, beyond the relatively stable protocols and boundaries that currently define the practice, eh?[90]

That this essay ends with a quote by 'me' but which was written by somebody else, as a commentary on my work about creative translation, seems to tally well with some of the mysteries of the *Canzoniere*. Did Laura really exist? Was she a literary translation of a real woman? Was she a hoax whom Petrarch dreamed up to fulfil his poetic fantasies? Was the great poet's literary self ever anything but a persona? Finally — what is a translation, or, indeed, a poem, ever able to be but a happy imagining?

Notes to Chapter 14

1. Francisco Petrarch, *Letters From Petrarch*, ed. and trans. by Morris Bishop (Bloomington: Indiana University Press, 1966), pp. 182–83.
2. Eliot Weinberger and Octavio Paz, *19 Ways of Looking at Wang Wei* (Kingston, Rhode Island, and London: Aspodel Press, 1987), p. 43.
3. Quoted in Sin-Wai Chan, and David Pollard, eds, *An Encyclopaedia of Translation: Chinese–English, English–Chinese* (Hong Kong: The Chinese University Press, 1995), p. 394.
4. Louis Zukofsky and Celia Zukofsky, *Catullus* (New York: Grossman, 1969), n.p.
5. John Dryden, *The miscellaneous works of John Dryden, Esq; containing all his original poems, tales, and translations... . With explanatory notes and observations. Also an account of his life and writings... .*, IV (London: J. and R. Tonson, 1760), p. 76.
6. Douglas Barbour and Stephen Scobie, *The Pirates of Pen's Chance* (Toronto: Coach House, 1981), p. 141.
7. Ibid., p. 141.
8. Ibid., p. 142.
9. Ibid., p. 140 (emphasis added).
10. Ibid., p. 24 (emphasis added).
11. Ibid., p. 142.
12. Ibid., pp. 142–43.
13. Ibid., p. 142.
14. Ibid., p. 1.
15. Ibid., p. 31.
16. Jack Spicer, *The Collected Books of Jack Spicer*, ed. Robin Blaser (Santa Rosa, CA: Black Sparrow Press, 1996), p. 111.
17. Ibid., p. 122.
18. Ibid., p. 123.
19. Ibid., p. 110.
20. Tim Atkins, *Petrarch Collected Atkins* (London: Crater Press, 2014), p. 220.
21. Francisco Petrarch, *Petrarch's Lyric Poems,* trans. by Robert Durling (Cambridge, MA, and London, Harvard University Press, 1976), p. 308.
22. Atkins, *Petrarch Collected Atkins* , p. 223.
23. Ibid., p. 83.
24. Ibid., p. 518.
25. Francisco Petrarch, *Petrarch's Lyric Poems,* trans. by Robert Durling (Cambridge, MA, & London, Harvard University Press, 1976), p. 551.
26. R. M. Rilke, *Duino Elegies & The Sonnets to Orpheus: A Dual-Language Edition*, trans. by Stephen Mitchell (New York: Vintage International, 2009), p. 3.
27. Ibid., n.p.
28. Ibid., n.p.
29. Robert Lowell, *Imitations*, New York: Farrar, Strauss and Giroux, 1961, p. xi.
30. Ibid., p. 51.
31. Ibid., p. 228.
32. Ibid., p. 202.
33. Ibid., p. 339.
34. Atkins, *Petrarch Collected Atkins* , p. 395.
35. Donny O'Rourke and Richard Price, *Eftirs/Afters* (Glasgow: Au Quai Press, 1996), n.p.
36. bp Nichol, *Translating Translating Apollinaire* (Milwaukee: Membrane Press, 1979), p. 1.
37. Ibid., p. 1.
38. Ibid.
39. Barbara Godard, 'O Vancouver: Translating Apollinaire after bp Nichol,' *Open Letter*, 13.1 (2007), 83–84.
40. Stephen Vincent, 'A Walk with Stephen Vincent', *Rain Taxi Online*, 3 August 2007.
41. Anne Carson, *If not, Winter: Fragments of Sappho* (New York: Knopf, 2002), p. 109.

42. Stephen Vincent, 'Sleeping with Sappho' onedit 7. 2007, <http://www.onedit.net/issue7/stephenv/stephenv.html>.
43. Anne Carson, *If not, Winter: Fragments of Sappho* (New York: Knopf, 2002), p. 327.
44. Stephen Vincent, 'Sleeping with Sappho' onedit 7. 2007,<http://www.onedit.net/issue7/stephenv/stephenv.html>.
45. Atkins, *Petrarch Collected Atkins*, p. 128.
46. Ibid., p. 50.
47. Ibid., pp. 290–91.
48. Dick Higgins, 'Towards An Allusive Referential', in *Claims for Poetry*, ed. Donald Hall (Ann Arbor: University Of Michigan Press), pp. 171–77 (p. 171).
49. Ibid., p. 171.
50. Ibid.
51. Ibid., p. 175.
52. Steve McCaffery, *Every Way Oakly* (Toronto: Book Thug, 2008), p. ix.
53. Steve McCaffery, 'Interview with Steve McCaffery', *Danforth Review*. 2009. Web. 20 September 2009.
54. Steve McCaffery, *Every Way Oakly* (Toronto: Book Thug, 2008), p. 1.
55. Francisco Petrarch, *Petrarch's Lyric Poems*, trans. by Robert Durling (Cambridge, MA, and London, Harvard University Press, 1976), p. 140.
56. Atkins, *Petrarch Collected Atkins*, p. 89.
57. Ibid.
58. Ibid., p. ix.
59. Douglas Barbour and Stephen Scobie, *The Pirates of Pen's Chance* (Toronto: Coach House, 1981), p. 141.
60. Francisco Petrarch, *The Canzoniere, Or Rerum Vulgarium Fragmenta*, trans. by Mark Musa (Bloomington and Indianapolis: Indiana University Press, 1996), p. 487.
61. Douglas Barbour and Stephen Scobie, *The Pirates of Pen's Chance* (Toronto: Coach House, 1981), pp. 141–42.
62. Ibid.
63. Francisco Petrarch, *The Canzoniere, Or Rerum Vulgarium Fragmenta*, trans. by Mark Musa (Bloomington and Indianapolis: Indiana University Press, 1996), p. 564.
64. Atkins, *Petrarch Collected Atkins*, p. 95.
65. Ibid., p. 191.
66. Arthur Rimbaud, *Selected Verse*, trans. by Oliver Bernard (London: Penguin, 1962), p. 10.
67. Steve McCaffery, 'Interview with Steve McCaffery', *Danforth Review*, 20 September 2009, p. 1.
68. Ibid.
69. Harry Mathews and Alastair Brotchie, eds, *Oulipo Compendium* (London: Atlas, 1998), p. 154.
70. David Melnick, *Men In Aida* (Berkeley: Tuumba, 1984), p. 1.
71. Tim Atkins, *Petrarch Collected Atkins* (London: Crater, 2014), p. 340.
72. Chang Tzu, Allison Cobb, Jennifer Coleman, and Burton Watson, 'Come Out of Works: A Physical Translation', *Chain*, 10 (2003), pp. 50–51.
73. Ibid., p. 44.
74. Ibid., p. 45.
75. Ibid., p. 46.
76. Ibid., p. 47.
77. Ibid., p. 48.
78. Ibid., p. 49.
79. Ibid., p. 50.
80. Roman Jakobson, 'On Linguistic Aspects of Translation', in *Theories of Translation*, ed. by John Biguenet and Rainer Schulte (Chicago: University of Chicago Press, 1992), p. 145.
81. Steve McCaffery and bp Nichol, *Rational Geomancy: The Kids of the Book Machine. The Collected Research Reports of the Toronto Research Group 1973–1982*, ed. by Steve McCaffery (Vancouver: Talonbooks, 1992) p. 42.
82. Kent Johnson, *Doubled Flowering* (New York: Roof Books, 1998), n.p.

83. Charles Bernstein, Fraud's Phantoms: a brief yet unreliable account of fighting fraud with fraud (no pun on Freud intended) with special reference to the poetics of Ressentiment', *Textual Practice*, 22.2 (2008), pp. 207–27.
84. Ibid., p. 210.
85. Ibid., p. 213.
86. Ibid.
87. Ibid.
88. Chang Tzu, Alison Cobb, Jen Coleman, and Burton Watson, 'Come Out of Works: A Physical Translation', *Chain*, 10 (2003), 43–51 (p. 45).
89. Charles Bernstein, 'Fraud's Phantoms: a brief yet unreliable account of fighting fraud with fraud (no pun on Freud intended) with special reference to the poetics of Ressentiment', *Textual Practice*, 22.2 (2008), pp. 207–27 (p.221).
90. Kent Johnson, 'Tim Atkins: Horace', *Chicago Review*, 53.4–54.1 (2008), 337–48 (p. 344).

CHAPTER 15

'Era il giorno ch'al sol si scoloraro': A Derivative Dérive into/out of Petrarch's Sonnet 3

Robert Sheppard

Petrarch was pretty clear that translation implied more than faithful reproduction of linguistic features. He warned, utilizing a conventional metaphor for translation drawn from apiculture, 'Take care [...] that the nectar does not remain in you in the same state as when you gathered it; bees would have no credit unless they transformed it into something different and better.'[1] This chapter involves attempting to trace the transformations involved in the writing of fourteen variations on a 'translation' I made of the third sonnet of Petrarch, *Petrarch 3* (2016), a partly conceptual, partly expressive, sonnet sequence, made under the sign of Oulipo, but informed by earlier poetic interests of my own, even early poems.[2] It is at once impersonal and personal. It is, arguably, both hugely derivative and original, though that last judgement is beyond the scope of my poetics as I define it as a 'speculative, writerly discourse'.[3] What I can say is that the process was immensely productive, though I would not dare to rise to Petrarch's aspiration concerning the betterment of the original. As a poet-critic, I believe that my literary criticism must inform my poetics — the mercurial writerly conversation that I have with myself in my journal, with others in explicit poetics pieces, and perhaps in this piece I am writing now — but I do not know how particularly, hence my use of the verb 'attempting' above. Indeed, one of the reasons I value writerly poetics is precisely because writers cannot read their own work, or even mislead themselves about what they are doing. I am therefore somewhat suspicious of the kind of practice-led research I am presenting here, but the creative story I have to tell is one that criss-crosses poetics, literary criticism, translation, and creative writing itself, and may reveal something about modes of transformation and translational processes.

My acquaintanceship with the innovative sonnet is a long one. I am represented in Jeff Hilson's anthology *Reality Street Book of Sonnets* (2008), which puts an excerpt from *Warrant Error* (2009), my book of 100 innovative poems concerned, as the title suggests, with the so-called 'War on Terror' of the early twenty-first century, alongside the poems of many others, from Ted Berrigan and Tom Raworth, through to my contemporaries Tim Atkins and Adrian Clarke.[4] But my use of innovative sonnet forms, which usually means sonnet aspirant, sonnet approximate, and sonnet deviant forms, poems that would not qualify as sonnets under the usual normative 'classroom' description, harks back to earlier work. Indeed, my long network *Twentieth Century Blues* (2008) contains many 14-line poems and I even invented a new form, the 100-word sonnet (a two word 'title' is followed by 14 lines of 7 words each, centre margined), which hailed from noticing this structure in one of Adrian Clarke's word-count poems of the 1990s, and adapting it for my poems and sequences.[5] Coincidentally, I have returned to this form, one dictated by a lack of punctuation and caesura and that develops a rhythmic celerity amid linguistic mix, in writing some poems that brood upon the disastrous vote of Britain to 'Brexit' the European Union. Indeed, this chapter is in some senses a poetics for my ongoing project of making sequences of innovative sonnet sequences, that mostly involve — though not exclusively — transformations of Petrarch's sonnets, beginning with *Petrarch 3* (the poet Richard Parker, who published *Petrarch 3*, declared this to be a 'corona of coronas' in conversation).

My predilection for the sonnet may be found even earlier. The opening poem of my first non-self-published booklet, *Dedicated to you but you weren't listening* (1979), is also a sonnet of sorts.[6] Using titles from recordings by the seminal British band Soft Machine as the start of each line (the book's title is also one of their compositions) the poem claims, in its subtitle, to be 'influenced' by the sonnets of Raymond Queneau and Jacques Bens, two members of Oulipo. In fact, in 1978 when I wrote the poems, like most Britons, I knew little of Oulipo, other than what I had picked up via the fortuitous possession of Simon Watson Taylor's *French Writing Today* of 1968, which anthologized both poets. Detailed knowledge of Oulipo evaded me until the mid-1980s, but the construction of innovative sonnets is obviously rooted deep in my practice, and the memory of my first brush with three of Queneau's now well-known 'Thousand Billion Sonnets', for example, and Bens' much less well-known mathematical use of *pi* as a determinant of rhyme-schemes in his 'irrational sonnets' — the 14 lines are arranged in stanzas dictated by the numerals of *pi* to the third point: 3, 1, 4, 1, and 5 — must have lain dormant.[7]

I embarked upon my recent critical volume *The Meaning of Form* (as I wanted to call it, though it now carries the search-engine-friendly *In Contemporary Innovative Poetry* after those emblematic words) under the sign of 'the turn to form'. The entire project is summed up in its opening statement: 'Poetry is the investigation of complex contemporary realities through the means (meanings) of form.'[8] The central methodology is introduced via a reading of the formalist criticism of Derek Attridge, Susan Wolfson, Peter de Bola, Angela Leighton, and others, though none of this criticism has addressed linguistically innovative poetry directly, which is strange, given its formally investigative strategies. These thinkers loosely share allegiance to a longer aestheticist tradition of regarding form as a *significant* force; Schiller is often read as the originator of the belief that 'the content should do nothing, the form everything'.[9] *Form* as a force and cognitive entity, particular *forms* as elements of poetic artifice, and *forming* as an event in active readerly engagement and transformation, are compared and differentiated, and all three italicized terms are used. Forms have to be formed in several ways, as Attridge puts it:

> The event of the literary work is a *formal* event, involving among other things, or rather among other happenings, shifts in register, allusions to other discourses, [...] the patterning of rhythms, the linking of rhymes, the ordering of sections, the movement of syntax, the echoing of sounds: all operating in a temporal medium to surprise, lull, intrigue, satisfy.[10]

We need to apprehend 'the eventness of the literary work, which means that form needs to be understood verbally — as "taking form", of "forming", or even "losing form"'.[11] The two counters of my title, meaning and form, are related in an original and distinctive way by Attridge, when he reminds us:

> Meaning is [...] not something that appears in defining opposition or complementary apposition to form [...] but as something already taken up within form; forms are made out of meanings quite as much as they are made out of sound and shapes.[12]

Form is an active and mercurial process, not a fixed product of poesis; it is poesis.

Beyond this theoretical framework (which is expounded in Chapter 1, the Introduction) two chapters are directly relevant to *Petrarch 3*, 'Convention and Constraint: Form in the Innovative Sonnet Sequence' and 'Translation as Transformation: Tim Atkins' and Peter Hughes' Petrarch'.[13] The first of these analyses both the history of the sonnet and its transformation in contemporary innovative practice (as exemplified by the *Reality Street Book of Sonnets*): the works of Ted Berrigan, Jeff Hilson, Philip Terry, Geraldine Monk, and Sophie Robinson are critiqued in detail. Questions of form (in terms of a consideration of the sonnet 'frame', as I rename what is commonly said to be sonnet 'form', its characteristic pattern or structure, its numbers of lines, its stanzas, its contrasting rhyme-schemes) are raised alongside issues of the historical form and its relation to politics and gender. The different 'frames' of the Petrarchan and Shakespearean patterns, for example, impose different structures of argument and rhetorical progress, and offer a simple example of the meaningfulness of form. The main business of the chapter is an examination of the breadth of experiment evinced in contemporary practice, in relation to the work of New York poetics, the Oulipo group, and quasi-concrete poetry experiments in a variety of visual 'sonnet' forms, and this prepares the ground for the chapter on Hughes and Atkins.

What could have been more fortuitous for my critical project, which hovers around notions of 'translation' as a formally investigative practice, than to discover, not one, but two, innovative 'translations' of Petrarch's *Canzoniere* appearing at around the same time by contemporary British writers? I put 'translation' in scare-quotes to alert the reader to the fact that neither project is a linguistic translation but each is a transposition of the original into contemporary modes. I have the two books on my desk now, two fat volumes (Atkins's slightly fatter because he tackles the complete *Canzoniere*, all 366 poems, while Hughes contents himself with the 317 sonnets), Atkins's *Collected Petrarch*, published by Crater Press in 2014, and Hughes's *Quite Frankly: After Petrarch's Sonnets*, published by Reality Street the following year. The titles are indicative of two facts that both projects share: the 'after' of Hughes's title emphasizes the fact of translation as transformation (with an emphasis, in my reading, on the presence of the word 'form' in that word), while Atkins's term 'Collected' alerts us to the fact that he had published selections and sections of his work as pamphlets with various small presses — as had Hughes — before these massive volumes appeared (Atkins's book is 544, Hughes's is 354, pages long). Crater Press and Reality Street are two of the most important independent presses that sustain linguistically innovative poetry in Britain.[14]

This minor fact of publication is vitally important to the fortuity of my deliberately modest Petrarch project (which also appears from Crater Press). In general terms, and without repeating my analysis, I conclude that while Hughes (who reads Italian) emphasizes his *difference* from Petrarch's originals (by relocating the poems to the Norfolk coast and modernizing their references, for example), Atkins (who does not read Italian) emphasizes his *distance* from the originals (largely through the use of post-Oulipo techniques and constraints, which he outlines in his chapter in the present volume). Hughes will eulogize his Norfolk love thus:

> imagination had me hovering
> with my lady in the Rings of Venus
> one of Fakenham's premier nite-spots
> she spoke although I couldn't hear a thing[15]

while Atkins is often more mysteriously disconnected, though in ways that often bring us close to Petrarch as a poet and then back us away into paradox,

> When you live 12 miles away from a lemon
> Wyatt adapts Petrarch's lament into his own
> Seeking shade from a shadow or a column
> Until it splashes up against the back of the front teeth.[16]

Both writers manage to reflect Petrarch's elegiac mode (Hughes notes 'yet another windswept friend of the dead | fixed petrol-station roses to the fence') while Atkins additionally injects a Buddhist negation of the things of the (contemporary) world that clutter his woeful lover's utterances: 'This is the Buddha life indeed | ... I is empty inside it.'[17] One unintended consequence of the publishing history outlined above was the quotation of my critical evaluation of the sequences in Atkins's volume itself. The manner in which I managed to sustain myself through the writing of *The Meaning of Form in Contemporary Innovative Poetry* was to write blog-posts on the developing project; one post (the most read, according to blogspot statistics) is about the two projects which I labelled 'The Petrarch Boys', rather cheekily it strikes me in retrospect. Jessica Pujol i Duran's Introduction to *Collected Petrarch*, 'Multi-Atkins', picks up on my prefatory post and tells us:

> Robert Sheppard worries; 'am I reading the poem, reading the tradition, or reading the *distance* between Atkins's poem and Petrarch' [...] We needn't really read *Petrarch* for the differences between Petrarch and Atkins, or indeed, their similarities — such concerns seem gleefully inessential for the British poet, in fact. The relationship between Italian 'original' and English 'version' forms a dialogue only at the point of our reception of the poems — not really during the creation of the works, when we would expect such a dialogue to develop.

> Thus we read Sheppard's '*distance*', aware that the measure of that distance is hallucinatory; that most of the time Atkins seems to be having a conversation with a neighbour, with a Zen master, or with 'fucking-Jeffrey-fucking-Hilson,' rather than with the fourteenth century Petrarch.[18]

Whether or not the distance is a chimera for the ordinary reader, holding only Atkins's book in his or her hand (and I suspect Pujol i Duran is right about the point of reception and about Atkins's gleeful anarchy, which is partly what I was signifying as 'distance'), this disregard between original and version was not for me, and would not be for others, engaged in critical and formal comparison, with Atkins's project to weigh against Hughes's, and with the need to contrast both with a 'straight' translation of Petrarch's poems; like Atkins, I do not have Italian. Robert Sheppard was more 'worried' than Pujol i Duran could have guessed. To establish my critical case about difference and distance, I needed to locate two poems for comparison; the methodology of reading for form required a lightly theorized close reading. If I were writing the chapter today, I would have 317 pairs of poems to choose from (which, with its dizzying possibilities, I am glad I did not have), but in 2012 or 2013 when I was writing the chapter, I had a small gathering of Hughes's and Atkins's pamphlets and one of the only paired poems I could locate was Petrarch's third sonnet, particularly as this was also translated in Mark Musa's *Petrarch: Selections from the Canzoniere and Other Works*.[19] The scene was set. Actually, the scene was this: my little work room, whose floor space is nearly completely covered with piles of books and pamphlets (each relating to a particular chapter), was excessively untidy when I palmed my way through these pamphlets, and Musa's translation was unlocatable, lost as surely was Laura to Petrarch it seemed, buried in the wrong pile perhaps, but obdurately not turning up in time for the formal reading (critical writing, like poetry writing, is a kind of performance for me, as Attridge suggests, an action that is also an event).

The first refuge of the disorganized is the internet, and I located Petrarch's original poem 3 and several translations of it online in a trice, but they seemed cloggy neo-Victorian takes, and not usable; I think one was a prose gloss. But I thought I could see enough of the original (perhaps I was as 'gleeful' as Atkins at this point) to make my own version from these (now also mislaid) translations. (I had also realized I might mitigate the large sums in permissions fees that my methodological insistence upon extensive quotation had inflicted upon my pocket, so even if Musa had turned up, I might have preferred my illegitimate version.)

Attridge posits a range of possible translational responses to an original, from 'diligent reproduction of characteristic features ... to inventive reworkings'.[20] Hughes and Atkins were undertaking the second of these options; at this stage, I was merely attempting the first. I took the frame as granted and draped the English through it, an amalgam derived from various translations operating like a trig point to confirm the target, to triangulate common denominators. Petrarch makes each stanza of the poem (as he may have thought of them) a complete sentence, and I reproduce this structure, though I was forced to make some amendments, either practical measures or egregious misrepresentations, depending on one's view.

> Era il giorno ch'al sol si scoloraro
> per la pietà del suo factore i rai,
> quando i' fui preso, et non me ne guardai,
> ché i be' vostr'occhi, donna, mi legaro.
>
> Tempo non mi parea da far riparo
> contra colpi d'Amor: però m'andai
> secur, senza sospetto; onde i miei guai
> nel commune dolor s'incominciaro.
>
> Trovommi Amor del tutto disarmato
> et aperta la via per gli occhi al core,
> che di lagrime son fatti uscio et varco:
>
> però al mio parer non li fu honore
> ferir me de saetta in quello stato,
> a voi armata non mostrar pur l'arco.[21]

I rendered this poem thus:

> *Era il giorno ch'al sol si scoloraro*
>
> That pitiful morning when the light of Heaven
> Was hidden for our mourning maker's sake,
> I saw you first that day, My Lady, but
> Was captured, disarmed, then bound to your stake.
>
> It didn't seem the time for shields and armour
> Against Love's arrows, his batters and blows;
> So, unsuspecting, I wept with the world,
> But that day my heartbreaks began, my woes.
>
> Love stalked me, found me, unarmed and weak,
> And opened my eyes, portals of tears, through which
> Sorrow flowed from the passage of my heart.
>
> But feeble was Love's triumph to triumph
> With his arrow over one so enfeebled,
> And to not even dare to flash you his dart.[22]

I use light rhyme, but on two occasions this distorts the sense. 'Bound to your stake' is an image of captivity that is loyal to the spirit of the poem but no 'stake' is mentioned. In the original poem Love shows his 'bow' but 'dart' was chosen to rhyme with 'heart' in my version (a decision that was to have consequences, as we will see), the possessor of both bows and arrows being Cupid. The 'pitiful morning' upon which the poem is set is Good Friday, the darkest day in the Christian year, and it was while the narrator 'wept with the world', participating in general mourning, that he was struck by Cupid's arrows: on Good Friday, 6 April 1327, Petrarch beheld the woman he called 'Laura' at mass in the church of Sainte-Claire d'Avignon. He was caught off-guard, like an ill-prepared soldier, but 'it didn't seem the time for shields and armour'. The result is extreme, and the tone at the *volta* is strident and emphatic: 'Love stalked me, found me, unarmed and weak'; these lines present the central emotive event of the poem. Only the composure of the final three lines recovers some dignity for the narrator. It was no victory at all to capture somebody so weak; I adopt wordplay to emphasize this sophistry: the repeated use of 'feeble' and 'triumph'. But the final line accuses Cupid of real cowardice: he smote the narrator but did not dare to show his bow and arrows to the beloved, who remains unsmitten. This account of my version is retrospective: I do not remember what I thought as I composed the text, though I was surprised that it came quickly. The poem is rhetorical, its argument follows the sonnet frame, its language colloquial but with heightened rhetoric at its climax, though of course such a capitulation to unrequited love is common to the tradition (and my previous encounters with hundreds of Petrarch-like English sonnets, whether Wyatt's close approximations or Shakespeare's innovations, lay behind my invention). The poem is addressed to the Lady (though Laura is not named in the poem) but she does not act in it. The only agency in the poem is invested in Love.

This version seemed workaday enough, segmented and analysed stanza by stanza, to use as an introduction to my comparison of the Hughes and Atkins sonnets. It is important to remember that *Petrarch 3* collects not so much my fourteen variations on the Petrarch original, but upon this rough 'translation', which is why I have sketched it out in its own terms. Almost as soon as I finished the 'translation' I found myself playing with it. Initial toying with Google Translate produced a far-too coherent version (the technology nowadays is too smart; it 'learns' through repeated use to refine its choices according to contexts), although perhaps it was the transposition of 'dart' into the Italian 'darto' and then back into English to provide the comical last line, 'And to not even dare to flash you his dick', that suggested I should work creatively with my crib.

If I am asked to name my favourite poem I cite Harry Mathews' 'Trial Impressions' (1977). This consists of thirty 'variations' or 'versions' of a poem (song) by John Dowland, one with a pronounced rhetorical structure that can be mimicked and transformed, engendering recognition on the part of the reader: 'Deare, if you change, Ile never chuse again'.[23] It is a classic Oulipean work, in that each operates by constraint. Some use simple constraints (an 'up to date', beginning, 'If you break our breakfast date, I'll go begging in Bangkok' or a 'haikuization': 'change/love/no/next/choice').[24] Some are procedurally elaborate ('Keep Talking' which is lengthy, or a poem of indeterminate duration formed by a multiple-choice narrative), through to the technically stunning (a palindrome, or the rendering of Dowland's 'doeful' song in the language of the King James Bible or as a sestina or traditional sonnet, the latter beginning, 'Who will in dearest love of Beauty change').[25] There are several sections that I have not unravelled (they operate, at least for me, as the sequence's clinamen, that necessary procedural 'spanner in the works' that renders all Oulipean works inoperative, like a Jean Tinguely construction hammering itself to pieces), and I confess myself an enthusiast for this sequence rather than a critic of it. (The early exposure to Queneau may have heightened this enthusiasm.) The same is true of Nicholas Moore's *Spleen* (1990), a collection of Moore's comic but disheartened pseudonymous multiple submissions to a competition to translate a single Baudelaire poem, 'Spleen', whose first line, 'Je suis comme le roi d'un pays pluvieux', can become 'I am the Pluto of a rainy hell' as well as 'I am like the T. S. Eliot of the new wastelands'.[26] In Moore's case, the multiplicity was intended to 'illustrate my own thesis of the impossibility of translation', but in fact, he demonstrates the joys of making (and reading) serial versions.[27] Both poets 'version' their original poem, to use a verb borrowed from dub reggae, and somehow I knew I wanted to attempt something analogous with my Petrarch poem. (I also avoided more mechanical Oulipo techniques like the S+7, which, in my practice at least, was losing its edge.) I knew even a failed attempt would be fun, though a residual guilt that realized my versions could not exist without Hughes and Atkins (even in the world of Kenneth Goldsmith's conceptual or 'uncreative writing') led me to acknowledge my debts, by dedicating the sequence to both poets, and to state that the work was 'in homage' to Mathews and Moore.[28] I also came up with the term 'derivative dérive' to describe the piece, by which I mean that the more derivative the pieces seem to become, of Petrarch, as well as of the works of the four cited poets, but not to them alone, as I shall show, the more wayward, off the beaten track, they become (and the more 'original' I hope readers will find them). Some became surprisingly and unexpectedly personal, as I gathered typical themes or returned to earlier works of my own to cohere around my Petrarch version.

In the first poem I turned to a familiar bête noire, Margaret Thatcher, and immediately twisted Petrarchan tropes, via medieval torture instruments and contemporary Sado-Masochist practices, to fit the image of 'The Iron Lady', who had died in 2013. (Postal workers were indeed observed in Liverpool pubs on the night of her funeral reprising their political chants from the 1980s.)

> *Iron Maiden*
>
> Latex skies. Low cloud obscuring celestial
> domination. I clapped my fuck-eye on you,
> which you then pierced on a glance, that day,
> and dragged me naked to your torture chamber.
>
> The funeral of Thatcher seemed the right time
> for your whip and irons. Posties brushed up their
> MaggieMaggieMaggie *chants and I cried onions-
> onions-onions*, stinging eyes fixed on your heels.
>
> You stalked me in your lace-up stockings, striding tight,
> and took my tears for real pain, yet can't you see desire
> burning under the dildo mask you've clamped on my kisser?
>
> Easy prey for your domination, bitch! Slap!
> I crumple to the floor. Would rubbery Love
> through his pouch dare to flash you his horn? (V.1: ll. 1–14)

This first version established a pattern that was repeated in some of the subsequent ones, as I realized I was probably approximating 'inventive reworkings' in Attridge's phrase.[29] The narrator is often a hapless 'lover', whether that is a pet dog (in the poem 'Pet'), a man watching soft pornography on TV, a losing poet at a prize-giving, or even myself on my first date with my future wife, to use four illustrative scenarios. Analogues to 'the pitiful morning', a particularized time for the poems' events, like Thatcher's funeral, recur across the sequence: the dog trots to Sefton Park, Liverpool, on 'Mad Friday' (it is also the Shortest Day of the year), defined as 'the Friday before Christmas, when Liverpool explodes in an orgy of drinking', in the words of an abandoned note I find on a computer file. The idle TV watcher is seeking 'Relief from *Comic Relief*', an annual charity televisual ordeal for some, which was

> found,
> flipping past *Russia Today* onto the *ADULT Section*,
> in fixing my eye upon *Babestation Academy*. (V. 13: ll. 1–3)

The poet on National Poetry Day cries out that Poet Laureate

> Duffy's
> droning on the radio (again) and you're on
> at the Poetry Society, whither I am headed
> to undress your double offbeats with my ears. (V. 14: ll. 1–4)

I return to the real events of the fortieth anniversary of Victory in Europe Day 1985; however, the poem is signalled as 'after Wayne Pratt', a fictional poet I invented in the 1980s to parody the mainstream poetry of the time, and so the tone is distorted though the story is true, and both are of their time, as it were:

> At the VE Night piss up, the gloom of the Blitz, the chill
> Of V2s, Goering's capture, Berlin scorched, were recalled.
> Then forgotten, the old girls squawking along with Al Bowly.
> On our first rendezvous we'd landed on this lot. (V. 11: ll. 1–4)

'It didn't seem the time for shields and armour', in my translation authorizes a sense of inappropriateness registered in some of my versions; 'But this wasn't the time for cockney triumphalism', the VE Day poem continues, though the (genuine) martial details are indeed surprising: 'The cheeky young man in the SS glad-rags | Tickled the dollies' flab' (V. 11: ll. 5–7). The series of metaphors concerning the clash of *armour* and *amores* is extended differently in other poems. For the dog in the park, unrequited love for a bitch is literally held in bondage by his owner, who plays the part of an ironical Cupid:

> You lifted your tail like a poodle, fluffy tart,
> Tripping past my flailing mass of muscle and lust.
> He didn't even notice, phone in hand, boot in my nuts. (V. 2: ll. 12–14)

The bored pornographer rises to the occasion with a metaphorical climax:

> I'm tossed into the refrigerated hold of factory-line phone sex!
> Unflipping catch, desire slipping through the net,
> I dream of you divested of logo, mobile, and smut.
>
> There's only one way that one way communication ends: a flick
> of the switch. My weak song at your tight thong corpses,
> like a weathergirl cracking a dirty joke by mistake. (V. 13: ll. 9–14)

The hapless poet 'praises' the prize-winning poet, Laura, whom he secretly loves, while recognizing, in similarly hyperbolic terms, the egotistical and stylistic awfulness of her National Poetry Day poem, 'your thumping Great I Am in clumping iambics' (a phrase I had been hoarding since the 1970s for this decisive moment) (V. 14: l. 9). Phallicism is never far away. The poem ends with the lines:

> You can't beat a posy conduit for poesy's soft con job;
> yet neither can you beat off love's stiff competition.
>
> Heads you win the laurels; tails I lose Laura;
> *my* name is reduced to a rhyme-scheme you use:
> the clapped-out alternative to you-know-whose. (V. 14: ll. 10–14)

This poem, the last of the sequence, is entitled 'You know' and the 'who' is, of course, Shakespeare, Petrarch's (assumed) rival in terms of sonnet frame invention (if only in the English sonnet tradition), and the final rhyming couplet is deliberately Shakespearean; but the palpable sense of unrequited love is mock-Petrarchan (and I ought to say I had no real-life model for this poet who has 'a voice like a spanked arse', but she is clearly a contemporary descendant of Wayne Pratt who narrates the 1985 poem; they are both voices of the detestable mainstreams of their times). Magically retranslated to 1985, 'I' may repeat the gloss of my 'translation', 'But it wasn't the time for cockney triumphalism', though all talk of triumph and cowardice is completely replaced at the end of the poem with a banal version of the recalled actuality: 'At dawn, we walked around the railings, Clissold Park. | Inside we could hear the parakeets sounding the all clear' (V. 11: ll. 13–14). (Retrospectively, I detect the tone of Eliot's *Four Quartets* here among the Pratt tropes and the ambiguity on the medical and military uses of 'all clear'; the narrator's 'excuse' to not make love is his 'scabies'.) As though I am darting between the differential and distanciating practices of Hughes and Atkins, I am not afraid to non-systematically *dérive* from my presented derivations, when occasion suggests. 'Such concerns seem gleefully inessential for the British poet', we might plagiarize Pujol i Duran; I seem 'to be having a conversation with "fucking-Wayne-fucking-Pratt"', 'rather than with the fourteenth century' poet.[30]

The poems also demonstrate something central to the poetics of Oulipo (and, in this local instance, in this project, to mine): that Petrarch's poem (or my pragmatic 'translation' of it) is but a potential realization from myriad possible versions. It would be possible to read the Wayne Pratt poem as the original of the 'dog' poem, should one wish, in a Borgesian shuffling of the records of composition; they might create their own precursors. That is before we think of adding all the other existent versions of Petrarch's poem, Atkins's and Hughes's included, to the roster. My limit of fourteen variations stops potentiality turning towards eternity (Nicholas Moore perhaps has too many versions; Mathews stops at thirty). There were two versions I rejected, a 'Chinese' version, 'Li Po Suction', though the pun of the title was more effective than the story of the morbidly obese 'Laura'), and 'Good Morning Blues', which was a blues song (I was particularly fond of the line, 'Beatrice got a phonograph; Laura don't exist', which seems to compare the beloveds of Dante and Petrarch (and suggests that the *Canzoniere* is completely fictional), but is in fact an amalgam of Robert Johnson's classic 'Phonograph Blues' and Johnny Mercer's standard love song 'Laura', which I suspect is in any case knowingly inflected with

Petrarchan tones. I occasionally perform this song at readings of the sequence with blues harmonica accompaniment. These poems are phantom limbs of potentiality; I can leave it to the reader to imagine more, which is the unspoken invitation of every Oulipean procedure.

To return to the main body of work, the sequence was influenced by two other studies in *The Meaning of Form*, to provoke a literary historical jest, and a return to an earlier homage. Working on Caroline Bergvall's sequence *Meddle English*, which involves numerous recastings of Chaucer's *The Canterbury Tales*, necessitated me reading and re-reading the Tales as background.[31] Then this appeared:

> The morwe biganne when hevene its bemes
> In routhe of our Lord hid al the lighte.
> My Lady I espeyde, she rent al my dremes,
> This wight bounden to wommens tendre myghte.
>
> It was nat the tyme for speres sharp and stronge
> Agan arwes of Love and his strook and smoot.
> Withouten sheeldes or defence I wep ful longe
> swich a love-longyne's desperaunce, as I woot.
>
> Love cam russhyng to smerte my peynes sorwe
> Fro the breethyng prisoun of my distempre hert,
> To open myn eyen and resolven the flo.
>
> Love's dominacion is yet deedly narwe
> Yif I am so wrecche, wounden bi a dart
> Whil you, unbuxomnesse Lady, escap his bow. (V. 3: ll. 1–14)

I was pleased with this 'Chaucerian' sonnet, a freak of literary history. My title 'Petrak: the first English sonnet, Good Friday 1401', suggests that somebody, not Chaucer, who knew Petrarch's work, adapted it, indeed 'introduced Petrarchan lyric into England over a century prior to the sonnets of Wyatt and Surrey', but never adopted the sonnet frame, and who died a year before the poem's supposed date, got there before him.[32] It is, of course, a joke at the expense of Wyatt and Surrey too (though I had no presentiment that I might turn to their sonnets at this point)!

The second poem derives from my chapter 'Stefan Themerson: Iconopoeia and Thought-Experiments in the Theatre of Semantic Poetry', with my study of the literary form invented by the Polish-British writer Themerson in his 1944 novel, *Bayamus: the Semantic Poetry Translation*.[33] In short, this proto-Oulipean procedure 'translated' a text word by word into its given dictionary definitions, and used lineation to orchestrate the results. When Themerson, whom I knew a little, died in the 1980s I attempted a Semantic Poetry Translation of one of my own poems, but it did not work (possibly because my original was asyntactic). The debt was finally paid by my deliberately prolix text that rearticulates, re-forms, Petrarch's poem; the last couple of lines of the poem become:

> But
> the exultation at the success
> of the deity of the devoted attachment
> to one of the opposite (or same) sex was

>   forceless
>   vacillating
>   faint
>   in its celebration of victory with pomp
>   not even bold enough to venture
>   to make show in a blaze of brilliant sparkles
>   of his pointed weapon
>   or toy
>   for throwing with the hand
>   or of a calcareous needle supposed to be used
>   as a sexual stimulus
>   by snails (V. 5: ll. 86–101)

The (almost) literal sting in the tail here is the introduction of a concluding definition of 'dart' that is at once deliberately inaccurate but sexual in a semi-appropriate way.

The implications of each word of my translation are considered (as in Themerson's prototypes), for example: Cupid is 'the deity | of the devoted attachment to one of the opposite (or same) sex'. However, my usually trusty 1970s Collins Dictionary omits references to same sex relationships so I augmented the definition. It is exactly this kind of slow-motion pondering upon the ideological constructions of words that Themerson's technique was attempting to effect. After such an excursion, it is perhaps not surprising that I contrasted this wallowing Behemoth with this fleet, tendrillar construction:

> dark morn
> sad god/sa
> w you/stak
> ed me/bad
>
> time for l
> ove's blow
> /wept woe/
> stalked my
>
> heart pou
> rs/weak Er
> os struck
>
> weak-me/no
> guts to s
> how a dart
>
> (V. 6: ll. 1–14)

Akin to an Oulipean haikuization, this is in fact a 'twittersonnet' (it contains 140 characters and spaces, the social medium Twitter's then word limit), and is described as 'after René Van Valckenborch', a reference to another fictional poet, the bilingual Belgian who dominates my volume *A Translated Man* (2013), and who supposedly invented this form.[34] Yet another intratextual reference to my work is woven into this 'derivative' structure. Somehow, in the writing of the translations (which came quickly between December 2013 and May the following year) I felt the need to link with other works of my own. 'Empty Diary 1327' goes further by adding an anomalous member to the series of 'Empty Diary' poems that runs through *Twentieth Century Blues, 1901–2000* (though I have since extended into the twenty-first century, though there had long been a science fiction 2055 poem), a sequence dealing with sexual politics, generally narrated from the point of view of a woman.[35] Here, Laura appears as an obscene vampiric vamp:

> His eye is pulled to the black hole
> at the centre of my white body. It's the reason
> I'm here this morning, snarling under my wimple... (V. 8: ll. 1–3)

This Laura wants nothing to do with the tradition within which she finds herself inserted, and she exposes the sexuality at the heart of her narrator's fawning religiosity. She rejects Petrarch and his Saviour: 'Trust a Florentine not to have seen where the fault lay: | the strung-up Megalomaniac rapping in riddles' (V. 8: ll. 13–14).

This poem could be thought of (in Oulipean terms) as the sequence's clinamen, but I would nominate instead the poem I call 'the Jimmy Savile' poem. It is actually entitled 'Now then now then then and now', playing on one of the dead, disgraced celebrity's insidious media catchphrases; he is open about his paedophilic operations and his inner psyche, as perversions of the love that sustains Petrarch:

> In my time I spun the grooves and groped the grubs
> from the milk bars of Leeds to the morgue at Broadmoor,
> consummate in the toilets of Broadcasting House. Now
> then: hate is when you're feeling Top of the Pops. (V. 9: ll. 5–8)

One of the covers of this man, probably Britain's most predatory paedophile, was his seduction of the establishment, and its catastrophic handing over of responsibility to this criminal; his threat to children, '*I'm the rock-hard tart who's pecked his way up Thatcher's snatch!*' is an imaginative recasting of a classic silencing device, the boasting of power by paedophiles: Savile was originally a disc jockey, and the closing, 'Yours is a request that will never be played', refers to his 'escape' from justice in death (V. 9: ll. 11/14). Although I generally eschew self-interpretation, I wish to be explicit about this poem's criticism of Savile to avoid any misunderstanding of my treatment of its controversial theme. Whenever I read this poem in public, I notice the audience is ill at ease, goes silent. Despite the sequence carrying the jocularity of a talking dog and a post-Chaucerian sonneteer, I want to show that 'versioning' can involve abrupt changes of tone, ones which are capable of considerations of the most serious subject matter of our time.

At this point I have been forced to renounce my writerly distance from the material, and — in contrast, and in respect to readers — I want to give a flavour of the rest of the sequence without too much comment. Running through the sequence are four poems which align Petrarch's sonnet with French symbolist poets (and sonnets). I think of them as impossibly 'half Petrarchan, half symbolist, and half me', to quote my characteristic introduction to them in performance. These poems again came about during the writing of *The Meaning of Form*. Critiquing Sean Bonney's political book *Happiness*, I referred repeatedly to Rimbaud's famous 'vowel' poem, which Bonney re-functions in various ways throughout his book, which is subtitled 'Poems after Rimbaud', although he warns: 'If you think they're translations you're an idiot.'[36] Rimbaud's 'Voyelles' begins with a statement of his famous and baffling alphabetic equation: 'A noir, E blanc, I rouge, U vert, O bleu, voyelles', and I realized I needed to concoct a partial translation to quote in the essay. (I do have *some* French.): [37]

> A black, E white, I red, U green, O blue, vowels,
> One day I'll tell of your latent spawnings;
> A: black velveteen belt of flies
> Blusters and clusters over the cruel stench,
> The shadowy gulf.[38]

In making my 'version', I could not resist injecting 'U LAUrA', impersonating the letter-play one finds in some of Petrarch's sonnets, and 'I another', a phrase that echoes (or parodies) Rimbaud's famous disavowal of self, or submergence into political community, in Bonney's fresh reading, which argues that 'For *I* is an *other*' is a prediction of 'the destruction of bourgeois subjectivity, yeh!' into collective consciousness.[39]

I offer, in this 'Symbolist Quartet', as I think of it, a vampire Baudelaire poem, derived from his famous 'A Une Passante', but which contains quotations from Robert Herrick and Bob Dylan; a Mallarmé poem that owes to Peter Manson's version of 'Angoisse'; my version of Rimbaud's 'Voyelles', which additionally has a reference to Barry MacSweeney's book title *Our Mutual Scarlet Boulevard*; and Verlaine's 'Luxures'. I offer this sequence within a sequence, as an appendix without further comment, my little authorial death being, I trust, the momentous birth of my readers.[40]

This tracking of the processes of writing *Petrarch 3* — which I perceive to be a peculiar species of poetics, a progress report for others — has convinced me that the subtitle, a 'derivative dérive', is in some senses accurate: the further I investigated my single poem with techniques borrowed from others (though with situations I devised myself, but sometimes suggested by those techniques, in endless interplay), the more I lost myself in the exploration of the suburbs of the poem, and the more I kept meeting myself, or rather, my aesthetic concerns, as I encountered Wayne Pratt, René Van Valckenborch or the voice of the 'Empty Diaries' sequence, which were unforeseen and could only have emerged from the formally investigative processes undertaken. The four poets named in its dedications inspired by example, Hughes and Atkins in their breath-taking breadth in taking on all of Petrarch (which I had to turn away from, a swerve from influence), and Mathews and Moore, by example of their consistent re-functioning of the same material, gnawing like dogs at a bone perhaps, or more like the performances of Thelonious Monk returning again and again to 'Monk's Mood' to mine fresh ore, rather than to mime with awe, from the same melody. I am also convinced that this has less to do with Petrarch than I had thought hitherto, although it has a great deal to do with the sonnet as a (continuing) obsession of mine, and in this piece I found new tones and voices *for me* (though I will not make claim to my nevertheless *hoped for* originality). Frankly, it allowed me to play with elements of poetic artifice that I usually eschew (rhyme and metre in particular), safe in my parodic frame. How does this meld with my formalist turn in my criticism? Strictly speaking, this is not for me to say, but Attridge argues

> The inventive artist is one who is fully in command of the materials and conventions of his art-form, or techne, but rather than simply producing a rearrangement of that material finds a way of making a space for the new, the other, the hitherto unthinkable or unperceivable. The scenario is exactly that of the hospitality of visitation: rather than inviting some already known idea or formal arrangement or quality of feeling into the work in progress, the successful artist finds a way of destabilizing the fixed structures of knowledge, habit, and affect, so as to make a *visitation* possible, and seeks to welcome the other, the *arrivant*, in a work that does justice to its singularity.[41]

I make no claims to invention in this specialized sense (neither do I refute it), but I wonder whether the gimp-masked submissive, Petrarch, the Scouse dog, Laura, even Jimmy Savile in his unmarked grave, are not arrivants in this hospitable sense? I believe I may have destabilized at least my own formal habits of writing and created something which is both a 'rearrangement' of the derivatively known and the making of a new space for dérive. No wonder my next set of sonnets were 'overdubs' of Milton's. Although I have written a number of other sonnet sequences since (including extending 'Empty Diary' poems to 2017), Petrarch was not absent for long, even if the next arrivant was Sir Thomas Wyatt. *Hap: Understudies of Thomas Wyatt's Petrarch* (2018) weaves Wyatt's versions of Petrarch, Wyatt's life as an endangered servant of that first Brexiteer, Henry VIII, and a modern day civil servant of the Brexit-obsessed administration of Theresa May, together into a satirical narrative.[42] History almost dictates that Henry Howard, the Earl of Surrey, should be submitted to a similar fate, and 'Surrey with the Fringe on Top', whose title suggests the growing irreverence of the enterprise, forages further into the dark undergrowth of Brexitland Britain, both in my versions of Surrey's versions of Petrarch (the seven poems of 'The Unfortunate Fellow-Traveller') and in my responses to seven of his occasional poems, 'Direct Rule', in which I operate a controlling meta-narrative over the poems, and its narrative of Surrey's hubristic behaviour in the face of the Henrician Terror that finally destroyed him, while presenting a comic post-Brexit Britain peppered with rural dogging sites and self-serving Brexiteers. I freely admit this process, begun in *Petrarch 3*, is addictive. Latterly, I have adapted female sonneteers, and taken the works of Charlotte Smith as transformational models: four of *her* versions of Petrarch preface responses to some of her 'Elegiac Sonnets' that evoke the Sussex countryside (where I was also born). At the time of writing, I am adapting some of Elizabeth Barrett Browning's 'Sonnets from the Portuguese' to the voice of a mistress of a Conservative MP.

If poetics is the speculative discourse about future possibilities for writing, then these sonnets, and this piece about them, suggest formal investigation of the sonnet frame in my work has not reached its limits. Poetics is, as Rachel Blau Du Plessis states, a 'permission to continue'.[43] What is unusual is that literary critical enquiries *suggested* the work, *informed* the work, but did not dictate (nor could it explain) the work.

Petrarch 3: The Symbolist Quartet

A Florentine Vampire in Paris

> Amid the rush of All Souls' Eve, the majesty of sadness
> (I'd waited 530 years for this translation, this transfusion)
> a woman mourned, passing slowly, lifted by the liquefaction
> of her clothes; holding fast the stake to my bloated heart.
>
> Like a wobbling lush, not feeling blows or blood,
> Under a livid sky of germs I fed off her grace,
> statuesque. I wept, drank deep from her softening eyes.
> Fascination weakens. Pain kills: pleasure bites.
>
> I've paid in blood but not my own, nor my words.
> Love flashed and she flooded, ensanguined and weak:
> bleak eternity escaped into the void vessel of her heart.
>
> Ever! There's no living beat in this unloving verse:
> O you whom I might have loved if I'd dared not to
> flash you my fangs! O you who'd read it all before! (V. 4: ll. 1–14)

Pale

for Peter Manson

> Tonight, I don't come to capture your body
> bearing my sins for the sake of the world; or,
> my Beast, to tear up a pitiful storm in your fuzz,
> from the incurable *ennui* I drop with the kiss of my verse;
>
> I demand of your bed dreamless sleep armoured against
> crepuscular amours, clouded in the curtains of unknowing;
> so you'll taste your own black lies, the batters and blues,
> you who know more about *le néant* than the dead.
>
> *Le Vice* stalked me, gobbled me, sucked out my grace;
> impaled, like you, sterile tears unflowing,
> while your stone breast is dressed to kill whose
>
> heart no glistening fang of crime unblesses,
> I run, run down, haunted by my shroud,
> afraid of dying in my sleep, in the poem, alone. (V. 7: ll. 1–14)

Vow

> A black, E blank, U LAUrA, I another, O Heaven,
> this last morning I'll tell of the vowels' latent spawnings;
> A, black velveteen corset of flies captivates,
> blusters and clusters over the cruel stench,
>
> A pit of shit; E, spears and shields, the filigree
> of glacial lace caught in my throat, an arrow-hook;
> I, blood-spit and anger, laughing beauty,
> I is a letter swept along the scarlet boulevard;

U, divine vibrations through viridian seas,
animal lusts flowing, alchemical sorrows
stitched into hardened arteries to derange me;

O, trumpet full of strange triumphs, blowing to bits
the silence of angels and cupids around the globe:
O, Omega, catch the violent dart of her azure eyes. (V. 10: ll. 1–14)

Lux! and Fux!

Flesh! under Heaven's dark light the sole fruit we bite,
Sweet and sour, juicing our teeth, My Lady; my soul
Hungry solely for Love, saw you just once and, gripped
By the throat, in the mouth your tart tart choked me,

Love! the sole emotion of those who weep not
At the world's dread. Love's stones grind and mill
The arrows of the rude, the shields of the prude, into hard
Wafer, my joy this Witching Hour, my woe this Eastertide.

Love, pretty shepherd boy in a pissed peasant's dream,
Herded me into a pastoral free of animal lusts, free
Of tears, but full of vile sweet white wine, unchilled!

Flesh is the peasant dreaming feebly that triumph
Will strangle the triumphant — this Holy Day or not.
Why let ecstasy's darts fall short, Love and Flesh? (V. 12: ll. 1–14)

Notes to Chapter 15

1. Susan Brigden, *Thomas Wyatt: The Heart's Forest* (London: Faber and Faber, 2012), p. 157.
2. Robert Sheppard, *Petrarch 3: a derivative dérive* (Izmir and Minneapolis: Crater Press, 2017). This is published in an unpaginated double-sided format (folded like a map). I will include references to the number of the variation (V.) and the lines (ll.) in the text.
3. Robert Sheppard, 'Poetics as Conjecture and Provocation: An Inaugural Lecture Delivered on 13 March 2007 at Edge Hill University', *New Writing: The International for the Theory and Practice of Creative Writing*, 5.1 (2008) 3–26 (p. 4).
4. Jeff Hilson, ed., *The Reality Street Book of Sonnets* (Hastings: Reality Street, 2008). pp. 226–28; Robert Sheppard, *Warrant Error* (Exeter: Shearsman, 2009).
5. Robert Sheppard, *Complete Twentieth Century Blues* (Cambridge: Salt Publications, 2008).
6. Robert Sheppard, *Dedicated to you but you weren't listening* (London: Writers Forum, 1979), p. 1.
7. Simon Watson Taylor, ed., *French Writing Today* (Harmondsworth: Penguin Books, 1968), p. 205.
8. Robert Sheppard, *The Meaning of Form in Contemporary Innovative Poetry* (New York: Palgrave, 2016), p. 1.
9. Friedrich Schiller, *On the Aesthetic Education of Man*. trans. by Reginald Snell (Mineola: Dover Publications, 2004), p. 106.
10. Derek Attridge, *The Work of Literature* (Oxford: Oxford University Press, 2015), p. 117.
11. Derek Attridge, *The Singularity of Literature* (London and New York: Routledge, 2004), p. 113.
12. Ibid., p. 114.
13. Sheppard, *The Meaning of Form*, pp. 47–84.
14. Tim Atkins, *Collected Petrarch* (London: Crater Press, 2014); and Hughes' *Quite Frankly: After Petrarch's Sonnets* (Hastings: Reality Street, 2015).
15. Hughes, p. 293.

16. Atkins, p. 344.
17. Hughes, p. 323; Atkins, p. 537.
18. Jèssica Pujol i Duran, 'Multi-Atkins', intro. to Atkins, p. xii.
19. Petrarch, Francesco, *Selections from the Canzoniere and Other Works*, trans. by Mark Musa (Oxford and New York: Oxford University Press, 1985), p. 23.
20. Attridge, *The Singularity of Literature*, p. 75.
21. Francesco Petrarch, *Canzoniere*, poem 3, at <http://petrarch.petersadlon.com/canzoniere.html?poem=3> [accessed 7 May 2014].
22. Sheppard, *Petrarch 3*: unpaginated, but this poem is, of course, printed before the fourteen variations.
23. Harry Mathews, *A Mid-Season Sky: Poems 1954–1991* (Manchester: Carcanet, 1992), p. 63.
24. Ibid., pp. 63 and 65.
25. Ibid., p. 68.
26. Nicholas Moore, *Spleen* (London: Menard Press, 1990), pp. 35 and 42.
27. Ibid., p. 12.
28. Kenneth Goldsmith, *Uncreative Writing: Managing Language in the Digital Age* (New York: Columbia University Press, 2011), pp. 1–13.
29. Attridge, *The Singulaity of Literature*, p. 75.
30. Pujol i Duran, 'Multi-Atkins', p. xii.
31. Caroline Bergvall, *Meddle English* (Callicoon, NY: Nightboat Boats, 2011).
32. William Rossiter, *Chaucer and Petrarch* (Cambridge: Boydell & Brewer, 2010), p. 25.
33. Stefan Themerson, Stefan, *Bayamus and the Theatre of Semantic Poetry* (London: Gaberbocchus Press, 1965).
34. Robert Sheppard, *A Translated Man* (Bristol: Shearsman Books, 2013).
35. Sheppard, *Complete Twentieth Century Blues*, pp. 94–152.
36. Sean Bonney, *Happiness: Poems after Rimbaud* (London: Ukant Publications, 2012), author's cover note.
37. Arthur Rimbaud, *Complete Works*, trans. by Paul Schmidt (New York, London, etc.: Harper Perennial 2008), p. 19.
38. Sheppard, *The Meaning of Form*, p. 113.
39. Rimbaud, *Complete Works*, p. 115; Bonney, *Happiness*, p. 64.
40. Translations may be found in Charles Baudelaire, *Selected Poems*, trans. by Jeffrey Wagner (London: Panther, 1971), p. 78–79; *Stéphane Mallarmé; The Poems in Verse*, trans. by Peter Manson (Oxford, OH: Miami University Press, 2012), p. 36–37; Rimbaud, *Complete Works*, p. 139); Paul Verlaine, *Selected Poems*, trans. by Martin Sorrell (Oxford and New York: Oxford University Press, 1999), pp. 128–29. MacSweeney's title is Barry MacSweeney, *Our Mutual Scarlet Boulevard* (London: Fulcrum, 1971).
41. Attridge, *The Work of Literature*, p. 304.
42. Robert Sheppard, *Hap: Understudies of Thomas Wyatt's Petrarch* (Newton-le-Willows: Knives Forks and Spoons, forthcoming). The other poems and sequences mentioned remain unpublished.
43. Rachel Blau DuPlessis, *The Pink Guitar, Writing as Feminist Practice* (New York and London: Routledge, 1990), p. 156.

APPENDIX

EUROPETRARCA:
The Relevance of a Database of Translations of the *Canzoniere*

Guillaume Coatalen

Petrarch is one of the most influential poets in Western literature. While few epics have been written since the 1950s — excluding Derek Walcott's *Omeros*, the sonnet is still thriving, placed as it is on the cutting edge of experimental poetry, in spite of its constraints, and perhaps thanks to them. The sonnet's popularity owes much to its brevity, adaptability, and fragmentary nature. Indeed, as shown elsewhere in the volume, the sonnet seems to be composed to be kept and quoted in parts even though the form has traditionally been praised by Wordsworth and other poets for being a harmoniously balanced whole. Readers have often recorded a quatrain, the concluding couplet or just a line for future personal use.

Petrarch established the most popular poetic form, the sonnet, and invented a comprehensive grammar of conventional images and situations for European lyric poetry. What is known as Petrarchism, the imitation of Petrarch's collection of lyric poems, the *Canzoniere* or *Rerum Vulgarium Fragmenta*, rapidly became one of the most widespread and rooted cultural phenomena and reached far beyond the confines of poetry. Petrarchism and its unique philosophy of love first fashioned court culture in Europe and then trickled down to the merchant and popular classes. In its restricted poetic sense, Petrarchism is defined by the borrowing of metaphors and allegories, the so-called Petrarchan conceits Petrarch developed in a systematic way in his *Canzoniere*. All love poetry since Petrarch has been written after the model he developed in his collection of songs and sonnets. It is not restrained to the Renaissance but still very much alive even if it takes other forms. Paradoxically, the avant-garde also recognizes Petrarch as one of its sources.[1]

The first decisive stage in the spread of Petrarchan poetics then and now rests on translations of the *Canzoniere* in vernacular languages. If our knowledge of Petrarchan conceits is extensive,[2] we know little about the translations, notably the later ones, simply because of their staggering amount. To understand Petrarchism thoroughly, it is indispensable to collect and examine translations carefully since the vast majority of poets and other writers who imitated Petrarch did it through these translations, not by returning to the original source. Often they did not understand Petrarch's Italian or were more interested in their native poetic traditions. This is certainly the case for Aragon, who worked on another French translation by Pierre-Louis Ginguené first printed in 1875 and made it sound more poetic without giving much thought to the Italian.[3] And he was not alone in doing this. Indeed, entire poetic traditions in other vernacular languages used French translations as the basis of their translations. German Romantic poets in particular had very little grasp of Italian but knew French as the most prestigious vernacular language from roughly 1700 to 1900.[4] The same may be said of Russian translators. Before that period, someone like Martin Opitz, whose work was decisive for German Petrarchism, was influenced by neo-Latin versions, when he translated *RVF* 132, 'S'amor non e, ehe dunque e quel ch'io sento?'.[5] Obviously, neo-Latin translations will have to be included in the database as essential sources for translations in the vernacular and interpretations of the source text in their own right.

Second, Petrarch like all literary models, from the beginning to the present age, has been reinterpreted and recreated anew by translators, depending on their period and more personal concerns. Translations often tell us more about social, political and more individual concerns than about the ever elusive meaning of the *Canzoniere*. Literature is by definition ambiguous[6] and the *Canzoniere* because of its allegorical nature even more so. The vast corpus of the *Canzoniere* in translation offers a multifaceted and rich portrait of a mythical figure. Petrarch is at once the prestigious humanist, the inspired love poet and a fierce critic of the Papacy. Only a fully integrated database can make it possible to grasp Petrarchism in its complexity.

Petrarchan studies are fragmented and divided according to language or geography. There are two main reasons for this. (1) The sheer amount of translations in certain countries — like France — has encouraged scholars to concentrate on particular periods, usually the origins, within the national corpus.[7] (2) The natural urge for scholars is to concentrate on their own literatures.

Moreover, there is a strong tendency among literary critics to examine Petrarch's influence on the biggest names in the canon such as Chaucer,[8] Sir Thomas Wyatt,[9] or Ronsard.[10] Most full or partial translations of the *Canzoniere* were however produced by lesser-known writers or even fairly obscure ones on whom very few critical studies exist, if any. Buried among the collections of European libraries, these rarely consulted works need to be properly assessed to further our understanding of the national Petrarchs and European Petrarchism as a whole. Precisely because this neglected body of translations is undistinguished, it will inform scholars on the established dominant practice of translation and literary *Zeitgeist*.

European Petrarchism does exist as a well-established topic in literary studies.[11] Yet, even when a European approach is taken, such works gather studies of national Petrarchs side by side with few attempts to make connections between them. Scholars tend to compare the best-known Petrarchan traditions like the English and French ones.[12] EUROPETRARCA will allow scholars to make multiple comparisons between several national Petrarchan traditions and ultimately improve our knowledge of the various Petrarchs in the vernacular. So far, I have gathered roughly 200 translations in 12 languages (including Latin). As an example, I have chosen Latin, German and Polish translations of *RVF* 132 printed in roughly the same period. These versions have never been considered together:

RVF 132[13]

    S'amor non e, che dunque e quel ch'io sento?
Ma s'egli è amor, perdio, che cosa et quale?
Se bona, onde l'effecto aspro mortale?
Se ria, onde sí dolce ogni tormento?

    S'a mia voglia ardo, onde 'l pianto e lamento?
S'a mal mio grado, il lamentar che vale?
O viva morte, o dilectoso male,
come puoi tanto in me, s'io no 'l consento?

    Et s'io 'l consento, a gran torto mi doglio.
Fra sí contrari vènti in frale barca
mi trovo in alto mar senza governo,

    sí lieve di saver, d'error sí carca
ch'i' medesmo non so quel ch'io mi voglio,
et tremo a mezza state, ardendo il verno.

Jeśli nie masz miłości, cóż jest, co ja czuję?
Jeśli miłość jest, co to przebóg takowego?
Jeśli dobra, skąd skutku nabywa tak złego?
Jeśli zła, czemu sobie mękę tak smakuję?

Jeśli gorę sam chcęcy, skąd te łzy najduję?
Jeśli rad nie rad muszę, na cóż me żałości?
O martwe życie! O ma bolesna radości!
Przecz mię tyranizujesz, jeślić nie hołduję?

Jeśli na to pozwalam, niesłusznie styskuję;
między sprzecznymi wiatry w niewarownwej łodzi,
bez wiosła jestem wpośród morza głębokiego,

która czcza wiadomości, pełna błędu chodzi,
nie wiem, czego chcę ani czego potrzebuję,
wśród zimy gorę, a drżę wśród lata samego.
Daniel Naborowski (1573–1640)[14]

Ists Liebe nicht: was ists, was ich empinde?
Ists Liebe — Gott, welch Ding? von welchem Schlage?
wenn gut: woher dann Tod und Trauertage?
wenn schlecht: woher dann jede Qual so linde?

    Brenn ich mit Fleiß: hat dann die Klage Gründe?
wenn wider Willen, dann — was nützt die Klage?
lebendiger Tod, o angenehme Plage,
wieso vermögt ihr, was ich unterbinde?

    Und stimm ich zu, ists Unrecht, daß ich klage!
Inmitten solcher Widerwinde finde
ich mich auf hohen Wogen ohne Steuer:

    so leicht Wissen, so beschwert mit Sünde,
daß ich, zu deuten was ich will, verzage:
im Sommer zitternd spür ich winters Feuer.
Martin Opitz (1597–1639)

> Quod si nil Amor est; quid me sentire putabo?
>> Sin aliquid; quaeso quale quid esse potest?
> Si bonus; unde malos effectus credis oriri.
>> Sin malus; unde ferax copia mellis adest.
> Sive volens uror; quorsum haec lamenta dolorque?
>> Sive aliter; nunquid plangere pro erit?
> O mors viva, malum non illaetabile[15], sive
>> Non consensus adest, quomodo tanta potes?
> Sin consensus adest, non recte conqueror amens:
>> Sub geminis ventis in rate fragili
> Dorsa maris rectoris egens incerta peragro,
>> Plenus et erroris, menteque tua vacuus;
> Ut non quid cupiam, detur mihi scire facultas,
>> Ipsa aestate tremens, ustus et ipsa hieme.
>> Guglielmus Canter (1542–75)[16]

General trends have long been established, such as the relative loss of influence of the Petrarchan model in the eighteenth century. What has never been offered is a clear pan-European picture of Petrarchism at any given place or moment.

Petrarch's dissemination across Europe is a complex one. To take just one example, early modern English translations of the *Canzoniere* rested just as much on French translations as they did on the original Italian text even if, according to George Puttenham,[17] Sir Thomas Wyatt and Henry Howard, the Earl of Surrey brought back the sonnet from their diplomatic missions in Italy. Before returning to England, the poets travelled through France, and most certainly stopped in Lyons, where they were probably in direct contact with Petrarch's poems, which circulated widely in numerous translations.

Thanks to the database, a far more nuanced picture of the spread of Petrarchism in Europe will appear. EUROPETRARCA will combine a more global approach by offering a pan-European view and the most detailed picture restricted to a place and time. This would bring to light new or rarely consulted material and would allow multiple comparisons which would otherwise be impossible to draw. National Petrarchan traditions have long been treated independently, with little regard for the more global European context. A multiple-entry database would enable a radically new approach by concentrating on the interactions between these national traditions which will no longer be seen as simply coexisting. By placing translation practices at the heart of the methodology, Petrarchism will be assessed as a multilingual cultural phenomenon, diachronically and synchronically. The well-known example of the triangular relationship between England, France and Italy may be expanded along other lines to the rest of Europe. Multiple relationships between various national Petrarchan traditions feeding one another will be tested as a core hypothesis. The circulation of texts in Europe and beyond has long been attested from the early modern period onwards[18] and explains why translators may have resorted to a number of translations in various languages in addition to consulting the original Italian. This is still true today. Tim Atkins notes he had recourse to a number of translations of Petrarch. In some cases, because translators did not master Petrarch's Italian, they did not read the *Rerum Vulgarium Fragmenta* in the original.

EUROPETRARCA is based on a truly multidisciplinary approach combining bibliography, palaeography, cultural history, literary criticism, translation studies, historical linguistics, and the latest advances in digital humanities.

The first step in collecting the data is to draw comprehensive chronological lists of translations of the *Canzoniere* for each vernacular language. This groundwork entails bibliographical knowledge since members of the project will have to work extensively in numerous repositories to track and consult not just printed volumes of the translations but journals — sometimes extremely rare ones — and manuscripts. The list will not only offer basic bibliographical information but will locate the poems or even individual verses within larger works precisely, be they printed or in manuscript form. This work has never been done before and will in itself be very useful to Petrarch scholars, as well as sonnet scholars in general. Palaeography is of course a necessary skill by which to identify the Petrarchan material before transcribing it. Early modern studies now take much more interest in works that only exist in manuscript form, especially works by women.

One aspect in Petrarchan studies which has not been fully grasped is the part played by anthologies of Italian verse in the transmission of the *Canzoniere*. More often than not, translators did not go back to full editions of the *Canzoniere* but chose instead selections in readily accessible bilingual or monolingual editions. They found it easier to work from a model in their own mother tongue. Paradoxically, some texts that may appear at first sight to be translations end up being rewritings of translations. EUROPETRARCA should make it possible to establish whether translations are disguised reworkings of earlier translations in the same language or another one. The addition of titles and commentaries will also be taken into account as essential material to understand how the collection was interpreted by translators and editors.

Petrarchism is not confined to literary studies, but constitutes one of the most significant cultural, social and even political phenomena in European history which extends far beyond literature. The obvious example is of course that of Queen Elizabeth I's court[19] where Petrarchan sonnets played a crucial part in complex relationships between the Queen herself and various prominent courtiers, and in diplomatic exchanges as well. In a later period in history, numerous Romantic artists — Franz Liszt comes to mind — were fascinated and highly influenced by Petrarch's sonnets. This fascination lasted well into the twentieth century with Arnold Schönberg's compositions. Beyond translations proper, ordinary Europeans composed Petrarchan sonnets to declare their love until the end of the nineteenth century.[20] Thus, Petrarch, or their own version of Petrarch, played a decisive part in their private lives. The late medieval Petrarch has often stood at the avant-garde of art.[21] The poet has also embodied nostalgia for an idealized past, but just as much the progressive revolt of the humanist intellectual against reactionary forces.

The most obvious tangible results will of course be in the field of literary studies and more precisely poetic studies across vernacular languages. The database will allow scholars to explore Petrarchism at any given moment or period in any of the languages included. EUROPETRARCA will answer simple core questions in Petrarchan studies. Who translated the *Canzoniere*? When? Which poems did they choose? What particular mode of translation, imitation or adaptation did they use? Did they write in metre or prose? Decades or years of intense translation and dissemination will be contrasted with less active periods. Since it is commonly accepted that all sonnets derive one way or the other from Petrarch's, the database should contribute to our knowledge of the sonnet in general, which is undoubtedly the most enduring and successful poetic form in the history of European verse, and still practised by poets like Peter Hughes or Tim Atkins.[22]

Historical poetics and metrical studies in particular will exploit the database by looking into the multiple ways in which translators have to negotiate with the Italian hendecasyllable and the presence of rimes, alliterations, metaphors and puns, to list just a few key features and problems to be tackled in translations. The evidence will bring to light chronological and national differences in translation choices. Significant patterns on imagery and metre should emerge.

Translation studies in general and literary translation studies in particular will benefit from the database directly. Petrarch's *Canzoniere*, because of its enormous influence in Europe, constitutes a seminal case study with which to explore the history of literary translation in general, from the end of the fourteenth century onwards. This is a fairly recent[23] but thriving field in the humanities, well represented by journals such as *Translation and Literature*, founded in 1992 and published by the Edinburgh University Press. The fully searchable data will allow scholars to analyse the translation of entire poems, verses, and even segments or simply single terms. Comparisons of the translation of particular terms will be possible in related languages, such as Romance languages, or Slavic ones.

Students and experts interested in historical linguistics will be able to use the corpus to conduct specialized studies in semantics, syntax or metre, for example. Those who wish to concentrate on a particular language will of course be able to do so. Through the radical or subtle changes introduced by translators, historians of European vernacular languages may study linguistic change in all its forms. The corpus of English translations could be added to corpora such as the Corpus Resource Database (CoRD) devised and hosted by Varieng at the University of Helsinki (http://www.helsinki.fi/varieng/CoRD/). The *Canzoniere* was used as the basic source for Italian–French dictionaries,[24] and translations will crop up in unexpected places such as letters and even speeches.

The project does not rest on a single theoretical approach but the concept of hybridity taken from cultural studies may provide a thread running through its various layers.

At the moment no such database exists. Databases fall into two categories:

(a) Databases containing digital images of manuscripts, printed books, prints, pictures and other artefacts such as LUNA, hosted by the Folger Library in Washington (http://luna.folger.edu/luna/servlet/FOLGERCM1~6~6) or EEBO, Early English Books Online, which offers pictures of books printed in England between 1470 and 1700.

(b) Full text searchable databases such as TCP (Text Creation Project) associated with EEBO.

Although EEBO and TCP belong to the same project, and even though they may be consulted at the same time, the sites are not connected.

EUROPETRARCA will be unique since it will combine digital pictures of the printed or manuscript translations and fully searchable diplomatic transcriptions.

An essential part of the work entails lengthy visits to numerous libraries and repositories across Europe. Another aspect is negotiating copyrights for more recent works. A substantial amount of the translations, notably nineteenth- and twentieth-century ones, have not been tracked down, let alone consulted. The *Canzoniere* contains 366 poems. According to a conservative estimate, the database when completed should record at least 500,000 pictures and translations. In certain instances, it is to be hoped that robotic book-scanners will be used, given the number of pictures to be taken.

Once the bulk of the digital pictures and transcriptions is uploaded, the data will be exploited according to the criteria. The most obvious studies will be linguistic ones in the broadest sense. They will address issues such as the history of lyric poetry and poetic form, metre, translation, rhetoric and historical linguistics. Comparisons will be chronological, but much finer studies will be made possible thanks to criteria such as the translator's age, gender, nationality and even profession, when applicable. Statistics on the popularity of certain poems in the *Canzoniere* should help us to understand their cultural function.

The data should help us to reassess the social, political and philosophical significance of the *Canzoniere* in Europe. Thanks to the translations in vernacular languages, the anthology played a major part from the Renaissance onwards in shaping social relationships between men and women, not least amorous ones, constructing national identities as a cultural icon, and providing theoretical and practical models for a vast range of emotions and ideas on love and faith.

This methodology may be adapted to other key authors in the European canon, and a similar project could take one of Shakespeare's plays, or even the entire Shakespeare canon, as a starting point, or Homer. The Chicago Homer does offer various English and German translations, but the site is far more limited in scope (http://homer.library.northwestern.edu/). The full extent of the influence of such major sources for European literature may only be measured thanks to such a massive and precise tool.

Free access will be granted to the database to encourage further studies in the academic community but also as a means to discover Petrarch's work and its influence for the general public. The possibilities are virtually limitless. Countless anthologies may be devised according to period, language or theme. Secondary schools across Europe could use the database to introduce Petrarch to students.

Notes to the Appendix

1. Tim Atkins, *Petrarch Collected Atkins* (London: Crater Press, 2014), Peter Hughes, *Quite Frankly after Petrarch's Sonnets* (Hastings: Reality Street, 2015).
2. Dolce Lodovico Petrarca, ed., *Il Petrarca* (Vinegia: G. Giolito de Ferrari, 1547); Leonard Forster, *The Icy Fire: Five Studies in European Petrarchism* (Cambridge: Cambridge University Press, 1969).

3. I owe the information to Riccardo Raimondo.
4. On the German debate on the French language, see William Jervis Jones, '"Französisch kauderwalsh macht unser Sprach falsch": Diagnoses of Gallomania", in his *Images of Language: Six Essays on German Attitudes to European Languages from 1500 to 1800*, Studies in the History of the Language Sciences, 89 (Amsterdam and Philadelphia: John Benjamins, 1999), pp. 111–70.
5. See Achim Aurnhammer, ed., *Francesco Petrarca in Deutschland. Seine Wirkung in Literatur, Kunst und Musik* (Tübingen: Niemeyer, 2006), pp. 189–210.
6. William Empson, *Seven Types of Ambiguity* (London: Chatto & Windus, 1930).
7. Joseph Vianey, *Le pétrarquisme en France au XVIe siècle* (Geneva: Slatkine Reprints, 1909, 1969); Jean Balsamo, ed., *Les poètes français de la Renaissance et Pétrarque* (Geneva: Droz 2004); Jack D'Amico, ed., *Petrarch in England: An Anthology of Parallel Texts from Wyatt to Milton* (Ravenna: Longo, 1979); Ève Duperray, *La postérité répond à Pétrarque: sept siècles de fortune pétrarquienne en France: actes du colloque tenu à l'Hôtel de Sade et à l'Université d'Avignon et des pays du Vaucluse, les 22, 23, 24 janvier 2004* (Paris: Beauchesne 2006); Edoardo Zuccato, *Petrarch in Romantic England* (Houndmills: Palgrave Macmillan, 2008).
8. William T. Rossiter, *Chaucer and Petrarch* (Cambridge: Brewer, 2010).
9. D. G. Rees, 'Sir Thomas Wyatt's Translations from Petrarch', *Comparative Literature*, 7.1 (1955), 15–24.
10. Jean Balsamo, ed., *Les poètes français de la Renaissance et Pétrarque* (Geneva: Droz, 2004).
11. Gino Belloni, ed., *Francesco Petrarca, da Padova all'Europa: atti del convegno internazionale di studi, Padova, 17–18 giugno 2004* (Rome: Antenore, 2007); Loredana Chines, *Il petrarchismo: un modello di poesia per l'Europa*, 2 vols (Rome: Bulzoni, 2006); M. Febbo, P. Salwa, eds, *Petrarca a jedność kultury europejskiej* (Warsaw: Wydawnictwo Naukowe Semper, 2005); Antero Meozzi, *Il petrarchismo europeo (secolo XVI)* (Pisa: Vallerini 1934),; Carlo Ossola, ed., *Pétrarque et l'Europe* (Grenoble: Jérôme Millon, 2006).
12. Stephen Minta, *Petrarch and Petrarchism: The English and French Traditions* (Manchester: Manchester University Press; Totowa, NJ: Barnes & Noble, 1980).
13. The text is taken from Petrarca, *Canzoniere*, ed. M. Santagata, (Milan: Mondadori, 1996).
14. Lucylla Pszczolowska, 'The Origins and Poetics of Polish Renaissance and Baroque Sonnets', *Europa Orientalis*, 18.2 (1999), 75–89.
15. I owe this correction to Riccardo Raimondo.
16. The text for the German and Latin versions is taken from Aurnhammer, ed., *Francesco Petrarca in Deutschland*.
17. George Puttenham, *The Arte of English Poesie* (London, 1589), 48.
18. Lucien Febre and Henri-Jean Martin, *L'Apparition du livre* (Paris: A. Michel, 1958).
19. Steven W. May, *The Elizabethan Courtier Poets: Their Poems and Their Contexts* (Columbia, MO and London: University of Missouri Press, 1991).
20. Stephen Burt and David Mikics, *The Art of the Sonnet* (Cambridge, MA and London: Belknap Press of the Harvard University Press, 2010).
21. Edoardo Zuccato, *Petrarch in Romantic England* (Houndmills: Palgrave Macmillan, 2008).
22. Tim Atkins, *Petrarch Collected Atkins*; Peter Hughes, *Quite Frankly after Petrarch's Sonnets*.
23. Theo Herman, ed., *The Manipulation of Literature: Studies in Literary Translation* (Abingdon and New York: Routledge, 1985).
24. Giovanni Antonio Fenice, *Dictionnaire françois-italien* (Paris, 1584).

INDEX

Apollinaire, Guillaume 172, 185, 188, 230–31, 242
Apollo 5, 74, 86, 104, 107, 109, 112–14, 163, 166
Aragon, Louis 5, 164–67, 169–70, 264
Ariosto:
   Capitolo 13
   Orlando Furioso 16, 21, 41, 44
   Rime 10, 41–42
Atkins, Tim, 6, 7, 32
   Petrarch Collected Atkins 171–90, 245–58, 266, 277
Attridge, Derek 246–47, 249, 252, 259, 261, 262
Augustine 1, 174

Baïf, Jean-Antoine de 44
Balsamo, Jean 45, 58- 60, 140, 148, 149
Barański, Zygmunt 194, 204
Barbour, Douglas 223–25, 233–34, 242–43
Barolini Teolinda:
   and Wayne Storey 2, 8
Barrett Browning, Elizabeth 259
Barthes, Roland 233
Barwin, Gary 237
Basho, Matsuo 237–38
Beard, Mary 21
Beaulieu, Derek 237–39
Bembo, Pietro 2, 4, 17, 40, 98, 193, 204
Benabou, Marcel 235
Benezet of Avignon 146, 148
Bens, Jacques 248
Bergvall, Caroline 255
Bernstein, Charles 240–41
Berrigan, Ted 229, 245, 247
Bertoli, Lide 140
Bible, the 2, 162, 195, 251
Boccaccio 2, 17, 115
Bök, Christian 239
Bonnefoy, Yves 6, 31, 156–58, 162, 188, 209–14
Boscán, Juan 63, 77
Bourgouin, Simon 51–56, 61
Bouvard, A. P. A. 143
Bowering, George 128–30
Brahms, Johannes 241
Brose, Margaret 202
Burns, Robert 230
Buron, Emmanuel 34

Cabadé, Ernest 144
Cage, John 232, 241

Camões, Luís Vaz de 66, 79
Canter, Guglielmus 266
Caproni, Giorgio 163
Carducci, Giosuè 193, 202
Carson, Anne 231
Casa, Giovanni della 103, 110, 119, 121
Cassin, Barbara 139, 145, 203
Castillejo, Cristóbal de 63
Catanusi, Placide 159, 162
Catherine of Aragon 200
Cavalcanti, Guido 39, 218, 234
Cecchetti, Dario 49
Cendrars, Blaise 187, 230
Cervantes, Miguel de 67
Cetina, Gutierre de 63
Chaperon, Jean 52
Char, René 200–01
Chartier, Alain 48
Chaucer, Geoffrey 2, 24, 217, 255, 257, 262, 264
Christ 88, 92
Cicero 8n, 45, 137n, 153
Cifarelli, Paola 48, 52
Cino da Pistoia 39, 234
Clarke, Adrian 245, 246
Cobb, Allison:
   and Jen Coleman 236–37
Cochin, Henry 141
Colonna, Stefano 200, 202

Daniel, Arnaut 38, 145, 234
Daniel, Samuel 23
Daniello, Bernardino 16
Dante 2, 15, 17, 25
   Divina Commedia 83, 95, 98, 100, 104, 199
   La Vita Nuova 15
Daphne 74
Dávalos, Diego 64
Dávalos y Figueroa, Pedro 64
Deschamps, Eustache 52, 54
Desnos, Robert 230
Desportes, Philippe 44
Dorat, Jean 36–37
d'Orazio, Sara 191, 193, 201
Doris, Stacy 175
Drayton, Michael 23
Drouy, Guillermo 66, 74
Dryden, John 223

Du Bellay, Joachim:
  L'Anterotique 36
  La Deffense et illustration de la langue françoyse 31–37, 40–41
  L'Olive 31–45
  L'Olive 3: 37–38
  L'Olive 4: 39
  L'Olive 8: 41–42
  L'Olive 33: 41–42
  L'Olive 45: 44
  L'Olive augmentée 31–32, 35–45
  L'Olive augmentée 35: 44
  L'Olive augmentée 77: 44
  L'Olive augmentée 90: 35
  L'Olive augmentée 93: 43
  L'Olive augmentée 113: 40
  Vers lyriques 36
Dubrow, Heather 7
Duchamp, Marcel 241
Duchess of Soma 63
Dufay, Guillaume 198
du Mans, Peletier 1, 2, 33, 36
Duperray, Ève 201
Durling, Robert 227, 233

Eliot, Thomas Stearns 252
  Four Quartets 199, 254
Erasmus, Desiderius:
  Adagia 15

Fiesco, Giulio 115
Forge, Georges de la 50–51, 53, 55
Fourest, Georges 220
François I 147
Fray Luis de León 78
Frye, Walter 198

Garcés, Enrique:
  Los sonetos y canciones del Petrarcha 63–81
  De Reyno y de la institución del que ha de Reynar 65–66, 68, 79
  Los Lusiadas 66
  'El traductor a su trabajo' 69, 76
  'Siendo este mi gran trabajo detenido' 67–69
  'Una dama debaxo de un verde lauro' 69–77
Gascoigne, George 17
Genot, Gérard 5, 154–56
Ginguené, Pierre-Louis 144, 159, 162, 264
Giolito de Ferrari, Gabriele 15, 39–42
Giovannelli, Ruggero 114–16
Godefroy, Hippolyte 159, 162
Goethe, Johann Wolfgang von 177
Goldsmith, Oliver 224, 252
Gómez de Tapia, Luis 79
Gréban, Arnoul 52
Green, Al 234

Groden, Suzy Q. 228
Guérin, Philippe 101
Guinizelli, Guido 218
Guittone d'Arezzo 215

Hainsworth, Peter 2, 14, 197
Harvey, Gabriel 18
Harvey, John 23
Henry II 31, 48
Henry VIII 200, 259
Herrera, Fernando de 63
Herriman, George 234
Hesiod:
  Theogony 42
Higgins, Dick 232
Hill, Geoffrey:
  Canaan 193, 195
  'September Song' 192
  Speech! Speech! 195, 200
  Al Tempo de Tremuoti 191, 197, 199, 200, 201, 202
  The Triumph of Love 193–203
Hilson, Jeff 172, 245–49
Hocquard, Emmanuel 6, 171–87
  Un Test de Solitude 171–87
Homer 33, 41, 269
Horace 31, 44, 227
  Ars poetica 67
Houédard, Dom Sylvester 238
Howard, Henry, the Earl of Surrey 13, 14, 21–22, 27, 266
Hughes, Peter:
  After Petrarch 7, 247–58, 268
Hume, Anna 41n
Hurtado de Mendoza, Diego 63

Index et catalogus librorum prohibitorum 66, 79 n. 18

Jakobson, Roman 237
Jerome, Saint 153
Johnson, Kent 240–41
Johnson, Dr 172, 181
Jonson, Ben 23, 192

Kennedy, William J. 8 n. 10
Kroetsch, Robert 234
Kulik, William 230
Kyd, Thomas 24

Labé, Louise 56
Ladmiral, Jean-René 153
Lafond, Edmond 147–48
Landi, Michela 157
Larue, Anne 204n
Lemaire de Belges, Jean:
  La Concorde des deux langages 58 n. 6
Leopardi, Giacomo 193, 199, 202

Liszt, Franz 4, 267
Lodge, Thomas 27
Lupacchino, Bernardo 115

Magny, Olivier de 44
Mahul, Emma 144–45
Marenzio, Luca:
  Primo libro de madrigali a quattro voci 103–21
Marguerite de France 31
Marot, Clément 49, 50, 56, 59, 156, 162, 164, 166, 169
Masson, Jean-Yves 1, 3, 5, 7, 156, 159–62, 166
Mayer, Bernadette 223
Maynier, Jehan, baron of Oppède 50–52, 54–55, 57
McCaffery, Steve 232–33, 235, 237
McLaughlin, Martin 2
Mellin de Saint-Gelais 33
Melnick, David 236
Menta, Francesco 115
Meschonnic, Henri 161
Mexía de Fernangil, Diego 64
Milton, John 198, 204, 295, 225, 259
Moncond'huy, Dominique 185, 186
Montaigne, Michel de 22, 26, 28
Montale, Eugenio 193, 201, 202
Montemayor, Jorge de 63
Montesquiou, Anatole de 145–46
Monteverdi, Claudio 103
Moore, Nicholas 7, 251–54, 258
Moscaglia, Battista 104, 118, 121
Mounin, Georges 199
Musa, Mark 234, 249

Naborowski, Daniel 265
Napoleon 141
Nichol, bp 230
Nida, Eugene 153

Oakeshott, Michael 218
Opitz, Martin 264–65
Orléans, Charles d' 50, 52
Ovid 31, 44, 55, 112
O'Hara, Frank 229
O'Rourke, Donny 230

Parker, Henry, Morley, Lord 200
Parker, Richard 246
Parussa, Gabriella 48, 49
Pasquier, Etienne 39
Pastior, Oskar 171
Patrizi, Francesco 65, 68
Pavese, Cesare 193, 201
Peacham, Henry 24
Peletier du Mans, Jacques 1–2, 33
Pergnier, Maurice 156, 158–59
Perloff, Marjorie 240
Pessoa, Fernando 240

Peter, Saint 147
Petrarch:
  life of 2, 83, 143, 172, 232
    in Avignon 142, 148, 250
  and Laura 2, 5, 14, 36, 83, 86, 92, 95, 127, 129–38, 177–78, 253
  and the Laureateship, 105, 191, 193, 201
  as literary myth 3, 5, 49, 57, 264
  as literary persona 2, 241
  and Europe 3, 14, 31, 183, 211, 215, 246, 266, 264, 269
  and Rome 1, 130
  Tuscan 1, 26, 33
  and Vaucluse 8n, 127, 135, 137, 141, 142, 147, 194, 227
Petrarchan themes and motifs:
  ars amandi 48
  anti-Petrarchism 3, 7, 30n
  blason 56
  catalogue, *see* list
  conceit 15, 18, 23, 26, 28, 192, 201, 263
  Cupid 83, 92, 102, 104, 250–53, 256
  death 1, 39, 74, 88, 99–102, 129–30, 142, 175–76, 194
  eyes 17, 35, 54–55, 72–76, 88, 131, 173, 185, 227
  golden hair 55–56, 75, 81
  Good Friday 7, 147, 250, 255
  innamoramento 171–89
  laurel 42–43, 70–75, 86–88, 92, 99, 139, 143, 192, 201–02, 254
  list 18, 50, 182–84
  love knot 52–53
  memory 22–26, 38, 51, 99, 127, 129–30, 137, 194, 222
  Petrarchan clichés 24, 58, 172, 180–81, 192, 204
  Petrarchism 3–7, 14–16, 25–26, 31, 34, 39–40, 49, 56, 95, 108, 128, 140–41, 146–48, 191–93, 201, 263–64, 266–67
  polysemy of Laura 139, 142–43
  puns 38, 143, 145, 151, 165, 186, 200, 268
  sighs 158, 193
  soldier 250
  tempus fugit 74
  Virgin Mary 194–98
RVF *Rerum vulgarium fragmenta*:
  RVF, *Canzoniere* as a whole 3, 15, 48–50, 64, 148, 155, 172, 202, 209–10, 233, 247, 254, 264
  RVF 1 'Voi ch'ascoltate in rime sparse il suono' 15, 168
  RVF 3 'Era il giorno ch'al sol si scoloraro' 7, 245–61
  RVF 5 'Quando io movo i sospiri a chiamar voi' 144, 145
  RVF 6 'Sí travïato è 'l folle mi' desio' 86
  RVF 7 'La gola e 'l sonno et l'otïose piume' 27
  RVF 20 'Vergognando talor ch'ancor si taccia' 20

RVF 22 'A qualunque animale alberga in terra' 21
RVF 23 'Nel dolce tempo de la prima etade' 18, 19, 25, 26, 99
RVF 24 'Se l'onorata fronde che prescrive' 44
RVF 29 'Verdi panni, sanguigni, oscuri o persi' 66, 69
RVF 30 'Giovene donna sotto un verde lauro' 63, 64, 69, 71, 76, 78, 80
RVF 33 'Già fiammeggiava l'amorosa stella' 83
RVF 34 'Apollo, s'ancor vive il bel desio' 86, 104
RVF 35 'Solo e pensoso i più deserti campi' 22, 111
RVF 38 'Orso, e' non furon mai fiumi né stagni' 137 n. 5
RVF 40 'S'Amore o Morte non dà qualche stroppio' 1
RVF 46 'L'oro et le perle e i fior' vermigli' 133
RVF 52 'Non al suo amante' 104
RVF 54 'Perch'al viso d'Amor portava insegna' 104, 122
RVF 55 'Quel foco ch'i' pensai che fosse spento' 150
RVF 56 'Se col cieco desir che 'l cor distrugge' 24
RVF 59 'Perché quel che mi trasse ad amar prima' 150
RVF 63 'Volgendo gli occhi al mio novo colore' 150
RVF 66 'L'aere gravato, et l'importuna nebbia' 83
RVF 70 'Lasso me, ch'i' non so in qual parte pieghi' 38
RVF 77 'Per mirar Policleto a prova fiso' 92
RVF 78 'Quando giunse a Simon l'alto concetto' 92
RVF 82 'Io non fu' d'amar voi lassato unquancho' 81
RVF 90 'Erano i capei d'oro a l'aura sparsi' 212
RVF 93 'Più volte Amor m'avea già detto: Scrivi' 121, 175
RVF 99 'Poi che voi et io piú volte abbiam provato' 150
RVF 100 'Quella fenestra ove l'un sol si vede' 219, 220
RVF 103 'Vinse Hanibàl, et non seppe usar' 217
RVF 105 'Mai non vo' piú cantar com'io soleva' 28
RVF 106 'Nova angioletta sovra l'ale accorta' 83, 104
RVF 113 'Qui dove mezzo son, Sennuccio mio' 128
RVF 114 'De l'empia Babilonia, ond'è fuggita' 66, 78
RVF 121 'Or vedi, Amor, che giovenetta donna' 104
RVF 124 'Amor, Fortuna et la mia mente' 102
RVF 126 'Chiare, fresche et dolci acque' 83, 84, 99, 140, 143, 149
RVF 127 'In quella parte dove Amor mi sprona' 93, 100, 104
RVF 128 'Italia mia, benché 'l parlar sia indarno' 92, 93, 94, 199
RVF 129 'Di pensier in pensier, di monte in monte' 19
RVF 132 'S'amor non e, ehe dunque e quel ch'io sento?' 216, 264, 265
RVF 134 'Pace non trovo, et non ò da far guerra' 18, 26, 217
RVF 136 'Fiamma dal ciel su le tue treccie piova' 66
RVF 137 'L'avara Babilonia à colmo il sacco' 66
RVF 138 'Fontana di dolore, albergo d'ira' 66
RVF 144 'Né così bello il sol già mai levarsi' 96
RVF 145 'Pommi ove 'l sole occide i fiori et l'erba' 27, 96
RVF 146 'O d'ardente vertute ornata et calda' 133
RVF 147 'Quando 'l voler che con duo sproni ardenti' 133
RVF 148 'Non Tesin, Po, Varo, Adige et Tebro' 138, 183
RVF 149 'Di tempo in tempo mi si fa men dura' 150
RVF 159 'In qual parte del ciel, in quale ydea' 132–33
RVF 164 'Or che 'l ciel et la terra e 'l vento tace' 81, 105, 122, 128
RVF 175 'Quando mi vène inanzi il tempo e 'l loco' 22
RVF 185 'Questa fenice de l'aurata piuma' 44
RVF 187 'Giunto Alexandro a la famosa tomba' 18
RVF 189 'Passa la nave mia colma d'oblio' 18
RVF 190 'Una candida cerva sopra l'erba' 81n, 173
RVF 194 'L'aura gentil, che rasserena i poggi' 145, 146
RVF 196 ' L'aura serena che fra verdi fronde' 145, 146
RVF 197 'L'aura celeste che 'n quel verde lauro' 145, 150
RVF 198 'L'aura soave al sole spiega et vibra' 145
RVF 199 'O bella man che mi destringi 'l core' 104
RVF 206 'S'i' 'l dissi mai, ch'i' vegna in odio' 21
RVF 207 'Ben mi credea passar mio tempo omai' 25
RVF 208 'Rapido fiume che d'alpestra vena' 38, 85
RVF 209 'I dolci colli ov'io lasciai me stesso' 21, 85, 86
RVF 214 'Anzi tre dí creata era alma in parte' 88, 90
RVF 216 'Tutto 'l dí piango; et poi la notte' 122
RVF 223 'Quando 'l sol bagna in mar l'aurato carro' 181
RVF 224 'S'una fede amorosa, un cor non finto' 21
RVF 228 'Amor co la man dextra il lato manco' 86

RVF 229 'Cantai, or piango, et non men di dolcezza' 43, 86
RVF 232 'Vincitore Alexandro l'ira vinse' 18
RVF 237 'Non à tanti animali il mar fra l'onde' 86, 101
RVF 239 'Là ver' l'aurora, che sí dolce l'aura' 145
RVF 245 'Due rose fresche, et colte in paradiso' 201
RVF 248 'Chi vuol veder quantunque pò Natura' 17, 21
RVF 256 'Far potess'io vendetta di colei' 91
RVF 257 'In quel bel viso ch'i' sospiro et bramo' 88, 91
RVF 259 'Cercato ò sempre solitaria vita' 128
RVF 262 '– Cara la vita, et dopo lei mi pare' 89
RVF 263 'Arbor victoriosa trumphale' 18, 88, 89
RVF 268 'Che debb'io far? che mi consigli, Amore?' 99
RVF 269 'Rotta è l'alta colonna e 'l verde lauro' 200
RVF 272 'La vita fugge, et non s'arresta una hora' 18
RVF 273 'Che fai? Che pensi? che pur dietro guardi' 202
RVF 274 'Datemi pace, o duri miei pensieri' 102
RVF 291 'Quand'io veggio dal ciel scender l'Aurora' 146
RVF 308 'Quella per cui con Sorga ò cangiato Arno' 14
RVF 310 'Zefiro torna e 'l bel tempo rimena' 105
RVF 314 'Mente mia, che presaga de' tuoi damni' 150
RVF 324 'Amor quando fioria' 105, 122, 150
RVF 325 'Tacer non posso, et temo non adopre' 97, 102
RVF 339 'Conobbi, quanto il ciel li occhi m'aperse' 87
RVF 342 'Del cibo onde 'l signor mio sempre abonda' 86, 87
RVF 366 'Vergine bella, che di sol vestita' 197
Triumphi (Trionfi):
 Triumphi as a whole 49, 195
 Triumphus Cupidinis (of Love) 51–56
 Triumphus Mortis (of Death) 52, 60
 Triumphus Pudicitie (of Chastity) 202
 Triumphus Temporis (of Time) 191
works in Latin:
 'Ad se ipsum' 202
 Africa 193, 204n
 Bucolicum Carmen 99
 Familiarum rerum libri 2, 16, 22
 Itinerarium 203
 De remediis utriusque fortunae 17, 200
Philieul, Vasquin 33, 50–55, 156, 218
Philip II, King of Spain 65
Pistoia, Cino 39, 234
Pizan, Christine de 52

Pléiade 36, 50, 160, 164
Poetics:
 ballad, ballata 105, 119, 121, 128, 176, 187
 canzone 3, 18–19, 26, 37–39, 46, 66, 69, 76, 78 104, 194, 198–99, 201–02, 205
 canzonetta 104–14
 cobla 215
 couplet 14, 19, 23–28, 133, 254
 fragment 13–28, 32–37, 45, 210, 228, 231
 haiku 229, 238 251, 256
 madrigal 103–21, 128
 metre 48–49, 59, 66, 71–75, 122, 219, 259, 268, 269
 motet 108, 110–11, 115, 198, 201
 narrative 5, 14, 82, 92, 98–99, 106, 116, 129–31, 180, 194, 203, 251, 259
 novel 83, 140
 novella 130–34
 part vs. whole 13–17, 24, 27–28, 32, 39, 116, 146, 161, 263
 poiesis 153
 rhyme scheme 64, 71, 80, 166, 203, 205, 246–47, 254
 sestina 44, 63–81, 83, 88, 128, 145, 251
 sonnet 9n, 28, 36, 109, 134, 145, 147, 156, 172, 186–87, 210, 215–21, 246–47, 256, 263
 Shakespearean sonnet 247, 254
 Sicilian sonnet 215–18
 tercet 25, 48, 55, 166, 215
 terza rima 18, 21, 48, 105–12, 199
 trobar clus 192–93, 198, 201, 204
 visual sonnet 185, 187, 247
Poliziano, Angelo 45
Poulenc, Joseph 146
Pound, Ezra 193, 196, 235
Price, Richard 230
Pujol i Duran, Jessica 248–49, 254
Puttenham, George 17, 19, 24, 27–28, 266

Queneau, Raymond 246, 251

Raimbaut de Vacqueiras 201
Ramírez Pagán, Diego 63
Rampo, Edogawa 235
Ricci, Bartolomeo 37
Ricœur, Paul 153
Riffaterre, Michael 53
Rigolot, François 33
Rilke, Rainer Maria 228–29
Rimbaud, Arthur 187, 235
 'Voyelles' 239, 257–58
Roche, Denis 185
Roche, Thomas P. 198
Rodefer, Stephen 223
Romei, Annibale 26–27
Ronsard, Pierre de 44, 56, 133, 140, 174, 264
Rore, Cipriano de 103, 108, 115, 198
Rossiter, William 205 n. 44

Rousseau, Jean-Jacques 140, 196

Sade, abbé de 5, 7, 131, 140–45, 164, 166
Saint-Gelais 33
Saint Gregory, William of 38, 234
Salutati, Coluccio 2
Sánchez, Luis 66
Sannazaro, Jacopo 15, 103–08, 110, 112, 114–16, 118–21
Sappho 228, 231
Scève, Maurice 27, 56, 140, 146–47
Schiller, Friedrich 246
Schleiermacher, Friedrich 153
Schönberg, Arnold 267
Scobie, Stephen 223–25, 233–34
Scott, William 23–24
Scotto, Fabio 157–58
Sébillet, Thomas 34
Seneca 195
Sennuccio 95
Shakespeare, William 193, 209, 211, 228, 251, 254, 269
Shelley, Percy Bysshe:
    The Triumph of Life 195–96, 199–200
Sheppard, Robert 6–7, 240, 248–49
Sidney, Sir Philip:
    Astrophel and Stella 15, 45, 71, 74
Silliman, Ron 240
Silvestre, Gregorio 63
Sismondi, Simonde de 143
Smith, Charlotte 259
Soupault, Philippe 230
Southwell, Robert 192, 198
Spanish Italianist poets 63, 78n
Speroni, Sperone 34
Spicer, Jack:
    After Lorca 225–26, 240
Spiller, Michael G. 196
Stein, Gertrude 177, 235
    Tender Buttons 232–33
Steiner, George 204
Stierle, Karlheinz 195
Suomela-Härmä, Elina 48
Surrey, Henry Howard, Earl of 13–14, 17, 21–22, 27, 200, 255, 259, 266

Taber, Charles R. 156
Tabios, Eileen 241
Tansillo, Luigi 115
Tasso, Torquato 24–25, 103, 110, 115
    Gerusalemme liberata 105, 119, 120–21
Tebaldeo, Antonio 40
Tennyson, Alfred Lord 241
Thatcher, Margaret 175, 252–53
Themerson, Stefan 255–56
Theocritus 107
Tofte, Robert 25
Toledo, Francisco de 23 n. 80

Toscanella, Orazio 16
Translation:
    as adaptation 3, 41, 72, 50, 57, 171, 181, 188, 193–94, 199
    as appropriation 5, 17, 141, 164, 184
    and commonplacing 4, 7, 13, 15, 19–28
    and copying 130, 213
    as domestication 225–30, 241
    ecclesiastical-religious meaning of translation 143, 146, 198
    and editing 2, 15, 225–28, 232
    erroneous 56
    as exegesis 4, 83, 88, 92, 156, 158
    and familiarization 156, 161, 164
    and genetics, genetic criticism 157
    as gloss 2, 15, 34, 192, 199, 249, 254
    as hermeneutics 4, 5, 127, 135, 152, 158, 162, 166
    homophonic translation 28, 75, 199, 235–37
    and imaginary 157–69
    and imagination 152, 166, 226, 234, 236
    as imitation 1–3, 7–8, 16–17, 21, 23, 28, 31–45, 57, 64, 140, 163, 192, 204, 213, 216, 226, 263, 268
    as interpretation 2, 4–5, 88, 92, 95, 98, 127, 131–34, 152, 157–58, 166, 237, 264
    and parody 6, 7, 174, 240, 253
    and plagiarism 218
    as re-creation 3, 5, 7, 136, 156–58, 162, 213, 264
    as rewriting 18, 53, 127, 140, 167, 172–74, 176, 180, 195–96, 201–03, 213, 267
    source vs target oriented translation 53, 64, 156, 158, 162–63, 235
    and subversion 5, 6, 171–72, 181, 187, 201
    traduttore traditore/betrayal 75, 155, 160, 192
    transcoding 156
    translation of meaning vs translation of form 5, 26–27, 34, 64, 69, 71, 73–76, 80–81, 143, 153, 158, 160–63, 166–67, 192, 222, 224, 226
    translation of style 106–08, 156
    transposition 44, 72–73, 95, 153–57, 247, 251
    untranslatable 7, 139–45, 191, 203
    as vernacularization 14–18, 27, 34, 45, 48–50, 200, 263–69
    as version 2, 19, 34, 41, 81, 191, 231, 248, 252
    as visualization 15n, 49, 76, 82–84, 185–87, 200, 212
Tyard, Pontus de 44
Tzu, Chuang 236–37

Vauzelles, Jean de 56
Vellutello, Alessandro 2
Vérard, Barthélemy 50–52, 54
Vico, Giambattista 153
Vincent, Steven 231
Virgil:
    Aeneid 44, 209, 234
    Georgics 42, 44
    Eclogues 44

Vitruvius 131
Vogelsgang, Arthur 240
Voltaire 5, 7, 140

Walcott, Derek 263
Watson, Burton 236–37
Watson, Thomas 17, 20–21, 217
Watteau, Jean-Antoine 241
Weinberger, Eliot:
    and Paz, Octavio, *Thirteen Ways of Looking at Wang Wei* 222

Willaert, Adrian 103, 108
William of St. Gregory 38, 234
Withye, William 24–25
Wordsworth, William 263
Wyatt, Sir Thomas:
    and Surrey 14, 17, 200, 255, 259, 266

Yasusada, Araki 240–41

Zuccato, Edoardo 140
Zukofsky, Louis 223

www.ingramcontent.com/pod-product-compliance
Lightning Source LLC
Chambersburg PA
CBHW080541090426
42734CB00016B/3169